Rural Microfinance and Microenterprise
Informal Revolution

About the MPRLP

Madhya Pradesh Rural Livelihoods Project (MPRLP), is DFID, U.K. Government funded project of Government of Madhya Pradesh, Department of Panchayat & Rural Development. MPRLP is operating on the Contemporary Sustainable Livelihoods Framework in remotest areas of eight tribal dominated districts of the State. MPRLP has the **Livelihoods Forum,** an autonomous high quality think tank for providing value addition inputs/high quality critical feedback to the Government/other stakeholders on matters concerning project implementation, policy prescriptions, sharing best practices, knowledge management, action research and documentation. In this initiative, the Forum has created a source book on sound learnings/sage advice/ successful experiments in the realm of Rural Microfinance & Microenterprise — within the sweep of a definitive Movement having the potential of a Revolution — in the informal segments of the society and economy.

About the Editor

Dr. Amitabh Bhatnagar is a development analyst and communicator, interested in — Rural Development/livelihoods generation/microfinance & microenterprise promotion/Human Resource & Institutional development/Project management/cross-cutting concerns — currently focused on convergent knowledge management initiatives to optimize the utilization of the global knowledge heritage in development interventions. He recently edited the critically acclaimed two volume '*Sage & Sound Recipes: Successful Experiments in Rural Development/Livelihoods.*'

RURAL MICROFINANCE AND MICROENTERPRISE

Informal Revolution

Edited by

Dr. Amitabh Bhatnagar

MPRLP

State Livelihoods Forum Coordinator

Foreword by

Mr. Jitendra Agrawal

In collaboration with

MPRLP-Livelihoods Forum, Bhopal

Published by

CONCEPT PUBLISHING COMPANY, NEW DELHI-110059

Cataloging in Publication Data—DK
Courtesy: D.K. Agencies (P) Ltd. <docinfo@dkagencies.com>

Rural microfinance and microenterprise : informal revolution / edited by Amitabh Bhatnagar ; foreword by Jitendra Agrawal. — 1st ed.
p. cm.
Contributed articles.
In Indian context.
Includes bibliographical references.
Includes index.
ISBN 13: 9788180695674
ISBN 10: 8180695670

1. Microfinance—India. 2. Rural development—India—Finance. 3. Rural development projects—India. 4. Small business—India. 5. Informal sector (Economics)—India. I. Bhatnagar, Amitabh, 1959-

DDC 338.642 095 4 22

ISBN-13: 978-81-8069-567-4
ISBN-10: 81-8069-567-0

First Edition 2008

Published and Printed by
Ashok Kumar Mittal
Concept Publishing Company
A/15-16, Commercial Block, Mohan Garden
New Delhi-110059 (INDIA)

Phones : 25351460, 25351794
Fax : 091-11-25357103
Email : publishing@conceptpub.com

Dedicated to

My Parents
Dr. Prakash Swaroop Bhatnagar & (Late) Mrs. Sarla Bhatnagar and family members
whose faith, support and love has been my beacon light

Dr. Amitabh Bhatnagar

Foreword

The Madhya Pradesh Rural Livelihoods Project (MPRLP) is a Government of Madhya Pradesh (GoMP) initiative managed by the Madhya Pradesh Society for Rural Livelihoods Promotion. It is funded by the Department for International Development (DFID), Government of United Kingdom. Initiated in 2004, the Project aims to enhance the livelihoods of marginalized/ disadvantaged communities in selected villages of eight predominantly tribal districts of M.P. The Project has entered into second phase from mid 2007. The details about the project can be accessed through *www.mprlp.in*.

The Project has successfully demonstrated the feasibility of working through the Gram Sabhas (village assemblies) and establishing people centered models of livelihoods promotion. It is a pioneering endeavour towards working out a sustainable model of democratic and decentralized governance to deliver economic development and social justice through the village communities as envisaged in the 73rd Constitutional Amendment.

Another distinctive feature of MPRLP is the Livelihoods Forum—an autonomous high quality think tank for providing critical feedback to the Government and other stakeholders on matters concerning project implementation, convergence, knowledge management, sharing best practices, policy initiatives and conducting action research and documentation, etc.

MPRLP—Forum has undertaken this initiative of putting together learnings related to Microfinance, Microenterprise and Informal Sector Development from a variety of contemporary multilateral/bilateral, government/non-government projects and programmes operational across the length and breadth of the country and beyond.

I am hopeful that this knowledge management/dissemination initiative of MPRLP-Forum would facilitate development practitioners, including MPRLP teams, in learning from and adopting proven good strategies concerning microfinance/ microenterprise sub-sectors from the studies/cases detailed in this collection. It is also anticipated that this will trigger documentation of other best practices in this and other related sub-sectors of development so that together we can take more meaningful steps to improve the impact of our development journey.

Madhya Pradesh Rural Livelihoods Project, Govt. of M.P.
Panchayat & Rural Development Department

Jitendra Agrawal
Project Coordinator
MPRLP

Contents

List of Contributors

Mr. Jitendra Agrawal is the Project Coordinator, Madhya Pradesh Rural Livelihoods Project, Bhopal.

Dr. Mukul G. Asher is Professor, Lee Kuan Yew School of Public Policy, National University of Singapore, Singapore. (sppasher@nus.edu.sg)

Ms. Sukanya Banerjee is Research Coordinator at the Foundation for MSME Clusters, New Delhi.

Dr. Amitabh Bhatnagar, editor of this publication is currently looking after the Livelihoods Forum at Madhya Pradesh Rural Livelihoods Project. (abhatnagr@hotmail.com)

Mr. Amit Kumar Burman is BDS Manager, Udyogini, a Microenterprise development NGO at New Delhi.

Dr. Keshab Das is Professor, Gujarat Institute for Development Research, Ahmedabad.

Mr. Mukesh Gulati is Executive Director, Foundation for MSME Clusters, New Delhi. (mukeshgul@gmail.com)

Ms. Marie Luise Haberberger is currently Programme Director, NABARD-GTZ Rural Finance Programme, GTZ, New Delhi. (Marie.Haberberger@gtz.de)

Dr. Sudhir K. Jain is Associate Professor, Department of Management Studies, Indian Institute of Technology, New Delhi.

Mr. Ashok Kumar is Director BDS and Enterprise Promotion, EDA Rural Systems Pvt. Ltd., Gurgaon (ashokkumar@edarural.com)

Ms. Alexandra Miehlbradt is an independent Consultant in micro, small and medium enterprise development and an International Trainer.

Ms. Melissa Nussbaum has worked on microfinance microenterprise, most recently with Save the Children US at Vietnam.

Ms. V. Prameela is MicroEnterprise and Livelihood Specialist at Sampark, an NGO based in Bangalore, India.

Dr. Smita Premchander is an International Trainer/Consultant for gender, microfinance/microenterprise and founder member of Sampark, an NGO at Bangalore. (smitapremchander@ gmail.com)

Dr. Joy Deshmukh Ranadive is Director, Indian School of Microfinance for Women, Ahmedabad. (joy@ismw.org.in)

Dr. Tamal Sarkar is Programme Director, Foundation for MSME Clusters, New Delhi.

Ms. Savita Shankar is an independent Researcher working on development issues (shankar.savita@gmail.com)

Ms. Frances Sinha is Managing Director, EDA Rural Systems Pvt. Ltd., Gurgaon, a leading development sector consultancy

Mr. K.K. Tripathy is Deputy Director, Ministry of Food Processing Industries, New Delhi, currently Research Scholar, Indian Institute of Technology (IIT), New Delhi. (tripathy123@rediffmail.com)

Dr. Vanita Viswanath is CEO, Udyogini, a New Delhi based microenterprise development NGO. (vanitaviswanath@udyogini.org)

Prologue

Rural Microfinance and Microenterprise: Informal Revolution—sage and sound recipes for sound Microfinance/Microenterprise/ Informal Sector Development-interventions based on the accumulated experience of versatile development practitioners/ well crafted projects interventions/successful experiments/best practices from a variety of contemporary multilateral/bilateral/ government and non-government sources.

Madhya Pradesh Rural Livelihoods Project (MPRLP) is DFID/ U.K. Government funded project of Government of Madhya Pradesh, Department of Panchayat & Rural Development operating on the contemporary Sustainable Livelihoods (S.L.) framework/approach in remotest areas of eight tribal dominated districts of M.P. The Project with its S.L. vision has put people (their capabilities, assets and activities) at the centre of development and has brought together in a holistic/partnership/ convergent perspective all relevant aspects of people's lives and multiple livelihoods.

The S.L. parameter of forging macro-micro links (higher level macro policy development/planning to be informed by lessons learnt/insights gained at the grassroots level) is delineated in MPRLP Livelihoods Forum. The Forum endeavours to provide high quality, critical feedback to the Government/other stakeholders on matters concerning project implementation, policy prescriptions, best practices, knowledge management, conducts documentation/action research and gives other value added inputs to the Project/development machinery of the State/others. The Forum had undertaken the Knowledge Management initiative of compiling sound learnings/sage advice from a wide spectrum of sources to create a ready referencer for the development practitioners—the two volume '*Sage and Sound Recipes: Successful Experiments in Rural Development/Livelihoods* (Co-publisher: M/s. Zenith Books International, New Delhi, Tel.: (91-011) 65925063, 91-9871068633, 91-9910385596, *E-mail*: zenith_book@yahoo.com).

Forum's present Knowledge Management endeavour is focused on a specific theme: Case Studies/Learnings from good and best practices/containing sage advice/food for thought and inspiration from sound interventions/research covering Microfinance/Microenterprise/Informal Sector development sub-sectors/cross cutting concerns, linkages, with a grassroots/national/global perspective. The purpose of this book is to attempt an overview of the varied dimensions/constraints, linkages, development best practices related to the rapidly evolving 'micro' informal segments of Rural finance/enterprise, along with holistic microfinance- microenterprise interconnectedness within the larger macro context (Indian/globally). While providing flavour of the field as a whole in the *Introductory Chapter, the subsequent nine chapters* of this book cover indepth some key/emerging focus areas with associated learnings/policy prescriptions, derived from multilateral/bilateral/national government, NGO, corporate sources. The vast, varied and intricate nature of the Informal Finance/Enterprise Sector under constant flux, makes the task of creating a sequential/well knit/comprehensive picture difficult. It is hoped, however that the snapshots given of the subject area (with capsules of summarized wisdom) would be extrapolated in combination with experienced learnings of the readers, for a better grasp of the nuances/anticipated future prognosis of the 'micro' movements and interventional 'food for thought'.

The Knowledge Management Principle: *Invent, Innovate but don't Re-invent*

The Global development journey in recent decades has seen the emergence/evolution of the Microfinance Movement, increased Enterprise Informalization, associated problems — for which a 'micro' revolution based on successful experiments/recipes on what works, can be adapted/replicated, the pitfalls to beware, is required to effectively meet the 2015 MDG (Millenium

Development Goals) timeline and India's Five Year Plan priorities. This will obviate the wasteful *'re-inventing the wheel'* syndrome—spending significant monetary and temporal resources in rediscovering (archival) knowledge through a battery of consultations, seminars and repeated bouts of capacity building. The existing storehouse of successful development recipes accessible from the global knowledge domain that would have led to sumptuous cuisine is not looked into — culinary attempts with many avoidable disasters resorted to, many recipes 'tried' on the long suffering beneficiary, and some of them abandoned on the way — with resultant greatly reduced effectiveness/output of the interventions. In contrast to the general trend this publication is an attempt to forge continuity with past initiatives/ learnings/successful experimentation in adherence to the Livelihoods Forum's *Knowledge Management Principle (KMP): if the know-how exists, access it, use it — go for further probing only when your investigations categorically confirm that new ingredients are required to make the existing recipe work in the new milieu/medium.*

Permanent Knowledge Management Mechanisms like this Forum are required to be created containing separate archives/ real and virtual libraries/resource centres containing details of structure/implementation/evaluation/project completion reports/ related ICE and extension material of past and ongoing interventions. These need to be maintained by the Planning Commission (GoI), State Planning Boards, Central and State development/research/training institutions and academies and should be provided with classified/rapid online access facilities, interconnectedness and networking to enable widest possible dissemination/access.

Contributors

As the readers would observe, the contributions to this series come from a *wide background*. Some of the contributions have been included without changes while others have been edited. Though most of the papers included in this work are recent/contemporary, the data have been retained in their original form (even where not latest) to provide *context continuity*. The *disclaimer* that the viewpoints expressed by the contributors are their own and do not in any way reflect the opinion of Govt. of M.P./DFID/MPRLP/

MPRLP-Livelihoods Forum applies to the contents of this publication. Livelihoods Forum does not endorse/validate the opinions/information conveyed by the writers/organisations in the contributions included in this selection (which nevertheless, adhere to high standards). The readers may appraise the papers as per their own experiences and adapt/innovate/replicate on the interventions/experiments/recommendations covered in this selection.

Acknowledgements

This series owes a lot to the generous support of the contributing institutions/individuals, their spirit of sharing/concern for the larger cause of development. MPRLP-Forum would wish to acknowledge valuable contribution from:

- The Project Coordinator, MPRLP, Jitendra Agrawal, MPRLP Project teams at the State/District/Cluster levels, Project's Technical Cooperation Project Support Unit (TCPSU) team and consultants. The Livelihoods Forum team (Mohan Raman, Owais Khan and Prakash Vishwakarma) endeavoured to make this series emerge within the prescribed timeline.
- The Department for International Development (DFID, Govt. of U.K.) which has been supporting/funding MPRLP from inception helped the Forum's initiative. Rachel Lambert, Rural Livelihoods Advisor and Moutushi Sengupta M.P. Programme Manager, DFID (I) New Delhi supported this publication.
- Govt. of Madhya Pradesh, Department of Panchayat and Rural Development and other Govt. Departments of M.P./ other States as well as the Central Government (Planning Commission, Ministry of Micro, Small Medium Enterprises, Ministry of Finance etc.) have provided critical inputs. Pradip Bhargava, Additional Chief Secretary and Development Commissioner, Government of M.P. and Wasim Akhtar, Secretary Rural Development, Government of M.P. provided considerable encouragement to our initiatives.
- National Bank for Agriculture and Rural Development

(NABARD) is the apex level development financial institution of India which has the mission to formulate/control/coordinate the developmental policy, planning, credit dispensation and regulatory operations for sustainable rural development of the country. The Project has initiated several valuable partnerships with NABARD. The apex institution's vast storehouse of learning (on microfinance/microenterprise development/rural non farm sector/tribal development/backward area development) have been disseminated among the Project teams/provided useful inputs for the publication.

- NGO partners have also contributed significantly to our initiative in several ways.
- Prof. P.K. Choubey (Indian Institute of Public Administration, New Delhi).
- Prof. M.S. Sriram (IIM, Ahmedabad).
- Ms. Marie Luise Haberberger (GTZ).
- Sujatha Viswanathan (Social Economist, Asian Development Bank, New Delhi).
- Geeta Gupta (Senior Information Officer, UNIFEM, New Delhi).
- Hideki Kagohashi (Enterprise Development Specialist) and Anandan Menon (Programme Officer), International Labour Organisation, New Delhi).
- S. Sriram (International Fund for Agriculture Development, New Delhi).
- Anand Kumar (Coordinator, United Nations Solution Exchange New Delhi). and Solution Exchange Communities.
- Alok Srivastava (Resource Person and Moderator, Solution Exchange Decentralisation Community, UNDP, New Delhi).
- D. Krishna Rao, Media Adviser and Dr. P.D. Kaushik, Associate Director (Rajiv Gandhi Foundation, New Delhi).
- Sandhya Venkateswaran (Director, Policy and Advocacy, CARE India, New Delhi).
- Uma Devi Swaminathan (Director, SEWA Gram Mahila Haat, Ahmedabad).
- Apoorva Oza (CEO, Aga Khan Rural Support Programme, Ahmedabad).

- Sanjay Sinha, Managing Director, Micro Credit Ratings International Ltd.
- Vipin Sharma (CEO, ACCESS Development Services, New Delhi).
- Anuradha Saxena, Learning Manager, United Nations Development Programme, New Delhi.
- Sanjeev Kaushal, Joint Secretary and Additional Development Commissioner, Ministry of Micro, Small and Medium Enterprises, New Delhi.
- Jaspreet Kaur Pal (Head of Operations, BBC World Service Trust, New Delhi).
- Prof. K.M. Shrivastava (Indian Institute of Mass Communication, New Delhi).
- S.N. Singh (International Development Research Centre, Regional Office for South Asia, New Delhi).
- Dr. Ajit N. Kanitkar (Ford Foundation, New Delhi).
- Dr. Sushil Kumar (ODI Consultant).
- Orlanda Ruthven (International Development Centre, University of Oxford, UK)
- Other scholars/practitioners provided valuable insights for this publication.
- The cooperation of Ashok K. Mittal and Concept Publishing Company team which made this co-publishing partnership possible is acknowledged with gratitude.

Summing Up

It is hoped that this publication will be *useful* to both the practicing development professionals (working from policy to grassroots levels) as also to the researchers/teachers and students of Development Studies courses (as Case Studies) in professional rural management/training/governance institutions. It is imperative for the practitioner/policy maker to be equipped with the fundamentals and contemporary status of concerned sub-sectors for and to form *mental checklists* of the parameters for their own/related sub sectors. For example, potential for micro-enterprise development has to be also gauged by farm/non-farm/

forestry sector specialists and is not the responsibility of MED specialist alone.

Readers are requested to convey their *feedback* and comments on the utility/content/vision of this initiative as also on possible areas for improvement which will help us in charting our future course. We shall also appreciate if readers will let us know *details of other* similar sage and sound existing experiments/studies/ research reports/think pieces/models etc. covering *good development/livelihoods practices* which we could cover in subsequent publications. Though considerable care has been taken in bringing out this publication, we would like to offer our apologies for inadvertent errors/omissions.

The development recipes/experiments/wisdom that have led to satisfactory outcomes in the field of microfinance/ microenterprise/Informal Sector development, have been highlighted in this book to motivate/provoke/enable other actors of the development arena to initiate their interventions with optimum effectiveness. It is hoped that Knowledge Management initiatives of MPRLP-Livelihoods Forum will continue to play a significant role in containing the reinvention of the development wheel.

MPRLP-Livelihoods Forum
Bhopal

Dr. Amitabh Bhatnagar
Livelihoods Forum Coordinator
abhatnagr@hotmail.com

1

Rural Microfinance and Microenterprise: The Informal Revolution Overview

AMITABH BHATNAGAR

I. FINANCIAL SECTOR: MICROFINANCE MOVEMENT

In the first decade of the millennium with the world stage dazzled by the blinding glare of globalisation—if we look at the backbenchers on the shadowy 'informal' fringes—groping for the MDG's (Millennium Development Goals) and beyond—we can feel the rustle of movement: in the 'micro' realms of money/finance, work, livelihoods and enterprise. It is evident that despite increase in industrialization, the informal economy has continued to expand globally due to capital intensification leading to a reduction of the workforce, "downsizing"—retrenched workers joining the ranks of either the unemployed or the informally employed, decentralization of production, subcontracting to smaller production units, some of which remain informal and cost cutting measures. In the last decade, increasing globalisation has accelerated the emergence/expansion of the informal economy—which however, is not a static but a moving entity, experiencing shifts and rustle. This rustle, its various connotations we shall attempt to understand in this chapter—the financial sector under the sweep of the microfinance movement, the 'informal' economy—unorganised micro and small enterprise sector. The trends in this 'micro' realm of finance and enterprise—inceased globalization induced informalization, parallel corrective movements for organizing the informal, within the formal structures—the movements in high momentum—constrained however from assuming the dimensions of a revolution. The backdrop, ground realities for the micro revolution to happen along with and a synoptic overview of the following chapters of this text (comprising of erudite papers covering dimensions of the subject area, related best practices, learnings) will be delineated in this chapter.

Financial Sector: Institutional Profile

The financial system of India comprises[1] of the system of borrowing and lending of funds or the demand for and the supply of funds of all individuals, institutions, companies and the Government. It includes the institutions and the mechanism which affect the generation of savings by community, the mobilization of savings and the effective distribution of the savings among all those who demand the funds for investment purpose. The Indian financial system consists of two parts, viz. the Indian Money Market and the Indian Capital Market. The Indian money market in which short-term funds are borrowed and lent deals in bills of exchange—trade bills and treasury bills and other instruments drawn for short periods. The capital market in India on the other hand is the market for medium term and long term funds.

The Indian Money Market comprises traditional and new financial institutions (Datta and Sriram) having informal/ unorganized and formal/organized sectors.

- Under the *traditional* financial institutions in the formal sector, we have government departments and institutions, Commercial banks and Regional Rural Banks (RRBs), Cooperative banks, Post Office Network, Insurance Companies, registered Non-banking finance companies. Under informal sector we have rural money lenders, traders, commission agents, indigenous bankers, unregistered local finance companies etc.
- Under the new financial institutions under formal 'non-profit' sector we have SHGs promoted by NABARD, NGOs, Government sponsored SHGs and Microfinance Organisations (registered as non-profit companies under Companies Act Section 25). Under 'for profit' category we

have rural non-banking finance companies and Mutually-aided Cooperative Societies (MACS) etc. The new informal sector organisations include self-managed unregistered financial bodies e.g. local chit funds.

- The formal/organized banking system in India can be broadly divided into three categories, viz. at apex level the Central Bank of the country, the Reserve Bank of India and apex Development Finance Institutions (DFIs—NABARD, IDBI, SIDBI etc.), the Commercial Banks (including RRBs) and the Cooperative Banks. The Reserve Bank of India is the supreme monetary banking authority in the country.
- Commercial banks which have been in existence for many decades, after the 1969 nationalization, are broadly classified into nationalized or public sector banks and private sector banks. The private sector banks include a small number of Indian scheduled banks which have not been nationalized and branches of foreign banks operating in India. The RRBs which came into existence since the middle of 1970s as low cost organisations with the specific objective of providing credit and deposit facilities particularly to the small and marginal farmers, agricultural labourers and artisans and small entrepreneurs are essentially commercial banks but their area of operation is limited to a few districts. Primary Cooperative Credit Societies (or Cooperative Banks) were originally set-up in villages to promote thrift and savings of the farmers and to meet their credit needs for cultivation. To support them, Central or District Cooperative Banks and above them State Cooperative Banks were established.
- The *Rural/Agricultural Banking sector* (elaborated in *Chapter* 3 of this Volume) consists of three institutions, viz. cooperative credit sector, commercial banking sector and RRBs: Primary Land Development Banks, branches of State Land Development Banks, Primary Agricultural Cooperatives, large sized Adivasi Multipurpose Societies, Farmers Service Societies, branches of RRBs and branches of commercial banks located at rural and semi-urban

centres and also some of the branches set-up at urban locations. In order to support, nurture and guide rural credit institutions in respect of planning, policy making, institution development and refinance operations, National Bank for Agriculture and Rural Development (NABARD) functions as apex level developmental financial institution.

- The *Post Office Network* provides savings as well as insurance services and sell the National Small Savings Organisation deposit instruments.
- The Life and General *Insurance* Corporations in the public sector along with a number of private sector insurance companies sell insurance products.

The large spread of the Indian financial system, and penetration of banking system across rural India, has not ensured satisfactory access of rural poor to formal finance—70 per cent of the rural poor lack a bank account and 87 per cent have no access to formal credit (World Bank—NCAER survey) and the informal sector lenders continue to deliver high interest finance to the rural poor. Research[2] demonstrates that in this scenario the 'use of informal mechanisms like reciprocal gifts, interest free lending and borrowing and taking credit in kind from shopkeepers, is widespread and does not decrease with increasing wealth..... Use of bank credit is open only to a minority whose landholding are generally above 5-7 acres'. This prevalent state of affairs of financial exclusion to a large majority of the disadvantaged section is despite almost four decades of bank nationalization, financial sector reforms since the 90s and operational LPG (liberalization, privatization and globalization) forces. For this, both supply and demand related factors are responsible. On the supply side, the formal banking sector is deterred by the high quantum of transaction costs/risks/uncertainty associated with servicing frequent/small loan transaction, without desired government support/conducive policy framework. On the demand side, for the poor rural clientele the banking sector's products and services are not consumer friendly on account of high costs, delays, difficult procedures, collateral requirements with leakages adding to the cost.

Microfinance Movement

This mismatch between demand and supply and the extortionary connotations of the traditional informal sector provided a conducive field for the emergence and growth of microcredit services, which over time attempted to move towards more comprehensive microfinance. This has assumed the dimensions of a Global Movement, the Microfinance Movement (MFM) across a large part of the developing world, including India, in the past decade.

Microfinance has been *defined* differently by different sources. Consultative Group to Assist the Poor (CGAP), the consortium of microfinance donors and practitioners set-up at the World Bank looks at microfinance as refering to 'any project or component thereof that supports delivery of (1) very small, uncollateralized or less-than-normally-collateralized loans, or (2) other financial services such as savings or insurance for low income clients.' For reporting purposes, CGAP, considers loans as microfinance if their average outstanding balance is not above US$ 5000 for Eastern Europe and NIS; $2000 for Latin America and the Caribbean, $1500 for the Middle East, North Africa, global and other projects and $ 1000 for Sub-Saharan Africa, Asia and the Pacific. For savings services, the cut-off may be one-third or one-quarter of the loan amounts. The Key Principles of Microfinance, as encapsulated by CGAP, which provide elucidation of the concept are provided in Box 1.1.

Box 1.1: The Key Principles of Microfinance

1. The poor need a variety of financial services, not just loans but also savings, cash transfers, and insurance that are convenient, flexible, and reasonably priced.
2. Microfinance is a powerful instrument against poverty as it enables the poor to increase incomes, build assets, reduces their vulnerability to external shocks. Microfinance allows poor households to move from everyday survival to planning for the future, investing in better nutrition, improved living conditions, and children's health and education.
3. Microfinance means building financial systems that serve the poor constituting the vast majority of the population in most developing countries. Yet microfinance continues to be seen as a marginal sector and primarily a development in order to achieve its full potential of reaching a large number of the poor,

(Contd.)

microfinance should become an integral part of the financial sector.

4. Financial sustainability is necessary to reach significant numbers of poor people to reach significant scale and impact far beyond what donor agencies can fund by reducing transaction costs, offering better products and services that meet client needs, and finding new ways to reach the unbanked poor.
5. Microfinance is about building permanent local financial institutions that can provide financial services to poor people on a permanent basis with diminishing dependence on funding from donors and governments—including government-financed development banks.
6. Microcredit is not always the answer as it is not appropriate for everyone or every situation. The destitute and hungry who have no income or means of repayment need other forms of support before they can make use of loans—small grants, infrastructure improvements, employment and training programmes, and other non-financial services.
7. Interest rate ceilings can damage poor people's access to financial services. It costs much more to make many small loans than a few large loans. At the same time, micro-lenders should not pass on operational inefficiencies to clients in the form of higher prices.
8. The government's role is as an enabler, not as a direct provider of financial services—in setting a supportive policy environment that stimulates the development of financial services while protecting poor people's savings, maintaining macroeconomic stability, avoiding interest-rate caps, refraining from distorting the market with unsustainable subsidized, high-delinquency loan programmes improving the business environment for entrepreneurs, clamping down on corruption and improving access to markets and infrastructure.
9. Donor subsidies should complement, not compete with private sector capital to build the institutional capacity of financial providers, develop supporting infrastructure (like rating agencies, credit bureaus, audit capacity, etc.), support experimental services and products where required provide subsidies to reach sparsely populated and otherwise difficult-to-reach populations.
10. The lack of institutional and human capacity is the key constraint as Microfinance is a specialized field that combines banking with social goals, capacity needs to be built at all levels.
11. The importance of financial and outreach transparency—accurate, standardized, and comparable information on the financial and social performance of financial institutions providing services to the poor is imperative.

Source: Consultative Group to Assist the Poor (CGAP), 2004 (extracts)

MFM: Achievements and Shortcomings

The MFM has propelled across a variety of pathways—the large outreach based SHG Bank Linkage Programme (wherein links have been created between commercial banks, NGOs and SHGs (informal local self help groups of poor segment of largely rural clientele) along with the other stream of Microfinance Institutions (MFIs) (mainly specialized small size/outreach based MFI initiatives). Looking at the achievements, the performance highlights of the Microfinance Movement can be encapsulated[3] as:

- The movement has reached the clientele that mainstream agencies had not reached effectively in the past.
- It has added/a new set of client groups—not only the poor, but also women.
- It has worked under a credit culture carrying the legacy of loan write-offs and political intervention and has till now shown itself to be an insular system with very high repayment rates.
- By including activities other than agriculture also in its portfolio it is helping people to diversify their livelihoods.
- It has worked under a paradigm of trust/social collaterals etc. thereby reducing transaction costs significantly.

Though successful microfinance interventions have demonstrated through these achievements that financial services can be an effective/powerful instrument for poverty reduction, assisting poor people to increase incomes, build assets, and reduce their economic vulnerability and there is now high acceptability of the key principles/best practices needed to make microfinance sustainable, yet, with few exceptions, MFM has not managed to reach massive scale. The MFM however, at its present stage of evolution across its different pathways, is limited: in its services portfolio (mainly credit, little of other financial services, viz. savings/insurance/remittances), client coverage (e.g. the poorest of the poor not within its ambit, geographical concentration (e.g. in South India), low efficiency/effectiveness of service delivery mechanisms (e.g. low quality of groups/MFI/others/high transaction costs), hostile regulatory/policy framework etc.

The Microfinance Movement has not fulfilled expectations related to scale/depth to the desired extent for a number of reasons[4], linked to problems with the service providers/facilitators—the financial institutions as well as the social service agencies/NGOs/MFIs:

Financial Institutions: When microfinance initiatives are run by banks or financial institutions, they often:

- create obstacles such as legal registration, personal guarantees, property title, and collateral requirements that effectively bar most potential clients;
- intimidate poor people, many of whom have never spoken to a bank officer or entered a bank;
- are expensive for the poor because of excessive documentation, repeated visits to the institution, and endless waiting for loans;
- provide credit ill-suited to the needs of the poor—too much credit extended for too long.

Social Service Agencies/NGOs/MFIs: When programmes are run by social service agencies, they often engender another set of problems. Typically,

- Staff have good community outreach skills, but little business experience, and often lack the ability to provide relevant advice;
- Welfare and business goals are often mixed so staff do not know whether to be social workers or business developers;
- Projects are often too complicated—involving complex marketing schemes or collective production plans, overwhelming the people they are trying to reach.'

Though projects run by social service agencies are expensive, highly subsidized, and limited in their capacity to serve clients, the few that have developed clear business goals and well-defined performance standards, operate successfully. Such programmes focus on upgrading existing economic activities and providing services geared to the needs of clients.

II. SOME KEY DIMENSIONS OF MFM: ASSOCIATED CONCERNS/SOLUTIONS

Certain key dimensions of the Microfinance Movement (in the Indian context and beyond), present status within the country, related concerns and solutions: SHG Bank Linkage Programme, Commercial Banks & Microfinance, Microfinance Institutions (efficiency/performance issues), issues concerning the access of poorest, technological delivery innovations, consumer protection, urban microfinance, MFM and rural finance (lessons and learnings) and future challenges—will now be highlighted.

NABARD and SHG-Bank Linkage Programme: The world's largest microfinance programme called the SHG Bank Linkage which is linking self-help groups (SHGs) to the formal banking system by focusing on the poor and especially women in the rural India was launched by the National Bank for Agricultural and Rural Development (NABARD) at national level to link SHGs with financial institutions with the objective of providing about one third of the rural poor with improved access to credit and savings services. This was to redress the situation where despite the presence of a diversified financial institutional infrastructure, the majority of India's rural population especially poorer households and women, do not have access to requisite savings and credit services through the formal banking sector.

NABARD launched SHG-Bank Linkage Programme is the predominant Micro-Finance (MF) model in the country. A proven method of financial inclusion, it has facilitated access of un-banked rural clientele to formal financial services from the existing banking infrastructure. The cumulative number of credit linked SHGs as on 31st March 2007[5] stands at 29,24,973 enabling an estimated 409.5 lakh poor households to gain access to MF from the formal banking system. To reduce the regional imbalances in the spread of the SHG-Bank linkage programme, NABARD has identified 13 States which have a large population of the poor for focused attention. NABARD extends financial support to RRBs, DCCBs, NGOs, Farmers Club and Individual Rural Volunteers (IRVs) for the promotion and nurturing of SHGs as Self-Help Promoting Institutions (SHPIs). NABARD facilitates in scaling-up the programme through various measures such as widening the programmes spatial distribution on a district-wise basis, training and capacity building of banks, NGOs, farmers clubs, government departments etc. widening the range of SHPIs associating village communities, peoples institutions, individual rural volunteers to participate in the programme as SHG promoters.

To provide comprehensive support to the Micro-Finance sector and keeping in view the important role played by Micro-Finance Institutions (MFIs) working in remote non-banked areas of the country, NABARD provides grant/loan based assistance to these institutions. NABARD has been extending Revolving Fund Assistance to select MFIs for on lending to SHGs. For the identification, classification and rating of MFIs and empowering them to intermediate between lending banks and clients, NABARD provides financial grant assistance to commercial banks and RRBs to avail the services of credit rating agencies such as M-CRIL, CRISIL, ICRA, CARE etc. for rating of MFIs. NABARD also provides capital/equity support to MFIs to enable them to leverage capital/equity for accessing funds from banks for providing affordable financial services to the poor and to enable them achieve sustainability in their credit operations over a period of 3-5 years.

The results of the impact studies[6] indicate that considerable socio-economic benefits are accruing from the fast growing Linkage Banking Programme (LBP) to small-scale farmers, rural micro entrepreneurs and landless labourers. The improved access of SHG members to sustainable microfinance services as well as the group approach and related human capacity building processes contribute with cross cutting outcomes in several direct and indirect ways to most impact aspects of MDGs 1 to 6. In groups effectively linked to banks at least one basic saving and lending product is generally being offered to SHG members. Most SHG members substantially increase their saving rates. In borrowing patterns a shift can be observed over time from consumption loans to loans for income generating purposes. Increased savings and capital formation improve the self-financing capacities and even out the household's cash flow. Generally higher risk absorption capacities and decreased vulnerability can be assumed. The access to formal financial services also contribute to a strongly reduced dependency on informal money lenders with positive effects on the reduction of capital costs. There is of course considerable regional variation in the SHG success story—with southern states like Andhra Pradesh in the lead with a considerably mature MFM (covered in *Chapter Five* of this book). The *major recommendations* resulting from the impact studies include:

(1) More efforts need to be geared towards institution building including the strengthening of group functioning in existing SHGs as well as the promotion of federal structures of SHGs.
(2) There is a need for the development of more effective management information systems to promote the further consolidation of sustainable financial service delivery through well performing SHGs.
(3) The future strategy should also focus more on training and capacity building of SHG members as it would improve the productivity of financial service delivery.
(4) For reducing apparent regional imbalances in Linkage Banking more emphasis should be put in future strategies on widening the outreach of the programme in the Central and Eastern Regions of the country. To increase the effectiveness such outreach strategies may have to include different delivery models.
(5) SHGs' role in development could be further enhanced through an increased involvement in development programmes in the area.

Formal Financial Sector/Commercial Banks and Microfinance

Institutions having large infrastructures, such as state owned commercial banks, credit unions, financial cooperatives are required to play a significant role in scaling up financial services for the poor/poorest. It has to be realized that financial services for the poor have to be part of the financial sector. The current situation where Microfinance has mostly developed outside the domain of the formal financial sector—with governments and donors while addressing financial sector reforms, not incorporating microfinance within its ambit, is not desirable. 'Large—scale sustainable microfinance can be achieved only if financial services for the poor are integrated into the overall financial systems of developing countries. This integration allows more access to capital, better protection of poor people's savings, and increased legitimacy and professionalization of the sector. The result is opening markets to increasingly poor and geographically remote clients. The challenge is to achieve this integration without compromising the social mission of microfinance[7].

For Microfinance Movement to be mainstreamed so that it is enabled to optimize its potential, it is imperative to ensure co-existence of wide range of delivery organizations with different objectives/services/delivery. Strong microfinance NGOs and national distribution networks of selected state banks, alternative delivery mechanisms such as post offices, providing demand driven wide array of flexible diverse financial services—savings, insurance, and remittance services in addition to credit, are required.

Owing to several potential competitive advantages in a number of areas, e.g. access to capital, recognizable consumer brand names, existing infrastructure/systems, the Commercial Banking Sector can play a more effective role in the microfinance sector and thereby optimize on both social responsibility and business opportunity at the 'bottom of the pyramid'. In view of realisation of the aforesaid in recent years Commercial Banks entering the Microfinance market in different ways can be divided into two main categories (CGAP): directly (by creating an internal unit or launching a separate company, such as a service company or specialized financial institution) or indirectly by working with existing microfinance providers (outsourcing retail operations, providing commercial loans to MFIs or providing infrastructure and systems). Each approach has its particular rationale, associated risks, success factors, and costs, and different factors may lead to a different choice of model. Commercial Banks looking to get into the microfinance market will need to take into account[8]—

- '*Commitment* from board and management, strong internal champions, and alignment with the bank's core commercial strategy.
- *Knowledge* of microfinance best practices and how to serve micro-clientele.
- *Infrastructure* located conveniently for clients.
- *Products* especially adapted for low-income and informal markets.
- *Systems and procedures* adapted to the microfinance operations, e.g., systems that support immediate follow-up on missed payments.

- Appropriate staff *training* and incentives on new clients, products, and delivery systems.'

Microfinance Institutions

It is necessary to create a supportive policy environment to encourage a diversity of efficient MF institutions in providing financial services to serve the poor, safeguard their money, promote competition, and build the technical capacities of their supervisory and regulatory authorities (elaborated in *Chapter Two* of this Volume).

Characteristics of Efficient MFIs: The most efficient MFIs in India have been identified[9] to be those that have the following characteristics:

- for profit non-bank finance companies or some form of cooperative,
- operate in an urban area,
- in South India,
- have had microfinance operations for more than 5 years,
- with portfolio size greater than only $ 125,000 (with average outstandings of $ 50-60 per borrower, this would result in MFI outreach of the order of 2,500 borrowers),
- portfolio growing at 50-60 per cent a year, and
- the average size of loans disbursed in excess of $ 125.

Measuring MFI Performance: While such MFIs may not reach large proportions of the absolute poor—those below the national poverty line—they 'certainly reach substantial numbers of low income families at levels of efficiency that are better than those achieved by similar institutions almost anywhere else in the world.' Qualitative database on the financial/social performance of MFIs are required to be created to facilitate effective supervision/audits/ratings, attract greater flows of commercial/private funding, allow microfinance providers to compare performance leading to better integration with the financial sector. Basic tools to measure *financial performance* of microfinance institutions (MFIs) in a few core areas have been listed as follows (CGAP: Core Performance Indicators for Microfinance):

1. *Outreach (breadth)*—how many clients are being served?
2. *Outreach (depth)*—how poor are the clients?
3. *Collection performance*—how well is the MFI collecting its loans?
4. *Financial sustainability*—is the MFI profitable enough to maintain and expand its services without continued injections of subsidized donor funds?
5. *Efficiency*—how well does the MFI control its administrative costs?

Social performance has been conceptualised[10] as the 'effective translation of an institution's social mission into practice'. The social value of microfinance refers to the way financial services improve the lives of poor and excluded clients and their families and widen the range of opportunities for communities. To create this value, the social objectives of a microfinance institution (MFI) may include objectives that:

- 'serve increasing numbers of poor and excluded people in an ongoing, sustainable way both by broadening and by deepening outreach;
- improve the quality and appropriateness of the financial services available to target clients through the systematic assessment of their specific needs;
- create benefits for microfinance clients, their families and communities that are related to social capital and social links, assets, reduced vulnerability, income, access to services and the fulfilment of basic needs; and
- improve the social responsibility of the MFI towards its employees, clients and the community it serves.'

Development indicators for assessing Social Performance of Financial Institutions/Progress towards the Millennium Development Goals: The five different dimensions of the Millennium Development Goals for which information should be collected, as also selected indicators relating to these dimensions, as recommended by CGAP are reproduced below:

1. Depth of Outreach

- use of targeting tools,
- per cent of clients living below USD 1.00 per day and USD 2.00 per day, and
- per cent of clients living below the national poverty line or the absolute poverty line.

2. Reducing Poverty and Hunger

- improvements in housing structure,
- increases in assets (land ownership or any simple, easily visible asset),
- employment generation (especially lean season employment),
- food security and consumption smoothening (sufficient food, especially in lean seasons),
- crisis coping (increased resilience to cope with crises), and
- access to emergency financing (loans and savings).

3. Schooling

- primary school attendance (% of eligible children).
- secondary school attendance (% of eligible children).

4. Access to Health Care Services

- access to messages on preventive care and to referrals.
- access to clean water.
- immunization and prenatal care.
- use of modern medical facilities (e.g., doctors or modern health care facilities at childbirth).

5. Women's Empowerment and Social Capital

- per cent of women clients,
- women's involvement in public sphere activities (e.g. elections or local adjudicating bodies),
- legal awareness (divorce, inheritance),
- women's networks (the development of social networks outside kin groups).

Impact studies[11] indicate that NABARD led national *SHG Bank*

Linkage programme has contributed with cross cutting outcomes directly and indirectly to most *impact* aspects of UN Millennium Development Goals (MDGs) 1 to 6. The improved access to financial services benefit households respectively individuals in maintaining, intensifying and diversifying their economic activities especially also in the non-agricultural sector with positive effects on income and employment generation. According to the overall study results average net income increases of more than INR 6000 or by about 32 per cent to nearly INR 25000 are realized per household. With the income increases substantial contributions are made to poverty alleviation. The share of households living below the poverty line is reduced from about 50 per cent in the pre-SHG situation to about 31 per cent in the post SHG situation. Thus, nearly 20 per cent of all sample SHG members are able to raise their income levels above the poverty line *(MDG 1: Eradicate extreme poverty and hunger)*. The financial services and their impact on incomes also raise the capacities of the beneficiaries of the programme to increase their household expenditure for basic needs such as better nutrition (MDG 1) as well as for education *(MDG 2: Achieve universal primary education)* and *health (MDGs 4 to 6: Objectives related to improved medical care)*. With about 90 per cent, a very high share of participants of the SHG Bank Linkage are women. Participation in SHGs contributes substantially to human capacity building and empowers women to become more self-confident and competent; they are also likely to participate more in family decision-making. It also promotes communication as well as co-operation among group members and improves the capacities for problem solving *(MDG 3: Promote gender equality and empower women)*.

MF Services and the Poorest

On considering the shortcomings of Microfinance, it has to be realised that all poor people, use and need a variety of financial services (such as savings, credit, insurance, remittance and money transfer services) that are 'convenient, flexible and reasonably priced.' However, the focus of the MFM has been largely on credit provision, making little headway in respect of other services. In the domain of Microfinance—Savings and Social Protection concerns, the need to mainstream micro-pensions has been emphasized in *Chapter Six* of this book. Even credit has reached a relatively narrow range of clients with the extremely poor and geographically remote clients not being serviced. Though Microfinance NGOs have played a crucial role in research/innovations/development of services, exhibiting that microfinance can successfully/sustainably reach poor clients, most of them have not become large scale or become independent of donor funding.

Furthermore, in most situations, microfinance does not reach the people at the very bottom of the socio-economic scale—the "poorest". Though many people living on less than a dollar a day (the "very poor") are already being served by microfinance institutions (MFIs), few MFIs reach the "poorest" customers at the bottom of the poverty scale (the bottom subset of this—the destitute, who do not have any reliable sources of earnings). Reasons for this exclusion are several. Extremely poor people may prefer not to borrow because they fear debt is more likely to hurt rather than assist them (self-exclusion), it may be exclusion by group members (unwilling to increase their own risk) and the exclusion may be driven by MFI policy (fearing loan default).

In addition, the poorest need non-financial support such as capacity building, food, grants or guaranteed employment before they are in a position to make effective use of loans/deposit services. Hence to help the poorest gain access to appropriate financial services a possible approach would be to commence with 'safety net programmes'[12] that will eventually help the poorest graduate to financial services.

"The challenge moving forward is to better understand the financial service requirements of those who are currently excluded from the financial system and ways to respond to these needs that have the potential to be self-sustaining. But better understanding is not enough. This understanding needs to be translated into permanent access to high-quality, affordable, and convenient financial services offered by a range of financial service providers. Only when supply begins to meet demand will poor people have the means to take control over their financial lives and chart their own paths out of poverty." (CGAP)

Microfinance Delivery and Technology

To serve the customers located in sparsely populated distant areas with frequent low volume transactions profitably, requires delivery channel/technologies that are inexpensive to set up, offer a wider range of financial services to poor customers, and are able to handle transactions at low cost. Some of the innovations may be found in information and communications technologies (ICTs)—low cost "direct banking" technology channels, such as internet banking and automated teller machines (ATMs), points of sale (POS) terminals (such as bankcard readers) at retail and postal outlets to deliver bill payment, savings, credit, insurance, and money transfer products and use of mobile telephones networks. Technology channels that replace bank branches will be profitable only if they service at each outlet a critical mass of customers and deliver a wide range of services to them, build strong relationships with clients and handle issues related to supportive infrastructure/ policies, consumer education, prevention of thefts/frauds, cash transfer etc.

MF Borrowers and Consumer Protection Issues

Attention to consumer protection issues such as high interest rates, indebtedness of borrowers and threats from potentially abrasive lenders have raised public concern for poor consumers in the Microfinance sector. The chief consumer protection measures are: disclosure requirements, consumer education, lender practice prohibitions/requirements, mechanisms for handling complaints/ disputes etc. whose principles are encapsulated in the following Pro Consumer pledge of ACCION International Microfinance Network (MFN) (www.bellanet.org/partners/mfn):

1. *Quality of Service*: MFN members will treat every customer with dignity and respect. Members will provide services in as convenient and timely a manner as possible.
2. *Transparent Pricing:* MFN members will give clients complete and understandable information about the true costs they are paying for loans and transaction services and how much they are receiving for savings.
3. *Fair Pricing:* MFN members will price their services at fair rates. Their rates will not provide excessive profits, but will be sufficient to ensure that the business can survive and grow to reach more people.

4. *Avoiding Over Indebtedness*: In order to avoid customer over indebtendness, MFN members will not lend any customer more than the customer can afford to repay.
5. *Appropriate Debt Collection Practices*: While debt collection practices must include energetic pursuit of defaulters, MFN members will treat customers with dignity and will not deprive customers of their basic survival capacity as a result of loan repayment.
6. *Privacy of Customer Information*: MFN members will protect the private information of customers from reaching others who are not legally authorized to see it.
7. *Ethical Behaviour of Staff*: MFN members will hold their employees to a high standard with respect to conflicts of interest and unethical behaviour, especially behaviour that harms customers (such as taking kickbacks). Employees who breach these standards will be sanctioned.
8. *Feedback Mechanisms:* MFN members will provide formal channels of communication with customers through which customers can give feedback on service quality. These channels will include mechanisms for responding to specific customers regarding their personal complaints.
9. *Integrating Pro-Consumer Policies into Operations*: MFN members will make pro-consumer orientation a hallmark of the way they conduct business, though efforts such as staff training and incentives, financial education for customers, customer satisfaction programmes and the like.

Urban Microfinance

In countries like India, Urban Microfinance has been slow to take-off despite[13] 'the prospects of (i) huge loan demand, (ii) larger average loan size and higher population density making for lower costs, (iii) the need to reach the growing numbers of the urban poor, and (iv) the example of Latin America where microfinance is predominantly urban,' due to apprehensions that the long association peer based/pressure dependent SHG model of rural areas may not find conducive conditions in urban slums/poverty areas which are relatively more heterogeneous/time constrained/transitory. There is need to upscale this sub-sector in the light of experience of pioneers like SEWA Bank and initial forays of rural MFIs/NBFCs moving into urban areas.

MF Insufficiency: Livelihood Finance

An important concern relates to insufficiency of present levels of microfinance in meeting long term, multipurpose livelihoods enhancement related financial requirements of the target population. It is stressed that a holistic view has to be taken of these requirements—higher financial assistance tailored to the specific circumstances of the borrower—livelihoods finance—is imperative.

FAO/CARE study[14] stresses the need to make the best possible use of existing options for *livelihood finance*. The target population has to be assisted to use the products that are available and identify the best way to invest money to improve their livelihoods. Assisting people to use available products, particularly from the commercial banks involves breaking down barriers on both sides and requires guidance from advisers. Mechanisms to reach people with advice and for financial institutions to reach out to people e.g. through farmers' clubs, self help groups, community centres and cooperatives are needed to be made more effective. Some practical recommendations arising from this study towards meeting the requirements of Livelihood Finance include the following:

(i) 'An assessment should be carried-out of the operations, strengths and weaknesses of various forms of livelihood resource centres in India with a view to producing guidelines on how these centres can best be structured and managed.

(ii) The concept of livelihood resource centres as a source of information, technical and financial advice should be encouraged and as far as possible established at district and block, mandal or cluster level.

(iii) All resource centres should be provided with a range of appropriate materials which can be used to facilitate discussion about financial and technical issues relevant to the location.

(iv) The concept of farmer's club should be revisited and

methods found to revitalize their role and create synergies with SHGs, MACs and other local associations.

(v) A concerted effort to provide useful and friendly information about financial products from banks, cooperatives and post-offices should be made with distribution of material through SHGs, farmers' clubs, NGOs, cooperatives and resource centres.

(vi) A strategy should be devised to improve the ability of village extension workers, SHG leaders and NGO personnel to explain livelihood finance and financial planning to poor households. The simplest visualizing tools should be selected, tested and taught via workshops at livelihood resource centres.

(vii) Bank and cooperative training institutes should review curricula to determine if changes should be made to incorporate a livelihood approach to analyzing the needs of customers and how this might impact on lending decisions. In service training on working with farmers' clubs and SHGs to help their members identify livelihood improvement opportunities and plan the use of their money should be introduced.'

MFI Delivery: Innovative Approaches

CARE-CASHE[15] is supporting research, development projects and pilot innovative initiatives of competent professional organisations in the country through the innovation fund. Description of some of such Projects supported by CASHE follows:

- *Money Remittances*: 'The objective of the innovation project is to establish an appropriate mechanism to transfer money of migrant workers of Orissa from Gandhidham (Gujarat) to their places of origin and to provide microfinance services to the families of migrant workers. Shramika Sahajog, a money remittance microfinance organisation was established in August 2002 by Adhikar an NGO in Orissa.... The initiative was supported by CASHE. About 410 migrant workers have been registered with the organisation in Gandhidham and are using this channel to make monthly remittances to their families in Orissa.

As a further innovation, savings and insurance products have been added to supplement the remittance activity. To address the emergency needs of the migrant workers, an emergency loan product is being formulated.'

- *Pension Fund*: 'An innovative Pension Scheme has been initiated by the activists for Social Alternatives, an NGO working with the rural poor of Tiruchirapally district of Tamil Nadu. The objective of the scheme is to mitigate the financial risks of members' families in their old age.'
- *Community Grain Banks*: 'Grain Banks aim at reducing food insecurity mobilizing food grains as savings from the community and utilizing this at times of scarcity. Learning from the success of a CARE supported grain bank project in Sangli district of Maharashtra, CASHE facilitated a similar project in the tribal districts of Orissa. Six grain banks have been formed covering 83 families. Members of the grain banks have taken jowar and bajra as loans.'
- *Computer Munshi*: 'This innovative project is developed by PRADAN with the support from CASHE. It aims to provide an efficient and independent SHG accounting system. It helps to take the accounting load from professional staff. Computer Munshi are village level people who provide their services to SHGs on a freelance basis. Since its inception in June 2003, training has been imparted to 153 computer munshis in the McFinancier software and they are in turn assisting about 1500 SHGs.'
- *Disability Project*: 'Pragathi Seva Samathi (PSS) a partner NGO of CASHE project has a strong base in Warangal district, Andhra Pradesh. PSS initiated a special innovative project to address issues of the people with disabilities to help them and their families achieve economic and social development. They created awareness on the need and problems of persons with disability, provided medical education, social and economic rehabilitation and promoted advocacy and empowerment... CARE-CASHE took-up the microfinance component of the project and provided support in institutional building and microfinance services. PSS organised 1878 person with disabilities into 251 qualitative SHGs. Various capacity building activities were organised on group formation and

> management, different products, loan policies and book keeping. Necessary trainings have also been organised for staff and community on their rights, various Acts and different entitlements meant exclusively for disabled persons.... Currently, members are getting loans from the group savings and have started their own livelihoods and few of them are upgrading their existing livelihoods... To enhance their bargaining power, SHGs were federated.'

To examine the adaptability of various *innovative credit delivery* mechanisms/systems, NABARD has been implementing various pilot projects. NABARD[16] has tested the concept of Joint Liability Groups (JLGs) and has formulated scheme for financing JLGs of tenant farmers to supplement the efforts of banks in the SHG-Bank linkage programme. NABARD has designed a pilot project for collaboration with Post Offices to appraise the efficacy of utilizing the countrys vast postal network for disbursement of credit to the rural poor on an agency basis. Under the project, Post Offices extend loans to SHGs at an interest rate of 9 per cent per annum repayable in 24 instalments by them. The department would retain the service fee of 3 per cent while the balance would be passed on to NABARD. NABARD has sanctioned pilot project to create a community based social security system for SHG members in rural areas for provision of a package of health/life insurance by paying premium generated through discounts offered by service providers like grocery shops, cloth merchants etc., in the project area.

An important innovative application of microfinance services has been suggested[17] in the field of education. In recent years, though the number of microfinance institutions (MFIs) offering microcredit has grown and at the same time NGOs/governments have enhanced efforts to increase literacy, traditionally, microcredit and education programmes have not worked with each other. *'Microfinance and education* can and should integrate. There is a very strong potential for microfinance to play an active role in helping developing countries increase their level of educational attainment... It is inherently harder to provide credit to build human capital. However, there are also strong reasons to think that developing credit markets for education, thus removing important demand-side constraints on its acquisition, is very important to help families get out of the vicious circle of poverty. Low and variable incomes lead to deficient levels of educational attainment, thus leading to the intergenerational transmission of poverty... Poverty is caused by many factors including lack of skills, entrepreneurship and human capital. If micro-credit is used for investing in education, it can have a deeper and longer impact through the creation of virtuous cycles out of poverty...' Some education related Microfinance products that MFIs can provide to fulfill the financial needs of poor parents wishing to send their children to schools have been suggested ranging from a loan of Rs. 3,000 for primary and secondary school to Rs. 15,000 to Rs. 30,000 per year for tertiary education to be re-paid after graduation.

MFM and Rural Finance: Lessons and Learnings

IIM Ahmedabad Workshop on Microfinance (2004) in which bankers representing the formal banking system and microfinance practitioners in India deliberated to examine where these two worlds meet and the learnings they could imbibe from each other came to the following conclusions[18]:

- 'Rural finance has suffered from interventions from the state in the past. While some interventions have been positive, they have harmed the sector when compromises such as write-offs have been made.
- Microfinance has emerged as an important mechanism to reach out financial services to the poor. There are interesting lessons from this for the banks to adopt.
- There are problems for the microfinance institutions in the form of regulatory and supervisory apathy. This leads to financial exclusion of large segments of the poor.
- There is a huge market for financial services—both loans and savings.
- Innovations across the world indicate important breakthroughs in delivery of financial services. These can be implemented provided the regulatory impediments are removed.
- The issue of risk management has to be systematically addressed.
- The role of the state, wherever positive, has been effective

and, therefore, this should be sharply defined to see how the state could contribute to this sector.

- The issue of interest rates continues to be vexatious and needs to be addressed urgently.'

Main *lessons derived from the informal (financial) sector* which are likely to be useful in creating a more inclusive Financial Sector as encapsulated by UNCDF/Microstat include the following:

- "*Work directly in the community*: Staff should visit villages and poor neighbourhoods almost daily, calling upon existing clients and explaining requirements to potential clients. They should hold meetings in the communities. If the project is operating in a rural area, staff should visit towns and villages, perhaps on a weekly basis;
- *Simplify application procedures*: There is little difference in the rate of loan repayment between projects that "write a book" on each applicant and those that reduce applications to one or two pages. At the microloan level, relying on peers to choose a client is an effective tool for loan security;
- *Extend credit quickly*: Loan applicants become discouraged if they have to wait months before receiving services. They are accustomed to moneylenders who dispense money on the spot. Well managed projects extend credit in less than a month and often within a week. They disburse subsequent loans even more quickly;
- *Do not require records and complex business plans*: Because only a small percentage of farmers, traders and micro-manufacturers keep written records of any kind, successful programmes refrain from asking for records or plans;
- *Do not require guarantees eliminating most potential candidates*: Alternative mechanisms, such as credit groups where business owners are mutually responsible for repaying loans, substitute effectively for conventional guarantees. The individual's reputation in the community is more important than collateral;
- *Work with existing economic activities, no matter how small, or work with start-ups appropriate to the community*: Launching larger enterprises is seldom successful and requires extensive inputs over months and often years;

- *Focus initially on the local market*: Local entrepreneurs and small farmers can find "niches" often invisible to outside experts. Efforts to find new markets are often costly and difficult;
- *Extend small, short-term loans primarily for working capital on simplified terms*: Small, short-term loans not only "test" the client's commitment to repay, but also allow the client to see whether or not a loan will, in fact, help the business grow. These loans should have frequent (weekly, bi-weekly, monthly) equal payments;
- *Provide larger loans based on successful repayment*: Virtually all successful programmes have a well defined system of providing increased loans based on successful repayment;
- *Charge a higher rate of interest than the market*: From the perspective of borrowers, quick credit is more important than a low interest rate. From the perspective of lenders, interest must cover transaction costs and the cost of operating the project;
- *Assume clients, with their network of friendships and their relationships within the community, will take a major role in promoting the project*: Clients form their own groups and provide one another with advice and assistance, reducing programme costs significantly. At the same time, this intensified interaction serves to develop a commitment among clients—to the project and to each other;
- *Develop large-scale, self-sufficient, profitable projects working in close coordination with local banks*: The involvement of the formal financial sector is vital if efforts are to reach a significant part of the rural and urban poor; and
- *Address the needs of poor clients*: Formal sector banking hours are often not convenient to the schedules of the working poor."

General *features of successful rural/agricultural microfinance*[19] which are derivable on the basis of these learnings from informal/ microfinance/related sectors have been summarised below and illustrated in the strategy statement of Inter American Development Bank.

- 'Poor families and especially poor farming families engage in a number of income-generating activities, have a number of financial coping strategies and use a variety of formal and informal financial instruments to manage their affairs. Although agricultural production may be the main source of revenue, it is seldom the only source.

- This revelation has allowed development finance initiatives, especially in the microcredit movement, to move away from the concept of loan repayments being tied to specific investment activities. Accordingly, the entire borrowing household is seen as an economic unit wherein income from different activities is mixed together to meet a wide variety of daily needs and repayment obligations. This shift has dramatically improved loan recovery rates and is probably a precondition for financial sustainability in most credit schemes for poor people.
- Successful agricultural microfinance providers have married the core principles of the microcredit movement—peer-based borrower selection and repayment enforcement, incremental lending, close follow-up on repayment and so on—with the technical expertise required to assess the agricultural competence of potential borrowers...
- Agricultural microfinance providers may modify loan terms and conditions to accommodate the more cyclical cash flows in farming households and the more demanding timing of credit needs for crop or livestock activities...
- One of the hallmarks of successful microcredit is that lenders diversify their loan portfolios into a large number of discrete, unrelated economic activities. Similarly, organizations seeking to engage in or expand lending in farming areas can limit their exposure by lending to a large number of households engaged in many distinct agricultural and other economic activities...
- In sum, with some significant—but not particularly daunting—adjustments, a lot of agricultural production can be financed using standard microcredit principles.'

As an illustration of policy formulation for provision of effective financial services in developing regions, the *rural finance strategy of the Inter American Development Bank's* (IADB) may be considered. This strategy[20] for Latin America and the Caribbean aims to 'systematically remove the constraints on both the demand for and the supply of financial services in rural areas, thereby allowing profitable intermediation and risk-sharing.' The recommended sequence of actions for the Bank (which depends on a suitable macroeconomic environment, overall banking sector strength, a high level of government commitment, and the presence of capable counterparts), is to engage in the following four steps:

1. 'removing biases in sectoral economic policies that have reduced the profitability and competitiveness of rural economic activities;
2. removing biases in the legal and regulatory framework that have increased the risk and cost of financial intermediation in rural areas;
3. strengthening and improving financial retail capacity for rural financial services; and
4. help to introduce new products and services for rural finance, once the policy environment is favourable and a number of solvent and capable financial intermediaries exist.'

Taken together, these four steps help address the problems of unmitigated risk, imperfect information and high transactions costs.

In India, though the ongoing decade and a half of *Financial Sector Reforms* has resulted in greater profit/market orientation, technological upgradation, reduced regulation, private sector induced competitiveness and gradual acceptance/promotion of MFM, a lot remains to be done, as discussed, for attaining desired financial inclusion and creating a successful rural microfinance model. Presently the governments's new *Microfinance Bill 2007* proposes an important (much needed) measure in allowing NGO-MFIs to mobilize savings—but by limiting savings to "thrift" (small/uniform/compulsory/member savings)—it doesn't offer the facility for small, variable frequency/amount based flexible saving facility suited to the poor microfinance borrowers. The Bill excludes from its purview MFIs registered as NBFCs and S.25 companies which account for nearly all the large MFIs in the country on the grounds that they are already regulated by the RBI. Consequently NBFC-MFIs will not be enabled to either accept public deposits or even the savings of their own borrower members either who will continue to have to depend on less profitable/ riskier saving instruments. It is desirable that MFIs may be allowed to mobilize public deposits with sound prudential measures. Furthermore, due to exclusion of NBFCs and S.25 companies from the proposed Act, several borrowers will not be able to access the protection of the ombudsman envisaged under the bill and the sector will not be able to build a universal performance standards/ comprehensive data base. The enabling role played by the government in Thailand in supporting microfinance (covered in *Chapter Four* of this Volume) offers useful learnings concerning the effective directions that the State can provide to the MFM.

Realising the MFM Potential: Future Challenges

Looking to the future, for extending the frontiers of finance difficult questions will have to be examined carefully: 'Will microfinance reach its full potential? Will financial systems become truly inclusive? Will there be access for all?' The answer to these questions can be in the affirmative if a number of *interlocking problems/challenges* are addressed. 'The myriad interlinked problems at all levels of the financial system add up to three core challenges that define the frontier of finance: scaling up to extend access to billions more people; reaching poorer and more remote clients; and reducing costs. A few additional cross-cutting issues pose particularly stubborn dilemmas and represent enormous opportunities. These issues include optimizing technology, leveraging money transfers and cross-border remittances, reaching farmers and remote rural clients, measuring social performance, and protecting poor consumers.' (Helms, 2006)

One of the important challenges[21] of the next decade will be 'political risk—the interference of politics in microfinance in a way that hampers the continued development of the industry... Some populist governments are already calling for interest rate ceilings, launching new government microfinance banks and bringing bank supervision back into the orbit of political leadership... challenge facing regulatory authorities involves the introduction of innovations such as the new technologies... are often outside existing regulatory frameworks, simply because they are so new. An example of regulators opening new channels is Brazil's programme of correspondent banks, through which banks can appoint retailers as agents to carry out transactions, thereby extending the reach of the financial system to remote areas... Cell phone banking is one of the most obvious question marks because both potential and risks are enormous. Banking authorities will have to decide whether cell phone banking and other innovations meet minimum standards of safety and security...'

In CGAP's recent *scenario-building exercise for the year 2015* (Financial Inclusion 2015: Four Scenarios for the future of Microfinance) to 'help anticipate and prepare for the global demographic, political, and technological forces that will shape the future of microfinance,' *four trends* that could help or hurt financial access were identified: wireless (new) technology, activist governments (political risk), new international actors, and international regulation. The most significant technological change that could open up access to finance for large numbers of excluded people is pervasive extension of wireless access, even in poorer countries. Wireless technology could radically reduce transaction costs and create anytime, anywhere access, even for very poor and remote clients. Subsidized state credit could drive many private MFIs out of business and destroy the general repayment culture (many borrowers see government loans as social and political transfers and do not feel compelled to repay them). International actors such as donors, technical assistance providers, and microfinance networks have played an important role in the growth of microfinance. An increasing number of international financial standards and codes already affect financial systems in developing countries. Measures such as Anti-Money Laundering and Combating the Financing of Terrorism (AML/CFT) initiatives, certifications by the Office of Foreign Asset Control, and the Basel Capital Accord aim to define a stable architecture for a global financial system. Know-your-customer rules require financial institutions to collect and report various identifying information for all customers. The expense of complying can make small transactions and accounts unviable, unless they are exempted from the requirement.

As the global Microfinance Movement is gathering momentum over its evolution (from microcredit to microfinance to inclusive financial systems) in many countries, through several innovative measures, one can discern positive signs of poor and low-income clients being integrated into their financial systems as can be observed from the following examples documented by CGAP[22]:

- '*In India and Brazil*—both enormous potential markets—commercial banks are experimenting with microfinance. They are forging alliances with agents as wide-ranging as supermarket chains, lottery outlets, and gas stations (Brazil) and with such local entrepreneurs as franchise owners and community-based MFIs (India). While relatively young yet, these experiments promise to reach large number of poor clients very quickly.
- More traditional microfinance markets like Bolivia, Bangladesh, and Uganda are becoming more competitive, spurring financial service providers to innovate by making their products more client-friendly (Bangladesh), broadening the range of services they can offer through transformation from non-governmental organizations to licensed intermediaries (Bolivia and Uganda), and introducing cost-saving technological advances such as intelligent automatic teller machines that allow illiterate people to more easily access basic banking services (Bolivia).
- Countries as varied as South Africa, the Philippines, and Kenya are introducing mobile phone banking that would allow poor clients to deposit funds, repay loans, pay bills, and transfer funds to relatives without necessarily having to leave their villages or open up formal bank accounts.
- Mainstream credit bureaus in countries as disparate as Bosnia, Peru, and Haiti have integrated microcredit borrowers into their databases.
- Donors and investors show an increasing commitment to making a difference with their funds by adhering to "what works" and expanding poor and low-income people's access to financial services.'

These and other examples help light the path for others to follow...Working together, financial service providers, governments, and the international development community can transform the dream of truly inclusive financial systems into a reality…to ensure access for all…. The future is uncertain and the scenarios are not predictions but they suggest some insights into where we can best focus our efforts to help make the positive stories come true and deflect the risks posed by the negative ones.'

However, for maximizing the potential of the MFM, it is also important to clarify common perceptions of—decision/policy makers, practitioners and consumers. Microfinance and MED should not become fads, to be offered as universal panaceas for handling economic distress. The following are *common myths*[23] among many poorly performing microfinance programmes which are hampering the progress of MFM and MED which need to be clarified so that a better understanding of the ground realities is appreciated.

Myth	*Reality*
Microentrepreneurs need to be cared for because they are poor.	Microentrepreneurs are knowledgeable about doing business in their local economy. They often have years of experience in their trade working with dedication and determination. Belief in the intelligence and business knowledge of clients is critical.
Microenterprises are redundant activities that should be replaced by larger businesses employing many people.	While often marginal, microenterprises are viable, locally important activities that should be upgraded. These small scale economic activities are valid business activities to be taken seriously.
Interest rates to the poor need to be subsidized.	Microfinance rates of interest must reflect operating costs to achieve sustainability. Organizations making large numbers of small loans will have high transaction costs and thus need to charge rates that are higher than commercial rates. However, microfinance rates are still significantly lower than the exorbitant rates charged by money lenders and other sources from whom the poor borrow.
Credit alone is useless. It must be packaged with training, marketing, technology, and other services.	Although programmes which package credit with other services may seem ideal, they require large subsidies and have proven to be largely unsustainable. The minimalist approach used by the Grameen Bank and many others has shown that clients can use credit in small amounts to start or improve the profitability of their microenterprises. Providing marketing and many other areas of services is valid, but best managed separately.

(*Contd.*)

Myth	*Reality*
The poor cannot be trusted with credit. The consumption needs of the poor are so pressing that any loan will find its way quickly to consumption.	The high repayment rate of millions of microfinance clients is empirical proof that the poor are credit-worthy.
The poor are unable to save.	The high rate of savings reported by many microfinance organizations demonstrates that the poor can value savings as much as credit.
Poverty has a crippling effect rendering the poor unable to improve their condition.	The remarkable success of institutions lending to over 10 million clients around the world, the vast majority of whom are below the official poverty line (usually defined by caloric intake), proves beyond any doubt the ability of the poor to improve their lives with their own ingenuity and drive.

Optimising the potential of the Microfinance Movement within larger financial sector reform framework is required for building *sustainable financial services systems* for poor men and women which is of critical interest from three perspectives[24]: 'First, from the point of view of *financial sector development*, people who have not been integrated into the formal financial sector because of low incomes, gender, ethnic identity or remote location often represent a large and potentially profitable market for institutions that can develop ways to reduce the costs and risks of serving them. Second, from the standpoint of *enterprise formation and growth*, the availability of stable sources of funding and deposit services contributes to successful start up and operations of micro and small enterprises. Third, from the perspective of *poverty reduction*, access to reliable, monetized savings facilities can help the poor smooth consumption over periods of cyclical or unexpected crises, thus greatly improving their economic security. Once some degree of economic security is attained, access to credit can help them move out of poverty by improving the productivity of their enterprises or creating new sources of livelihood.'

For the outreach of the MFM to be scaled up in a significant way so as to be in a position to provide sustainable mass financial access for the deprived rural clientele so as to cater to the diverse financial requirement (credit, saving, remittance, insurance etc.) of the poor rural consumers through flexible services/products on cost effective terms, it has to overcome the several impediments/

constraints discussed, facilitated by an enabling state policy/ infrastructure support.

While optimizing on the potential of microfinance a quick/ simple mode for delivering financial services, the perspective strategy[25] for scaling-up access to finance for India's rural poor (outlined in Box 2) should be to evolve microfinance clients to avail the services from formal finance institutions. Since presently the formal financial institutions are not in a position to offer convenience flexibility and reliability desired by the poor segment customers, it is imperative to reform the vast network of India's rural financial institutions to enhance the efficiency and design services/products which are suited to the requirements of microfinance customers. 'To become a force for change, banks will need to increase their outreach, even within the agricultural sector and to develop policies and products which promote innovation...' (Orlanda Ruthven and Sushil Kumar, 2002). The long term financial inclusion strategy has necessarily to be holistic and endeavour to improve the effectiveness of the formal sector at "banking the poor" even while it is working to strengthen the delivery of the microfinance movement.

Box 1.2: Scaling-Up Access to Finance for India's Rural Poor

- Reducing minimum start-up capital requirements to facilitate the transformation of MFIs into NBFCs. The minimum start-up capital requirement for registering as an NBFC in India is high beyond the reach of most MFIs.
- Encouraging multiple sources of equity for MFIs which have problems raising equity because (i) NGOs are restricted to invest in MFI equity and (ii) the minimum amount for equity investment by foreign donors, development finance institutions and non-resident Indians in an MFI is far too high.
- Facilitating MFIs to raise debt—while Indian banks have been lending more easily to MFIs than earlier, the supply is still limited.
- Permitting MFIs to mobilize savings, with safeguards—arguments for allowing MFIs to mobilize deposits, at least from their members, center on the importance attached to savings by poor households, and also on the need for MFIs to mobilize deposits in order to achieve financial sustainability.
- MFI representatives have also made the case that the regulator, jointly with the MFIs, could consider developing a set of prudential

(*Contd.*)

norms that are more appropriate to institutions serving the poor, and set up supervision mechanisms around those.

- Attention to quality, and the importance of financial sustainability—scaling-up SHG Bank Linkage requires attention to the quality and sustainability of groups, their promoters and lenders (banks). A strong focus on the quality of SHGs by their NGO promoters was a key factor in the success of this model in its pilot phase. But in recent years, growing concerns have emerged about group quality as well as the ability of partner banks to properly assess, monitor and manage risk on their SHG portfolios. Going forward, if SHG Bank Linkage is to be scaled-up, NABARD and its partners face several challenges, key among which include ensuring that high quality groups are created and maintained, and that concerns over numeric targets of group creation and linkage do not override attention to group quality and resilience... Equally, efforts need to focus on ensuring that banks price their loans to SHGs at rates that would cover their costs and ensure financial sustainability of SHG banking... Similarly, attention is needed to ensure the quality of MFIs. Many Indian MFIs suffer from weak governance and management structures, and the absence of adequate internal controls and financial discipline.
- Clear targeting of clients—the dual pursuit of social ends and financial profits is an ongoing tension... mission drift is a common fear as pressures mount to serve richer clients with larger loans.
- Appropriate products and services, and good staffing is critical to ensuring effectiveness—the stretching of rules is kept in check by other practices... how products are designed, how staff are compensated, what messages are delivered from headquarters, and who is recruited onto staff.
- Inclusiveness and competition in the microfinance sector can generate high payoffs—partnership between government, NGOs, and a range of rural banks (commercial banks, RRBs, cooperative banks) has already generated a strong payoff... new private sector banks, most notably ICICI Bank, but also UTI Bank and HDFC Bank are pursuing innovative approaches to microfinance—as a potential business and not merely as a social or priority sector lending obligation.
- Overcoming geographic concentration if microfinance (in the South)—the general malaise in the economy of the central, eastern and north eastern states, with very little resultant demand for credit among the subsistence poor, and the absence of good quality NGOs... overall economic growth has to pick up in these

(Contd.)

states. Investments are required in areas such as watershed development, small-scale irrigation, livestock up gradation and forest regeneration... The experience of the Rashtriya Gramin Vikas Nidhi and the Rashtriya Mahila Kosh in supporting hundreds of small NGOs all over the eastern region is useful in this regard and lessons from such experience need to be taken into account. Another proposal has been to incubate MFIs in poorer districts under the guidance of established MFIs.

- Longer-term Reforms in Rural Financial Markets and Institutions to Scale-up Access—efforts to promote microfinance should go hand-in-hand with efforts to make the formal sector better at "banking the poor", and government can play a critical role in this context. Government to revisit its policy of setting interest rate "caps" on rural lending rates and "floors" on the deposit rates... Government should also consider revisiting its policy on priority sector lending requirements imposed on banks...... Government needs to do what it takes to create an environment that would make it possible and profitable for interested private banks to enter the rural finance market.
- The Private Sector help in delivering rural finance for the poor—Banks and MFIs do not need to sit around and wait until the ideal policy, legal and regulatory environment has been created by government. They should continuously innovate to reduce costs, improve financial sustainability, and expand outreach. This would involve introducing new products, services, technologies and low-cost ways of reaching the rural poor and better managing risks and recovery. For instance, they can use technology to drive down their transactions costs.

III. INFORMAL ECONOMY: UNORGANISED MICRO AND SMALL ENTERPRISE SECTOR

The informal economy today accounts for a significant share of employment and output and is comprised[26] of traditional forms (e.g. casual jobs) and self-employment (e.g. home-based microenterprises, street vending) new forms (e.g. temporary and part time jobs) and self employment (e.g. high tech home based work). It is being increasingly recognized that the Informal Economy a large segment of which is made up of micro/small enterprises (MSEs) and which is serviced largely by informal financial sector including Microfinance is here to stay, in both new and old forms. Having acquired an overview/insight into the

Informal Sector's financial segment, it's interrelation with the formal systems and the dynamics of the Microfinance Movement sweeping across it—we shall now consider this sector's MSEs segment in which various parameters including finance, interact.

The MSEs have been defined variously. The term 'small enterprises' covers a wide range of enterprises 'disagregated into microenterprises as well as small and medium sized enterprises (SMEs) with the specific definition depending on the purpose or country context.' The Micro, Small and Medium Enterprises Development Act, 2006 (Govt. of India) has classified *manufacturing* enterprises on the basis of investment in plant and machinery—micro (not exceeding Rs. Twenty five lakhs), small (more than Rs. twenty five lakhs but not exceeding Rs. five crores), medium (more than Rs. five crores, not exceeding Rs. ten crores) and *services rendering* enterprises on the basis of investment in equipment as micro (not exceeding Rs. Ten lakhs), small (more than Rs. ten lakhs, not exceeding Rs. two crore), medium (more than Rs. two crores, not exceeding Rs. five crores).

In view of the challenges/opportunities of globalization, a sick small scale industry sector, an almost stagnant agriculture sector, the spread/acceptance of group/community mode of development, proven success trails—realizing the full potential of Micro and Small Enterprise Sector is imperative for developing countries like India to cross the poverty line and join the ranks of middle developed countries. The utility/effectiveness of Microenterprise programmes is because they use locally available skills, are labour-intensive, create significant employment are simple to operate, can serve as a basis for community participation/clients empowerment and improve the income of the working poor, especially poor women. In this section we shall take an overview of the MSE arena, particularly in the Indian context, the international/national/other initiatives, approaches and models for MSE development, innovative approaches, limitations and policy issues.

Micro and Small Enterprise Sector

Micro-entrepreneurs initiate very small scale, isolated rural and urban businesses usually with no outside support. The operating costs are kept low by working from home (home-based workers) using handmade machinery/tools and family labour. These micro-entrepreneurs have virtually no access to capital beyond sources from family, relatives, friends or professional moneylenders and usually have low access to business development services. Many of these enterprises could evolve into substantial enterprises, if they could access productive resources.

In India, the MicroSmall Enterprises Sector[27] has the second largest share of employment after agriculture and spanning a wide range, including small-scale, *khadi*, village and coir industries, handicrafts, handlooms, sericulture, powerlooms, food processing and other agro/rural industry segments. It affects the livelihoods of the weaker and unorganized sections of the society—more than half of those employed being women, disadvantaged and the marginalized. Agro-food processing, sericulture and other village enterprises have the potential of checking rural-urban migration by gainfully employing people in villages and also taking pressure off agriculture. The MSE sector can provide significant opportunities in regions like the North-East and hill states where large industries cannot be set-up due to inadequate infrastructure and environmental considerations.

Despite the importance of this sector for India (about 40 to 60% of economically active population in Indian cities work in the Informal Sector and in rural areas, off-farm employment accounts for 30 to 45% of the work force) the micro-enterprise sector continues to struggle with difficult business environment—lack of adequate credit/training in business management/marketing, obsolete product design/technology/operational conditions, ,a plethora of mostly piecemeal sporadic/uncoordinated/outdated state interventions.

In a UNIFEM, New Delhi sponsored three state studies[28] on the Informal Sector's home-based workers covering certain sub-sectors, it has been found that 'the situation of *home-based workers* is complex and has to be addressed at various fronts'. The most important needs of home-based workers that emerged from the survey were: timely payments, more work, minimum wage, market information, credit facilities and skill training. The study revealed that 'several home-based trades are being challenged in the fast changing economic and production context and workers are marginalised as a result. Decreasing vulnerability for home-based workers requires clearer articulation of the sector they are involved in and the impact of changing economic policies and urbanization on the sectoral demand and supply chains.' The study also highlights the dismal living conditions of home-based workers in the trades mapped, majority of whom are living below the poverty line and unable to access any social protection measure. For home-based workers, the home is also the workplace, but they lack proper housing and basic sanitation facilities. As the home is also the workplace, home-based workers are required to pay for many of additional costs—such as electricity, defects in raw materials etc. Workers surveyed suffer from a variety of ailments related to their work. Lack of sanitation and safe drinking water and low nutritional status result in a cycle of low productivity. The study concludes that 'awareness about safer working process and conditions could go a long way in augmenting the productivity and well-being of female home-based workers.'

Micro and Small Enterprise Development

Micro and Small Enterprise development includes all assistance programmes (concerning access to financial resource/business and technical know-how/a market for products and services etc.) directed to increase the ability of the self-employed poor and owners of very small business in the informal/non-farm/off-farm unorganised sectors to provide income for their families and for those of their employees and thereby escape poverty through market driven, productive activities.

It is important to make an in-depth analysis of the current status of micro-enterprise sector, the constraints under which it is functioning and identify the conditions/interventions necessary for the growth and development of this sector—favourable regulatory and policy environment, vibrant, sustainable institutions for providing financial and non-financial business development services to this sector, improve access of low-income and disadvantaged micro-entrepreneurs (including women, youth and deprived people) to these services. A holistic country/region specific model (working on principles of synergy/convergence/ cross-cultural/global best practices) is required for Micro and small enterprise development which will have the potential for minimizing the mass poverty, build linkages with livelihoods/ microfinance, boost the formalization of the Informal Sector and place developing countries in the ranks of middle developed countries. This discussion, though more concentrated on the micro segment, has relevance for small and medium enterprise development as well.

To support small enterprise creation/expansion, *key interventions* include: a supportive policy, regulatory and legal environment that is simple, fast, inexpensive and free from leakages, low cost and accessible finance, access to efficient/market oriented affordable business development services, workers who are trained in appropriate skills, basic health and education for optimizing human capital, entrepreneurship, supportive culture, access to domestic/international markets on equitable basis with large enterprises and reliable infrastructure (energy, transport, telecommunications etc.).

Microfinance is a *support for microenterprise development*—enterprise development being an important factor behind initiation of microfinance as a strategic tool for poverty reduction in the developing world. The subsequent spread of microfinance initiatives has occurred to incorporate other components/issues due to the horizontal growth of financial access. An important goal of a microfinance project is to create income/employment in poor sections of societies through the development of local micro/small enterprises and consequently improve the financial well-being of the borrowers and the community at large.

Microfinance is required to support micro enterprise development as it comprises several components of enterprise building market orientation, project/product identification and meeting some of enterprise credit requirements. For micro enterprises to get established, however, along with financial resources, other supplementary/business development resources are also important—many enterprises fail not because of a lack of finances but because of the lack of supportive business environment initiatives. By providing just financial support without the necessary infrastructure/skills in education, marketing linkages and social capital, the credit becomes a financial liability. The issue of establishing business linkages of micro-small enterprises with the larger business chains has to be carefully addressed so as to reduce the small entrepreneurs vulnerability by strategizing their fit into the larger production/supply/market business chains.

NGOs working as MFIs and/or promoting microenterprise have to work as facilitators in enabling microfinance beneficiaries to evolve into micro-entrepreneurs as manufacturers/processors and also as contract service providers for established corporates, providing backward/forward linkages including business development services, technical and marketing tie-ups, entrepreneurship, training, skills upgradation, credit assessment/ procurement, convergence between various agencies/departments etc.

MFIs offering microfinance are mostly not working in a manner conducive to enterprise development. The strategy, staff capacity etc. in most institutions do not show livelihood finance/ enterprise orientation. Process changes, product design, new skill sets for staff, reoriented organisational mission and long term financial resources access would all be needed for microfinance to act as enterprise finance.

The dynamics of group entrepreneurship managing finances/ risks with capacity building, identifying product technology, competitive marketing niche, assessing credit needs and locating affordable fund sources, the livelihood pattern of the group members and their performance as a management team through appropriate organisational structure (e.g. member owned cooperative or producers company) are some of the other parameters to be considered to understand/facilitate MicroEnterprise Development. For promoting group entrepreneurship, capacity building is required for the existing SHGs which have a group identity, have savings and borrowing and are in the stage of readiness being motivated to use their savings productively. In the total development of the unit-enterprise development, awareness building of both facilitating NGOs and groups to promote product specific and skill related selling points, high quality goods production with adoption of appropriate technology, design innovations for specific markets, procurement/production/packaging/quality control/marketing tasks allocation among group members have to be looked into.

An all inclusive/holistic approach for considering the poor family as a unit for microfinance intermediation would consider its other needs to make it socially/economically empowered: income generating employment/activities, information on marketing/technology upgradation and government schemes, linkages with state social security/HRD programmes such as universalize access to primary education/health, computer education and e-services, sanitation, vocational training etc.

Though capital is not the only factor that allows for enterprise growth/creation, it is very significant as without it drive and innovation cannot result in material actions for millions of people around the world who work for themselves—weavers, carpenters, mechanics, artisans, wood-workers, street vendors etc. who (along with several other skill based entrepreneurs) comprise a majority of the workforce in developing countries. Most of these micro-entrepreneurs operate without adequate financial resources—business credit risk coverage or a safe avenue for savings—and so are unable to expand their enterprises beyond the barest survival level.

Business development services (BDS) have to be provided, in addition to the state initiatives by market based private providers, where required on a fee paying basis. These services can include: credit, training and capacity building services, marketing promotion, technology development and transfer, information provision and business linkage assistance. In developing markets, business associations, donors and NGOs initiate and support the demand for and supply of business development services such as training of private trainers in delivering requisite courses, financial services such as micro-credit needed by poor entrepreneurs, organising trade, business fairs and linkages programmes. The case study on integrating microenterprise into markets through Business Development Services (*Chapter Nine* of this book) is instructive.

An important method to facilitate and provide business development services to micro and small enterprises is setting up and managing financially sustainable *business centres*. ILO's InFocus Programme on Boosting Employment through Small Enterprise Development (IFP/SEED) has established several business centres in post-crisis regions (political conflict and transition economies) in Eastern Europe where private BDS provision was almost non-existent. It has been found[29] that the goal of financial sustainability can only be achieved if business centres offer BDS services tailored to the specific needs of microentrepreneurs that attract a fee-paying clientele. This however is a difficult proposition for BDS providers since their targeted clients are usually micro-entrepreneurs with little resources, inadequate awareness of the benefits of BDS and low inclination to remit fees.

The *Donor Committee for Enterprise Development*[30] (comprising of bilateral/multilateral donor representatives working towards promotion of small enterprises in developing countries) recommends that development agencies should support business environment reforms that—

(1) Provide broad incentives for the private enterprises to grow.
(2) Support government leadership by providing flexible support, guidance, information and by encouraging government to take full ownership of reforms efforts.
(3) Support reform interventions integration to ensure that change in one aspect of the policy, legal, regulatory or organizational framework is consistent with other changes.
(4) Support reforms that are strategically focused by assigning a high priority to those areas of the business environment that have 'a strong bearing on the cost of doing business and are doable in specific country conditions' since 'the greatest impact of reform will come from focusing on the most binding constraints to business activity and addressing the factors that contribute to this.'
(5) Stress that initial reform efforts should be prioritized on the areas that are easiest or have the most immediate (rather than greatest) impact on the business environment, building the ground for scaling-up the reforms.
(6) Reemphasize the importance of implementation—the need to address issues associated with poor governance, organizational weaknesses and corruption.

Strengthening Informal Sector worker's *training and improving their skills* are important measures towards decent work/job security/enhanced incomes. The necessity of adopting a 'capabilities and entitlement's approach for entrepreneurial capacity building in order to minimise the globalisation created inequalities has been exemplified in *Chapter Eight* of this book. Some conclusions and policy suggestions emerging from an *ILO/Chinese Study*[31] of a country whose consumer goods have in the past decade acquired worldwide presence:

- 'Vocational training targeting employment in the informal sector should enhance the skills and business start-up capacities of people working in the informal sector.
- Planning of employment training for the informal sector should be integrated in the nation's comprehensive vocational training plan. Task forces should be set up to conduct studies on the current situation of workers in the informal sector. Localities should formulate training programmes that effectively respond to market demand and employment priorities.
- Integrated policy measures on employment training for the informal sector should be undertaken.
- Provide differentiated vocational training for informal sector in recognition of specificities of those working in this sector. Training institutes should provide differentiated training workshops targeting enterprise laid-off employees and the unemployed of different ages, skills levels, education levels and their job preference.
- Adopt flexible training forms in connection with the conditions of laid-off employees and the unemployed. Full-time, half-day training forms can be complemented with night school vocational training.
- Make active efforts to secure the funding of training programmes and improve the practice of government purchasing training results. Government pays training institutes based upon their participants' training passing rate and their participants' re-employment rate in a certain time period.
- Strengthen employment services and enhance training effectiveness with communities as bases for such activities—communities are where informal sector workers live. Community employment service institutions should be strengthened. Data collection on job openings, as well as projections, should be institutionalized.
- Strengthen collaboration between government agencies—collaboration between labour and social security departments with departments of education, finance, chambers of industry and commerce, taxation offices, should be strengthened.
- Continuously promote and improve business start-up

training—these courses should pay special attention to the development of jobs in the community-based service sector and be provided by designated training institutes and community employment service agencies. Where conditions permit, vocational training institutes can form alliances with enterprises.

- Strengthen vocational (rural) training planning: rural labour force development and employment in a comprehensive *manner*. Thus, employment for rural surplus workers should include both internal transfers within the agricultural sector and transfer to non-agricultural sectors (such as non-agricultural production and trading activities).
- Building up institutional capacity of vocational training institutes—a network of city, district/county, township and village-level training institutes should be established.'

Women face both general and gender related barriers in starting or expanding enterprises which have to be addressed through specific projects and through the mainstreaming of gender equality in micro small enterprise promotion activities. Women micro entrepreneurs despite playing important economic roles are often not taken into account by policymakers and have to rely on their own efforts and the support from their families/friends in developing income generating enterprises. Programmes such as ILOs women's entrepreneurship training package (GET Ahead) assist poor women entrepreneurs by developing their management skills and also addressing personal, confidence building and other entrepreneurial qualities. The gender dimension/women's empowerment issues in microfinance/microenterprise development programmes is analysed in *Chapter Ten* of this book.

In view of the high unemployment rate for young people between the ages of 15 and 24—twice as high as the rate for adults, increasing/special attention is required on the problem of *youth* unemployment and seeking to devise effective employment strategies as entrepreneurship promotion for this category. In collaboration with the government/workers and employers organizations, programmes such as Start Your Business are now used for training young people in the education system, along with Know About Business, to teach students in vocational training poverty, revitalizing distressed communities and assisting budding entrepreneurs to gain entrance to the financial system. Yet there are some looming dark clouds on the horizon that the field is already beginning to confront. How it weathers this storm will determine the future of the movement in the years ahead. There are seven key challenges faced by the field that are discussed briefly below... accompanied by a review of one or more innovations that the practitioners in the field have introduced to meet these challenges:

1. *There is a huge gap between the potential market and the number of customers currently being reached*: What is required to better understand why this gap exists and to begin to close it? We suggest these areas of endeavour to be pursued:
   - Conduct additional market research to better understand the dynamics of the market and what microentrepreneurs need to start and grow their businesses.
   - Create more strategic marketing partnerships. Most non-profit organizations simply do not have enough resources to effectively and consistently market their products. Organizations should look to partner with banks and corporations that service the small business community such as office supply stores, self-employment trade associations.
   - Diversify the product mix offered to microentrepreneurs based on market research. The standard working capital term loan may have limited appeal and other financial products such as lines of credit, stored value cards, and credit builder loans, may find more demand.
   - With the collaboration of various funders, FIELD has recently funded very specific marketing research projects to better understand the changing nature of the field and the needs of microentrepreneurs.
2. *The market place has changed dramatically since the field began in the early 1990s*: Several trends have occurred in the market place that pose both a threat and a potential opportunity for the field. First, the conventional banking and financial sectors have moved downstream in their loans and financial products. Another phenomenon that has appeared in the last ten years is what, in the United States, is known as "fringe banking" or alternative financial service providers... They include check cashing companies, payday lenders, pawnshops, rent-to-own stores, signature loan companies and others. Many are "one-stop" shops

(*Contd.*)

training—these courses should pay special attention to the development of jobs in the community-based service sector and be provided by designated training institutes and community employment service agencies. Where conditions permit, vocational training institutes can form alliances with enterprises.

- Strengthen vocational (rural) training planning: rural labour force development and employment in a comprehensive *manner*. Thus, employment for rural surplus workers should include both internal transfers within the agricultural sector and transfer to non-agricultural sectors (such as non-agricultural production and trading activities).
- Building up institutional capacity of vocational training institutes—a network of city, district/county, township and village-level training institutes should be established.'

Women face both general and gender related barriers in starting or expanding enterprises which have to be addressed through specific projects and through the mainstreaming of gender equality in micro small enterprise promotion activities. Women micro entrepreneurs despite playing important economic roles are often not taken into account by policymakers and have to rely on their own efforts and the support from their families/friends in developing income generating enterprises. Programmes such as ILOs women's entrepreneurship training package (GET Ahead) assist poor women entrepreneurs by developing their management skills and also addressing personal, confidence building and other entrepreneurial qualities. The gender dimension/women's empowerment issues in microfinance/microenterprise development programmes is analysed in *Chapter Ten* of this book.

In view of the high unemployment rate for young people between the ages of 15 and 24—twice as high as the rate for adults, increasing/special attention is required on the problem of *youth* unemployment and seeking to devise effective employment strategies as entrepreneurship promotion for this category. In collaboration with the government/workers and employers organizations, programmes such as Start Your Business are now used for training young people in the education system, along with Know About Business, to teach students in vocational training poverty, revitalizing distressed communities and assisting budding entrepreneurs to gain entrance to the financial system. Yet there are some looming dark clouds on the horizon that the field is already beginning to confront. How it weathers this storm will determine the future of the movement in the years ahead. There are seven key challenges faced by the field that are discussed briefly below... accompanied by a review of one or more innovations that the practitioners in the field have introduced to meet these challenges:

1. *There is a huge gap between the potential market and the number of customers currently being reached*: What is required to better understand why this gap exists and to begin to close it? We suggest these areas of endeavour to be pursued:

   - Conduct additional market research to better understand the dynamics of the market and what microentrepreneurs need to start and grow their businesses.
   - Create more strategic marketing partnerships. Most non-profit organizations simply do not have enough resources to effectively and consistently market their products. Organizations should look to partner with banks and corporations that service the small business community such as office supply stores, self-employment trade associations.
   - Diversify the product mix offered to microentrepreneurs based on market research. The standard working capital term loan may have limited appeal and other financial products such as lines of credit, stored value cards, and credit builder loans, may find more demand.
   - With the collaboration of various funders, FIELD has recently funded very specific marketing research projects to better understand the changing nature of the field and the needs of microentrepreneurs.

2. *The market place has changed dramatically since the field began in the early 1990s*: Several trends have occurred in the market place that pose both a threat and a potential opportunity for the field. First, the conventional banking and financial sectors have moved downstream in their loans and financial products. Another phenomenon that has appeared in the last ten years is what, in the United States, is known as "fringe banking" or alternative financial service providers... They include check cashing companies, payday lenders, pawnshops, rent-to-own stores, signature loan companies and others. Many are "one-stop" shops

(*Contd.*)

offering multiple services including remittance services, payment of utility bills, purchase of money orders etc.

These outlets offer a real alternative to those who have traditionally been outside the financial mainstream or immigrants who may not trust banks based on their experience in their home countries. The advantages of these entities for the customer include locational convenience, few requirements, rapidity of loan decisions, and multiple services. The disadvantages primarily relate to the high fees and interest rates charged which can lead to a perpetual cycle of indebtedness for some.... ACCION New Mexico has pioneered a strategy for partnering with banks in the state. The organization has enlisted the staff of several banks to serve as ACCION "facilitators", informing potential customers about the programme, helping them fill out loan applications and assisting in loan closings.

3. *There are simply too many organizations in the microenterprise field*: In spite of so many organizations operating, there is very little real collaboration among them, little specialization and no economies of scale. Each one tends to operate independently, often offering a wide range of services, and duplicating.... This state of affairs cannot be maintained. The inefficiencies that result drive up the cost of product delivery to an unsustainable level. There are some hopeful signs that this scenario is beginning to change. As the field looks to the future it should rapidly evolve by:

   - Promoting the merger and consolidation of some of the organizations.
   - Promoting further specialization so that organizations can become better and more efficient at providing one or two services. This means separating out the lending from the training function so that organizations can focus on one activity.
   - Exploring the use of a centralized "back office" to process loans for multiple organizations to carry out other common functions.
   - Pooling loan funds so that each organization is not managing its own but has access to a common fund based on its performance.

4. *The service delivery methodologies of most organizations, both lending and training, are too expensive and too labour-intensive*: Relatively little innovation has occurred on either the lending side or the training side that has resulted in significant cost reductions.

(*Contd.*)

NABARD has launched a pilot project for promotion of micro-enterprises among members of matured SHGs which is being implemented by NGOs acting as 'micro-enterprise promotion agency' (MEPA) under the technical guidance of a resource organisation Marketing and Research Team (MART). MEPAs completed detailed district surveys to identify existing opportunities and supply and demand patterns for farm/non-farm activities that can be taken-up on a project basis for sustainable income generation in the identified areas. The identification of suitable activities has been carried-out through participatory processes in consultation with SHG members and Action Plans finalized on the basis of the survey findings are being implemented.

➢ *Micro Enterprise Development* at *Aga Khan Rural Support Project India AKRSP(I)*[35] works for the enhancement of livelihoods for those rural communities that are too poor to be benefited by development programmes which are mainly land-based and also to developing certain key sectors such as animal husbandry that have the potential for creating wide-spread economic linkages/multipliers in rural incomes, across social strata. AKRSP(I) MED Programme finds markets for the existing skills/product of poor communities, builds upon their limited skills, and act as a source of livelihoods oriented knowledge/ information to them. Interventions range across the farm, off-farm and non-farm sectors though the majority of work has focused on farm-based initiatives. Animal Husbandry, Fishing and Organic Compost making are some of the more successful activities that have been supported. Village-level federations enabling rural people to purchase agricultural inputs and sell their produce collectively have also been supported though not falling strictly within the domain of 'micro-enterprise'.

AKRSP(I) strongly believes in offering *loans—and not grants*—to its poor MED beneficiaries despite the fact that grants are often available to the not-so-poor, due to the belief that loans create the 'strong sense of ownership amongst beneficiaries that is necessary for MED interventions to grow. First-time borrowers are extended

loans at zero-interest while for subsequent loans rate of interest is similar to the one charged by government banks. Loan repayments result in an increasingly large pool of money-formal revolving funds in the operational villages to act as receptacles for all loan repayments as well as sources of new MED loans are proposed to be created to make the entire operation self-sustainable.

The challenges envisaged by AKRSP(I) MED programme are (1) the need to design a standardized system whereby the economic viability of new MED proposals may be assessed in a logical manner rather than on ad-hoc parameters; (2) the need for an MED-specific MIS to be developed which will 'capture relevant parameters of on-going enterprises and facilitate continual analysis of their progress'—currently data is collected sporadically in non-standardised formats; (3) in view of the example of large subsidies in many government funded programmes, it becomes difficult for AKRSP to insist on high contribution levels from the partnered communities; (4) for involving the private sector in efforts to alleviate rural poverty special efforts 'to harness its energies for development purposes in a positive manner' would be required, in view of the corporate sectors own priorities; and (5) other problems include finding adequate working capital sources to see activities through the lows of business cycles, enhancing the limited skills of rural beneficiaries and creating an enabling environment for rural businesses to thrive in areas of poor infrastructure.

Models/Approaches for MED: What Works

What are the effective approaches for implementing MED in the globalised world of today? To answer this query different strategies/approaches/view points have been proposed—innovative models like the indigenous Grassroots to Global (G^2G) model, studies challenging the status quo ('self-employment microenterprise programmes may not be suited to all the jobless', 'targeting of better off regions rather than poorer regions for creating entrepreneurial infrastructure') or innovative propositions ('support larger enterprises in labour intensive industries rather findings should not lead to a simple rejection of all targeting approaches which can be effective for certain interventions such as welfare programmes. Instead of applying targeting in all poverty reduction projects, there is a need to 'differentiate poor households and poor regions. For the poor without working capacity, welfare programmes should be designed to take care of this group on a long-term basis and targeting is an effective mechanism to channel public subsidies to the poor and minimize the leakage of the benefits to others. To effectively reduce poverty among the productive poor, however, project interventions need to be tailor-made to mitigate the key constraints on poverty reduction in the particular project areas.' While bringing small and temporary benefits to the poor such projects failed to lift them out of poverty in the cases studied. To be effective, projects aiming to reduce poverty among the productive poor should target the key causes of poverty instead of poor households or poor regions. 'Solutions that effectively reduce poverty in the poor regions may require public investment in non-poor regions to promote economic growth as well as participation of non-poor individuals in job creation.' In regions with high potential to generate significant employment, such as areas with sufficient land and well-endowed for commercial agriculture, infrastructure projects may elicit large inflows of private capital and substantial job creation. Such investments may not be effective, however, in remote and poorly endowed regions, which, in the cases studied, remained unattractive to private investors even after projects upgraded rural roads. Without private investment to generate long-term jobs, the projects may temporarily improve living conditions for the poor without actually lifting them out of poverty. In contrast, 'interventions to facilitate the orderly migration of surplus rural labour from the poor regions to areas with dynamic growth, including measures to reduce migration costs, may be a more effective alternative.'

MF/MED Vs. Larger Enterprises: In view of the limitations of microfinance, the problems associated with MED including absence of entrepreneurial skills in many and the remarkable economic success of countries like China and South Korea through larger labour intensive enterprises, the proposition to support such high quality/productive larger enterprises instead of focusing

heavily on microfinance/microenterprise development is also gaining ground (Box 1.4).

Box 1.4: Microfinance Misses its Marks[40]

- Despite the 'hoopla' over microfinance, it doesn't alleviate poverty/which however stable jobs do. For really helping the poorest of the poor, societies should stop investing in microfinance and start supporting large, labour—intensive industries. At the same time, governments must fulfil their development responsibilities, for market-based solutions will never be enough.
- Microloans are more beneficial to borrowers living above the poverty line than to borrowers living below the poverty line.
- Microloans sometimes even reduce cash flow to the poorest of the poor.... If poor clients cannot earn a greater return on their investment than the interest they must pay, they will become poorer as a result of microcredit, not wealthier.
- Although some microcredit clients have created visionary businesses, the vast majority are caught in subsistence activities. They usually have no specialized skills, and so must compete with all the other self-employed poor people in entry-level trades. Most have no paid staff, own few assets, and operate at too small a scale to achieve efficiencies, and so make very meager earnings. In other words, most microenterprises are small and many fail.
- Most people do not have the skills, vision, creativity, and persistence to be entrepreneurial. Even in developed countries, about 90 per cent of the labour force is employees, not entrepreneurs.
- Microcredit is... a genuine innovation that has provided some positive impact to its clients, particularly to women's non-economic empowerment. It also helps the poor during cyclical or unexpected crises, and thus reduces their vulnerability. But the critical issue is whether microcredit helps eradicate poverty And on that front, it falls short. China, Vietnam, and South Korea have significantly reduced poverty in recent years with little microfinance activity. On the other hand, Bangladesh, Bolivia, and Indonesia haven't been as successful at reducing poverty despite the influx of microcredit.
- Most microcredit clients are not microentrepreneurs by choice. They would gladly take a factory job at reasonable wages if it were available... Creating opportunities for steady employment at reasonable wages is the best way to take people out of poverty.

(Contd.)

by type of enterprise...formal or state sanctioned institutions are more likely to succeed when they build on existing informal arrangements...' For moving towards formalization of the informal sector, certain critical questions have to be answered such as: 'What is the appropriate balance between positive sanctions and enforcement and how might it change during the process of formalization? How might business associations and large firms be persuaded to cooperate with informal sector enterprises? And how should the policy approaches to informality be adapted to the differing needs of lower and middle-income countries or post-conflict environments and to the situation of firms in different economic sectors?' (Kenyon, 2007).

IV. SYNOPTIC OVERVIEW OF CHAPTER CONTENTS

It is thus evident that the task of 'organizing' a micro-revolution in finance/enterprise, particularly in the difficult rural domain of the developing world, is an onerous one and requires careful strategizing, judicious utilisation of 'best practices'/success stories/ learnings from misguided interventions. In the following chapters of this volume, erudite development practitioners/scholars have explored some of the key issues related to this 'formalization' process and highlighted valuable learnings emerging from global/ national/government and non-governmental initiatives/ innovations. While some of the themes emerging in our overview find elaboration/validation in these papers, several challenging propositions/issues have been raised for which there are no easy solutions.

Now for a preview of the following chapters of this book, for a better picture of the microfinance movement, the reengineering imperatives of the micro small enterprise development sector, interrelatedness, stark connotations as well as subtle nuances of the 'informal to formal' transformation.

Chapter 2: MFIs and the Maturing of Indian Microfinance

This study forms a part of the National Microfinance Support Project (NMFSP), being implemented by SIDBI Foundation for Micro-Credit (SFMC), a department of Small Industries Development Bank of India (SIDBI), in collaboration with the heavily on microfinance/microenterprise development is also gaining ground (Box 1.4).

Box 1.4: Microfinance Misses its Marks[40]

- Despite the 'hoopla' over microfinance, it doesn't alleviate poverty/which however stable jobs do. For really helping the poorest of the poor, societies should stop investing in microfinance and start supporting large, labour—intensive industries. At the same time, governments must fulfil their development responsibilities, for market-based solutions will never be enough.
- Microloans are more beneficial to borrowers living above the poverty line than to borrowers living below the poverty line.
- Microloans sometimes even reduce cash flow to the poorest of the poor.... If poor clients cannot earn a greater return on their investment than the interest they must pay, they will become poorer as a result of microcredit, not wealthier.
- Although some microcredit clients have created visionary businesses, the vast majority are caught in subsistence activities. They usually have no specialized skills, and so must compete with all the other self-employed poor people in entry-level trades. Most have no paid staff, own few assets, and operate at too small a scale to achieve efficiencies, and so make very meager earnings. In other words, most microenterprises are small and many fail.
- Most people do not have the skills, vision, creativity, and persistence to be entrepreneurial. Even in developed countries, about 90 per cent of the labour force is employees, not entrepreneurs.
- Microcredit is... a genuine innovation that has provided some positive impact to its clients, particularly to women's non-economic empowerment. It also helps the poor during cyclical or unexpected crises, and thus reduces their vulnerability. But the critical issue is whether microcredit helps eradicate poverty. And on that front, it falls short. China, Vietnam, and South Korea have significantly reduced poverty in recent years with little microfinance activity. On the other hand, Bangladesh, Bolivia, and Indonesia haven't been as successful at reducing poverty despite the influx of microcredit.
- Most microcredit clients are not microentrepreneurs by choice. They would gladly take a factory job at reasonable wages if it were available... Creating opportunities for steady employment at reasonable wages is the best way to take people out of poverty.

(Contd.)

by type of enterprise...formal or state sanctioned institutions are more likely to succeed when they build on existing informal arrangements...' For moving towards formalization of the informal sector, certain critical questions have to be answered such as: 'What is the appropriate balance between positive sanctions and enforcement and how might it change during the process of formalization? How might business associations and large firms be persuaded to cooperate with informal sector enterprises? And how should the policy approaches to informality be adapted to the differing needs of lower and middle-income countries or post-conflict environments and to the situation of firms in different economic sectors?' (Kenyon, 2007).

IV. SYNOPTIC OVERVIEW OF CHAPTER CONTENTS

It is thus evident that the task of 'organizing' a micro-revolution in finance/enterprise, particularly in the difficult rural domain of the developing world, is an onerous one and requires careful strategizing, judicious utilisation of 'best practices'/success stories/ learnings from misguided interventions. In the following chapters of this volume, erudite development practitioners/scholars have explored some of the key issues related to this 'formalization' process and highlighted valuable learnings emerging from global/ national/government and non-governmental initiatives/ innovations. While some of the themes emerging in our overview find elaboration/validation in these papers, several challenging propositions/issues have been raised for which there are no easy solutions.

Now for a preview of the following chapters of this book, for a better picture of the microfinance movement, the reengineering imperatives of the micro small enterprise development sector, interrelatedness, stark connotations as well as subtle nuances of the 'informal to formal' transformation.

Chapter 2: MFIs and the Maturing of Indian Microfinance

This study forms a part of the National Microfinance Support Project (NMFSP), being implemented by SIDBI Foundation for Micro-Credit (SFMC), a department of Small Industries Development Bank of India (SIDBI), in collaboration with the

Department for International Development (DFID), UK and the International Fund for Agricultural Development (IFAD), Rome. It was conducted by the Research Team of EDA Rural Systems Pvt. Ltd. (a leading development sector consultancy: focus areas—microfinance and microenterprise) under the leadership of Frances Sinha.

The study covers a sample of 20 MFIs of SIDBI and explores key impact questions, exploring issues of outreach, use of microfinance services and their contribution to different dimensions of poverty reduction.

The Chapter is structured as follows:

I. Microfinance Context: MFIs in India
II. Research Design
III. Outreach
IV. Use and Contribution of microfinance: Microfinance and Enterprises
V. Microfinance and Poverty Reduction
VI. Microfinance and Vulnerability
VII. Microfinance and Women's Empowerment
VIII. Alternative Financial Services
IX. Feedback on MFI Services
X. Implications for Practice
XI. Implications for Policy

Chapter 3: Agricultural Finance in India: Microfinance Innovations

Though the outreach and access to total bank credit has been improved by bank nationalization, the delivery of agricultural credit is weak-affected by credit scarcity, higher transaction costs, staff shortage and dominance of non-institutional credit markets. Micro-finance delivery models have emerged as possible panacea for these problems. This paper reviews the trend, status and issues of agricultural credit in India and appraises the implementation/ sustainability issues of the government-run micro-finance model Swarnjayanti Gram Swarozgar Yojana (SGSY, also analysed in *Chapter Ten* of this Volume) towards increasing universal access, ensuring procedural efficiency and cost effectiveness in financing rural credit (An analytical study on improving SGSY in Madhya

Pradesh conducted by MPRLP-TCPSU and included in livelihood Forum's earlier publication[43]).

The paper has been jointly written by K.K. Tripathy, Deputy Director, Ministry of Food Processing Industries, New Delhi currently Research Scholar, Indian Institute of Technology (IIT), New Delhi and Dr. Sudhir K. Jain, Associate Professor, Department of Management Studies, IIT, New Delhi.

The chapter is structured as follows:

I. Introduction
II. Trends in the Supply of Rural Credit/Progress of Rural Banking in India
III. *Microfinance*—An Alternative Rural Credit Delivery System
IV. SGSY Model of Microfinance
V. Analysis of Field Study in Rural Orissa
VI. Conclusions and Policy Implications

Chapter 4: Enabling Role of Governments in Microfinance Development : Experiences from Thailand

This GTZ (German Technical Cooperation) study provides a critical appraisal of the functioning of BAAC (Bank for Agriculture and Agricultural Cooperatives), a major provider of micro and rural finance services in Thailand and the role played by the Thai government in this context. It is a useful case study to facilitate development practitioners in learning from "one of the most successful examples of Financial System Development in Thailand."

This paper has been written by Marie Luise Haberberger, currently Programme Director, NABARD-GTZ Rural Finance Programme, New Delhi.

The Chapter is structured as follows:

I. Introduction
II. The Macro Economic Environment
III. The Bank for Agriculture and Agricultural Cooperatives (BAAC)
IV. Conclusions
V. What lessons can be learnt

Chapter 5: Andhra's Women SHGs : Participatory Poverty Alleviation

This paper makes a comprehensive analysis of the primarily women-based self-help groups (SHGs) movement in the state of Andhra Pradesh, India where the state, in partnership with NGOs has taken pro-active measures in mobilizing the SHGs as a primary force for poverty alleviation and development. While highlighting the comprehensive social mobilization approach to create/sustain SHGs that has been adopted by the State which has resulted in Andhra occupying a leading position among the Indian States in this area, the study also deliberates upon the lessons learned from the Andhra experience and the limitations to be overcome to maximize the potential of the SHG movement.

The paper has been authored by Dr. Joy Deshmukh-Ranadive, Director, Indian School of Microfinance for Women, Ahmedabad. This paper was originally prepared for the World Bank under the guidance of Dr. Deepa Narayan, Senior Adviser, World Bank.

The chapter has been structured as follows:

I. Introduction: Implementation Process
II. Impact Analysis
III. Driving Factors
IV. Learning and Experimentation: Lessons Learned

Chapter 6: Micro Pensions in India : Towards Mainstreaming

At a time when developing countries like India are emphasizing the area of Social Security including pension reforms, this topical paper on micro-pensions (in the domain of microfinance savings) provides valuable inputs for policy consideration. The paper has been written by Dr. Mukul G. Asher, Professor, Lee Kuan Yew School of Public Policy, National University of Singapore, Singapore jointly with Savita Shankar, Researcher.

The Paper has been structured as follows:

I. Introduction
II. The Nature and Design of Micro-Pensions
III. Channels for Expanding Coverage
IV. Reform Directions

Chapter 7: Clustering for Progress: The Road Travelled and the Way Ahead

When micro, small and medium enterprises (MSME) deal with 'same, similar or complementary range of goods and services in the local area,' the commonality of interests makes it more viable to respond to the challenges more effectively and efficiently through the approach of industrial or micro-enterprise clusters. Enterprises in clusters have shown higher productivity and have stimulated regional industrial growth. Hence it is necessary to understand clusters, how they operate and find ways to encourage their role in enterprises. This document, which reviews the developments linked to the arena of cluster development and provides policy inputs for cluster based MSME development in India is an initiative of Foundation for MSME Clusters, New Delhi. The Foundation, set-up by Entrepreneurship Development Institute of India with technical support drawn from United Nations Industrial Development Organisation, stimulates new thought in the area of local economic development, particularly with regard to clusters.

The document has been jointly authored by Dr. Keshab Das, Professor, Gujarat Institute for Development Research and a 'Foundation team' comprising of Mr. Mukesh Gulati, Executive Director, Dr. Tamal Sarkar, Programme Director and Ms. Sukanya Banerjee, Research Coordinator, with support from the Swiss Agency for Development and Cooperation (SDC), New Delhi.

The chapter is structured as follows:

I. Clusters, their relevance and need for policy,
II. Clustering Development Experience: Significance in India and Abroad,
III. Policy Challenges—Viewpoints of Stakeholders, and
IV. Policy Agenda for Way Forward.

Chapter 8: Entrepreneurial Capacity-Building: A model for Inclusive Growth in an Era of Globalisation

To address the inequity created by globalisation created growth trajectory in which the poor, specially poor women in India and other developing countries lacking requisite capabilities/resources have not reaped the benefits of economic growth a 'capabilities and entitlements' approach is required. This paper describes and analyses the experience of women's entrepreneurial capacity building initiative for inclusive growth by 'Udyogini' (in a field location in Madhya Pradesh).

The paper has been authored by Dr. Vanita Viswanath, CEO, Udyogini, which is a New Delhi based microenterprise development NGO that is working towards empowering women through enterprise development in the backward states of North-West and Central India. The paper's co-author is Amit Kumar Burman, BDS Manager, Udyogini.

The Chapter is structured as follows:

I. Introduction
II. Growth with Equity: Key Challenges
III. Entrepreneurship for Inclusive Growth: Udyogini's Experiences

Chapter 9: Integrating Microenterprise into Markets through Business Development Services: SEEP Network/USAID Case Study

Sustainable Business Development Services are essentially required to complement financial/microfinance inputs for development of micro, small enterprises and for their profitable integration into local/regional/global markets. To examine this issue in weak market conditions in order to discern effective service provision business models and related learnings this study of the leather footwear sub-sector in Rajasthan was undertaken by EDA Rural Systems Pvt. Ltd. (a Private Consulting Company in Gurgaon, India) under the SEEP Network (USA) Practitioner Learning Programme in Business Development Services Market Assessment Programme with support from Microenterprise Development Office of USAID. The study has been authored by Melissa Nussbaum (Micro finance/Microenterprise Professional), Ashok Kumar (Director BDS & Enterprise Promotion at EDA Rural Systems) and Alexandra Miehlbradt (Consultant and International Trainer).

The chapter is structured as follows:

I. Introduction
II. EDA's intervention

III. Service Provision Business Models
IV. Lessons Learned and the way forward

Chapter 10: Microfinance Microenterprise Programmes and Women's Empowerment

This report attempts to examine the role of finance and credit in relation to the impact on women's empowerment.[44] The report analyses some government and NGO initiated policies and programmes (viz. IFAD/World Bank funded Swashakti Project, GoI's Swayamsiddha Programme, GoIs Swarnajayanti Gram Swarozgar Yojana, Rashtriya Mahila Kosh etc.) within the context of women's social, political and economic empowerment. This report is an abridged and updated version of the study originally sponsored by CARE India (New Delhi) to bring to light findings relevant to ensuring that microcredit is able to meaningfully and sustainably impact the lives of marginalised women not merely by increasing access to resources but also in shifting firmly entrenched gender norms that limit women's social and political capabilities.' (Sandhya Venkateswaran, Director, Policy and Advocacy, CARE India).

The report has been prepared by V. Prameela, MicroEnterprise and Livelihood Specialist at Sampark, an NGO based in Bangalore, India and Dr. Smita Premchander, International Trainer and Consultant for gender, microfinance/microenterprise and founder member of Sampark.

This Chapter is structured as follows:

I. Introduction
II. Empowerment objective in four women's microcredit/ microenterprise/programmes
III. Lesson from NGO Microfinance/Microenterprise Experiences
IV. Designing Microfinance/Microenterprise Programmes that Empower Women

NOTES

1. Bhatnagar, Amitabh: Re-Engineering Millenniums Indian Banking Sector (New Delhi: Anmol Publications 2000).

2. Ruthven, Orlanda and Kumar, Sushil—Fine Grain Finance: Financial Choice and Strategy among the Poor in Rural North India—IDPM, University of Manchester UK Finance & Development Research Programme—Working Paper Series 2002).
3. Colloquium: *Rural Finance in Contemporary Times*: interface with Microfinance R. Srinivasan, (Faculty, IIM Bangalore) and M.S. Sriram (Faculty IIM Ahmedabad) VIKALPA Volume 30 No. 2 April-June, 2005.
4. Micro Start: A Guide for Planning, Starting and Managing a Microfinance Programme: *United Nations Capital Development Fund* (www.uncdf.org/English/microfinance/microstart/guide).
5. National Bank for Agriculture and Rural Development: *Annual Report, 2007*: NABARD, Mumbai 2007.
6. Hannover, Wolfgang: Impact of Microfinance Linkage Banking in India on the Millennium Development Goals: *National Bank for Agriculture & Rural Development/GTZ India (NABARD/GTZ)*: 2005.
7. CGAP: Helping to improve Donor Effectiveness in Microfinance: CGAP, 2003.
8. CGAP Focus Note: Commercial Banks and Microfinance: Evolving Models of Success CGAP, 2005.
9. Sinha, Sanjay: Efficiency with Growth: The Emerging Face of India's Microfinance: ADB Newsletter: *Finance for the poor—September 2007 Vol. 8*, Number 3.
10. IFAD: Assessing and Managing Social Performance in Microfinance.
11. Hannover, Wolfgang: Impact of Microfinance Linkage Banking in India on the Millennium Development Goals: National Bank for Agriculture & Rural Development/GTZ India (German Technical Cooperation) (NABARD/GTZ) (2005).
12. CGAP Focus Note No. 34 (2006) Graduating The Poorest Into Microfinance: Linking Safety Nets And Financial Services.
13. Ghate, Prabhu & Others: Microfinance in India: A State of the Sector Report, 2007: Microfinance India, New Delhi: 2007.
14. Moving from Micro-credit to Livelihood Finance—A report prepared by CARE India in collaboration with FAO Livelihood Support Programme: *FAO Italy* (Rome)/CARE India (N. Delhi): 2007.
15. CARE-CASHE: Promoting Sound Practices & Inovations in Microfinance—CASHE TIER II Mandate: CARE India (N. Delhi).
16. National Bank for Agriculture and Rural Development. *Annual Report 2007*: NABARD (Mumbai) 2007.
17. Botero, Cataline Robledo: Demand-side financing of education: Role for Microfinance. Rajiv Gandhi Foundation, New Delhi: *Annual Report* 2006-2007.
18. Colloquium: Rural Finance in Contemporary Times: Interface with Microfinance (IIM, Ahmedabad) *VIKALPA: Volume 30* No. 2 April-June 2005.

19. Christen, Robert Peck & Pearce, Douglas: Managing risks and designing products for Agricultural Microfinance—Features of an emerging model (IFAD Occassional Paper, 2006) (extracts).
20. Wenner, Mark Inter-American Development Bank: Rural Finance Strategy IADB: 2001.
21. Rhyne, Elisabeth and Otero, Maria: Microfinance through the Next Decade: Visioning the Who, What, Where, When & How ACCION:2006.
22. Helms, Brigit: Access for All—Building Inclusive Financial Systems: CGAP: 2006.
23. Micro Start: A Guide for Planning, Starting and Managing a Microfinance Programme: United Nations Capital Development Fund (www.uncdf.org/English/microfinance/microstart/guide).
24. Bennett, Lynn & Cuevas, Carlos E: Sustainable Banking with the Poor: World Bank.
25. Srivastava, Pradeep and Basu, Priya: Scaling-up Access to Finance for India's Rural Poor: IBRD/*The World Bank*: 2004 (extracts).
26. Chen, Martha Alter, Jhabvala, Renana & Lund, Francis: Supporting Workers in the Informal Economy—A Policy Framework: ILO Working Paper on the Informal Economy: ILO: 2002.
27. Planning Commission Approach to Eleventh Five Year Plan: Planning Commission, GoI (2007).
28. UNIFEM/Institute of Social Studies Trust, New Delhi: Policy Recommendations for Home-based Workers.
29. Sievers, Merten, Haftendorm, Klaus & Bessler Astrid: Business Centres for Small Enterprise Development—Experiences and Lessons from Eastern Europe: ILO (Geneva) SEED Working Paper.
30. Donor Committee for Enterprise Development: Supporting Business Environment Reforms: Practical Guidance for Development Agencies: *Donor Committee 2007*.
31. Research Group of the Department of Training & Employment, Ministry of Labour and Social Security, People's Republic of China: Skills Training in the Informal Sector in China: ILO InFocus Programme on Skills, Knowledge & Employability (extracts).
32. Planning Commission Approach to Eleventh Five Year Plan: *Planning Commission*, GoI (2007).
33. Burrus, William: Innovations in Microenterprise Development in the United States: ACCION, USA (extracts).
34. National Bank for Agriculture and Rural Development. *Annual Report 2007*, NABARD (Mumbai): 2007.
35. Aga Khan Rural Support Project (India), Ahmedabad: Micro Enterprise Development at AKRSP (I)—A Quick Glance (Note) and personal communication.
36. Gupta, Anil K.: Grassroots to Global: Online Incubation of Grassroots

Innovations based enterprises—IIM, Ahmedabad: *Working Paper No. 2007-07-07*, July 2007.

37. Prahalad, C.K. and Hammond, Allen: What Works: Serving the Poor, Profitably: A private sector strategy for Global Digital Opportunity: *MARKLE Foundation*/World Resources Institute.
38. Vishwanathan, Sujatha and Srivastava, Ravi: Learning from the Poor—Findings from Participatory Poverty Assessments in India: Asian Development Bank (Manila) (2007).
39. Asian Development Bank: Special Evaluation Study on Pathways out of Rural Poverty and the Effectiveness of Poverty Targeting, *Asian Development Bank* (Manila) 2006.
40. Karnani, Aneel: Microfinance Misses its Mark: *STANFORD Social Innovation Review*' Summer 2007 (Extracts).
41. Chen, Martha Alter, Jhabvala, Renana & Lund, Francis: Supporting Workers in the Informal Economy—A Policy Framework: *ILO Working Paper on the Informal Economy*: ILO: 2002.
42. Kenyon, Thomas: A Framework for Thinking about Enterprise Formalization Policies in Developing Countries: *World Bank Policy Research Working Paper: 2007*.
43. Bhatnagar, Amitabh (ed.): Sage & Sound Recipes—Successful Experiments in Rural Development/Livelihoods—Volume I: MPRLP-*Livelihoods Forum* (Bhopal)/Zenith Books International (N. Delhi): 2007.
44. CARE India/CASHE Strategic Impact Inquiry Study (2006) on the extent of impact of CASHE on women's empowerment was covered in our earlier publication: Bhatnagar, Amitabh (ed.): Sage & Sound Recipes—Successful Experiments in Rural Development/Livelihoods—Volume II: MPRLP-Livelihoods Forum (Bhopal)/Zenith Books International (N. Delhi): 2007.

2

MFIs and the Maturing of Indian Microfinance*

FRANCES SINHA and EDA RURAL SYSTEM TEAM

I. MICROFINANCE CONTEXT: MFIS IN INDIA

In India there is a diversity of approaches to microfinance, involving banks, government agencies, NGOs, cooperatives. There are now specialised microfinance institutions (MFIs), many still registered as NGOs or cooperatives, a few 'transformed' into Non-Banking Finance Companies or Section 25 Companies. Their purpose is to extend the provision of financial services (credit, savings, insurance) whilst building their own financial sustainability.

Over 100 MFIs in India have been credit-rated. These MFIs have a combined outstanding portfolio of Rs. 380 crores ($ 87 million) with cumulative disbursements of Rs. 1,560 crores ($ 360 million). Total clients of these MFIs are an estimated 2.3 million.[1]

Table 2.1: MFIs in India (M-CRIL database December 2004)

MFI model	*No. of MFIs*	*No. of clients*	*% clients by model*	*MFI borrowers as % of clients*
SHG	76	1,434,900	62	30
Grameen	19	783,400	34	79
Individual	9	91,500	4	67
Overall	104	2,309,800	100	47

* Study of the National Microfinance Suppprt Project implemented by SIDBI Foundation for Micro Credit in Collaboration with DFID, U.K. and IFAD, Rome

Most MFIs use groups as intermediaries for financial transactions, but there are different ways of working with groups. These may be broadly classified as the Self Help Group model (SHG) and Grameen replicators and Cooperatives. The SHG model predominates with 62 per cent of total clients. The Grameen model covers a smaller proportion (34%) of total clients but has a larger share of outstanding portfolio, and a higher number of borrowers, due to its more regular cycle of loan disbursements. The Individual Banking (IB) model accounts for 4 per cent of clients.

MFIs in the NMFSP

The MFIs associated with the National Microfinance Support Project (NMFSP) of SIDBI Foundation for Micro-Credit (SFMC), represent the more established microfinance institutions in the country. As at March 31, 2005, SIDBI had a loan portfolio of Rs. 199.36 crores ($ 46 million) with over 70 partner MFIs.[2]

This study has sampled 20 of these MFIs. Most follow the SHG model and have microfinance experience of at least 4 years, and up to 10 years. Based on data for the sample MFIs, some operational features that are typical of the three different models are presented (over page) showing variations in approach, focus and type of products.

Table 2.2: Study Sample: 20 MFIs

Model	*MFIs*
SHG	APDMACS IASC LEAD OUTREACH RASS SNF SWDMACTS LUPIN Shramik Bharati
GRAMEEN	ASA SKS Spandana CASHPOR RGVN VWS
INDIVIDUAL BANKING/SECTOR COOPERATIVE	BASIX SIFFS Pustikar VSSU YVU

Table 2.3: Operational Features of Microfinance Models in India

Operational features	*SHG*	*Grameen*	*Individual Banking*
The 'model'	10-20 member groups save regularly: group loans to members from savings; jointly liable fro external loans—from MFI or bank	5 clients per group organized into 'centers'; assume joint liability for regular MFI loans	Individual clients receive loans on condition of minimum savings deposit
Main Clients	Women	Women	Men (usually)
Targeting	'The poor'—broadly described as the weaker sections of 'BPL'	'The poor'—specifically defined in terms of housing, other assets, type of employment	General; non-poor and poor
Service focus	Saving and credit	Credit—regular	Credit
Transactions	Monthly meetings	Weekly meetings	Individual—often daily
Saving deposit	Rs. 20-100 ($0.40 -2.20)/month	Rs. 5-25 ($0.10-0.60)/week	Flexible, above a minimum (usu. 10% of loan amount)
Interest on savings	Bank rate (4.25%) + profit share	6-9%	6%
Initial loans size (MFI)	Rs. 5-10,000 ($110-225)[a]	Rs. 2-5,000 ($ 45-110)	Rs. 5-15,000 ($ 110-330)
Effective interest rate (usual range)	24-28%	32-38%	23-38%
Insurance	At a preliminary stage: usually loan linked; sometimes linked to national companies		
Development services	Some lined programmes	A few small projects	Enterprise support (occas.)

Source: Data for sample MFIs

Note: [a] Also, internal group loans range from Rs. 200-2,000 ($ 5-45) in new groups; up to Rs. 10,000 ($ 225) in established groups.

Credit rating information for the sample MFIs at the time of the field study, show by model that: the Grameen MFIs are larger scale and growing extremely fast, with 30,000 clients on average, 23,000 borrowers. Sustainability was high (average Operational Self Sufficiency of 106%)[3] with moderate portfolio quality (PAR_{60} 7%)[4] resulting in an average rating of β. SHG MFIs are longer established organisations, with an average 24,000 clients but lower incidence of borrowing from the MFI (4,000 active borrowers on average). This is reflected in lower OSS ratios (68% on average) and, with lower portfolio quality; the average rating is β. IB MFIs are relatively young with 13,000 clients on average, 10,000 active borrowers and high sustainability resulting in an average rating of α-though portfolio quality is variable.

II. RESEARCH DESIGN

The study aims to *document impact* of microfinance services at the end user level and improve practice by understanding the processes of MFIs' intervention and their relevance. Impact is defined as *'change that can be plausibly associated with involvement in a microfinance programme'*.

The research questions are:

1. Who is being served by microfinance? Are the poorest getting left out?
2. How is microcredit used? Does microfinance contribute to enterprise growth and incomes?
3. Does microfinance lead to a reduction in poverty: is it sufficient to move poor families out of a situation of poverty and vulnerability? Indirectly, does it enable the better off to provide employment opportunities to the very poor?
4. Does women's role as microfinance clients translate into their empowerment? Or is there focus on women clients instrumental, i.e. a means to ensure repayments and group discipline?
5. What effect does microfinance have on other systems or sources of finance both formal (local banks) and informal (moneylenders, traders)?
6. Which products and services are effective in reaching the poor and responding to their financial needs?

In line with recent developments in impact assessment and poverty analysis methodologies, the research combines quantitative and qualitative tools. Questionnaire data enables us to quantify and correlate results on different indicators. Qualitative information (from Focus Group Discussions and Case Studies) helps us to ground the data in an understanding of the situations that people face, how they use and perceive microfinance.

Box 2.1: Poverty Analysis

Different methods (PRA, household asset index, estimated household income) were combined to arrive at a household wealth rank. The wealth ranks assigned are comparable in different areas whilst reflecting local perceptions and a range of indicators (including housing quality, assets, type of employment, incidence of ill health, alcoholism). Four wealth rank categories were applied: very poor, poor, borderline, non-poor.

Indicators for different wealth rank categorizes

	Very poor	Poor	Borderline	Non-poor
Housing	Small Kuccha (thatched) houses	Mostly small houses, either kuccha or mixed (tin)	Medium size, usually mixed or pucca (concrete)	Mostly lagre, pucca houses
Assets	No major assets, basic utensils only	Marginal land (<1 acre), few small animals, cot, radio, cycle	Small (1-5 acre) land holding, 1-2 milch cattle, small animals, B&W TV, fan, bicycle, radio, some furniture, old two-wheeler	Large (>5 acres) landholding, >2 milch cattle, tube well, TV, phone, fridge, motorcycle, car
Food security	Usually one meal a day— basic creates only	Just able to manage two meals a day—but variable	2 meals a day but sometimes face problem (a few weeks in a year)	Regular family diet—(2 meals/day and 'quality' items)
Income sources	Low paid casual wage labour, single earner	Regular wage labour, one-two earners	Seasonal business; low paid jobs; May sometimes depend on skilled wage labour	Assured regular income, e.g. established. business or high pay job
Poverty line	Below*		Above: may slip into poverty in case of an 'income shock'	Above

Note:* The poverty line is based on rural and urban levels for each State, estimated by the Planning Commission, updated to 2003-4 prices using the appropriate consumer price index (rural agricultural labourers, urban industrial workers); for the time of the field survey, the estimates for the study States were Rs. 9.26-13.20 (rural) and Rs. 12.31-18.31 (urban) per capita per day. The international poverty line ($ 1.08/day at purchasing power parity) works out to Rs. 14.54 (rural/urban 33 cents) which is roughly comparable to the local poverty line.

The 20 MFIs sampled for the study reflect the main models of microfinance delivery and their relative presence in different regions of India. The sample covers the States of Andhra Pradesh, Tamil Nadu, Karnataka and Kerala in the South and Uttar Pradesh, Rajasthan, Assam and Manipur in the North/East.

From each MFI, two to six clusters (villages or urban areas) were randomly selected from village/area lists. All MFI clients within a cluster were surveyed for a client sample size of at least 130 per MFI providing a statistical confidence level of 95 per cent. Non-clients were sampled as a comparison group. The large baseline sample provides strong evidence for the study findings.

Study sample: > 5,000 households

- 4,000 clients (74% rural)
- 1,400 non-clients
- 280 dropouts
- 150 case studies
- 200 + focus group discussions

III. OUTREACH

Box 2.2: Hypothesis: MFIs are Extending Financial Services to the Poor and Other Disadvantaged People not Reached by Formal Sector Finance of

Mixed Findings—MFIs are:

— mainly operating in more developed areas of the country
— reaching the unbanked
— serving all castes and communities including socially marginal groups (Scheduled Castes)
— reaching women headed households
— catering to all economic levels, not only the poor

Microfinance is more concentrated in the South of India: Based on national data for the NMFSP, the majority of microfinance clients (89%) are in the more developed Southern region districts of the country, including some in the West; just 11 per cent of clients are in the less developed North and East. Programmes are mainly rural with 77 per cent rural clients (90% in the case of Grameen and IB model MFIs).

Depth of outreach: Based on sample data, MFI services are 'reaching the unreached'—81 per cent do not have formal savings in a bank or post office, 92 per cent have not had a bank loan.[5] The client profile includes vulnerable and socially marginalized groups such as scheduled castes, scheduled tribes and women headed households.

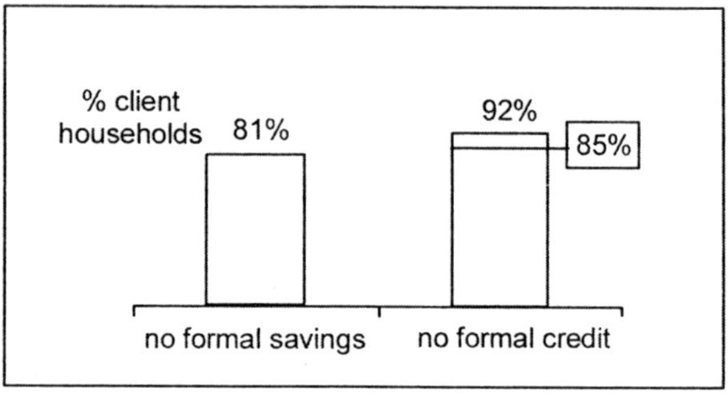

Fig 2.1: No Formal Financial Service

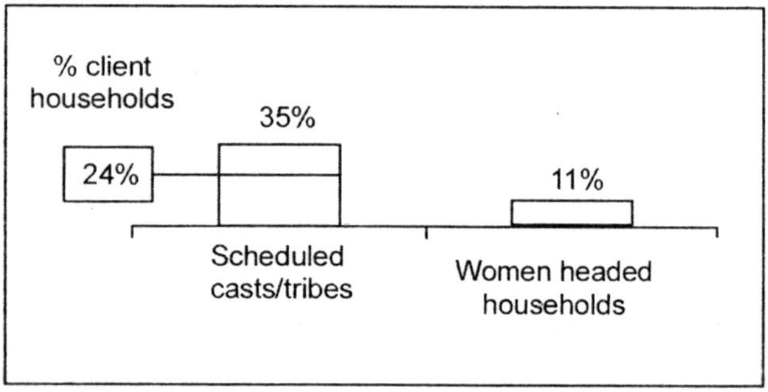

Fig 2.2: Socially Marginal Clients

Key: % All India (from secondary sources: All India Debt and Investment Survey, Census, Planning Commission).

Nevertheless the data shows that MFIs are catering to a mixed clientele that includes both poor and non-poor. Given the very limited outreach of formal financial services, it cannot be assumed that all those without access, and needing financial services, are poor.

This pattern of outreach is much broader than that generally assumed: that most microfinance clients fall in a band around the poverty line. In the current debate about focusing on the poor, we do not believe that this finding necessarily represents a negative feature. As a practical strategy for operational sustainability, MFIs are tending to diversify their clientele, whilst at the same time including poorer clients. A more critical issue, as we see later, is the scope to provide services that meet clients' varying financial needs, including for poorer clients.

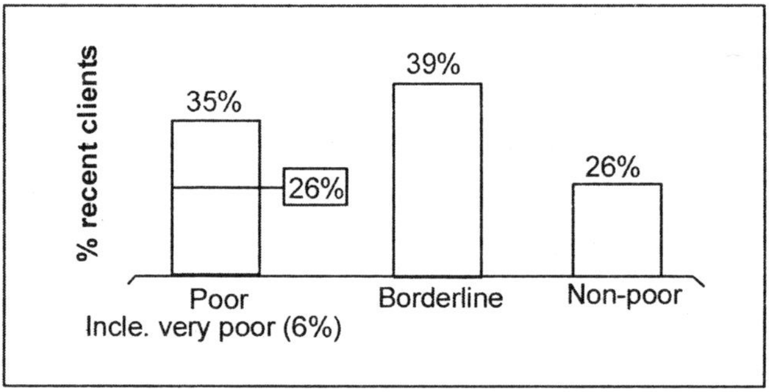

Fig. 2.3: Targeting the Poor?

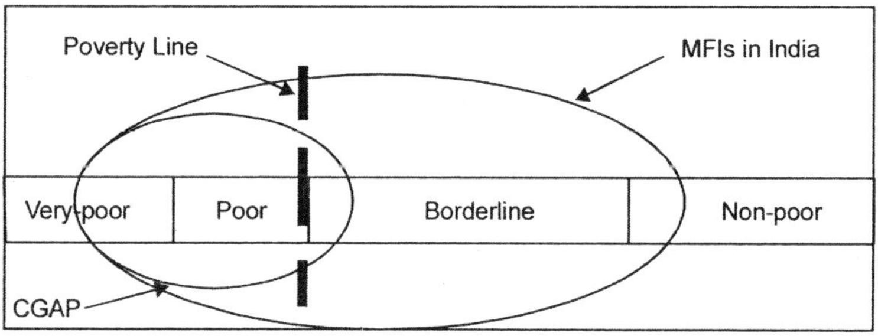

Fig. 2.4: Pattern of Microfinance Outreach
Adapted from CGAP [Donor Brief no. 13, July 2003]

Depth of outreach and MFI performance: The data broadly supports the general perception that there is a trade-off between outreach to the poor and operational self-sufficiency. Most clearly in the case of IB MFIs, strong OSS is combined with low depth of outreach. Both SHG and Grameen MFIs have considerable range of outreach. On OSS, the sample SHG MFIs are weaker (due to smaller portfolios relative to scale of operations) while the

Grameen MFIs tend to be stronger (large portfolios, high staff productivity in terms of client: staff ratio). Yet, there are interesting exceptions: 2 SHG MFIs and 2 Grameen MFIs combine sustainability with substantial depth of outreach.

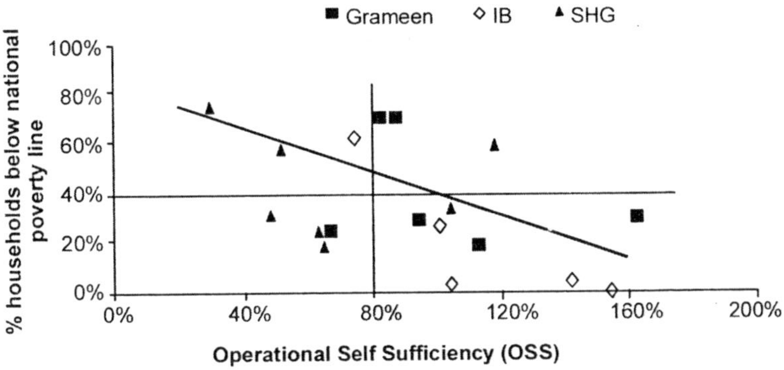

OSS line at 80% (approaching Operational Self-Sufficiency) Depth of outreach line at 40% of clients below national poverty line. Trend line overall: $R^2 = 0.24$.

Source: Survey data & M-CRIL reports (19 MFIs, OSS data not avialable for one MFI (SHG/South).

Fig. 2.5: Operational Self Sufficiency and Depth of Outreach (Recent Clients)

At least part of the explanation for greater outreach to the poor lies in operations in a poor region combined with effective targeting. In the two SHG examples, both sustainability (lower costs of group formation, higher staff productivity) and depth have been achieved (in a relatively short time) through providing microfinance services to SHG groups established under long standing NGO programmes.

Depth of outreach and MFI products: The data does not support another assumption, that small loans and lower interest rates are determining factors for deepening outreach. They may suit the poor, but do not in themselves serve to exclude the non-poor. Rather it is responsiveness to client financial needs in terms of the range of products offered that is the main factor (along with operations in poor areas).

IV. USE AND CONTRIBUTION OF MICROFINANCE: MICROFINANCE AND ENTERPRISES

Use of Microfinance

Box 2.3: Hypothesis: Micro-Credit is Used for Investment and for Other Household Needs

> SUPPORTED
> — focus on direct investment,
> — more diverse use in SHG model, including internal lending from group savings.

The main use of MFI loans is direct investment, although the actual use is slightly less than the recorded use (85%). There is greater focus on such investment in Grameen and IB model MFIs, compared to SHGs. The Figure shows client use of total micro-credit borrowed over the previous two years, including internal lending from group savings in the SHG model. 'Investment' refers to directly productive use—in non-farm enterprise, animal husbandry and agriculture. Micro-credit is also being used for a range of 'other household purposes'—including family events (especially marriage costs), housing, medical care, household purchases and schooling. These 'other' purposes also represent a form of investment but they are usually considered separately by MFIs (and by SIDBI).

Such use is partly due to 'fungibility', depending on household credit requirements at the time of loan disbursement, despite MFI insistence on loan use for enterprise although some MFIs are now introducing other products.

The use of micro-credit for direct investment increases with wealth rank. Poorer clients use a higher proportion of micro-credit for other household needs (48% compared to 28% by the non-poor).

Micro-Credit Support to Enterprises

Box 2.4: Hypothesis: Microfinance Increases Enterprise Activity

> SUPPORTED
> — new and expanded non-agriculture enterprises with some increase in (self-) employment,
> — contributes to reported increase in enterprise income.

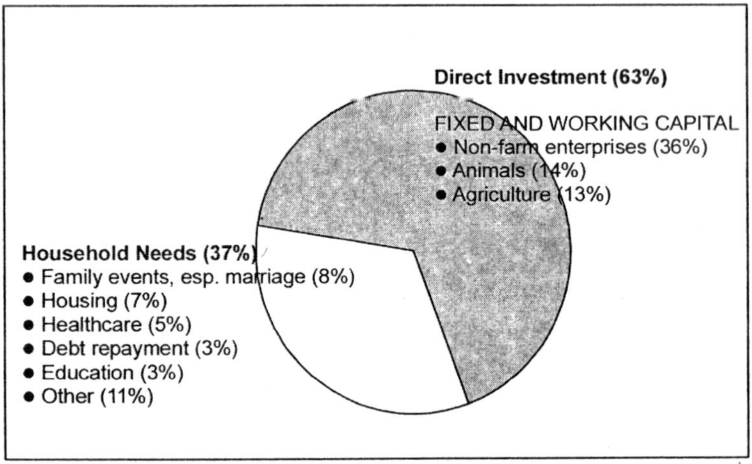

Fig. 2.6: Use of micro-credit (MFI loans and internal group lending)

Table 4: Different Scales of Enterprises

Enterprise type	*Income Generating Activities-IGA*	*Micro-enterprise ME*	*Small enterprise SE*
Scale	Low investment [Rs. 2-15,000 ($ 45-330)] Part-time Seasonal Family labour Supplementary income	Investment up to Rs. 35,000 ($ 800) Full-time Some seasonality Mainly family labour Secondary/primary income source	Investment up to Rs. 2 lakhs ($ 4,500) Full-time Regular Some hired labour Primary income source
Examples	Animal husbandry (small animals, 1-2 dairy animals) Seasonal vending Home based tailoring/petty shops	(A few larger scale animal units) Provision shops, Tea shops/Tiffin centres, Transport (Cycle rickshaw), Home based manufacturing	Large scale trading/business Repair units—electrical separate manufacturing units powerlooms
MFI model support	SHG and Grameen, some IB		IB, some Grameen

Enterprises of different scales—requiring different levels of capital (fixed and working)—are using micro-credit. Group-based MFIs provide small loans for use in 'income generating activities' and 'micro-enterprises'. IB MFIs usually provide larger loans for 'small enterprises'.

The majority of supported enterprises are rural. The main sector is non-farm. The Grameen and IB MFIs support a high proportion of non-farm enterprises. Animal husbandry is common in more remote rural areas, where there are fewer alternative opportunities for enterprise.

Table 2.5: Enterprises using Micro-Credit

Selected enterprise parameters		*By model*			*Over all (wted. avg.)*
		SHG	*Grameen*	*IB*	
% By Sector	Non-farm	29%	66%	80%	44%
	Animal husbandary	42%	21%	8%	34%
	Agriculture	29%	13%	12%	23%
% New enterprises		28%	45%	7%	32%
Employment*/supported enterprises		1.05	1.25	1.66	1.14
	Family	0.99	1.13	1.26	1.05
	Hired	0.06	0.12	0.40	0.10
% Reporting increase in income		55%	82%	81%	64%
% Closed down		7%	11%	2%	8%

* 'Employment' includes self-employment.

Nearly one third were new enterprises started with micro-credit, primarily by poor and by borderline clients. This proportion is higher for the Grameen model and in animal husbandry. Enterprises with credit from group based MFIs are usually owner-operated, sometimes involving more than one member of the family, often part-time (they are typically IGAs and micro-enterprises). Small enterprises—which typically have IB credit—have more employment that is mostly full-time and partly hired. New employment—both women and men—has been generated mainly through new enterprises (not expansion of existing enterprises). New employment has been generated mainly through new enterprises. Half of the additional employment is of women, 5 per cent is of children less than 15 years.

Client households reported an increase in income following micro-credit support in two-thirds of supported enterprises. This proportion is significantly higher in the Grameen and IB models reflecting more non-farm enterprises supported in these models, and a regular cycle of credit. Income increase was mainly due to expansion and improved quality and range of products or services. Lower reported increase in the SHG model partly reflects more uncertain returns to agriculture (which is more prominent in SHG lending).

Box 2.5: Diversifying Income Sources Through Micro-Credit

> **Prabhavati** and her husband were both agricultural labourers. After she joined the MFI group (Grameen) in 2001 she invested her first loan of Rs. 5,000 ($ 115) in a *tiffin* business for which there was good local demand. The business did well and Prabhavati has reinvested some of her earnings to buy sheep. Both livelihoods provide a year round income. Prabhavati no longer works as an agricultural labourer. She is proud of the fact that she is running her own business and not working for anybody. And, life is more stable without difficulties she used to face during lean agricultural seasons.
>
> *[Borderline, Grameen client, rural South India]*

Nevertheless, micro enterprises are susceptible to risks. Risks may relate to personal situations (especially illness and cash flow difficulties), market constraints and competition, natural conditions, and other wider factors (technological change, political or regulatory factors). Clients reported problems in over 30 per cent of supported enterprises (36% of non-farm, 25% of animal units). Problem incidence was higher for the very poor and poor who are more likely than other wealth ranks to report illness, have less experience in enterprise activities and (in case of the very poor) are less likely to report an income increase. The rate of closure is 8 per cent, again higher for poorer clients, especially those who used micro-credit to start new enterprises, as reflected in the higher rate of closure for the Grameen model.

V. MICROFINANCE AND POVERTY REDUCTION

Box 2.6: Hypothesis: Microfinance Contributes to a Reduction in Poverty

> MIXED FINDINGS
>
> — improvement in economic indicators: financial, productive and physical capital,
>
> — more diversified income sources,
>
> — for social capital: some evidence for higher enrolment of children at primary level, but not at secondary level or above, where gender imbalance continues,
>
> — substantive conclusions will depend on endline comparison of clients/non-clients, and
>
> — nevertheless, over one-third of older clients (with microfinance programme >5 years) are still poor, some very poor.

The data shows that microfinance can directly improve access by the poor to finance that supports productive activities and asset development. Micro-credit has enabled client households (all wealth ranks, including the poor and very poor) to invest in productive assets (37% of client households invested in the previous two years, compared to 17% non-clients) and to diversify their livelihoods (73% of client households have multiple sources of income, compared to 59% of non-clients). Sixty per cent of households who acquired a productive asset have reported income increase. On other (non-income) dimensions, client households have been able to build financial capital (savings), physical capital (household assets and improved housing though the difference with non-clients here is not so large) and human capital in terms of sending children to primary school (but no increase seen in girls' attendance or in education at secondary levels and above).

On practically all indicators, a comparison with non-clients shows more significant effects for poorer households.

Table 2.6: Poverty Reducing Effects

Households	*Very Poor & Poor*			*Borderline*		
	Client	*Non-client*	*Difference*	*Client*	*Non-client*	*Difference*
Income related indicators:						
% acquiring a productive asset in last two years	36%	14%	21%	41%	17%	24%
% with multiple sources of income	67%	50%	17%	77%	62%	15%
Dependency ratio*	2.70	2.93	-0.23	2.58	2.84	-0.26
% reporting increase in HH income	45%	26%	19%	48%	35%	13%
Financial capital						
% with savings	98%	28%	70%	97%	55%	42%
Physical capital						
% investing in housing in last two years	23%	20%	3%	23%	22%	1%
% acquiring a household asset in last two years	23%	17%	6%	34%	31%	3%
Human capital						
% girls (6-14 years) going to school	82%	76%	6%	89%	87%	2%
% boys (6-14 years) going to school	89%	83%	6%	90%	85%	5%

*Note:** Total number of members (including earning members) per earner in the household.

Direct poverty effects are prominent in the Grameen model, which combines substantial poverty outreach with a focus on credit for direct investment. The IB model has a similar focus, whilst catering more to the borderline and non-poor. In this model the use of micro-credit to promote small scale enterprises that hire non-family labour can have an indirect poverty effect by supporting income-earning opportunities for non-clients, though the data shows that any increase in labour is mostly for family members joining the enterprise and less in terms of hired labour.

Table 2.7: Poverty Reducing Effects by Model

(In percentage)

Client households	*SHG*	*Grameen*	*IB*	*Overall [wtd. avg.]*
Acquiring a productive asset in last two years	23	51	39	33
With multiple sources of income	67	82	71	72
Reporting increase in HH income	41	70	67	52
Investing in housing in last two years	21	25	32	23
Acquiring a household asset in last two years	29	33	44	31
Supported enterprises with hired labour	4	6	25	6

Microfinance is contributing to livelihoods but is it sufficient to move households out of poverty? More will be known about the impact of microfinance through a client/non-client comparison at the endline stage of the study. Cross-sectional analysis of the baseline data (comparing older with more recent clients) suggests movement of client households into less poor wealth rank categories in four MFIs, with a possible shift out of poverty (to non-poor) for around 20 per cent of the sample in these MFIs.

This is supported by case-study examples.

Box 2.7: MFI Loan Helps a Widow to Grow Her Business and Plan Future Expansion

When Saraswathiamma's husband died she was forced by her son and daughter-in-law to live separately and fend for herself. She borrowed Rs. 1,000 ($ 25) from her neighbours (interest-free) and opened a tiffin centre in her house where she serves idli/sambar and tea, seven days a week. Business was good and she soon repaid the startup capital. She was looking for more credit to expand the enterprise when some of her neighbours suggested she join the MFI group.

(Contd.)

She joined a new group of the MFI in 2000. Within the same year she took a loan of Rs. 4,000 ($ 90) which she used to purchase an electric grinder, to save her time, allowing her to do several other tasks. The second loan of Rs. 5,000 ($ 110) she used to purchase material in bulk, enabling a discount from the retailer, involving one weekly visit to the market in town, instead of the earlier daily visits. Saraswathiamma has repaid both loans on time. Now she is thinking of starting a new hotel outside the village (on main road), though not for herself but for her son.

[*(Now) non-poor SHG client in rural South India*]

Box 2.8: Client's Husband Invests a Series of MFI Loans in his Manufacturing Unit

For over 25 years **Mataprasad** worked as a carpet weaver—employed on other's looms for export. He was earning Rs. 2,500 ($ 55) a month quite regularly until carpet exports declined and many carpet units closed down. For a year or so, the family managed on his occasional earnings—with difficulty (they could not afford a school uniform for their growing son every year; they did not replace their cow when it died). The alternative option was unskilled labour. But, weaving was the skill that Mataprasad knew, and over the years he had developed connections in the industry. But to set up his own loom, he needed credit, and he did not have the collateral for a loan—whether from a bank or a pawnshop.

Then, when his wife Sita joined an MFI group (Grameen) in 2001, she was able to obtain a loan of Rs. 6,000 ($ 135). Adding Rs. 2,000 ($ 45) from his savings, Mataprasad used the micro-credit to purchase a loom. This was the start of his carpet-manufacturing unit and, with two more MFI loans, he added another two looms. Now, Mataprasad has a bank account, the family owns a cow, and his son has two new sets of uniform each year. And Mataprasad employs six other men from his village-weavers who had earlier lost their jobs, just like him.

[*Borderline, Grameen client in rural North/East India*]

Nevertheless, even in these four MFIs, for which the sample includes a substantial number of clients with the microfinance programme for 5 years or more, 30 per cent of such 'high involvement' clients are below the local poverty line (including 12% very poor). Across the entire sample, one third of high involvement clients are still poor. Involvement in microfinance therefore may reduce poverty for some clients, but not for all, the greatest challenge remaining to reduce the poverty of the poorest.

VI. MICROFINANCE AND VULNERABILITY

Box 2.9: Hypothesis: Microfinance Builds the Capacity of Individuals, Households and Enterprises to Manage Risks

Mixed Findings:
- '*ex ante*': livelihood diversification and physical capital helps build resilience.
- weak protective role (savings not withdrawable, insurance services not yet developed).
- '*ex post*': significant contribution to small scale emergency credit needs, (especially from internal lending in SHG model) but limited contribution when large sums required for emergencies.

Vulnerability is intrinsically linked to poverty both as cause and symptom. It is defined as susceptibility to risk, risk being understood as the chance of a loss (in income, livelihood, health, housing) or the loss itself. In case of risk, micro-credit strengthens the coping strategies of its clients *ex ante* (in advance) mainly through livelihood diversification and asset building. Protection through financial intermediation is weaker.

Ex post (after risk occurs), client households, especially the poor and the very poor continue to borrow to meet the costs of risk related needs. These include medical costs, marriage, debt redemption and emergency needs (such as for food, house repair). Micro-credit contributes quite substantially to the latter needs, especially through the small flexible loans usually available in the SHG model, and specific products of some (mainly Grameen) MFIs, as well as through general products that may be used for such needs (fungibility). Given the (small) size of micro-credit, it is not surprising that it contributes less to larger needs (marriage, medical costs). Clients are going to moneylenders for such loans, but the dependence on them in case of risk is less compared to that of non-clients.

Microfinance contributes to the coping strategies of its more vulnerable clients (the very poor, scheduled castes, women headed households). Though the most vulnerable (those with irregular income sources, existing indebtedness) are also the least creditworthy. Such households do sometimes struggle as MFI clients (illustrated by the story of Chinnapillai later in Section 8) and their vulnerability can lead to dropout. In case of enterprise risks, microfinance support is marginal, if any. In fact, where micro-credit is being provided for enterprise use to clients with limited skills or previous experience, this is contributing to increased vulnerability.

Box 2.10: Role of Microfinance in Coping Strategies

	Very Poor	*Poor*	*Borderline*	*Overall*
% client households borrowing for risk	66%	64%	53%	53%
Median borrowed (Rs.)	2,000	3,000	4,000	4,000
% HHs borrowing for risk from				
moneylenders: —Client	28%	35%	37%	34%
—Non-client	52%	62%	56%	53%
Use of mircro-creadit for risk needs	*SHG*	*Grameen*	*IB*	
% risk borrowings —MFI	6%	26%	14%	
—group	42%	—	—	

Two MFIs in the sample are examples of co-variate risk. In these MFIs, all clients are affected by adverse economic conditions (prolonged drought in one case, increasing costs of production in the other). When clients in substantial numbers default (on both loan repayments and saving payments) or need large credit sums to meet investment costs, an MFI's portfolio is constrained and cannot respond to the additional financial needs of its clients.

VII. MICROFINANCE AND WOMEN'S EMPOWERMENT

Box 2.11: Hypothesis: Microfinance Contributes to Women's Empowerment at Individual, Households and Community Levels

Mixed Findings—MFI approach instrumental rather than transformative

- opportunity to save, access credit and earn—a first for many women
- supports women managed enterprises—mainly IGAs
- women benefit from peer interaction and support in mature groups
- enhanced status within household for some women but constrained by patriarchal relationships

All group based MFIs, and some IB MFIs and Sector Cooperatives, target women as clients of microfinance.

Table 2.8: Women Clients of Microfinance

	SHG & Grameen	*Sector Coop.*	*IB*	*Total*
% clients who are women	99%	54%	23%	95%
Number of women clients (millions)	2.20	0.006	0.02	2.22

Source: M-cril data base (December, 2004).

In practice, this does not necessarily reflect an empowering strategy for women in the fullest or *transformative* sense of enhancing women's capabilities and addressing fundamental gender inequalities. Rather, MFIs may target women because it is easier to organise women than men and thereby increase programme outreach and impose discipline. This reflects a *neutral* or instrumental approach to women's empowerment. The SHG model—which promotes more autonomy and responsibility within women's groups—shows more scope for *support to* developing women's opportunities and skills.

Table 2.9: Approaches to Women's Empowerment

	Neutral	*Supportive*	*Transformative*
Orientation	Women as clients for financial transactions	Support to women clients to build skills to take advantage of new opportunities	Transforming gender relations which reflect patriarchal values
Assumptions	Women are easier to organise, will come to meetings and be disciplined about repayment	Women benefit from specific support (through group interaction/responsibilities and skill development); need to build confidence and abilities as part of an empowering process	Ensuring women's access to and control over an economic resource (finance) is part of a transformative process to give women an equal say within the household, in their communities and within financial institutions
By model, typically	Grameen and IB	Some SHG MFIs	[none in the sample]

This study explores women's empowerment largely through indicators identified by women clients, and using data for women clients and their households. (Data on indicators of women's empowerment in households of men clients shows little change).

An underlying theme is the difference between the north and the other regions of the country. The scope for women's empowerment and economic activity is conditioned significantly by sociocultural factors and livelihood opportunities which are more favourable in the south, and in urban areas. This is reflected in differences in women's involvement in economic activities.

Box 2.12: What Women Say?

Women's priorities

- A better quality of life that will come only if,
- employment and incomes are stable,
- children are educated, and
- social evils—such as alcoholism—are eradicated

Indicators of change for women through microfinance

Objective

- Ability to save and access loans
- Opportunity to undertake an economic activity
- Mobility—opportunity to visit nearby towns
- Increased financial awareness
- A role in community activities (some MFIs)

Subjective

- Increased self-confidence
- Ability to command respect within the household and have a say in household decision making

Source: FGDs.

In terms of individual empowerment, targeting women as clients of microfinance has provided for many women (including women heads of households) an option to save and access credit for the first time. However, basic awareness of micro-finance related issues (products and terms, banking procedures) appears to be limited, particularly for very poor women. An aspect linked to low literacy rates 60 per cent of women clients have had little or no schooling. Women like to be part of a group. They draw moral support from their peers and develop a sense of confidence from interaction at group meetings. The group mechanism thus contributes to women's options, mobility and skill development, though this contribution is strongest for group leaders, and in the SHG model.

At the household level, involvement in microfinance is contributing to women's recognised owership of assets (mainly for productive assets, to some extent for housing); women are involved in the management of enterprises for which they obtain micro-credit, especially in the southern sample though typically in activities that are micro-scale, require low investment and are home-based (animal husbandry, petty trading). A number of enterprises depend on 'joint management' with the common pattern being that men negotiate the more public markets and handle major cash transactions (for example purchasing a milch animal, buying stocks from wholesale markets).

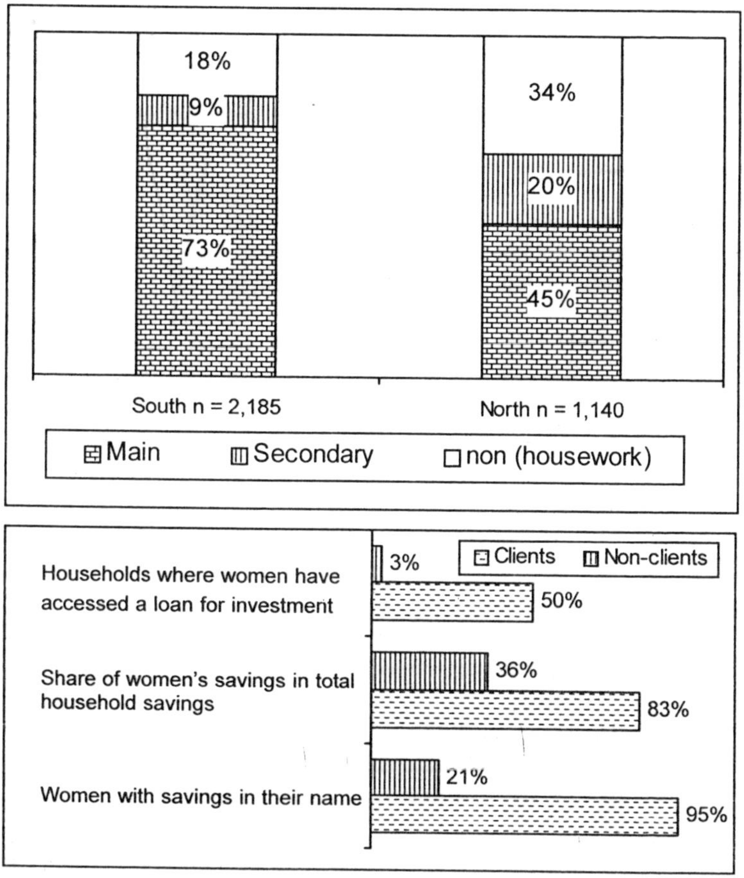

Fig 2.7: Women Clients' Economic Activity

There are also cases of 'loan pass': 27 per cent of supported enterprises in the southern sample, over half of the northern sample. In such cases, women are pleased to be contributing to household income. For women themselves, it is less important who manages an enterprise activity, than that it generates additional income for the household. Thus, gender roles remain the same, with women continuing to be dependent on their husbands for money for repayments and savings deposits.

Table 2.10: Indicators of Women's Status at Household Level

	Clients n = 3,128		*Non-clients n = 1,141*	
	South	*North*	*South*	*North*
% of productive assets purchased in women's name	43%	31%	22%	9%
% of housing assets purchased in women's name	19%	10%	12%	6%
Loan pass—% enterprises supported by loan in women's name but not involving women in management or employment	27%	53%	—	—

Note: Survey data for 16 MFIs that target women clients.

On subjective aspects related to a woman's 'status' in the household, the qualitative information gathered through case studies and FGDs suggests that many women clients have a sense of self-worth that arises from an enhanced ability to earn, to save and to contribute to the welfare of the household.

Box 2.13: Micro-Credit helps Women to Contribute to Household Income

Behind the scenes....

Jabamani's husband was running a small tiffin centre in the village in 1998. But he ran into debts, sold the shop and worked as a labourer in a brick kiln. Jabamani earned a small income from beedi rolling. By 2001, they had saved enough to restart the tiffin centre. Her husband manages the tiffin centre, Jabamani prepares the food items and cleans the place. Everyday around 50 people come for tiffin. Tea is a key item for the centre for which they require around 11 litres of milk everyday. Her husband decided to buy a cow for which Jabamani took a group loan (Rs. 3,000/$ 70) and he added another Rs. 3,000 ($ 70) from their earnings. Jabamani is proud of her contribution to the enterprise and her husband is openly appreciative.

[Borderline, SHG client in rural South India]

Increased status...

Saraswati's family used to depend on their one-acre land (growing jute and rice) and her husband's seasonal casual employment. The income was barely sufficient to meet the needs of the family including her young son and in-laws. Three years ago, she joined an MFI and within six months took a loan for Rs. 2,000 ($ 45). She and her husband decided to use it to start a home-based silver ball-making unit (used for making artificial jewellery). Her husband spent some time with other units in the area to pick up the technique. The business has expanded with two more loans from the MFI (last loan Rs. 5,000/ $ 115). Repayments have been on time and the business yields a monthly income of ~Rs. 2,000 ($ 45). Saraswati works about six hours each day in the unit along with her husband (no longer going for casual labour). She and her mother-in-law have also started husking paddy as an additional income source. Saraswati's husband is respected in the community as a successful entrepreneur. Saraswati also feels that her status in the family has improved as she is part of family decisions on enterprise or other family matters. With the next MFI loan cycle she has plans to expand the business further.

[Borderline, Grameen client in rural North/East, India]

The picture though is mixed. It seems most positive in clients of mature SHG groups in the South, and especially for group leaders. And in Grameen clients (South and North-East) who have been able to use credit to enhance their economic activity. For these women, access to micro-credit has helped them to a sense of financial responsibility, sometimes even autonomy; and discussions during group meetings have given them more awareness about financial matters and opportunities (though this could be increased further). But the path to enhanced status is not clear-cut or uniform. Other women clients (in the North, but in the South too) say that they do not perceive any change in their role in decision-making. Men continue to take all decisions; including those regarding financial matters and women may or may not be consulted on other household decisions.

Case studies also illustrate the barriers that women face when they have to make a living for themselves. Women are disadvantaged by lack of exposure to the world of business and enterprise, and assumptions about what women can do and where. In such situations, credit may be available but credit alone is not a solution.

Box 2.14: Micro-Credit... may only Lead to Micro-Earnings but What are the Options?

Two Grameen clients [in rural, North/East India]

Surata is 30 years old, and a widow since her husband Haider Ali died of cancer. The family had to mortgage their one-acre land with a moneylender to meet the costs of Haider Ali's treatment. And since her husband died, Surata has had to earn, finding work as a casual labourer. An MFI client for one year, she has taken her first loan of Rs. 1,000 ($ 25) which she on-lent to a shopkeeper. He pays her interest of Rs. 40 ($ 1) per week, leaving her Rs. 6 (10 cents) after paying the weekly MFI instalment of Rs. 34 (80 cents). Not much of a difference. She is thinking about the next MFI loan and wants to use it for a more substantial enterprise, but she is not sure what that might be...

[Very poor]

Dipti Das (50) is a widow, living with her daughter and her family. Her son-in-law works in a jewellery shop. Dipti used to work as a casual labourer but shifted to making puffed rice (*muri*) at home for sale. She has been an MFI client for 3 years and has used loans through 3 cycles (Rs. 2,000-5,000/$ 45-110) both for her rice processing and for household needs. Costs are low, but the returns are not high either, may be up to Rs. 250 ($ 6) a week, and often with sales on credit. Even with further credit, Dipti does not see how she can expand her business (many women in the area are selling *muri* now) nor what could be an alternative enterprise option for a woman.

[Poor]

At community level, the study found just a few examples of group based action in the community (one in the urban south—for cementing a road, one in the rural north—an unsuccessful attempt to stop liquor sales in the village). We found no instances of women clients getting actively involved in wider community forums (such as *panchayati raj*). New initiatives are however opening up new responsibilities for women at an institutional level—in SHG Federations (SHG model) and in Mutual Benefit Trusts (at a very preliminary stage in some Grameen MFIs).

VIII. ALTERNATIVE FINANCIAL SERVICES

Box 2.15: Hypothesis: Microfinance Improves the Terms, Conditions and Accessibility of Other Local Financial Services

MIXED FINDINGS:
— increase in access to bank services mainly through bank-SHG linkage programme.
— few instances of change in terms and conditions available from informal lenders, at present level of MFI activity.
— informal moneylenders, though costly, provide timely and flexible credit.

Alternative financial services are available through various formal and informal delivery channels. Variety and access is greater in the south (both rural and urban) where banks offer loans against gold deposits, and the informal sector includes small pawnshops, finance companies, ROSCAs and chit funds. In the north/east, the options are fewer.

As a credit provider, moneylenders have a strong presence, generally seen to be exploitative and high cost (with annual interest rates as high as 200 per cent, and lump sum repayments which are difficult to make) but nevertheless meeting diverse credit needs for large numbers of people. Personal informal sources (relatives, neighbours) are also a source of credit—usually at no or very low cost. Banks and post offices have a widespread infrastructure, but they continue to be relatively inaccessible. Banks do attract savings (from the better-off) and offer relatively large loans at notionally low cost (~12% annual interest), but credit-deposit ratios are low especially in rural areas. Microfinance is an additional 'semi-formal' financial service that lies in between the formal and informal in terms of cost and availability.

Few client households have access to formal financial services (as individual savings and credit accounts). Individual access is higher for the better-off, but does not increase with involvement in microfinance. Primarily as a result of NABARD's initiatives for SHG-bank linkage, bankers are positive about extending services to the poor through groups. They are comfortable about lending to groups promoted by MFIs, but there are emerging issues relating to: the level of guidance/escorting required for the groups, who should provide this, for how long, the costs involved, and competition with MFIs on interest rates.

Table 2.11: Use of Alternative Credit Options Client Households/Last 2 Years

	Formal Banks	*Microfinance MFIs/Govt. programmes*	*Money-lenders*	*Friends/ relatives*
Effective Interst Rate	8-29%	18-47%	60-200%	-0%
% households borrowing	8%	82%	36%	34%
Median borrowings (Rs.)	13,000	3,000-8,000	10,000	5,000
Share in total-borrowings	10%	42%	30%	18%
Share by use—Investment	11%	61%	20%	8%
—Housing	18%	25%	34%	23%
—Household needs	4%	28%	41%	27%

An important feature of microfinance as a financial service is the concern to reduce the need to borrow from costly informal moneylenders. A comparison with non-clients shows that fewer client households are borrowing small loans from moneylenders, and their average interest burden is lower (a difference especially significant for the poor, though we should bear in mind that high outstanding debt can be a reason for not being able to join a microfinance programme).

Nevertheless, over one-third of client households continue to borrow from moneylenders, especially for larger amounts (needed for example to meet marriage obligations) or for amounts needed urgently (for example for medical costs). Microfinance, so far, has not reduced either the business or the terms of moneylenders. There is some evidence for the reverse, that microfinance may in fact increase informal money lending, if clients need to 'top up' micro-loans, or borrow to repay according to the instalment schedule.

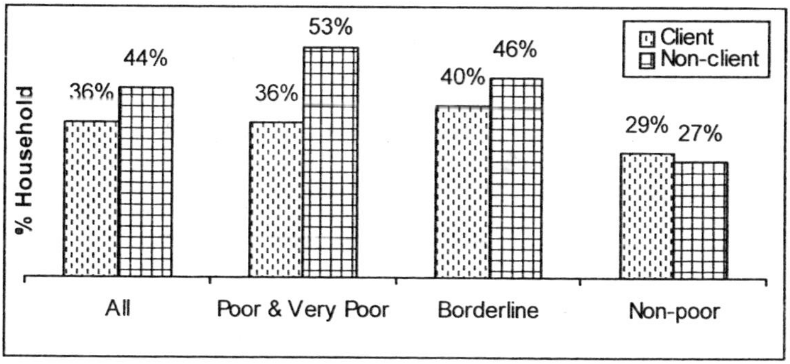

Fig. 2.8: Borrowing from Moneylenders

Box 2.16: A vulnerable Group Member Turns to a Moneylender

> **Chinnapillai,** is a widow living by herself in a small unelectrified hut on one side of the village. She has seen better days. When her husband was alive, they lived in a *pucca* house and traded rice from the local mill to the main city market. Now her son and his wife have taken over the house. Chinnapillai supports herself working in a rice mill, the evening shift—7 p.m. to 4 a.m. She earns Rs. 30 (70 cents)/ day, but the work is seasonal. So there are certain months (April and May) when there is no work. At this time she has to borrow to meet her daily needs. She borrows from a moneylender under a '10-week scheme', paying 25 per cent interest for the period, deducted up front.
>
> When SHGs were being formed 2 years before, the opportunity to save and get small loans seemed ideal. Chinnapillai joined, but, she says the group does not lend to her since they doubt her ability to pay: "*When I can borrow from a moneylender and repay why can't I repay a group loan? The moneylender is more flexible, he lends me money when I need it and would expect my son to repay if necessary.*" Maybe part of the problem is that she can't make it regularly to the evening meetings. She has been to 2 of the monthly meetings in the past year. In the other months, she gives her savings deposit (Rs. 50/$ 1.10/month) separately to the group leader. However, she does not know her savings, since the group leader keeps all the passbooks. She would like to be able to draw on her savings at times when the rice-mill closes—but savings are not withdrawable for 5 years. Ironically, Chinnapillai did become eligible for a larger MFI loan (Rs. 3,000/$ 70). But she didn't need such a large sum—so the loan was allocated to another member. In the meantime, she has borrowed Rs. 400 ($ 9) from the moneylender.
>
> [*Very poor, SHG client in Rural, South India*]

Informal sources continue to play an important role on account of their almost immediate accessibility and speed, and flexibility in purpose (how the credit can be used), amount and terms, even though costs may be high.

Comparing different providers on these parameters, microfinance scores over banks (on all parameters barring cost) and over moneylenders (on cost and repayment terms). MFIs score less well on credit purpose and timeliness, and sometimes on repayment terms. Overall, the Self Help Group mechanism emerges as a preferred option, if the group is managed well. For, as groups mature and the savings fund accumulates, members are able to obtain internal group loans of varying amounts, quite fast and for whatever they need at a relatively low cost (with the interest going back into the group fund).

IX. FEEDBACK ON MFI SERVICES

Feedback on microfinance services was obtained through FGDs and open-ended questions in the questionnaire—from clients and drop-outs.

Table 2.12: Feedback Summary

Positive aspects		*SHG*	*Grameen*	*IB*
Savings				
A convenient option to save		↑	↑	↑
Loans —	low interest	↑	—	↑
—	availability	↑	↑	↑
—	easy repayments	↑		↑
Group interactions (women)		↑	—	—
Less positive aspects				
Savings				
Not withdrawable		↓	↓	—
Not clear about interest payable		↓	↓	—
Loans				
Lack of flexibility in purpose		↓	↓	↓
Lack of flexibility in amount		↓	↓	—
Size does not suit credit need		↓	↓	—
High cost		—	↓	↓
Strict weekly repayment		—	↓	—
Insurance				
Compulsory—inadequate information		↓	↓	↓
Time spent in microfinance (est. hours/year)				
Clients		17	53	16
Group/centre leaders		102	95	NA

Source: Survey data and FGDs.

By model, SHG services score well, especially through the flexibility of internal group lending and clients appreciate the system of monthly repayments. In the Grameen model, clients say the strict schedule of weekly payments is sometimes difficult to meet in the context of varying cash flows; and in all but one MFI in the sample, find the flat interest rate high. In both group based models, clients are not clear about the interest payable on their savings and would like to be able to withdraw some of their savings.

In the IB model, clients appreciate the range of savings options available (in 3 MFIs in the sample) and loan availability and terms, (which can include daily doorstep transactions). The less positive feature in this model from the client perspective is the guarantor requirement and loan processing charges.

Across all models, insurance is an issue. MFIs introducing insurance products tend to impose compulsory premium payments as an additional payment or packaged as an upfront loan deduction. Clients are not fully aware of the terms and conditions, and do not necessarily perceive a future benefit to themselves from paying the premium. This is partly because they are not provided records of the premiums they have paid, also there are not many examples of successful insurance claims as yet.

Estimates of time spent in microfinance transactions indicate the highest amount of time for ordinary Grameen clients (54 hours/year due to weekly meetings), and highest of all cover 100 hours/year for group or centre leaders in both group-based models.

In terms of costs to clients, the SHG loan at 27.8 per cent has the lowest EIR. The Grameen loan, repaid in equal instalments at a 'flat' rate of interest, has a higher EIR of over 36 per cent, largely from the conversion into a declining interest rate, but also from relatively high service charges. The IB model loan has a relatively high EIR on average at 35.8 per cent due to the savings collateral requirement and the costs associated with having a guarantor (obtaining a letter from a government employee, paying for guarantor to accompany the client to the MFI office). Time as a transaction cost is not included here.

Overall, group-based models appear relatively standardised, although a few MFIs are beginning to introduce different products and the internal group lending of the SHG model provides flexible access to credit, especially as groups mature. IB MFIs appear the most responsive, if not innovative, service providers, with a range of products adapted to clients' different (investment) needs and cash flows. IB MFIs are more likely to assess the economic viability of the enterprises they support and adapt loan products accordingly.

Finding out why clients dropout, and who they are, is another form of feedback on a microfinance programme. The concept of 'dropping out' is applicable to all MFIs that aim to retain members and build their transactions. (Of course, there could also be 'fly-outs' as graduates to formal banking, though none such in this sample). The drop-out rate in the sample clusters (calculated as ratio of number of dropouts in the previous two years to the total number of clients (+dropouts) at the time of the survey) was a relatively low 6 per cent, with not much difference between models, but a somewhat higher rate amongst the very poor (8%). There was often a combination of reasons for dropping out, including (for the sample of 229 ex-clients): unable to save regularly (50%), default on loan repayments (30%), group disagreements (23%), and no time for meetings (15%).

X. IMPLICATIONS FOR PRACTICE

Outreach to Different types of Clients

MFIs need to review their strategies in relation to the following:

- They are effectively catering to a range of clients, with different livelihoods and financial needs and capacities. This translates into a variety of savings and credit needs; clients may or may not need credit for investment, and, if they use credit for enterprise, different scales of investment may be appropriate;
- Rural and urban contexts directly affect livelihood options and financial needs. MFIs operating across different contexts need to segment their markets and adapt their products accordingly;
- The very poor and the poor are more likely than the better-off to need small sums for consumption smoothening; flexible and withdrawable savings would be a useful facility for this, and small seasonal loans;
- The very poor and the poor are also interested in credit for investment. However, and especially when they are undertaking new enterprises for the first time, there is considerable risk involved. Specific elements of risk (for example, market saturation for certain enterprises, quality of a dairy animal purchased) need to be identified and combined with the finance strategy in order to ensure viability. In this context, insurance may be a fall-back but is not the solution;
- The group mechanism has proved to be an effective

strategy for accelerating outreach whilst targeting women. The viability of the groups was not a specific focus of this study, but there are emerging issues relating to ensuring effective management, accountability and impartial leadership, and the level of facilitation required to achieve this;

- The drive for growth is likely to involve some degree of a trade-off between catering to existing clients (consolidating the client base, diverse and larger loan sizes) or catering to more, new, clients (usually starting with smaller loans). In some MFIs there is a danger of playing the numbers game, that is achieving outreach, but at the expense of improvement in services to existing clients and potential impact;
- On the other hand, as part of an exit strategy, MFIs operating successfully with clients over a number of years should consider graduating established, better-off clients to formal sources of credit.

Providing a Responsive Financial Service

The basic challenge facing MFIs, whatever their mission or model, is to balance what is practical and sustainable for them as service providers with what is responsive to their clients' needs (including the needs of poorer clients). Suppliers of microfinance services need to maintain manageable and cost-effective systems (e.g. few products, same terms, equal repayment instalments, higher revenue, emphasis on credit discipline and repayments). But this contrasts with clients' preferences that include: flexibility, match with household cash flows, lower cost and hassle.

Table 2.13: Supplier (MFI) and Client Needs

Services	*What suits practitioners*	*What clients prefer*
Savings Amount	*One size fits all*—same amounts at same intervals—simplifies accounting	*Flexible* amount so that they can save according to varying cash flow patterns (taking into account irregular income sources and varying expenditure needs at different times of year)

(*Contd.*)

Services	*What suits practitioners*	*What clients prefer*
Withdraw ability	*Compulsory, unwithdraw able* savings provide low const and steadily accumulating funds for portfolio lending	Though clients appreciate the option to save, they would prefer savings to be *withdrawable*
Interest	Lower interest reduces portfolio costs	Higher interest
Credit Purpose	Enterprise/direct investment use assuming repayment from resulting income flows; some housing loans for established clients (with low cost funds from HDFC).	Credit not just for direct investment, but to meet a range of different needs, regular or emergency (food/consumption smoothening, school costs, medical expenses); repayments are possible from existing income sources.
Size	"One size fits all"—helps to streamline loan administration, simplify decision making and operations, minimize operational costs.	Variable loan sizes, based on need and repayment capacities—small for the poor and larger for those with higher repayment capacity.
Interest rates; associated processing and service charges	Interest rate (and associated charges) should be high enough to cover costs, including risks, cost of funds, operational costs and growth	Lower effective interest rates—(especially when serving in group/MFII not withdrawable).
Repayment terms	Standardised repayments—easy for clients and MFI field staff to understand, simplifies accounting and MIS	Variable repayment terms that match cash flows for available income sources (not only from the micro-credit supported enterprise)
System of guarantee	(a) group based models: group savings are the basic collateral (b) IB MFIs ask for a guarantor—either a government officer or an existing client with adequate savings in the MFI	IB clients who are not so well off or know the right people, would prefer a less costly alternative
Insurance	Make insurance compulsory since coverage of a clients' life, health and asset risks represents a security against loan default, especially if repayment of outstanding loan is the first call	Insurance which could be quickly provided when required would be ideal; benefits not perceived if there is no call and premiums have to be renewed without accumulating as a form of savings—or as a compulsory upfront dedication on loans
Programme related: Group meetings	Meetings planned at various times during the working day to suit times and security of the MFI field staff who, especiatly in the Grameen model, have to cover several clusters in a day	Schedule meetings at times which are convenient to clients and especially for those who are casual labourers, need not lead to loss of a days earnings

Some suggestions of how these could be balanced are listed below:

Table 2.14: Balancing Supplier (MFI) and Client Needs for a More Responsive Service

Services	*Some options*
Savings Amount	Flexibility in savings amount (around a minimum compulsory amount over a specific period of say 4 months)—allows clients to save more, depending on their cash flow
Withdraw ability	After 1 year, allow withdrawal of interest and a proportion of savings too
Credit Purpose	A more flexible mandate which encourages enterprise use but does not exclude other uses; repayment does not only come from a credit supported enterprise, therefore assessment of creditworthiness would take account of different household income sources
Size	Link loan amounts to understanding of specific requirements, as well as creditworthiness; scope will depend will depend on availability of funds to MFI for on-lending and strategy for expansion (larger loans for existing clients or small loans for new clients)
Interest rates; associated processing and service charges	Explore scope for bringing down EIR by reducing associated transaction costs SHG MFIs have reduced their direct costs through linking in to established NGO-based programmes (as banks do in the NABARD linkage model) Grameen MFIs (not linked to NGOs) push for high growth, high repayments and portfolio turnover (strong emphasis on discipline with pressure on field staff)
Repayment terms	Find out more about cash flows of different livelihoods, and see how loan repayment terms can be adapted; dairying is a common loan use, instalments can be adapted to the milking cycle
System of guarantee	(a) Group collateral needs clearer explanation to the groups (as the basis of peer lending) (b) IB models could try joint liability groups with individual savings
Insurance	Try forms of insurance that accumulate as savings (as in LIC); clearer communication is necessary, and may become easier once claims are seen to be honoured; but the challenge will be to enable speedy access whilst retaining prudential norms/checks
Programme related: Group meetings	Draw up the meeting schedule with reference to the time constraints faced by both sides, and obtain agreement of all group members (not just the leader).

Microfinance and Vulnerability

This study identifies key risks and financial pressures faced by vulnerable households. Microfinance is supporting the coping strategies of its clients, but it could do more. Currently, it is informal finance (that is moneylenders who can provide different amounts of credit, fast—and at high cost) who are meeting these financial needs, including for older clients, and especially for the poor who are less likely to have the sort of friends and relations who can help.

What can MFIs do to improve the protective role of microfinance and contribute more to the coping strategies of client households, especially the the poor and the very-poor? Some of the options are set out (next page), covering *ex ante* support and *ex post provisioning*. The list necessarily extends to aspects that go beyond the provision of financial services, though for some of these there is not an obvious solution.

Microfinance and Empowerment

In the context of socio-cultural limitations on women's roles and agency, targeting women for financial services is a good start on the road to women's empowerment in terms of redressing the usual inequitable gender balance. Women have certainly become more 'visible' as microfinance clients, but being a client does not translate 'automatically' into her 'empowerment'—her individual growth, her economic activity, her status in the household or the community.

A close look at various microfinance practices, suggests certain strategic features that could make MFI practice more empowering for its women clients. The first and basic requirement is clear and systematic communication on microfinance services and options. A key challenge for MFIs targeting women is that their clients are often illiterate. The majority of women clients (60% in the sample) have had very little or no schooling. Such clients in a few MFIs, have learnt to sign their names (though not necessarily to read them). Though MFIs do claim that they communicate regularly with clients on products and terms, women clients' awareness is not as strong as it should be. The communication flow is either irregular or limited to group leaders who do not pass on the

Table 2.15: Helping Households Cope with Vulnerability—Microfinance, and Beyond

	Risks	What can microfinance do?		And beyond microfinance—a 'wish list'
		Ex ante—promotional/protective		
Household-Specific Risks	Ill health in the family/accidents	Health insurance—for family (not just client)	Emergency loan for medical expenses	Health awareness Cost-effective medical services
	Major family events—marriage, death, birth	Savings (special product)	Special life cycle loans	A campaign to reduce social expectations
	Alcoholism and gambling among men and boys	Collective pressure by groups		
	Loss of husband/main income earner	Savings in women's name Withdraw able savings to meet small consumption needs	Investment and flexible small consumption loans Peer support and example—through group mechanism	More equitable employment options for women
	Recall of outstanding debts by moneylender		Loans to redeem debts	
Livelihood Risks	Loss of enterprise asset (shop burned down, animal dies)	Asset insurance	Additional loan to restart/ repair/replace business	
	Enterprise failure	In case of enterprise loan, link sanction to viability assessment (household skills, market environment) – and assistance, if possible Asset insurance		Alternative employment
	Loss of job (factory closes/labour retrenched)		Investment loan	Alternative employment
Co-variate Risks	Seasonal difficulties (summer/monsoon)	Withdraw able savings	Seasonal loans	
	Technology change—affecting an economic sector		Larger investment loans - if viable	Alternative employment
	Natural hazards (drought/floods), deteriorating natural resources	Insurance	Limits to MFI viability and therefore ability to respond	A major challenge beyond financial services

information. Leaving aside a transformative vision of empowerment for women, their understanding of the transactions they are being committed to is a basic requirement for any finance programme that aims to serve its clients.

Table 2.16: Strategies to Support Women's Empowerment

Strategies	*Components—within microfinance*	*And in addition—a 'wish list'*
Support to women as clients	• Gender sensitivity of staff (whether men or women) • Clear and systematic communication about the programme to all clients	Economic • Guidance on finance management • Support to undertake viable enterprises Social • Social programmes/guidance wider social/community participation • Exposure/opportunities in new forums
Support to women's groups	• Leadership development/capacity development • Groups guided to have more responsibility/autonomy	• Leadership rotation • Women interact with external financial institutions

Other dimensions include support to group development, as well as a 'wish list' of wider issues. These would need to be adapted to different cultural contexts—especially in north. Nevertheless, it is important to realize that there could be powerful synergies between the provision of financial services to women and other non-financial services.

The challenge before MFIs that are concerned about women's empowerment is how to build such 'extra' inputs into or around their delivery of financial services.

XI. IMPLICATIONS FOR POLICY

The provision of financial services by MFIs is beginning to fill the gap between the relatively low cost but inaccessible formal banking sector, and the more accessible, but high cost informal sector. Microfinance represents a range of financial services to large numbers of people without access to the formal banking system. This is happening across the country but predominantly in the Southern region where the NGO base is strong. The North and East are underserved. The *first challenge* is to support the outreach of microfinance to under-served and poorer areas.

Microfinance is essentially a financial service. Its micro scale (small savings deposits, small loans) means that its role may in some situations, for some clients, be promotive (increasing income, reducing poverty) in other situations, for other clients, its role is more protective (consumption smoothening, helping to meet emergency needs). Different clients, especially the poor, need different kinds of finance at different times. The **second challenge** therefore is to enhance the range of products provided under microfinance so as to cater to the different needs of its clients, including the poor.

Substantial numbers of the poor and large numbers of women are microfinance clients, especially in the SHG and Grameen model. This has given rise to strong expectations in terms of poverty reduction and women's empowerment. Given the complexity of both—the multiple dimensions of poverty and the socio-cultural constraints to women's empowerment—it is unrealistic to expect a financial service alone to make the difference, especially a 'micro' one.

At the policy level, this means recognising the serious and continuing need for other development interventions—in infrastructure, cost-effective health care, education, employment. Within microfinance, there are approaches and supporting mechanisms which can be built in as MFIs work on getting to know their clients and their financial needs better. Suggestions on improving practice relating to this are given below. Alongside the process of formalising microfinance institutions, policy makers can support such practices, recognising specifically

(i) The strong supportive role that microfinance can play in providing an accessible option for safe savings—for the poor and for women, and
(ii) If MFIs are to be able to respond to a range of different credit needs and to cover their costs, the rate of interest they charge will be higher than that charged by banks for larger loan amounts.

NOTES

1. This data (for December 2004) is from the database of Micro-Credit Ratings International Ltd, a specialist microfinance rating agency. Established in 1998, M-CRIL has carried out nearly 300 ratings of

MFIs in India and neighbouring countries of South, South-East and Central Asia. M-CRIL is an associate company of EDA.

2. SIDBI provides need-based financial assistance by way of loans to partner MFIs for meeting their on-lending requirements. In addition, partner MFIs are provided an annual customised package of capacity building grant to build their operational, financial and institutional capacities and to achieve self sustainability in due course. SIDBI also offers: short-term loans to its partners for meeting their temporary liquidity constraints; a Transformation Loan product for NGO-MFIs who are transforming their operations into a regulated and formal entity; and equity funding to eligible MFIs.
3. Operational Self Sufficiency = Ratio of total income (interest on portfolio, other income—fees, investments) to total costs for the year (cost of funds, operating expenses).
4. Portfolio at risk at 60 days (PAR) = Ratio of the principal balance outstanding on all loans with overdues greater than or equal to 60 days to the total loans outstanding on a given date.
5. Overall percentages here and in subsequent Tables are the weighted average based on client distribution by model (SHG = 0.62, Grameen = 0.34, Individual Banking = 0.04).

MFIs Participating in the Research

APDMACS	—	Andhra Pradesh Dalitbahujan Mutually Aided Cooperative Societies Federation, Andhra Pradesh
ASA	—	Activists for Social Alternatives, Tamil Nadu
BSFL	—	Bhartiya Samrudhi Finance Ltd. (BASIX), Andhra Pradesh
CFTS	—	Cashpor Financial and Technical Services, Uttar Pradesh
IASC	—	Indian Association for Savings and Credit, Kerala/ Tamil Nadu
LEAD	—	League for Education and Development, Tamil Nadu
LHWRF	—	Lupin Human Welfare and Research Foundation, Rajasthan
Outreach	—	Karnataka
Pustikar	—	Pustikar Laghu Vyaparik Pratishthan Bachat and Sakh Sahakari Samiti limited, Rajasthan
RASS	—	Rashtriya Seva Samithi, Andhra Pradesh
RGVN	—	Rashtriya Grameen Vikas Nidhi, Assam

Shramik Bharati	—	Uttar Pradesh
SIFFS	—	South Indian Federation of Fishermen Societies, Kerala
SKS	—	Swayam Krishi Sangam, Andhra Pradesh
SNF	—	Sarvodaya Nano Finance, Tamil Nadu
SWD	—	Swayamkrushi Women's Development, Andhra Pradesh
MACTS	—	Mutually Aided Cooperative Thrift Society, Andhra Pradesh
VSSU	—	Vivekananda Seva Kendra O Sishu Uddyan, West Bengal
VWS	—	Village Welfare Society, West Bengal
YVU	—	Youth Volunteers Union, Manipur

ABBREVIATIONS

BPL	—	Below Poverty Line
EIR	—	Effective Interest Rate
FGD	—	Focus Group Discussion
HDFC	—	Housing Development Finance Corporation
HH	—	Household
IB	—	Individual Banking
IGA	—	Income Generating Activity
LIC	—	Life Insurance Corporation of India
MFI	—	Micro Finance Institution
M-CRIL	—	Micro-Credit Ratings International Ltd.
NABARD	—	National Bank for Agriculture and Rural Development
NGO	—	Non Governmental Organisation
NMFSP	—	National Micro Finance Support Project
OSS	—	Operational Self Sufficiency
PAR	—	Portfolio At Risk
ROSCA	—	Rotating Savings and Credit Association
SFMC	—	SIDBI Foundation for Micro Credit
SHG	—	Self Help Group
SIDBI	—	Small Industries Development Bank of India

$ exchange rate applied: ~Rs. 44

3

Agriculture Finance in India: Microfinance Innovations

K.K. TRIPATHY and S.K. JAIN

I. INTRODUCTION

Despite a mere 18.5 per cent contribution[1] to the gross domestic product (GDP), agriculture still provides livelihood support to about two-thirds of the country's population. Quite appropriately, agricultural development has been given due importance right from India's First Five Year Plan (1951-56). No doubt, the country has taken notable strides in the agricultural sector during the last four decades of economic planning where the contours of Indian agriculture started showing improvement gradually after the mid-1960s with the introduction of High Yielding Varieties (HYV) of crops. The subsequent emphasis, on the development of agricultural infrastructure for supply of agro-inputs like irrigation, power, water, seed, credit and fertilisers, creation of storage and marketing facilities and provision of adequate and fair distribution of food-grains however could not give an appropriate boost to the growth of agricultural productivity.

The key problem of those dependent on agriculture, specially the poor, small and marginal farmers and weaker sections of the society, is finance. Therefore, in each Plan period, there has been a continued emphasis on rapid and progressive institutionalisation for supply of timely and adequate credit-support to enable those engaged in agriculture to adopt modern agricultural technology and improved agricultural practices for enhanced growth, production and productivity. The traditional concern about accessibility of agricultural credit to the needy rural inhabitants is still alive even after increasing bank branch network, improving Co-operative Banking structure, evolving specialised rural banking institutions (i.e., Regional Rural Banks) and the setting up of various financial agencies like the National Bank for Agriculture and Rural Development (NABARD) in 1982.

The impressive quantitative expansion of bank branches and other rural formal financial intermediaries has not really helped in developing an atmosphere of hassle-free qualitative credit flow in the rural economy. We have been focusing on co-operative movements, priority sector lending, operation, supervision and monitoring of rural credit by designated rural financial agencies for the smooth, adequate and timely flow of credit to the rural people. With the disappointing result of these formal agencies, we have now started depending on an innovative model of credit delivery mechanism, popularly known as micro-finance. This micro-finance (MF), after the Grameen Bank revolution in Bangladesh, is the buzz-word these days and is treated as a suitable alternative to formal banking in rural India keeping in view its cost-effectiveness, easy and hassle-free accessibility and in-built process for loan allocation and its recovery. Micro-finance which includes, *inter alia*, micro credit and micro savings, is increasingly advocated by country planners to ensure timely and adequate credit to small and marginal farmers and to alleviate poverty. It is treated as an effective employment generator in rural areas having capability to sustain the income of the households by ensuring their opportunities to work. A preliminary analysis of the number of loans distributed through a high budgeted government-operated micro-finance programme, Swarnjayanti Gram Swarozgar Yojana (SGSY)[2], by purpose, across the States in India indicates that 65 per cent of the total number of loans has been advanced to take up primary activities. The number of loans taken for service and secondary sectors is 15.3 and 19.7 per cent respectively (Annexure I). This revelation has provoked us to examine the implementation of this micro-finance programme and gauge its impact on the field level farmer clients.

In this backdrop, this paper tries to review the trend, status and issues of agricultural credit in India and explores whether the present day formalisation of informal micro-finance can increase universal access and bring in efficiency and cost effectiveness to loan financing in rural areas. The objectives of the paper are to:

- review agricultural credit policies followed in India and assess the trends and progress in credit flow and access;
- examine the suitability of government-directed micro-finance activities as an alternate tool to the formal credit delivery mechanism in enhancing access to credit in rural areas; and
- analyse the issues relating to sustainability of the micro-finance programme in rural areas of India.

The paper looks into the above-mentioned objectives by examining the trend of progress in the flow of agricultural credit from the formal financial institutions. Secondary data on trends in agro-rural credit outreach have been collected from Reserve Bank of India (RBI), Ministry of Agriculture, Directorate of Economics and Statistics, Ministry of Finance and Planning Commission of Government of India (GoI). Field level observations of the implementation of the government-directed micro-finance programme in one of the backward most Indian States, Orissa have been analysed. Since the programme aims at removing poverty by increasing access to bank credit and other financial services, it is expected that the same may have facilitated the already enlisted poor families shift to relatively profitable occupations for income enhancement and poverty alleviation.

Section II of the paper deals with rural credit growth since bank nationalisation in the country. Credit flow and credit deployment in the priority sector of Agriculture have been analysed and the issues and problems in the access to rural finance irrespective of growth in bank branches and credit extension have also been explained in this section. **Section III** looks into the aspect of the emergence of micro-finance as an alternative rural credit delivery mechanism and reviews various models of innovative micro-financing approaches followed in India. While in **Section IV** aspects relating to outreach and ground level implementation of SGSY has been assessed by analysing secondary data on physical and financial progress under the programme in the country, the survey results of the programme in two districts of Orissa are discussed in **Section**

V. **Section VI** concludes with suggestions and policy implications for micro-finance model of credit delivery in rural areas.

II. TRENDS IN THE SUPPLY OF RURAL CREDIT

Immediately after the country's independence, the central bank and Government authorities focused on the prevention of bank failures and restoration of public confidence in the formal banking system. While the amended Banking Regulation Act of 1949[3] tried to consolidate the Indian banking network in the pre-bank nationalisation era, the attempt of bank-nationalisation in India in 1964 gave a new direction to the structure, operations, policies and practices of commercial banks in the country through features like social control and directed bank credit to priority sectors. Implementation of the service area approach and the lead bank scheme[4] during 1969 envisaged to bring in a consortium of bank leaders for ensuring a co-ordination between the co-operative banks, the commercial banks and the other financial institutions in their geographic jurisdictions for the development of credit-starved regions to its fullest. Although the post-nationalisation period in the Indian banking yielded significant changes in the operational policies and practices of the formal financial agencies in the rural areas, yet it failed to make a significant dent in the age-old attitude of the rural bankers towards financing the so-called less creditworthy but productive poor farmers. The increased outreach and access to agricultural credit in the post bank-nationalisation period coupled with augmented demand due to the Green Revolution of 1960s and enhanced focus on directed priority sector lending[5] could not correct the weaknesses in the rural financial delivery system over the years which adversely affected the viability and sustainability of these institutions (Mohan, 2006). Further, the security-orientation of loans and the economic and social status of the rural borrowers were the major constraints in requisite credit mobilisation irrespective of branch expansion in rural areas.

Progress of Rural Banking in India

As on 31-3-2005, there were 606 districts covering 7,27,911 villages which had 10.60 crore land holdings; the average size of the holding being only 0.88 hectare. The GoI's policy initiatives for strengthening the rural credit delivery mechanism has, therefore, laid emphasis on enhancing flow of credit at the grassroot level through an appropriate credit planning, adoption of region-specific strategies, rationalisation of lending policies and procedures and reduction of cost of rural borrowings. Keeping in view the constraints in the accessibility of rural finance by the farmers of the country, the credit policy emphasised on the disbursement of rural credit through a multi-agency network consisting of Commercial Banks (CBs), Regional Rural Banks (RRBs) and Co-operatives. The organisation of rural credit is explained in Figure 3.1:

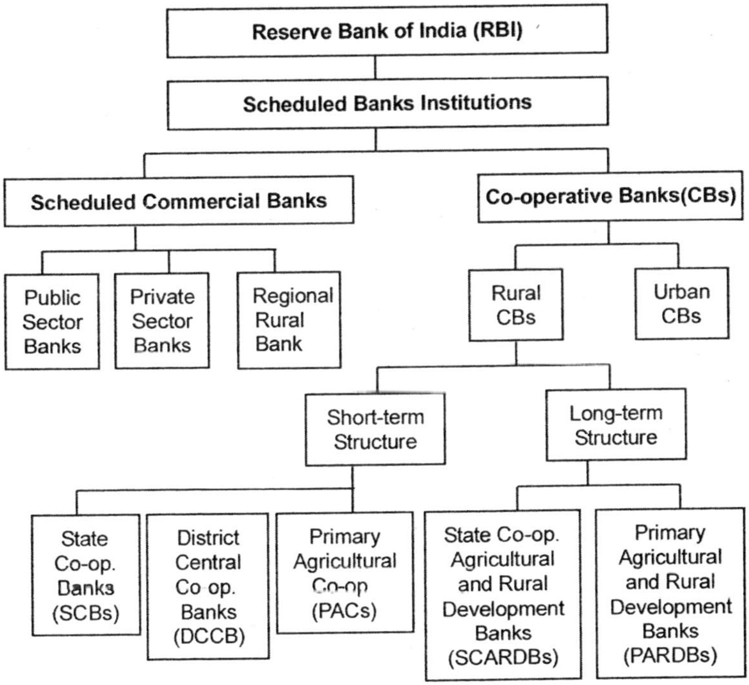

Fig. 3.1: Organisation of Rural Credit

By the end March 2006, there were approximately 1,08,779 village level Primary Agricultural Credit Societies (PACs), 367 District Central Co-operative Banks (DCCBs) with 12,858 branches and 31 State Co-op. Banks (SCBs) with 953 branches providing primarily short term agricultural credit in the country. The long term co-operative structure consists of 20 State Co-operative Agricultural and Rural Development Banks (SCARDBs) with 2609 operational units, comprising 788 branches and 727 Primary Agricultural and Rural Development Banks (PCARDBs) with 1049 branches (RBI, 2006). By the end-June 2006 there were 30,754 rural Commercial Bank branches out of which 21,713 were Public Sector Bank Branches.

The inadequacy of credit flow to rural areas during mid-1960s continued to draw attention of the RBI and compelled the Government to constitute a Rural Credit Committee[6] to have a comprehensive review of flow of agricultural credit. The Committee and the subsequent Committees on Rural Credit felt the need of a vibrant rural banking system with active and complementary role of Commercial Banks along with Co-operatives in extending rural credit. The opening up of rural bank branches was not only due to the supply-side push through government's social control over rural banking but also due to the increase in demand because of population increase and diversification of agro-products in the post-green revolution era. This is evident from Table 3.1 where one can see that the initial growth in spread of rural branch-banking in India during 1980s faded with time and followed a downward trend after 1991.

Table 3.1 shows the distribution of rural population and rural bank offices in India from 1971. There were 4,817 rural bank branches during 1971 catering to almost 33 crore rural people. The corresponding figures for 2006 were 30,750 and 79 crores respectively. While the percentage of rural bank offices to total bank offices was the highest (58.5 per cent) at the end of 1991, it gradually reduced to 44.5 per cent during 2006. The downward trend of post-1992 era (Banking reform era) in the opening up of bank offices in rural areas may be due to the excessive pressure on the banking system to follow prudential norms on income recognition, asset classification and their provisioning. Profit considerations in the liberalised and globalised scenario have taken priority over expansion of the bank spread in rural areas.

Table 3.1: Year-wise Distribution of Population and Bank Offices in India

Year	Population (in '000)		% of Rural Population to Total Population	Bank Offices		% of Rural Banks to Total Banks
	Rural	Total		Rural	Total	
1	2	3	4	5	6	7
1971	329932	439046	75.1	4817	13622	35.4
1981	364404	523867	69.6	17656	35707	49.4
1991	411281	628836	65.4	35206	60220	58.5
2001	742490	1028610	72.2	32562	65919	49.4
2002	752506	1045547	72.0	32380	66190	48.9
2003	762345	1062388	71.8	32303	66535	48.6
2004	772006	1079117	71.5	32121	67188	47.8
2005	781488	1095722	71.3	32082	68355	46.9
2006	790786	1112186	71.1	30750	69118	44.5

Source: Handbook of Statistics on the Indian Economy (RBI), 2005-06, Census Statistics, 1971, 1981, 1991, 2001 and Population Projection Report of National Population Commission (GoI), May 2006 .

The increase in bank credit in the last few years has been a heartening phenomenon in India's banking sector which reflects the economic reform policies followed since 1990s. The financial sector reform measures have yielded desired results and strengthened financial positions of the banks. The overall higher order credit growth in the banking system has not supported the desired expansion of agricultural credit and credit to small-scale industries sector (Roy, 2006). As we can see from Table 3.2, while the Bank Credit disbursed during 1970-71 as a percentage to the Agriculture GDP was 0.57, the same increased to 12.13 during 2000-01 and to an all-time high of 49.5 percentage points during 2005-06. However, while 2.04 times increment in the credit disbursement in Indian Agriculture could lead to an increase in 1.11 times of the agri-GDP during 1970-71 and 1975-76, the growth in credit disbursement and Agri-GDP between the years 2000-01 and 2005-06 shows that the same were 4.73 times and only 1.16 times respectively. This clearly indicates that though the credit disbursement in rural areas has increased manifold the same has not affected any increment in the agricultural GDP. This may be due to a continuous decline in the total factor productivity in Indian Agriculture (Rao & Gulati, 2005) caused by the absence of a suitable technological breakthrough in Indian agriculture in the post-green revolution era.

Table 3.2: Agricultural Credit, Agriculture GDP, Total GDP and Total Commercial Banks' Credit

Year	Agricultural Credit Disbursed (Rs. Cr.)	Agri-GDP (Rs. Cr.)	Credit Disbursed as a % of Agri-GDP	Total GDP (Rs. Cr.)	Agri-Credit as a % of Total GDP	Total Bank Credit Disbursed by CBs (Rs. Cr.)	Agri-credit as a % of Total CBs' Credit
1	2	3	4	5	6	7	8
1970-71	818	142581	0.57	296278	0.28	4684	17.5
1975-76	1675	159337	1.05	343924	0.49	10877	15.4
1980-81	3436	167770	2.05	401128	0.86	25371	13.5
1985-86	7159	198353	3.61	513990	1.39	56067	12.8
1990-91	10188	242012	4.21	692871	1.47	116301	8.8
1995-96	23692	275153	8.61	899563	2.63	254015	9.3
2000-01	38127	314252	12.13	1203079	3.17	511434	7.5
2005-06	180486	364576	49.51	1680343	10.74	1507077	12.0

Source: Handbook of Statistics on the Indian Economy (RBI), 2005-06, Economic Survey (GoI), 2006-07, Annual Report (Ministry of Agriculture)

Rural Credit in Post-Reform Era

In the post-financial reform period, rural credit got less than the desired level of attention from the CBs and RRBs. To augment credit flow to the agriculture and allied sectors the RBI had introduced the target of 18 per cent of the net bank credit for lending to agriculture in 1989 which the banks were required to meet by March 1990. Unfortunately only 19 per cent of total public sector commercial banks and 7 per cent of total private sector commercial banks could achieve it by 2003 (Patil, 2005). There are also other alarming trends like the rural borrowers' accounts and the credit deposit ratio in rural areas in addition to the decline in the number of rural offices in post-1992 period (RBI, 2006).

Region-wise ground level credit disbursements under Agriculture and Allied activities highlights that there is tremendous variation in the credit flow amongst the regions (Annexure II). Figure 3.2 indicates that while the agro-credit flow to the Northern, Southern and Western regions are quite acceptable, the same for North Eastern and Eastern was far below satisfaction.

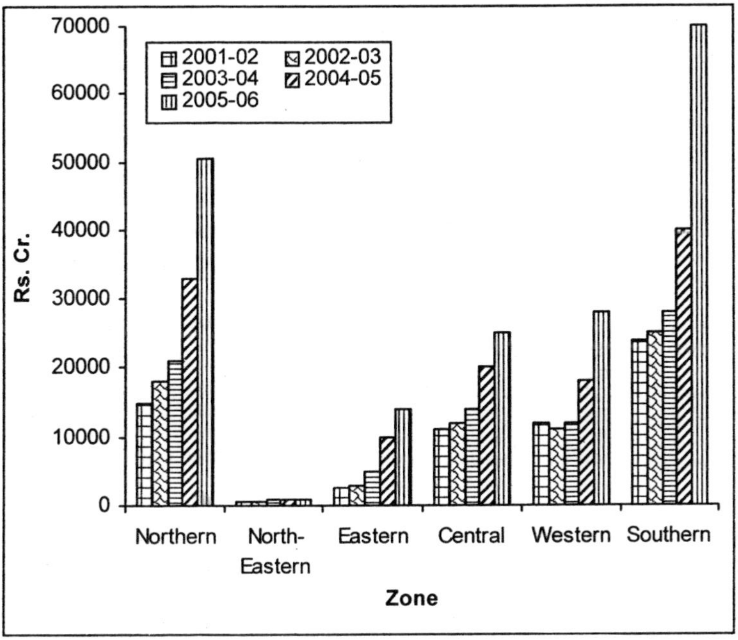

Fig. 3.2: Ground Level Credit Disbursement to Agriculture and Allied Activities (2001 to 2005)

Rural Co-operative Credit Societies

Initiated way back in 1904 through the enactment of Agricultural Credit Co-operative Societies Act, Co-operative Institutions expanded rapidly in the post-independence era and became an important vehicle for implementation of various government programmes. The structure of the three-tier rural credit co-operative institutions has not been uniform across the States. The multi-level regulatory structure, heterogeneous nature of operations and problems of incentives faced by the co-operative sector have been the main constraint in the development of this banking network (RBI, 2005).

Primary Agricultural Co-operative Societies[7] (PACS), the grassroot level arms of the three-tier cooperative credit delivery system in India, have been engaged in delivering credit to the poor and weaker sections of the society. As on March 31, 2005, as many as 7.27 lakh villages in India are covered with co-operative credit societies (Table 3.3). However, the physical and financial performance of the PACS across various zones has not been symmetrical. While there are 30,332 PACS operating in the western region of the nation, there are as low as 3,628 PACs operating in North-Eastern zone. The village to PACS ratio was 2 for western zone and 13 for Central Zones. Similarly, the per cent of profit making PACS to total PACS was highest in Northern Zone and lowest in North-Eastern zone. The percentage of loss making PACS to total PACS was 86 for North-Eastern region and 42 for Northern zone.

Table 3.3: Select Indicators of Primary Agricultural Co-operative Societies (As at March 31, 2005)

Region	*No. of PACS**	*No. of Villages*	*No. of Profit Making PACS*	*No. of Loss Making PACS*	*Village-PACS Ratio*	*% Profit Making PACS to Total*	*% Loss Making PACS to Total*
1	*2*	*3*	*4*	*5*	*6*	*7*	*8*
Northern	14997	91238	8334	6230	6	56	42
North-Eastern	3628	32045	490	3138	9	14	86
Eastern	29182	270859	14634	14548	9	50	50
Central	15329	195555	7425	7904	13	48	52
Western	30332	57907	12138	18194	2	40	60
Southern	15303	80308	3994	11309	5	26	74
All India	108779	727911	47015	61323	7	43	56

Note: * Includes no-profit—no-loss PACS as well.

Source: Report on Trend and Progress of Banking in India (RBI), 2005.

The aggregate institutional credit (Short Term and Long Term) issued for agriculture and allied activities in India by co-operatives constituted as high as 70.9 per cent during 1975-76 (Table 3.4). This marked a sharp decline trend and was as paltry as 21.8 per cent of total credit disbursed during 2005-06. While the loans issued by State Governments and Regional Rural Banks (RRBs) were 4.9 and 0.1 per cent during 1975-76, the same was 0.2 and 8.4 respectively during 2005-06. The loans issued by Commercial Banks to total disbursement in 1975-76 and 2005-06 were 24.2 and 69.5 respectively.

Table 3.4: Institutional Credit for Agriculture and Allied Activities (ST & LT)

Year	*Loans Issued (as a percentage of Total)*					*Loans Outstanding (as a percentage of Total)*			
	Co-ops.	*State Govts*	*RRBs*	*SCBs*	*Total*	*Co-ops.*	*SCBs*	*RRBs*	*Total*
1	*2*	*3*	*4*	*5*	*6*	*7*	*8*	*9*	*10*
1975-76	70.9	4.9	0.1	24.2	100	74.9	25.1	NA	100
1980-81	59	4.2	NA	36.8	100	57.2	40.4	2.4	100
1985-86	51.3	4.9	5.6	38.1	100	42.8	51.8	5.4	100
1990-91	47.3	3.5	3.3	45.9	100	35.9	58.1	6	100
1995-96	52.7	2.3	5.8	39.1	100	41.6	50.9	7.5	100
2000-01	45.2	1.3	10.4	43.1	100	34.7	54.9	10.4	100
2005-06	21.8	0.2	8.4	69.5	100	NA	NA	NA	NA

NA: Not Available.

Source: Handbook of Statistics on the Indian Economy (RBI), 2005-06, NABARD, 2006 and Economic Survey (GoI), 2006-07.

Table 3.5: Agricultural Loan Outstanding (ST & LT)

Year	*Loans Outstanding (as a percentage of Total)*			
	Co-ops.	*SCBs*	*RRBs*	*Total*
1	*2*	*3*	*4*	*5*
1975-76	74.9	25.1	NA	100
1980 81	57.2	40.4	2.4	100
1985-86	42.8	51.8	5.4	100
1990-91	35.9	58.1	6.0	100
1995-96	41.6	50.9	7.5	100
2000-01	34.7	54.9	10.4	100

NA: Not Available

Source: Handbook of Statistics on the Indian Economy (RBI), 2005-06, NABARD, 2006 and Economic Survey (GoI), 2006-07.

The loans outstanding as a percentage of total disbursement for co-operative banks were 74.9 and 34.7 respectively during 1975-76 and 2000-01 (Table 3.5). The same for CBs were 25.1 and 54.9 respectively during the corresponding period.

The ever-increasing overdues, failure of formal financial institutions in recovering the credit from the farmers has led to the emergence of severe indebtedness amongst the rural farmers. Table 3.6 highlights that the institutional credit which was increasing in the pre-financial reform period declined after 1991. The Non-institutional borrowings have increased to 42.4 per cent in 2003 from 30.6 per cent in 1991. This trend coupled with the rising indebtedness amongst farmers in the country raises questions about the sustainability of the formal financial agencies and their method of operation in the rural areas. There is a positive co-relationship between the credit accessibility and indebtedness (Annexure III).

Table 3.6: Relative Share of Borrowing of Cultivator Households from Different Sources (in Per Cent)

Sources of Credit	*1951*	*1961*	*1971*	*1981*	*1991*	*2003*
1	*2*	*3*	*4*	*5*	*6*	*7*
Non-Institutional, *of which*	92.7	81.3	68.3	36.8	30.6	42.4
Money Lenders	69.7	49.2	36.1	16.1	17.5	25.7
Institutional, *of which*	7.3	18.7	31.7	63.2	66.3	57.6
Co-op. Societies/Banks	3.3	2.6	22	29.8	35.2	19.6
Commercial Bank	0.9	0.6	2.4	28.8	35.2	35.6
Unspecified	0	0	0	0	3.1	0
Total	100	100	100	100	100	100

Source: RBI (2000 Series of Bulletins) & NSSO (2006).

As rural credit deals with millions of small borrowers, it requires not only a constant attention of the policy-makers and grassroot implementers but also the active base-level participation of the client farmers for appropriate utilisation of their loaned amount. Considering the importance of flow of credit to rural areas in the alleviation of multi-dimensional poverty in the respective regions, the RBI in 1996 included financing to small informal groups of poor called Self-Help Groups (SHGs) as a mainstream activity of banks under their priority sector lending through various models of micro-finance. Subsequently the GoI bestowed national priority to the micro-finance initiatives through its recognition in the Union Budget 1999. In addition to the introduction of innovative credit schemes like Kissan Credit Card (KCC) and Crop Insurance Schemes, the government felt the emerging need of developing micro-finance sector in the country. While the RBI was in charge of formulating regulatory guidelines for the Micro-Finance

Institutions, the Government allocated budgetary support through setting up of Micro-credit Development Fund.

Further, as part of poverty alleviation measures, the GoI launched government-operated micro-finance driven self-employment Scheme called Swarnjayanti Gram Swarozgar Yojana (SGSY) with effect from 1.4.1999 where the major emphasis has been on SHG formation, social mobilisation and economic activation through micro-credit finance. Simultaneously, the Government supported NABARD to take up such activities like group formation, micro-finance and economic activation. The government felt the need of the implementation of such a programme in India as various studies have indicated that this model of finance has the capability to ensure accessibility of credit plus services. Though the micro-finance programmes may not constitute the sole panacea for economic growth, yet they may ensure definite causal links between increased credit access, growth and poverty reduction (Mor, 2005) and are expected to provide access to credit to over 500 million people in India who are deprived of access to financial services.

Gradual emphasis on small doses of credit support based on absorption approach in general and after the Bangladesh Grameen Bank's revolutionary micro-financial activities in particular, the common perception about the poor's ability to pay back the loan underwent a change. What the poor need now is not only the access to credit but also the access to various credit related services. This is why, micro-credit emphasises on bringing-in the necessary credit related knowledge to the needy and poor farmers who will save first to take the advantage of credit. Yunus (2004) found that micro-credit programmes provide a wide range of services to meet economic and extra economic needs of the citizens. The micro-credit effort in Bangladesh through Grameen Bank shows that this is effective in helping the poor people to use their own efforts and creativity to meet their basic needs in a sustainable manner.

III. MICRO-FINANCE—AN ALTERNATIVE RURAL CREDIT DELIVERY MECHANISM

Concentration of monopolistic power, higher interest rates on loans, insistence on collaterals and exploitation through undervaluation of collaterals have been the trademarks of the informal financial sector. The inherent limitations of the formal and informal financial sectors in providing financial services to the needy and poor have led to the emergence and extension of micro-credit programmes in the developing world. The micro-credit programme was initiated with the objective of providing poor people with credit removed collaterals. Thus, micro credit has been defined as the extension of small loans to be given in multiple doses based on the absorption capacity of the needy beneficiaries, who are too poor to qualify for formal bank loans, as they have no assets to offer as collateral security against loans.

SHG and Micro-Credit

Micro-credit has worked largely through SHGs in general and women groups in particular. Since the SHG is a small group of 10 to 20 persons drawn from relatively homogenous backgrounds, the members, who join the group, know what benefit they would attain from the group through micro-credit. Micro-credit has to be utilised in such a way that it benefits the SHGs to improve the quality of life of their members and their productivity to earn a sustainable income. The SHGs need to firm up their financial and economic norms meant for selection of appropriate beneficiaries and subsequent disbursement of credit to the needy.

The borrowing member chooses economic activities for income-generation purposes and knows clearly the goals or objectives he has to attain for his own sustenance and stability of the group which he/she belongs to. Here, the members through participative decision-making process prioritise their goals in terms of their urgency. All the members are aware of their individual needs so as to converge their needs with the group objective. They can utilise team effort in addressing their problems and issues while approaching their target. Unity, group effort and team-work help them in achieving their goals.

Models of Micro-Finance

There are several models of micro-finance prevalent in India. Out of these, the most important ones are—Model I where SHGs are financed directly without the intervention/facilitation of any Non-Government Organisation (NGO); Model II, wherein SHGs are financed directly with the facilitation extended by formal or informal agencies Self-Help Promoting Institutions[8] (SHPIs), viz., Government, Commercial Banks and Micro Finance Institutions (MFIs) like NGOs, Non-Bank Financial Intermediaries (NBFIs) and Co-operative Societies; in Model III financing takes place through NGOs and MFIs as facilitators and financing agencies and Model IV is the Grameen Bank Model, similar to the model followed in Bangladesh.

In India, Model II of micro finance constitutes as much as three-fourths of the total micro-financing where SHGs are formed and nurtured by facilitating agencies like the Government and NGOs and are linked directly with banks for the purpose of receiving credit. The SGSY model of delivering micro-finance is based on this linkage approach which is quite unique to India. The linkage is vital for securing the SHGs timely micro-finance.

The following chart indicates that micro-credit adds to the group corpus[9] and is sourced from Government, NGOs, Banks etc. While funds from the Government enrich the group corpus by way of subsidy, the NGOs and Banks supply credit as per the needs of the group. The group is then involved in inter-loaning activities for consumption and production purposes. By pursuing productive economic activities, the group enhances its income, repays the loan amount to the bank and spends on basic health, education etc. so as to drive itself out of the poverty trap. (Figure 3.3)

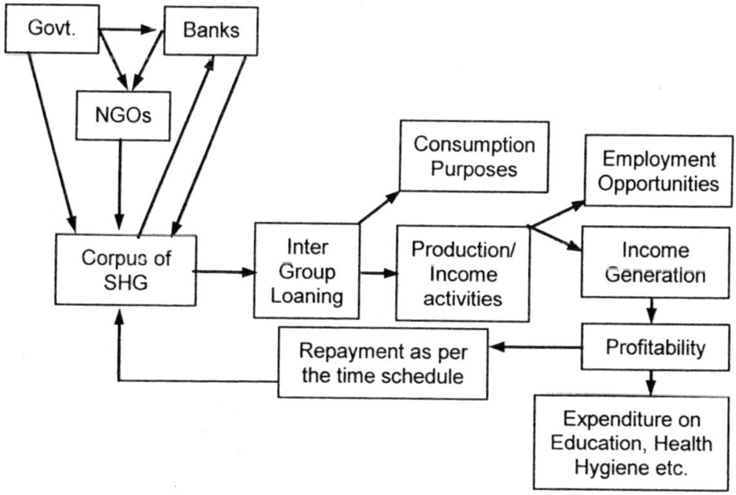

Fig. 3.3: Role of Group Corpus

Studies conducted on the income impact of micro-credit on the clients drawn from poverty line have indicated that most households are better off with micro-credit, but income impacts vary in magnitude and durability, and a sizeable proportion of clients find that their post-credit incomes stagnate or fall (Copestake, Bhalotra & Johnson, 2001). However, studies conducted on the programmes implemented in Bangladesh for the poorest of the poor indicated that micro-credit programmes are not suitable for all categories of the poor. For those trapped in chronic food insecurity with no asset base to protect themselves from the myriad web of shocks, micro-credit can be ineffective and sometimes counterproductive (Matin & Hulme, 2003).

Micro-credit institutions are indeed effective weapons in the war against rural poverty (Mwenda & Muuka, 2004). However, micro-credit schemes alone cannot alleviate the broader, non physical symptoms of poverty which deprive the poor of a full social existence through effective participation in various patterns of the everyday life of a society. The battle for total eradication of poverty from the lives of more than one billion poor, worldwide, requires combining micro-credit schemes with parallel, complementary programmes at the local, national, regional and multi national levels. SHGs formed to enforce rights or improve their economic/social/political position through micro-financing have a chance to improve the position of their members, by creating and enhancing cohesive identities and enhancing a sense of self-worth as well as by improving the participations' economic position (Throp *et al.*, 2005).

IV. SGSY MODEL OF MICROFINANCE

A Committee of the Planning Commission[10] on poverty alleviation and employment generation programmes of the GoI recommended to restructure the earlier self-employment programmes and redesign the credit delivery system in the rural areas. This led to the introduction of a microfinance driven self-employment programme called Swarnjayanti Gram Swarozgar Yojana (SGSY) on April 1, 1999 in all the rural areas of the country. The programme design of SGSY emphasises the linkage between banks and SHG and envisages enhancement of self-employment avenues for rural poor. While provision of credit at multiple doses is an important focus of the programme, subsidy is treated as an enabling element. The microfinance component of the programme is referred to as a small-scale financial intermediation, inclusive of savings, credit, insurance, business services and technical support.

The SGSY envisages increasing outreach of microfinance through small and informal SHGs formed with the support of 5 to 20 persons from relatively homogenous economic backgrounds. Microfinance is extended under the programme to only those SHGs which have passed a subjective grading test and are involved in regular thrift and credit activities for not less than six months. To assess whether SHGs can be considered for financial assistance, grading tests are done in phases considering the maturity of the groups, member composition, regularity and participation in meetings, regularity and quantum of savings, utilisation of loans, etc. These activities are mandatory for inculcating banking habits in unaccustomed members of the SHGs. To improve the productivity of the SHGs, the programme tries to firm up the financial and economic norms meant for selection of appropriate beneficiaries and subsequent disbursement of credit to them. The borrowing member under SGSY chooses economic activities for income-generation purposes which are already notified by the State Governments concerned to be considered for finance by the formal banking institution. Here, the members are expected to prioritise their goals in terms of their urgency through participative decision-making process. Individual needs of all the members of an SHG are expected to converge with the objectives of their group.

The corpus of a group consists of its cash balances, all outstanding loans, interest on loans, its savings with the bank and interest on balance in the savings bank account. While funds from the Government enrich the group corpus by way of subsidy, the NGOs and Banks supply credit as per the needs of the group. The group is then involved in inter-loaning activities for consumption and production purposes. By pursuing productive economic activities, the group enhances its income, repays the loan amount to the bank and spends on basic health, education etc. so as to drive itself out of the poverty trap.

SGSY in India: Performance and Outreach

An analysis of the trend of SHG formation under SGSY between 2000-01 and 2006-07 in the country indicates that the number of

Table 3.7: State-wise SHGs Formed and Assisted under SGSY (2001-02 and 2006-07)

States	SHG Formed		SHG Assisted		% SHG Assisted to Formed	
	2001-02	2006-07	2001-02	2006-07	2001-02	2006-07
1	2	3	4	5	6	7
Andhra Pradesh	219943 (42.7)	19921 (8.73)	4123 (15.7)	62917 (48.99)	1.87	315.83
Assam	12307 (2.4)	15511 (6.79)	663 (2.5)	5837 (4.55)	5.39	37.63
Bihar	17390 (3.4)	17977 (7.87)	3757 (14.3)	6540 (5.09)	21.60	36.38
Gujarat	9565 (1.9)	4051 (1.77)	655 (2.5)	946 (0.74)	6.85	23.35
Haryana	2105 (0.4)	2120 (0.93)	171 (0.6)	1262 (0.98)	8.12	59.53
Himachal Pradesh	2033 (0.4)	497 (0.22)	646 (2.5)	511 (0.40)	31.78	102.82
Jammu & Kashmir	943 (0.2)	518 (0.23)	330 (1.3)	349 (0.27)	34.99	67.37
Karnataka	13403 (2.6)	7271 (3.18)	1441 (5.5)	3498 (2.72)	10.75	48.11
Kerala	19633 (3.8)	6549 (2.87)	756 (2.9)	1395 (1.09)	3.85	21.30
Maharashtra	36029 (7.0)	19546 (8.56)	1477 (5.6)	6401 (4.98)	4.10	32.75
Orissa	29040 (5.6)	16032 (7.02)	1169 (4.4)	5647 (4.40)	4.03	35.22
Punjab	1223 (0.2)	509 (0.22)	176 (0.7)	617 (0.48)	14.39	121.22
Rajasthan	3326 (0.6)	5076 (2.22)	32 (0.1)	1769 (1.38)	0.96	34.85
Tamil Nadu	43985 (8.5)	37475 (16.42)	4712 (17.9)	3528 (2.75)	10.71	9.41
Uttar Pradesh	37466 (7.3)	16884 (7.40)	227 (0.9)	18132 (14.12)	0.61	107.39
West Bengal	7794 (1.5)	36590 (16.03)	1235 (4.7)	2513 (1.96)	15.85	6.87
Pondicherry	285 (0.1)	163 (0.07)	1 (0.004)	117 (0.09)	0.35	71.78
TOTAL	515691	228290	26317	128417	5.10	56.25

Note: The summation of SHGs formed/assisted in the selected few States would be less than the All India total.

Figures in parentheses indicate percentage to total.

Source: Ministry of Rural Development (2006).

SHGs formed in 2006-07 (228,290) was only about 44 per cent that of the number of SHGs formed during 2001-02 (5,15,691) (Table 3.7). However, the number of SHGs assisted increased more than four-fold from 26,317 in 2001-02 to 1,28,417 during 2006-07. Accordingly, from being merely 5.1 per cent in 2001-02, the number of SHGs assisted as a percentage of number of SHGs formed increased to about 56.25 per cent during 2006-07.

The distribution of SHGs formed and assisted under the programme across the various States of the country, however, is quite uneven. The number of SHGs formed during the two financial years, 2001-02 and 2006-07, declined in 13 out of 18 States which are under review. The States of Andhra Pradesh, Uttar Pradesh, Maharashtra, Kerala, Orissa and Madhya Pradesh recorded substantial decline in the number of SHGs formed between 2001-02 and 2006-07. The decline is quite conceivably due to the setting up of alternate micro-finance bodies run by steadily evolving NGOs and NBFIs which stress on financing credit to the poor without any subsidy component attached to it. Indeed, the emergence of alternate micro-finance delivery models may have overshadowed the importance of the subsidy-led credit supply model under SGSY. Contrary to this, in States like Orissa, NGOs are yet to become vibrant and as of now, SGSY has no alternatives.

In States like Andhra Pradesh, Himachal Pradesh, Punjab and Uttar Pradesh, the number of SHGs to which assistance has been provided during the financial year 2006-07 is more than the number of SHGs formed during that year. This may be due to the fact that assistance has been extended during 2006-07 to SHGs formed in earlier years. Besides, assistance may also have been extended to those SHGs which have been formed under programmes implemented by the NABARD, NGOs, NBFIs etc., and not necessarily under SGSY. A glance at columns 6 and 7 of Table 3.7 brings out clearly that assistance extended to SHGs is picking up. With the exception of Tamil Nadu and West Bengal, all other States show that from 2001-02 to 2006-07 an increasing number of SHGs have been assisted, as a proportion of the number of SHGs formed.

SGSY credit disbursement has not been proportionate to the poor living in most of the backward States (Table 3.8). During 2006-07, Bihar, Gujarat, Madhya Pradesh, Uttar Pradesh and West Bengal, with 19.48, 2.06, 11.25, 21.32 and 9.32 per cent of India's rural poor received 5.01, 0.65, 7.31, 18.40 and 1.75 per cent of SGSY credit, respectively. The largest gainer of the SGSY credit was Andhra Pradesh (23.88) followed by Uttar Pradesh (18.40), Orissa (7.51), Maharashtra (6.14), Bihar (5.01), Tamil Nadu (4.88), Assam (4.79) and Karnataka (4.38). The per capita SGSY credit disbursement to the poor during the year was only Rs. 92.7 in the country.

The comparison of the proportion of SHGs assisted during 2006-07 (Table 3.7) and the per cent distribution of SGSY credit across States/UTs (Table 3.8) conveys a vast mismatch. For instance, while Karnataka accounts for 4.38 per cent of SGSY credit distribution, the proportion of SHGs assisted in the State accounts for only 2.72 per cent of the country's total SHGs assisted. For Madhya Pradesh the respective figures are 7.31 per cent and 5.01 per cent. Similarly, for Maharashtra, the respective figures are 6.14 and 4.98 per cent and for Orissa are 7.51 and 4.40 per cent.

Table 3.8: State-wise Poverty and SGSY Credit Flow (2006-07)

States/UTs	*Total Rural Poor (Lakh)**	*State's Share in Total Rural Poor*	*SGSY Credit Disbursed (Rs. Cr.)*	*Per cent Distribution of SGSY Credit through SHGs*	*Per capita SGSY Credit Disbursed to poor (in Rs.)*
1	2	3	4	5	6
Andhra Pradesh	58.13	3.01	427.66	23.88	735.7
Assam	92.17	4.77	85.74	4.79	93.0
Bihar	376.51	19.48	89.69	5.01	23.8
Gujarat	39.8	2.06	11.71	0.65	29.4
Haryana	11.94	0.62	34.64	1.93	290.1
Himachal Pradesh	4.84	0.25	12.25	0.68	253.1
Jammu & Kashmir	2.97	0.15	5.99	0.33	201.7
Karnataka	59.91	3.10	78.41	4.38	130.9
Kerala	20.97	1.09	27.93	1.56	133.2
Madhya Pradesh	217.32	11.25	130.93	7.31	60.2
Maharashtra	125.12	6.47	109.97	6.14	87.9
Orissa	143.69	7.44	134.52	7.51	93.6
Punjab	10.2	0.53	12.68	0.71	124.3
Rajasthan	55.06	2.85	65.34	3.65	118.7
Tamil Nadu	80.51	4.17	87.32	4.88	108.5
Uttar Pradesh	412.01	21.32	329.56	18.40	80.0
West Bengal	180.11	9.32	31.41	1.75	17.4
Pondicherry	0.64	0.03	2.37	0.13	370.3
All-India	1932.43	100.00	1790.7	100.00	92.7

Note: * As per latest Below Poverty Line Census conducted by Ministry of Rural Development.

Source: Ministry of Rural Development (2006).

V. ANALYSIS OF FIELD STUDY IN RURAL ORISSA

A field visit to two districts, viz., Jagatsingpur and Nuapara of one of the most backward States of India, Orissa was undertaken to review the implementation of SGSY. Out of the two study districts while Jagatsingpur is well-known as the cultural heart of the State, the other district Nuapara is infamous for acute poverty, severe malnutrition and widespread destitution. While the total population of Jagatsingpur district is 10.15 lakh in 1,391 villages of 8 Community Development Blocks[11] (CDBs), Nuapara has 5.3 lakh population in 663 villages of 5 CDBs. Though the former is a relatively better-off district than Nuapara, yet both are backward in terms of infrastructure development like road network, markets, banks and technical institutions.

A study was conducted by the authors in 32 Gram Panchayats (GPs) in two CDBs in each of these districts during June 2006 to April 2007. Basic information on occupation structures, income and asset ownership, programme structure and participation of members in the programme was collected through a structured schedule from 64 SHGs. The sample size for each of the CDBs was 16 SHGs. These CDBs were chosen through a stratified random sampling by SHG penetration.

The number of SHGs formed in Jagatsinghpur and Nuapara till 2006-07 was 4,124 and 2,206, respectively (Annexure IV). The credit to subsidy ratio was 2.5 and 1.8 respectively while the same for the whole state recorded only 1.8. As per the results of the survey, SHGs in these districts are exclusively women groups with an average member size of 17. The monthly savings of members range between Rs 30 and Rs. 60. The responsibility of formation and nurturing of SHGs lies with the village level workers[12] (VLWs).

Out of the total 256 respondents, 99.6 per cent was found to be reeling under poverty line. Further, an overwhelming proportion of the SHG members in these districts was found to be illiterate (48 per cent) or had studied till standard five, i.e. primary school (26.2 per cent). The illiteracy among the SHGs in Nuapara was as high as 41.4 per cent (Table 3.9). Under SGSY, the presumption is that the poor members of SHGs would acquire basic skills of accountancy, book-keeping, management, leadership and team-work to manage their own business unit for their income-generation (MoRD, 2003). So, the illiteracy of members may pose a grave challenge for the future survival and sustainability of these SHGs, which have to be self-reliant and cannot be permanently dependent on SHPIs for their day-to-day work.

Table 3.9: Socio-Economic Background of the Beneficiary Households

	No. of Respondents		
	Jagatsingpur	*Nuapara*	*Total*
1	*2*	*3*	*4*
Education			
Illiterate	17 (6.6)	106 (41.4)	123 (48.0)
Primary	47 (18.4)	20 (7.8)	67 (26.2)
Upper-primary and HS	33 (12.9)	2 (0.8)	35 (13.7)
Intermediate	30 (11.7)	0 (0.0)	30 (11.7)
Graduate and above	1 (0.4)	0 (0.0)	1 (0.4)
Total	128 (50.00)	128 (50.00)	256 (100.0)
BPL status			
BPL	128 (50.0)	127 (49.6)	255 (99.6)
Non-BPL	0 (0.0)	1 (0.4)	1 (0.4)
Total	128 (50.00)	128 (50.00)	256 (100.0)

Source: Survey Data.
Figures in the parentheses refer to the percentage to total.

Table 3.10: Land Property of the Beneficiary Households

Land (Range in Acres)	*No. of Respondents*		
	Jagatsingpur	*Nuapara*	*Total*
1	*2*	*3*	*4*
No land	33 (12.9)	48 (18.8)	81 (31.6)
Upto 1	74 (28.9)	72 (28.1)	146 (57.0)
2-3	8 (3.1)	7 (2.7)	15 (5.9)
3-4	2 (0.8)	1 (0.4)	3 (1.2)
above 3	11 (4.3)	0 (0.0)	11 (4.3)
Total	128 (50.0)	128 (50.0)	256 (100.0)

Source: Survey Data Figures in the parentheses refer to the percentage to total.

It was observed that 88.6 per cent of the members were either landless or possessed land of less than 1 hectare (Table 3.10). Around 97.6 per cent of the members belonged to the lowest income group, i.e. less than Rs. 1500 per month (Table 3.11), thereby corroborating the fact that the beneficiary selection under SGSY had been as per the programme guidelines that lays emphasis on selection of people living below the poverty line. It was also found that there has been an increment in income of the respondents in the reference periods. While 95.3 per cent were earning upto Rs. 750 per capita per month in pre-1999 period, the same has reduced to 52.7 per cent as on 2006-07. While 4.3 per cent of the respondents in the pre-SHG period were earning between Rs. 750 to Rs. 1,500 a month in the pre-SHG period, the same has increased to 44.9 per cent in the post-SHG period indicating a positive income impact of the micro-finance programme.

Table 3.11: Income Profile of the Beneficiary Households (Pre and Post-SHG)

Income Range (in Rs/day)	*No. of Respondents (Pre-SHG)*			*No. of Respondents (Post-SHG)*		
	Jagatsing-pur	*Nuapara*	*Total*	*Jagatsing-pur*	*Nuapara*	*Total*
1	*2*	*3*	*4*	*5*	*6*	*7*
upto 25	116 (45.3)	128 (50.0)	244 (95.3)	39 (15.2)	96 (37.5)	135 (52.7)
25-50	11 (4.3)	0 (0.0)	11 (4.3)	83 (32.4)	32 (12.5)	115 (44.9)
51-100	1 (0.4)	0 (0.0)	1 (0.4)	4 (1.6)	0 (0.0)	4 (1.6)
101-150	0 (0.0)	0 (0.0)	0 (0.0)	2 (0.8)	0 (0.0)	2 (0.8)
above 150	0 (0.0)	0 (0.0)	0 (0.0)	0 (0.0)	0 (0.0)	0 (0.0)
Total	128 (50.0)	128 (50.0)	256 (100.0)	128 (50.0)	128 (50.0)	256 (100.0)

Source: Survey Data.
Figures in the parentheses refer to the percentage to total.

The SHGs which have been in existence for a period of at least 6 months in the study area were found to have the potential of utilising small amount of credit upto Rs.50,000 per group. However, arbitrary fixation of savings amount per member, irregular meetings and member absenteeism in these meetings failed to augment the corpus of the group. This also failed to inculcate banking habits in the members, since the frequency of thrift and credit activities within the group was severely limited.

It was also observed that the SHG-bank linkage framework of SGSY suffered because of the lackadaisical attitude of the grassroot level implementing authority. The groups were not sensitised about the participation and self-help approach and were aware only of the subsidy component of the programme. The basic tenet of self-help was lacking in the study groups. Around one-third of the sample SHGs were neither graded nor linked with micro-credit, though these had existed for more than two years. It was also observed that an SHG in the study area waited on an average upto 18 months for the first ever subjective grading after which corpus linked micro-credit assistance was provided to the groups concerned from the banking institution. The delay in the grading test of the SHGs was due to the lack of co-ordination between the implementing district and village level government officials, SHPIs and Bank officials. The investment per SHG varied from below Rs. 25,000 to Rs. 5 lakh. While more than 40 per cent of the total SHGs in Nuapara had a range of investment between Rs. 1 to 5 lakh per group under SGSY (Table 12), none of the respondent SHG members in Jagatsinghpur had an investment above Rs. 1 lakh.

Table 3.12: Investment in the SHGs

Investment Range (in Rs)	*No. of Respondents*		
	Jagatsingpur	*Nuapara*	*Total*
1	*2*	*3*	*4*
upto 25,000	40 (15.6)	12 (4.7)	52 (20.3)
25,001 to 50,000	24 (9.4)	4 (1.6)	28 (10.9)
50,001 to 1 lac	64 (25.0)	8 (3.1)	72 (28.1)
1 to 5 lac	0 (0.0)	104 (40.6)	104 (40.6)
above 5 lakh	0 (0.0)	0 (0.0)	0 (0.0)
Total	128 (50.0)	128 (50.0)	256 (100.0)

Figures in the parentheses refer to the percentage to total.

Source: Survey Data.

It was found that as many as 59 per cent of total member respondents perceived finance as their greatest problem in the successful implementation of their self-employment activities. While around 30 per cent of the respondents indicated marketing, product and quality as major problems, 8.2 per cent and 2.3 per cent of the respondents cited infrastructure and facilitators' support respectively as the problem areas (Table 3.13).

Table 3.13: Difficulties Faced

Difficulty Categories	*No. of Respondents*		
	Jagatsingpur	*Nuapara*	*Total*
1	*2*	*3*	*4*
Marketing	29 (11.3)	10 (3.9)	39 (15.2)
Finance	51 (19.9)	100 (39.1)	151 (59.0)
Product and Quality	29 (11.3)	10 (3.9)	39 (15.2)
Infrastructure	14 (5.5)	7 (2.7)	21 (8.2)
Facilitator's Support	5 (2.0)	1 (0.4)	6 (2.3)
Total	128 (50.0)	128 (50.0)	256 (100.0)

Source: Survey Data Figures in the parentheses refer to the percentage to total.

An analysis of the beneficiaries' occupational pattern before and after joining the programme was undertaken to find out the reasons behind the low credit off-take under SGSY. The respondents were asked about their pre and post-SGSY activities. It was found that more than 17 per cent of members were involved in household chores before joining the programme in Jagatsinghpur. However, there was a complete shift from household and other works to various types of income generating activities in the post-SGSY period. While in the pre-1999 period there were 34.4 and 67.2 per cent people engaged in agriculture or related activities, with the initiation of programme, the occupational share in agriculture and related activities in Jagatsinghpur increased by 23.4 percentage points. The shift from agricultural activities to other activities in Nuapara was very marginal. These reflect that under SGSY the micro-finance is used mostly for agro-related activities in rural areas. While in Jagatsinghpur there is a shift towards agriculture from household industries, in Nuapara, the shift of occupation to household industries from trade and commerce and transportation and communication services was evident (Table 3.14).

It was observed that the low growth in self-employment in household industrial activities are because of growing demand of SHG members for meeting consumption expenditure on medicine, school education and on less productive economic activities like agriculture, livestock and trading activities.

Table 3.14: Occupational Status of Members Before and After Joining SGSY

Occupation	*Before Pre-99 Period*		*After 1999-2006-07*	
	Jagatsinghpur	*Nuapara*	*Jagatsinghpur*	*Nuapara*
1	*2*	*3*	*4*	*5*
Agri and Related	34.4	67.2	57.8	64.1
Household Industries	39.8	26.6	15.6	35.2
Trade and Commerce	0.0	0.0	17.2	0.8
Transport and Communication	8.6	0.0	9.4	0.0
House work/others	17.2	6.3	0.0	0.0

Source: Survey Data.

It was also observed that SHG members prefer to extend agriculture or agro-based activities without weighing their future prospects and without diversifying their agricultural activities. Further, the SHG members were found to have undertaken activities other than those identified by the Government. Though the SGSY guidelines stress on the identification of a maximum of ten activities in each block, it was observed that each block had identified varieties of activities[13] for assistance under SGSY without taking into account their forward and backward linkage effects. Besides, these activities were not identified through a participatory process involving SHPIs and prospective members of SHGs. Many activities had been selected without taking into account the details of existing local resources, the aptitude and skill of the people in the area concerned. Lack of convergence amongst various Government institutions, market and bank infrastructure had resulted in defeating the very purpose of the programme in ensuring a holistic community development in rural area. The monitoring and assessment mechanism of the programme was less effective than expected as the grassroot level government functionaries themselves did not have complete knowledge about the programme objectives and benefits.

VI. CONCLUSION AND POLICY IMPLICATIONS

The key to the effective implementation of any rural based project lies in a series of rigorous monitoring of pre-envisaged end-activities of the project. The success of the rural micro-finance programme, therefore, lies in the formation of quality groups, adequate and timely credit support along with the identification of appropriate and profitable economic activities. The credit-to-subsidy ratio under the programme has to be at least in the ratio of 3:1. In phases the subsidy component has to be withdrawn and more and more emphasis is to be laid on credit for elimination of subsidy dependence syndrome from the soil of rural India.

Field level studies reveal that a lot more is required by way of co-ordination among the different tiers of implementing agencies, viz. bankers, government officials and SHPIs. The in-built co-ordination and monitoring mechanism within the programme has to be reviewed and redesigned ensuring the active involvement of programme implementing agencies. Due to the lack of focus on the location-specific key activities, additional employment and income have not been effectively generated in the rural areas. This has dampened the enthusiasm within the beneficiary communities.

The selection of activities in a particular area should be determined by the availability of physical resources, skills and aptitude of the people and market demand. For optimum forward and backward linkages the number of key economic activities should not exceed five. Moreover, excess capacity should not be created by too many people taking up the same activity at a time leading to over crowding of units in a particular area. Further, the selected activities should have the potential of generating incremental income sustained over a period of time which would enable the beneficiaries to cross the poverty line. Project reports for assistance under SGSY should stress on the availability and access to training, credit, technology, infrastructure and marketing facilities. Before any beneficiary is financed, the feasibility of the activity for the group members should be assessed.

The role of SHPIs in sensitising and motivating the poor cannot be undermined. With the right assistance from SHPIs, SHGs graduate from being mere groups to being profitable micro-entrepreneurial ventures. The absorption and repayment capacity of the members should determine the amount of financial support to be extended to them. Consumption loans should definitely be discouraged. Before extending any loan, even for productive purposes, an assessment by the group in consultation with all the programme implementing authorities is a must. Emphasis should be laid on participatory decision making while mapping the local resources, identifying and selecting economic activities. Periodic monitoring should be carried out not only of the progress made by the beneficiaries but also of the quality of operation of the SHGs.

Rural bank network needs to be expanded so that they become more accessible to SHGs. Besides, an improvement in marketing and technical infrastructure for the SHG units is required. In the era of globalisation, the SHGs need to upgrade their methods of production to be able to survive in a competitive market. The stage is set just right for the SHG-bank linkage model of economic development to get the appropriate boost.

NOTES

1. The share of Agriculture in GDP has declined over the years. During the years 2000-01 and 2005-06, the average contribution of agriculture to GDP was estimated to be 22 per cent. However, during 2006-07, the share of agriculture further declined to 18.5 per cent while the share of industry and services improved to 26.4 per cent and 55.1 per cent respectively.
2. SGSY being a micro-finance driven rural employment generation programme seeks to bring the needy rural poor families above the poverty line through an integrated action of various district and village level agencies—District Rural Development Agencies (DRDAs), banks and other Self-Help Promoting Institutions (SHPI) like Non Government Organisations (NGOs), Panchayati Raj Institutions, Rural Branches of Commercial Banks, Regional Rural Banks, Co-operatives, Corporate bodies, private sector companies and individuals.
3. To prevent bank failures and to restore public confidence in the banking system in the post-independent India, Banking Regulation Act of 1949 was enacted with a view to weeding out small and non-viable banking units, formulating prudent and sound bank practices, ensuring greater protection to the depositors. This later on proved to be an effective control tool of the RBI for setting up of a strong, unified and compact base for Indian banking system.
4. Observations made by Prof. D.R. Gadgil Study Group of National Credit Council on "Organisational Framework for the Implementation of Social Control Objectives" and the recommendations of Nariman Committee of Bankers facilitated the way to implement a Lead Bank Scheme in the country at the end of 1969. Under this scheme districts were allotted to localised major

public sector banks to act like consortium leaders to ensure co-ordination between co-operative banks, the commercial banks and other financial agencies in the districts to intensively develop the identified area.

5. As per the RBI's Circular No. BPD(PCB)MC. No.8/09.09.01/2004-05 dated August 11, 2005, the banks are required to lend on priority basis to Agriculture and Allied Agricultural Activities, Small Scale and Ancillary Industries, new and renewable sources of energy, Cottage Industries, Khadi & Village Industries, Artisans and Tiny Industries, Small Scale Service & Business {Industry Related} Enterprises (SSSBEs), Food and agro based processing and forestry, Small Road and Water Transport Operators, Retail Traders, Small Business Enterprises, Professionals and Self-Employed Persons, Weaker Sections.
6. All India Rural Credit Review Committee was constituted under the Chairmanship of Shri B. Venkatappiah in July 1966 to review the supply of rural credit in the context of Fourth Five Year Plan (1969-74) of India in general and the requirements of the intensive programmes of agricultural production in various parts of the country in particular.
7. A PACS may be started with ten or more persons, normally from a particular village. The value of share to become a member is very nominal and management rests with an elected body comprising president, secretary and treasurer. Loans are given for short periods, normally less than 365 days with low interest rates for carrying out agricultural activities. Profits of PACS are not distributed as dividends but are used for the welfare activities of the village.
8. Facilitating agencies or catalysts working closely with the poor at the grassroot level who can sensitise and motivate the poor about the advantages of organising themselves into groups for their socio-economic progress. The SHPI spectrum includes NGOs and other community based organisations, various government rural development institutes, Panchayati Raj Institutions, Rural Branches of Commercial Banks, Regional Rural Banks and Co-operatives, Corporate bodies and private sector companies, individuals like school teachers, retired government employees, health workers, village development workers and even unemployed educated youth.
9. The corpus of a group consists of cash balances with the group, group savings as per the balance in the savings bank account of the group, the sum of all outstanding loans against the members of the group, interest earned on the loans to members and interest on balance in the savings bank account.
10. In February 1997, the Planning Commission, Government of India set up a Committee to review and rationalise schemes for poverty

alleviation and employment generation under the chairmanship of S.R. Hashim. A detailed report of the committee was submitted to the Government in April 1997. For details, see Report of the Committee to Review and Rationalise Centrally Sponsored Schemes for Poverty Alleviation and Employment Generation, Government of India, Planning Commission, April 1997.

11. For development and cohesion between the people in a community, nearly 100 villages with 60,000 to 80,000 population have been grouped together to constitute a Community Development Block (CDB).
12. VLWs act as community builders by socially mobilising poor women from various households in a village to form informal cohesive groups. They are required to monitor the group, its day-to-day function, internal lending and banking habits.
13. Some of the activities identified under SGSY in the study blocks were dairy farming, poultry, goat rearing, pisciculture, floriculture, vegetable cultivation, chilli cultivation, betel binding, plantation, cane and bamboo cultivation, *agarbati* and detergent powder making, coir products, tent house with brass band, golden grass, palm products, mushroom cultivation, fruit processing, spices, soft toy making, terracotta, oil-making, *dal*-processing and dry fish making.

Annexures

ANNEXURE I: NUMBER OF LOANS TAKEN UNDER SGSY BY PURPOSE (DURING 2006-2007)

States	Primary Sector	Secondary Sector	Tertiary Sector	Total	% Activities to Total		
					Primary	Secondary	Tertiary
1	2	3	4	5	6	7	8
Andhra Pradesh	394859	138962	105022	638843	61.8	21.8	16.4
Arunachal Pradesh	612	259	6	877	69.8	29.5	0.7
Assam	28918	20856	4880	54654	52.9	38.2	8.9
Bihar	65355	19678	26021	111054	58.8	17.7	23.4
Chhattisgarh	17062	6568	10039	33669	50.7	19.5	29.8
Goa	711	0	NA	711	100.0	0.0	0.0
Gujarat	19576	3296	4365	27237	71.9	12.1	16.0
Haryana	11439	2076	642	14157	80.8	14.7	4.5
Himachal Pradesh	4403	590	912	5905	74.6	10.0	15.4
J & K	3328	3241	1336	7905	42.1	41.0	16.9
Jharkhand	30491	8559	22536	61586	49.5	13.9	36.6
Karnataka	34618	7644	394	42656	81.2	17.9	0.9
Kerala	11069	5518	5800	22387	49.4	24.6	25.9
Madhya Pradesh	35176	15005	9536	59717	58.9	25.1	16.0
Maharashtra	60674	4484	10628	75786	80.1	5.9	14.0
Manipur	1225	1118	NA	2343	52.3	47.7	0.0
Meghalaya	2926	369	33	3328	87.9	11.1	1.0
Mizoram	565	23	16	604	93.5	3.8	2.6
Nagaland	2317	887	49	3253	71.2	27.3	1.5
Orissa	51828	11066	5793	68687	75.5	16.1	8.4
Punjab	4738	3052	2742	10532	45.0	29.0	26.0
Rajasthan	28376	4695	5374	38445	73.8	12.2	14.0
Sikkim	1363	34	0	1397	97.6	2.4	0.0
Tamil Nadu	28481	19516	5512	53509	53.2	36.5	10.3
Tripura	5821	3344	386	9551	60.9	35.0	4.0
Uttar Pradesh	197813	31283	28481	257577	76.8	12.1	11.1
Uttrakhand	9763	608	193	10564	92.4	5.8	1.8
West Bengal	15154	11448	1649	28251	53.6	40.5	5.8
A&N Islands	89	0	120	209	42.6	0.0	57.4
Lakshadweep	36	0	NA	36	100.0	0.0	0.0
Pondicherry	935	355	NA	1290	72.5	27.5	0.0
TOTAL	1069721	324534	252465	1646720	65.0	19.7	15.3

Source: Ministry of Rural Development (2006).

(Contd.)

Note: Primary Sector includes cultivation, irrigation and land development activities and Milch cattle Secondary Sector includes handicraft, handlooms and village industries. Tertiary Sector includes services arising in village and agro-based industries (NA: Not Available)

ANNEXURE II: REGION-WISE GROUND LEVEL CREDIT DISBURSEMENTS UNDER AGRICULTURE AND ALLIED ACTIVITIES (RS. CR.)

Zone	*Year*				
	2001-02	*2002-03*	*2003-04*	*2004-05*	*2005-06*
1	*2*	*3*	*4*	*5*	*6*
Northern	14815	17455	21819	32125	50448
N-Eastern	116	154	300	407	936
Eastern	3292	3869	5047	7238	12216
Central	8461	10030	12487	17142	23134
Western	9668	9142	10122	14111	26178
Southern	19749	21558	26137	36819	63463

Source: Ministry of Agriculture (2006-07) & NABARD (2006).

ANNEXURE III: STATE-WISE POPULATION PER BANK (IN '000) AND PERCENTAGE OF FARMER HOUSEHOLDS INDEBTED (MARCH 2005)

State	*Population per Bank (in '000)*	*Per cent indebted*
1	*2*	*3*
Andhra	14.7	82
Arunachal Pradesh	16.9	5.9
Assam	22.9	18.1
Bihar	24.7	33
Chhattisgarh	21.3	40.2
Gujarat	14.5	51.9
Haryana	13.5	53.1
Himachal	7.9	33.4
Jammu & Kashmir	13	31.8
Jharkhand	19.2	20.9
Karnataka	11.2	61.6
Kerala	9.5	64.4
Madhya Pradesh	18.6	50.8
Maharashtra	15.9	54.8
Manipur	32.3	24.8

(Contd.)

State	Population per Bank (in '000)	Per cent indebted
1	2	3
Meghalaya	13.3	4.1
Mizoram	11.9	23.6
Nagaland	30.1	36.5
Orissa	16.9	47.8
Punjab	9.4	65.4
Rajasthan	17.8	52.4
Sikkim	10.4	38.8
Tamil Nadu	13.3	74.5
Tripura	18.4	49.2
Uttar Pradesh	21.6	40.3
Uttrakhand	10.2	7.2
West Bangal	18.6	50.1
Group of UTs	NA	50.8
All India	16	48.6

Source: RBI (2006) & NSSO (2006). *NA*: Not Available.

ANNEXURE IV: DISTRICT-WISE SHGS FORMED, PER FAMILY INVESTMENT AND CREDIT-SUBSIDY RATIO IN ORISSA

District	SHG Formed Since 1999	Per Family Investment	Credit-Subsidy Ratio
1	2	3	4
Angul	8400	29191	2.1
Balasore	9721	28647	2.3
Bargarh	3889	30064	2.4
Bhadrak	5120	19478	2.5
Bolangir	6761	25180	1.8
Boudh	765	24453	1.7
Cuttak	4915	23191	1.6
Deogarh	726	21879	1.4
Dhenkanal	9570	21799	1.3
Gajapati	2974	24808	1.5
Ganjam	14717	27875	1.6
Jagatsinghpur	4124	35040	2.5
Jajpur	6175	26652	1.9
Jharsuguda	864	37872	3.1
Kalahandi	1460	26201	1.6
Kendrapara	2940	23092	1.6
Keonjhar	6443	24220	1.6
Khurda	5327	30778	2.1

(*Contd.*)

District	SHG Formed Since 1999	Per Family Investment	Credit-Subsidy Ratio
1	2	3	4
Koraput	3773	30534	2.0
Malkangiri	2269	27286	2.1
Mayurbhenj	14819	21834	1.3
Nabarangpur	8491	30318	2.1
Naupada	2206	25262	1.8
Nayagarh	4341	23070	1.5
Phulbani	1531	22815	1.4
Puri	2600	20014	1.3
Rayagada	6873	24244	1.6
Sambalppur	3748	29626	2.1
Sonepur	2859	27170	2.0
Sundergarh	6477	29709	2.0
TOTAL	154878	26048	1.8

Source: Economic Survey, Government of Orissa (2006-07) & Ministry of Rural Development, GoI (2006).

REFERENCES

1. Claessens, Stijn. (2005, February). Universal Access to Financial Services: A Review of the Issues and Public Policy Objectives. *Paper presented in the Fifth Services Experts Meeting of OECD-World Bank,* OECD, Paris, France.
2. Copestake, J., Bhalotra, S., & Johnson, S. (2001). Assessing the impact of microfinance: A Zambian case study. *Journal of Development Studies,* 37, 81-100.
3. Government of India. (1971-2001). *Census of India,* Office of the Registrar General & Census Commissioner, New Delhi.
4. Government of India. (1991). Report of the Committee on the Financial System, M. Narasimham (Chairman), *Ministry of Finance,* New Delhi.
5. Government of India. (1997). Report of the Committee to Review and Rationalise Centrally Sponsored Schemes for Poverty Alleviation and Employment Generation. *Planning Commission,* New Delhi.
6. Government of India. (2003), Guidelines: Swarnjayanti Gram Swarozgar Yojana. *Ministry of Rural Development,* New Delhi.
7. Government of India. (2005). Task Force on Revival of Rural Cooperative Credit Institutions, A Vaidyanathan (Chairman), *Ministry of Finance,* New Delhi.
8. Government of India. (2005-06 & 2006-07). Annual Reports.

Department of Agriculture & Cooperation, *Ministry of Agriculture*, New Delhi.

9. Government of India. (2005-06 & 2006-07). Annual Reports. *Ministry of Rural Development*, New Delhi.
10. Government of India. (2006). Economic Survey, *Ministry of Finance*, New Delhi.
11. Government of India. (2006). Household Assets Holding, Indebtedness, Current Borrowings and Repayments of Social Groups in India (as on 30.06.2002). *All-India Debt and Investment Survey Report* No. 503(59/18.2/4). NSS 59th Round, Delhi.
12. Government of India. (2006, May). Report of the Technical Group on Population Projections Constituted by the *National Commission on Population*, Office of the Registrar General & Census Commissioner, New Delhi.
13. Government of Orissa. (2006). Economic Survey, Directorate of Economics and Statistics, *Planning & Co-ordination Department*, Bhubaneswar.
14. Matin, I. & Hulme, D. (2003). Programme for the Poorest: Learning from the IGVGD Programme in Bangladesh. *World Development*, 31, 647-665.
15. Mohan, Rakesh (2006). Agricultural Credit in India Status, Issues and Future Agenda. *Economic and Political Weekly*, 41, 1013-1021.
16. Mor, Nachiket (2005). Expanding Access to Financial Services Where Do We Go from Here? *Economic and Political Weekly*, 40, 1122-1126.
17. Mwenda, K.K. & Muuka, G.N. (2004). Towards best practices for micro finance institutional engagement in African rural areas—Selected cases and agenda for action. *International Journal of Social Economics*, 31, 143-158.
18. NABARD. (2005-06 & 2006-07). *Annual Reports*. Mumbai.
19. Patil, B.V. (2005). Rural Banking Problems of Localised Banking Institutions. *Economic and Political Weekly*, 40, 1224-1228.
20. Rao, C. H. H., & Gulati, Ashok. (2005). Indian Agriculture: Emerging Perspectives and Major Policy Issues, Indian Economy and Society: In C.H. Hanumantha Rao, B.B. Bhattacharya and N.S. Sidharthan (Eds.), *Indian Economy and Society in the Era of Globalisation and Liberalisation — Essays in Honour of prof. A. M. Khusro*.41-60, New Delhi: Academic Foundation.
21. Reserve Bank of India, (2000) *Reserve Bank of India Bulletins*, Mumbai.
22. Reserve Bank of India, (2005). *Draft Technical Paper on Priority Sector Lending*. RPCD, Mumbai.
23. Reserve Bank of India, (2005). *Handbook of Monetary Statistics of India*. Mumbai.
24. Reserve Bank of India, (2006). *Handbook of Statistics on the Indian Economy*. Mumbai.

25. Roy, M. (2006). A Review of Bank Lending to Priority and Retail Sectors. *Economic and Political Weekly*, 41, 1035-1040.
26. Throp, R., Frances, S. and Amrik, Heyer (2005). When and How Far is Group Formation a Route Out of Chronic Poverty?, *World Development*, 33, 907-920.
27. Yunus, Muhammad (2004). Grameen Bank, Microcredit and Millennium Development Goals. *Economic and Political Weekly*, 39, 4077-4080.

4

Enabling Role of Governments in Microfinance Development: Experiences from Thailand

MARIE LUISE HABERBERGER

I. INTRODUCTION

The extent to which governments should engage in the development process remains a subject for discussion. Many pro-government economists believe that the role of governments should be confined to providing the institutional framework within which financial systems can operate but do not support the active involvement of governments. The debate about the role of governments in institutional development has hitherto focused solely on the question, whether, and to what extent governments should intervene. But even if we agree that efficient institutions do not emerge automatically as a result of an evolutionary process and further that governments have to intervene in order to compensate for market deficiencies, there is still no certainty that government intervention will take place at the right time with the right means. However, we all agree that development—economic, social and sustainable—is impossible without an effective government. Let us take a look at Thailand and the well-known BAAC (Bank for Agriculture and Agricultural Cooperatives) a major provider of micro and rural finance services and the role of the Thai government.

Thailand has a population of about 63 million people occupying an area of some 513,000 square kilometres. The Gross

Domestic Product in 2003 was US$ 142.3 billion and the per capita income was US$ 2,241. Over the last five years, the annual inflation rate in Thailand has fluctuated between less than one to 1.5 per cent.

Between 1980 and 1995, the share of agriculture in GDP declined from 23 to 11 per cent. This decline was matched by an increase in the share of industry. These changes had a significant effect on settlement patterns, with the proportion of urban population more than doubling, from 17 per cent in 1980 to 36 per cent in 1995. 50 per cent of the urban population lives in Bangkok.

There has been a drastic reduction in poverty in Thailand in recent years; official estimates suggest that the incidence of poverty has fallen again after the financial crisis to around 12 per cent of the population. However, there is considerable regional variation. A long-term trend towards greater income inequality has been evident since the mid-70s.

II. THE MACRO ECONOMIC ENVIRONMENT

Favourable Growth Rates

In the fourth quarter of 2003, the economy expanded by 7.8 per cent, accelerating from the previous quarter. Seasonally adjusted GDP growth increased by 2.7 per cent—an indication of on-going economic expansion. Strong domestic demand, both consumption and investment, were the main driving forces of the economy. Greater domestic consumption and investment have expanded the range of production activities for the grassroots population, providing small entrepreneurs the opportunity to enter the market and earn more income.

Low Inflation Rates

Over the last five years Thailand has experienced its lowest inflation rates of less than one to 1.5 per cent. These low inflation rates have been conducive to economic stability and growth. Under the inflation targeting system used since 2000, the Monetary Policy Committee of the Bank of Thailand sets short-term interest rates with a goal of sustainable growth while keeping core-inflation within a range of zero to 3.5 per cent. With inflation on the lower side of the target and a relatively strong external position thanks to a good export performance, the monetary policy fully promotes the recovery process.

Poverty Reduction Through Improved Export Markets for Rural Products

The Thai government has recognised the importance of local rural production. In order to promote local products, the One Tambon One Product (OTOP) initiative was launched at the beginning of 2001 (a *tambon* is a group of villages or a sub-district) to enable each community to develop and market its own local products based on traditional indigenous expertise and local know-how. The government is further prepared to provide additional assistance in terms of appropriate modern technology and new management techniques to promote marketing through domestic and international outlets with a good retail network. The booming Thai tourist industry complements and fosters the sale of rural or locally produced goods. The OTOP initiative aims to channel income into local communities in Thailand, thereby helping to raise standards of living throughout the county.

Infrastructure and Bank Branch Networks

Road infrastructure is fairly well developed in Thailand and road conditions are quite satisfactory. Rural clients reach the nearest branch within 15 to 30 minutes of travelling time. Clients living in remote locations are few. BAAC alone, which has an outreach of 92 per cent[1] throughout its large rural network, is operating in nearly 600 branches and 888 field or service units.

Interest Rates

A general ceiling of 15 per cent interest is applied to loans. This ceiling is specified in the Civil and Commercial Code, and applies to all bodies and transactions unless they are specifically excluded. Exceptions are as follows: Since 1992, almost all financial institutions regulated by the Bank of Thailand are free to charge interest rates based on market conditions. However a few Specialised Financial Institutions (SFIs), thrifts and credit cooperatives are excluded and are subject to an interest rate ceiling of 19 per cent, but their interest rates have yet to reach the ceiling.

The interest rate ceilings impact differently on various institutions and could be a constraint to the development of microfinance, particularly when the costs of funds are increasing. Given the higher transaction costs associated with microfinance, the chances of the ceiling acting as an impediment should be closely monitored.[2]

Thailand's Financial Sector

The formal financial sector in Thailand consists primarily of commercial banks, non-bank financial institutions, Specialised Financial Institutions established by the government and cooperatives. By 2002, there are 13 Thai commercial banks, 5 credit financial companies (type of finance company), 18 finance companies and 18 full foreign commercial bank branches, and 29 BIBFs (Bangkok International Banking Facility). There are 3632 bank branches throughout the country, all under the supervision of the Bank of Thailand.

There are nine specialised financial institutions (SFIs—four banks and five companies) supervised by the Ministry of Finance (MoF) and inspected by the Bank of Thailand. Most notable among these in regard to micro and rural financial services is the Bank for Agriculture and Agricultural Cooperatives (BAAC) with 588 branches and sub-branches.

III. THE BANK FOR AGRICULTURE AND AGRICULTURAL COOPERATIVES (BAAC)

General

BAAC is a front rider' with regard to outreach: 92 per cent of farm households in Thailand have been reached directly or indirectly by BAAC. However outreach is meaningful only if it remains sustainable.

The Bank of Agriculture and Agricultural Cooperatives (BAAC) was established in 1966 as a government-owned agricultural development bank. The mandate of the bank has been to provide agricultural credit to farm households and agricultural cooperatives. Since the expansion of the branch network in 1988, the number of borrowers has doubled. By 2003, more than five million farm households were registered as BAAC's direct and indirect clients while 2.7 million of them are active BAAC borrowers. This represents about 92 per cent, respectively 46 per cent of the total farm households in Thailand. Savings accounts totalling almost 9.6 million provide significant proof that there is a high demand among rural clients for BAAC's financial services. BAAC's pro-active rural savings mobilisation[3] has brought about what is virtually a revolutionary change in the financial resource base. BAAC has become financially self-reliant and has been able to significantly reduce its dependence on loans from domestic and foreign sources. By 2003, or in just a decade, the deposit-to-loan ratio has reached 100 per cent.

An ongoing process of change is underway at BAAC and reforms are far from complete; important lessons can be learned from BAAC's experience. BAAC has gone through several evolutionary steps. For many years it tried hard to secure an amendment to the 1966 BAAC Act and to obtain permission to expand its lending operations to non-farm activities in rural areas. In 1993, a first window was opened when BAAC was allowed to provide loans for farm-related activities and, as a second step in early 1999, the government approved amendment to the BAAC Act. GTZ, as part of its technical cooperation with BAAC, was helping the bank to develop a system for non-farm lending and to conduct testing in selected branches.

BAAC has generated positive returns on assets and equity throughout the 36 years of operations. During this time BAAC has been able to cross-subsidise its lending business with interest income from investments and, more recently, from fee-based income and has managed to maintain its overall profitability. BAAC has benefited from various types of hidden incentives and indirect subsidies, such as an exemption from minimum reserve requirements and income tax.

Since 1998 it has been evident that the financial crisis in Thailand has not left BAAC unaffected and consequently matters concerning prudential regulation by the central bank and diversifying into non-agricultural lending have become serious issues. In 2003, the MoF as supervisor and owner decided that BAAC should implement more realistic provisioning rules to ensure the long-term sustainability of its operations.

Governance, Ownership and Interventions

BAAC is categorised as a so-called specialised bank providing financial services in rural areas. Ownership has hitherto largely remained with the government. More than 99 per cent of the shares in the Bank are held by the Ministry of Finance, with the balance mainly in the hands of agricultural cooperatives.

BAAC operates under the supervision of the Ministry of Finance, as do all other SFIs, while the commercial banks are supervised by the Bank of Thailand (BoT). The State Audit Office, a government agency, performs the annual external audit. In addition, BAAC's performance is annually assessed by the Thai Rating and Information Service (TRIS) within a framework designed for state-owned enterprises which focuses on five aspects (operational effectiveness and efficiency, stakeholder issues, management, organisational development, good governance).

BAAC has an internal audit department for the ongoing financial and management audit of its operations. Periodic reports from the provincial and branch offices are channeled to BAAC's senior management in order to monitor the sources and uses of funds.

BAAC is governed by a fifteen-member Board of Directors. The Board controls the policies and business operations of the Bank. The composition of the Board is outlined in the BAAC Act of 1966 to include representatives of the Prime Minister's Office, the Ministry of Finance, Ministry of Agriculture and Cooperatives, Cooperative Promotion Department, the Agricultural Land Reform Office, the Bank of Thailand and one representative from the agricultural cooperatives. The president of BAAC is an ex-officio member of the Board. The Finance Minister is officially the chairman of the Board, but the Deputy Finance Minister is assigned to act on his behalf. In general, the Board comprises mainly public officials representing the interests of the government.

The composition of the Board has several important implications. First, it implies a primarily short-term agenda, which may not support the long-term objectives of financial health and sustainability of the institution. Second, major internal policies are based on well-intended and general development considerations, rather than financial business principles. Third, due to its highly emphasised policy status as the major agricultural arm of the government, BAAC has to accommodate the particular interests of ministries and government agencies by implementing a considerable number of 'special projects', in addition to its regular lending operations.[4]

Such 'development projects/programmes' have often had a negative impact on the financial viability of the Bank. In response, BAAC has adopted a strategy of 'interventions against compensations' through negotiations with the government and members of parliament. The latest and most significant programme implemented through BAAC was debt suspension for all borrowers with an outstanding loan of less than Baht 100,000 (US$ 2,300) with BAAC. Under the programme, borrowers who choose the debt suspension are permitted to suspend loan principal and interest payments for three years.

The government compensates BAAC for the interest payments not made. Borrowers under the debt suspension programme cannot borrow from BAAC during the three-year period. The government expects the policy to boost the purchasing power of those given temporary relief from loan repayment. When farmer borrowers join the programme, they are supervised and helped by the committee to improve and restructure their operations. The programme was launched at the beginning of 2001. About 50 per cent of eligible farmers opted for debt relief and their suspended loans accounted for around 21 per cent of BAAC's total loan portfolio. Borrowers who opted out of the programme are entitled to a privilege card—a mark of their good credit standing. This is a powerful incentive to keep up the discipline of the credit system, while ensuring that those in real need of debt relief have an option. The debt suspension has definitely been an obstacle on BAAC's path towards viability and poses a potential threat to its long-term sustainability. An increase in the reserves by BAAC became unavoidable.

In the past, government interventions were mainly confined to policy level, ensuring that the operational level enjoyed a high degree of autonomy. BAAC has managed to resist the pressure from political interest groups as well as interference from local governments with regard to borrower selection and lending decisions. However, the government-directed debt suspension programme in 2001 affects the autonomous nature of BAAC's operations. BAAC thoroughly monitors the existing status of debt suspension and has established adequate reserves in an effort to prepare its 'firewall' for any eventual moral hazard.

By 2004, the Ministry of Finance and the Bank of Thailand had implemented new prudential measures on the basis of Basel II for BAAC.

Major Restructuring Initiated by Policy Changes Lead to Remarkable Results

One of the core elements of BAAC's reform process has been the fundamental restructuring of the sources of funds. The restructuring of the liability side progressed over a period of 30 years.

In its early years, BAAC operated almost exclusively with government funds. The major share (about 60 %) came as equity contribution and a minor share (about 20 %) was in the form of a special credit facility on preferential terms from BoT.

Ten years later (1975-1987), mandatory deposits from commercial banks were the major source of funds (about 40 %), following the agricultural credit policy issued in 1975. At the same time, BAAC started borrowing from international financial agencies, which made this source the second most important (about 30 %) in the 1980s. Finally, deposit mobilisation from the general public started to gain importance towards the end of the 80s. In 1987, deposits mobilised by BAAC already accounted for one-fourth of BAAC's funds.[5]

The period from 1988-2001 brought another major change in the funding structure. During this time, BAAC made deposit mobilisation a major activity of its banking operations and, consequently, deposits mainly from the rural areas evolved into the single most important source of funds. The liberalisation of the agricultural credit policy caused commercial banks to reduce their mandatory deposits with BAAC, which led to a substantial stimulation to BAAC's savings mobilisation efforts. While borrowings fell to a low of 4.6 per cent in 2003, BAAC suffered considerable losses as a result of exchange rate fluctuations associated with foreign loans and adopted a more cautious stance towards borrowings from abroad.

By 2003, BAAC's source of funds consisted of only 4.6 per cent from borrowings, which is divided into 28 per cent from foreign loans (JBIC) and 72 per cent from local borrowings.

In the last 13 years, BAAC has become increasingly self-reliant in financial terms and has been able to significantly reduce its dependence on government funds, mandatory deposits from commercial banks and loans from domestic and foreign sources.

In just a decade, the deposit-to-loan ratio doubled to 100 per cent in 2003.

Since 1995 GTZ has been supporting this major restructuring process at BAAC by jointly planning and implementing a savings mobilisation strategy, savings product development and a savings delivery system.

Policy Changes Lead to Innovations in Financial Service Delivery

Savings Mobilization: During the first twenty years of operations, BAAC concentrated almost exclusively on credit services while savings—as in many agricultural development banks elsewhere—largely remained the 'forgotten half' of rural finance. In the early years, BAAC implemented a compulsory savings scheme for borrowers, requiring each borrower to deposit an amount equivalent to 5 per cent of the loan value in a savings account. The scheme was costly to administer, and was terminated in 1979.

Only since the mid-1980s has BAAC recognised the importance of voluntary savings mobilisation, not only from its own perspective of deposits as a stable and reliable source of funds, but also from the viewpoint of its rural clients, who need safe, liquid and convenient deposit facilities. The Bank realised that there is a strong demand for deposit facilities, especially among farm households that are forced to synchronise income and expenditure in the course of the agricultural production cycle. Furthermore, savings act as a buffer against the uncertainty governing the rural economy. In the wake of unforeseen events and emergencies, financial savings perform a basic insurance function.[6]

Over the, past decade, the Bank has campaigned effectively to mobilise rural savings. The branches were instructed to set annual mobilisation targets, and savings mobilisation became one of the major criteria for evaluating branch performance. As a result, BAAC has achieved remarkable success in deposit mobilisation. Deposits from the general public grew at average annual rates of 17 per cent and increased from only Baht seven billion (US$ 280 million) in 1986 to more than Baht 321 billion (US$ 7.3 billion) in March 2004.

Demand-Oriented Savings Products: In 1995, BAAC introduced an innovative savings product, called *Om Sap Thawi Choke* or 'Save and Get a Chance', primarily targeted at the low-income market. This product was developed by BAAC Savings Promotion Division together with the GTZ-supported Microfinance Linkage Project. The minimum opening deposit is only Baht 50 (US$ 1.15) and, although the interest rate of 0.75 per cent (2002) paid on deposits is one per cent below the standard rate, BAAC pays for savings accounts, and the account holder is entitled to participate in semi-annual tombola-drawing parties offering goods popular in rural areas as prizes. After successful pilot testing in selected branches, the product was launched nationwide in early 1996 and, by the end of 2003, had attracted more than 2.5 million depositors with an average deposit of Baht 3,800 per account holder (US$ 87).

The most recent product introduced in 1997, with the objective of attracting medium-term funds is the BAAC Savings Bond (Thawi Sin). The savings bonds have a nominal value of Baht 500 (US$ 11.40) each and a term of three years. The three-year bonds carry an interest rate of only 1.33 per cent per annum (2002) but—as a compensation for the low yield—bond holders participate in a highly publicised prize draw at the national level.

More than 75 per cent of BAAC's deposits are generated mainly through four core products, which include the two mentioned above. The two other products are Time Deposits and Passbook Savings.

Institutional deposits are made up of a relatively small number of accounts with large amounts. They are held in both savings and fixed deposits on an almost equal balance. Furthermore, institutional deposit accounts are subject to considerable fluctuations, depending on budget allocations and expenditures, which exposes the Bank to a considerable liquidity risk.

Table 4.1: Change in BAAC's Sources of Funds Structure, 1967-2001 (%)

	1967	*1973*	*1980*	*1987*	*1993*	*1998*	*2001*	*2003*
Deposits from the public	11	17	12	25	48	62	76	83
Mandatory deposits from CBs	—	—	39	39	7	1	—	—
Borrowings	19	22	35	29	32	25	13	4.6
Shareholders' equity	66	57	12	6	8	7	7	8.4
Other liabilities	4	4	2	1	5	5	5	4
Total	100	100	100	100	100	100	100	100
Deposit-to-loan ratio	14	19	21	38	66	83	98	100

Deposits from individuals have generally been much more stable. More than 90 per cent of deposits from private individuals were held in simple savings accounts including *Om Sap Thawi Choke,* a pattern typical of rural customers. The number of savings accounts increased from 4.1 million in 1994 to 9.5 million in 2002—an increase of about one million savings accounts a year.

The size distribution of savings accounts by number and volume reveals a considerable concentration. The vast majority (97%) of the savings accounts have a balance of less than Baht 50,000 (US$ 1,140). This may indicate that the majority of BAAC depositors belong to the lower-income segment. However, these accounts generate 36 per cent of the deposit volume, while a few large depositors (slightly above 10,000 clients or 0.1 per cent in 2002) account for 24 per cent of the volume.

Service-Oriented Mindset

BAAC pays attention to the quality of its service and continuously stresses the importance of a service-oriented-mindset among its work force. This emphasis reaped positive results in the TRIS (Thai Rating and Information Services) annual performance appraisal: 90-95 per cent of BAAC's clients appreciate the Bank's services. The annual TRIS evaluation is a tool used by the MoF to control BAAC's overall quantitative and qualitative performance. Client satisfaction is highly valued and assessed every year. One should bear in mind that the TRIS evaluation result impacts on BAAC staff remuneration. The 'BAAC Service Culture' which is an Organisational Development Intervention has become internalised in the entire bank as a permanent subject. It has been progressively developed further. While the initial focus was only on behaviour, it has more recently also encompassed competency such as product and customer knowledge. Although BAAC has hundreds of products, as is the case with the financial products of many other banks in the world, the so-called Pareto rule also applies to BAAC: about 20 per cent of the products and services generate almost 80 per cent of the business. That explains the focus on the products that account for the 20 per cent, as they enhance profitability and efficiency.

BAAC has an outreach (direct and indirect) of 92 per cent (2001) to rural families. The more direct outreach is that 46 per cent of the rural families in Thailand have one active BAAC borrower. In every rural household, there is a BAAC savings account. BAAC holds a market share of 34 per cent of rural deposits (Table 4.2) and 5.5 per cent on a nationwide basis[7].

Table 4.2: Customer Orientation

	1999	2000	2001
Number of loan products	—	2	2
Number of savings products	5	5	5
Number of other financial services	—	5	5
Loan Portfolio			
Number of active borrowers (000's) of which rural borrowers (000's)	2,686	2,676	2,738
	2,685	2,676	2,738
Number of accounts (000's)	4,556	4,281	4,413
Outstanding gross portfolio in US$ (000's)	6,257,975	6,007,649	6,120,851
Average outstanding loan balance in US$	1,345	1,355	1,321
Average outstanding loan size/per capita income in %	66.7	64.9	62.5
Average loan processing time	2 weeks	2 weeks	2 weeks
Percentage of rural population served	8.7	8.5	8.5
Savings Portfolio			
Number of savings accounts (000's)	8,298	8,633	9,570
Portfolio size in US$ (000's)	2,036,458	1,960,920	2,586,757
Average deposit balance in US$ (000's)	245	227	270
Average deposit balance/per capita income in per cent	12.2	10.9	12.8
Percentage of rural population served	27	27	29

Source: BAAC.

Branches Become Profit Centres

Profitability—expressed by return on assets (ROA)—is becoming an important criterion for measuring branch performance. In 1997, BAAC introduced the transfer price mechanism. Transfer price is the internal interest rate applied on funds transferred between the branches and the head office. When a branch requires funds for its lending operations, it borrows from the head office and is charged the transfer price, and *vice versa*: when a branch mobilises savings and deposits, then head office pays, based on the transfer price. In principle, the transfer price is set by the management in accordance with the market cost of funds. It can also be used as an important policy instrument.

BAAC with the support of GTZ and the German Bankakademie has introduced a new Branch Management Information System (BMIS) in all its branches. It provides a complete framework for managing a branch network, based on a decentralised branch-controlling concept. This new BMIS includes monthly provisioning, transfer pricing and realistic cost allocations for the branches. This instrument supports the head office with its central treasury department and the branches in implementing the overall bank strategy.

The fully computerised Branch Management Information System (BMIS) has been operational since early 2003.

Government-Secured Tending *Versus* Viable Credit Products

Government-Secured Lending: In addition to its normal lending business, BAAC grants a large number of government-secured loans or so-called 'special agricultural development projects and policy lending programmes'. There are around 200 'special projects and programmes', some nationwide, some of them regionally concentrated. However, these special projects entail a heavy workload. First results from the decentralised branch controlling (BMIS) indicate that they are loss-making products. Moreover, they divert the attention of credit officers from their mainstream lending activities. Most special lending programmes supported by government departments carry preferential interest rates, which have occasionally caused some confusion among clients. BAAC is compensated by the government in the form of fees and interest compensation. 'Special loans' with its old supply-driven approach or 'old paradigm' accounted for 7.3 per cent of the total net loans in 2003.

A research study conducted in 1996 by the well-known TDRI (Thai Development Research Institute) confirmed the following:

- Loans under government-secured lending programmes do not reach the poor farmers for whom they were designed, but rather the better off and more informed farmers who know the officers of the Agricultural Extension Service.
- Subsidised loans are not tailored to the needs of poor

farmers, because they are designed by agricultural department officials who think they know what is best for poor farmers.

- Most government-secured or subsidised loans create moral hazard or unwillingness to repay the loan. This results in low repayment performance. These subsidised loans also create confusion among other BAAC borrowers.

Shift from Wholesale to Retail Lending

The initial success of direct lending to farmer clients organised in small Joint Liability Groups on the one hand and the problems experienced in lending to agricultural cooperatives on the other caused a shift in the lending policy in the late 70s. BAAC decided to focus mainly on retail lending to farmer clients. From the founding of BAAC until today, the share of wholesale lending through cooperatives dropped from 70 per cent to only six per cent in 2003.

Client Orientation Through Credit Technology

The development of the Joint Liability Groups concept dates back to the founding of BAAC in 1966. As few Thai farmers had land title documents to use as collateral in the 60s, BAAC adopted joint liability as the principle form of security for small loans. Joint liability has been at the heart of the BAAC's lending ever since.

Joint Liability Groups are formed by people who know and trust each other. They vary in size from a minimum of five to a maximum of 30 and usually average about 15 members. In general, Joint Liability Groups are primarily client groups and not what is normally understood as Self Help Groups with organisation and administration. BAAC Joint Liability Groups do not function as financial intermediaries. Individual loans up to Baht 150,000 (US$ 3,400) are granted on the basis of joint liability. Loans above this amount must be secured by tangible collateral, usually through mortgage of land and buildings.

All transactions are conducted between BAAC and the individual members; the group leader has no role in disbursements or recovery of loans and is responsible for distributing repayment notes and reminding the members of their obligations.

Since in the more recent years the majority of the BAAC borrowers earn income from agricultural and non-agricultural activities, the loan assessment has to be in line with the total household cashflow of the borrower and not just follow agricultural harvesting schedules.

BAAC's New Market Segment—Cashflow-Based Lending

For many years, BAAC has tried hard to secure an amendment to the 1966 Act and to obtain permission to expand its lending operations to non-farm activities in rural areas. While a first window was opened in 1993, when BAAC was allowed to provide loans for farm-related activities, as a second step, in the beginning of 1999, the government approved amendment to the BAAC Act. This allowed the expansion of lending operations into non-farm activities for farmers—up to 20 per cent of the total portfolio. BAAC with the support of GTZ has developed a system and a credit product for cashflow-based lending which is in line with the total household cashflow of the borrower. In 2003, the Thai cabinet decided that BAAC was a Rural Development Bank and no longer restricted to agricultural lending.

IV. CONCLUSIONS

Although BAAC is now self-sufficient in its source of funds, and subsidised credit programmes have dwindled, elements of the old and the new paradigm coexist. At the Sri Lanka Conference, on "The Challenge of Sustainable Outreach: How can Public Banks Contribute to Outreach in Rural Areas?" there was evidence that the 'paradigm shift' in rural and microfinance—in particular after the financial crisis—is becoming increasingly evident in Thailand. BAAC is now focusing on economic viability and sustainability, as well as on the outreach of financial services.

BAAC has managed to resist the pressure exerted by political interest groups as well as interference from local government with regard to borrower selection and lending decisions. The government-directed debt suspension programme in 2001, however, affects the autonomy of BAAC's operations. BAAC thoroughly monitors the existing status of debt suspension and has established adequate reserves in an effort to prepare its 'firewall' for any eventual moral hazard.

In the wake of the financial crisis, an important and positive change was initiated in October 1998 when the government decided in principle to place BAAC under the prudential regulation of the BoT. Prudential regulations and banking standards in line with international standards set out in the Basel Agreement have been developed by the BoT to take effect in the new Thai Banking Law. An on-going dialogue with the Ministry of Finance about the preparation of prudential measures has been concluded and the measures implemented.

The implementation of the decentralised branch controlling system, with its BMIS, is a strong tool to delegate more responsibilities and accountability to branch managers and is a step in the right direction. BAAC knows the financial performance of each of its core products. Moreover, the bank knows that government-secured loans are loss-making for BAAC. This leads to a more appropriate compensation through the government.

Streamlining all BAAC products by identifying the most important ones or core products is a positive step towards accelerating product knowledge and cross-selling among staff.

Reform processes at the BAAC are gradually on-going over a period of 36 years, which is very different from other Agricultural Banks where reforms are implemented quick and massive. At times, the reform processes in the BAAC move slowly, but gain momentum in other periods. In terms of focus and content, reform processes have been directed at the transition from agricultural credit to rural microfinance and at the institutional transformation of BAAC from a specialised credit institution to a diversified rural bank. The gradual diversification of financial services is a clear indication of this evolution.[8]

The BAACs pro-active rural savings mobilisation has caused revolutionary changes to the financial resource base. The BAAC has become financially self-reliant and has significantly reduced its dependence and cut down on loans from domestic and foreign sources. In just a decade, the deposit-to-liability ratio has reached 83 per cent, and the deposit-to-loan ratio 100 per cent. This can be assessed as an outstanding result.

The BAAC has developed a fundamental eagerness for cost effectiveness, productivity and efficiency. BAAC's management pays constant attention to branch performance. The delegation of authority and responsibility to managers at all levels and the implementation of profit centres in the branches contribute to this achievement.

V. WHAT LESSONS CAN BE LEARNT?

Political Interventions and Government-Subsidised Loans

Populist political interventions carry a high prize for governments and must be compensated by those who initiate them. A government has to be thoughtful in initiating relevant policies that meet the needs of the lower income groups. The providers of financial services must operate in a sustainable manner and refrain from wasting scarce taxpayers money and depleting their own funding base. Governments should not underestimate the risk of moral hazard which some interventions can cause for a very long time.

Of interest in the Indian context could be the finding of the TDRI research, confirming that loans under the government-secured lending programmes do not reach the poor farmers for whom they were designed, but rather the better off and more informed farmers who know the officers of the Agricultural Extension Service. The subsidised loans are not tailored to the needs of the poor farmers, because they are designed by officials who think they know what is best for poor farmers. Most of the subsidised loans create moral hazard or an unwillingness to repay, which is resulting in low repayment performance.

A decentralised branch controlling system or BMIS can become a powerful tool which is essential for a financial institution in its negotiations with governments when it comes to presenting the government with a bill for intervention.

The Painful Lesson of Borrowing from Abroad

The experience of borrowing from abroad has been mixed. BAAC was required to take on the foreign exchange risk on most of the loans and, as a consequence, suffered substantial losses due to exchange rate fluctuations. The losses were severe in the wake of the financial crisis and the devaluation of the Thai currency when half of the bank's equity was wiped out. This was a painful lesson.

Relevance of a Favourable Macro-Economic Environment

A stable macro-economic environment, including favourable growth rates, low inflation rates and positive interest rates on (small) savings, poverty reduction strategies, good road infrastructure and bank branch network are of relevance for the growth of sustainable rural finance and microfinance.

BMIS or Branch Controlling System

The new Branch Management Information System (BMIS) in all BAAC branches provides a complete framework for managing a branch network, based on a decentralised branch-controlling concept. This new BMIS includes monthly provisioning, transfer pricing and realistic cost allocations for the branches. This instrument supports the head office with its central treasury department and the branches in implementing the overall bank strategy. The fully computerised BMIS can also be implemented on a manual basis. BMIS could be interesting for the Indian banking sector, as it enables branch managers to manage their branches in a timely and effective manner. Simultaneously it can also be used by the management of a bank's head office to insert its policies efficiently.

Successful Mobilisation of Small Savings Leads to a Revolutionary Change of the Funding Structure

Demand-driven approaches to rural financial services offer opportunities for success. There is a large demand for savings facilities in rural areas, so that the self-financing of rural lending is entirely possible. Safety and convenience rather than high interest rates are the main concerns of potential depositors. The success in small savings mobilisation is rooted in BAACs ability to provide a balanced combination of what small savers want and need: safety, convenience, liquidity and positive yields. BAAC has successfully addressed these four elements in its savings mobilisation. An accelerated and voluntary savings mobilisation in the rural areas could also be of interest in India, especially in the context of upgrading SHG members or when they require a more flexible liquidity arrangement. Accelerated and voluntary savings mobilisation could also be an important source of funds for a financially healthy credit cooperative structure.

The Joint Liability Group Concept—A Low Cost Credit Delivery System

The BAAC experience of more than three decades with the Joint Liability Group concept as the core credit product of the bank deserves attention. In the past, few Thai farmers had land title documents to use as collateral, which is why BAAC adopted joint liability as the principle form of security for small loans. Joint Liability, which has been at the heart of the BAAC's lending since 1966, is a highly cost-efficient credit delivery model and has contributed substantially to BAAC's remarkable outreach. The majority of BAAC's borrowers are served through Joint Liability Groups. The concept of Joint Liability could become a viable alternative to the SHG Linkage Banking in India.

Cashflow-Based Lending—A New Credit Delivery System for Small Borrowers

The cashflow-based lending technology is BAAC's latest credit delivery system and is geared very much to its future. This credit product corresponds fully with the cashflow of the small enterprise/small farmer combined with his/her household, as 90 per cent of the rural borrowers have income from agriculture and non-agriculture. This relatively new BAAC credit product suits the changes in rural Thai society, which is no longer just agriculture based. Income from non-agricultural sources plays a more significant role while 'rural' and 'urban' are coming closer. Cashflow-based lending calls for substantial capacity building, as it brings about a change from stereotypical agricultural lending to a more need-oriented cashflow-based lending. In the Indian context, there are important similarities to the Kisan Credit Card. This is where the capacity building of the BAAC cashflow-based lending could be studied.

Connecting Qualitative and Quantitative Performance to Remuneration

Total performance-based evaluations like the TRIS in Thailand are impacting on staff remuneration. A possible option could be to build in performance indicators for government-owned banks which have an influence on staff remuneration.

Joint Cooperation Results in Significant Leverage

The BAAC-GTZ cooperation in the context of microfinance has served as a laboratory for developing and testing innovative features, products and approaches in selected branches. This cooperation has shown high leverage in supporting BAAC in its savings mobilisation, improving staff competence, developing a decentralised branch controlling system and the system and instruments for cashflow-based lending.

NOTES

1. BAAC has a direct or indirect outreach covering 92 per cent of the farm households in Thailand.
2. Bank Indonesia-GTZ High Level Policy Meeting on Micro and Rural Finance in Asia, Yogjakarta, Indonesia, February 26-28, 2004.
3. The Thai-German Microfinance Linkage Project supported BAAC in its savings mobilisation efforts.
4. Maurer, Klaus. *Rural Finance.* Working Paper No. B 6, IFAD.
5. Haberberger, Marie-Luise; Wajananawat, Luck; Kuasukul, Nipath. January 2003. *The challenge of Sustainable Outreach* (GTZ/BAAC), the *Case of the Bank for Agriculture and Agricultural Cooperatives* (BAAC), Thailand.
6. Maurer, Klaus. *Rural Finance.* Working Paper No. B 6, IFAD.
7. Haberberger, Marie-Luise; Wajananawat, Luck; Kuasukul, Nipath. January 2003. *The Challenge of Sustainable Outreach*(GTZ/BAAC), the *Case of the Bank for Agriculture and Agricultural Cooperatives (BAAC),* Thailand.
8. Maurer, Klaus: *Rural Finance,* Working Paper No. B 6, IFAD.

REFERENCES

BAAC, *Annual Reports,* various issues.

Bank Indonesia and GTZ, (February 2004). Proceedings of the High Level Policy Meeting on Microfinance and Rural Finance in Asia. Yogjakarta, Indonesia.

Bank of Thailand, (2002). Economic and Financial Statistics.

Haberberger, Marie-Luise; Wajananawat, Luck. Various publications in the Bangkok Post from 1999 to 2002.

Haberberger, Marie-Luise; Wajananawat, Luck; Kuasukul, Nipath (2003). *The Challenge of Sustainable Outreach, the Case of the Bank for Agriculture* and *Agricultural Cooperatives (BAAC).*

Maurer, K. (1999). *Rural Finance,* Working Paper (1999) No. B 6, Draft for IFAD.

Thailand Development Research Institute Foundation (TDRI), 1998.

The Rural Finance in Thailand, 1996.

World Bank, (May 2002). *Economic Monitor,* Thailand.

Yaron, J. (1992). *Assessing Development Finance Institutions: A Public Interest Analysis.* World Bank Discussion Paper No. 174.

Yaron, J. (1992a). *Successful Rural Finance Institutions.* World Bank Discussion Paper No. 150.

5

Andhra's Women SHGs: Participatory Poverty Alleviation*

JOY DESHMUKH RANADIVE

I. INTRODUCTION/IMPLEMENTATION PROCESS

This case study focuses on Andhra Pradesh, India, where state initiative has extensively used the 'self-help group' (SHG) as a tool of poverty alleviation and empowerment. A SHG is a small group of persons who come together with the intention of finding a solution to a common problem with a degree of self-sufficiency.[1] Within development initiatives, SHGs can be formed around various issues related to livelihoods and resources. One sees groups around watershed management, forest management, livelihood generation, etc. However, largely, the SHG is the conduit through which *micro credit* is routed to the poor in the belief that it will prove catalytic in helping them to pull out of poverty.[2] Andhra Pradesh is the fifth largest state in India, with a population of 76 million, of which three-fourths live in the 26,500 rural villages. According to the Survey of the Ninth Five Year Plan (1997-2002) carried out by the Government of Andhra Pradesh (GoAP), the state is among the poorest in India with many indicators below the national level. Income poverty has been reduced in the second half of the 90s but at a slower rate compared to the rest of the country. On the positive side, Andhra Pradesh has been pursuing economic reforms to step up growth and alleviate poverty.

---

* From the paper originally prepared for the World Bank under the guidance of Dr. Deepa Narayan, Senior Adviser, World Bank.

Significant strides have been made in participatory management of land, water and forest resources.

It is within this state of India that the SHG has constituted a primary route towards poverty alleviation and development. Both state and NGO initiative have recognized the value of forming small groups of poor people who have a common desire to generate livelihood options. Further, micro credit is seen as the key to unlock the poverty trap. SHGs are also supposed to empower women. Currently Andhra Pradesh has mobilized and organized 48 lakh poor women in the rural areas into 3.7 lakh groups. These women's groups have built up a corpus fund of Rs. 750 crores consisting of their savings, borrowings from banks and revolving funds from government programmes. The major poverty alleviation project through which SHGs are promoted is the state-sponsored *Velugu*[3], working in over 860 *mandals*[4] in 22 districts, aiming to reach 29 lakhs of the poorest of rural poor.

Upscaling with Innovation

In Andhra Pradesh, the use of SHGs to route and implement poverty alleviation programmes has to be seen as an evolution over time of government initiative, national and state, as well as NGO efforts. The evolution goes back to 1979, with the national implementation of the Integrated Rural Development Programme (IRDP), that targeted the poorest of the poor, under which as a sub-component in 1982-83, the Government of India (GoI) started the Development of Women and Children in Rural Areas programme (DWCRA).[5] The aim of this programme was to provide self-employment, empower and incorporate rural poor women into the development process. Under DWCRA, women living in neighbourhoods with similar socio-economic background formed SHGs of 25 members each, to choose and collectively undertake one economic activity suited for their skills and resources. Groups were provided with a maximum matching grant of Rs. 15,000 to be used as a revolving fund to undertake the group's economic activity, which was increased to Rs. 25,000 in 1994-95.[6] Besides money, DWCRA SHGs received training and their products were also distributed to *Bazaars*, providing them an opportunity to access diverse markets.

In spite of well-formulated designs, however, when

implemented, programmes do not always fit the requirements of the field. Gaps need to be ascertained and modifications made to make them more meaningful. The district of Ananthpur proved exemplary in this context. DWCRA was being criticized for being too rigid in its stipulations, since groups had to have a minimum of 25 persons that wanted to undertake the same activity. This was, first, difficult to find, and second, it was problematic for the village to absorb the production of 25 persons conducting the same activity. Further the guidelines were rigid requiring that the money be used only for the activity that the group conducts. The administration of Anantapur made three modifications in an attempt to salvage the programme. The size of the group was reduced, people from other castes and communities were permitted to join the same groups and different economic activities were pursued within the same group. This, however, caused a problem in that, the homogeneity of background and economic activity, which had initially formed a cementing factor, was no longer present. Hence an alternate binding force was introduced through thrift and savings in women SHGs. Between the late eighties and early nineties, this programme picked up in momentum and was also upscaled to the extent that it covered 30,000 women, which constituted almost one fourth of the poor women in Anantapur.[7] Over time, DWCRA groups all over the state were strengthened.

Government initiative and sponsorship of SHGs link more recently to what are called the SAPAP SHG groups. In 1996, the South Asia Poverty Alleviation *Programme* (SAPAP) a pilot project was conducted in three districts of Andhra Pradesh.[8] The programme has covered 66,000 households, who constitute 34 per cent of the total households of the project area and 64 per cent of the total target group households. Subsequent to the success of SAPAP, the processes in Andhra Pradesh have generated a successive upscaling of SHG promotion. The GoAP incorporated the 'social mobilization approach' into its major poverty reduction project, *Velugu* comprising in the first phase of the Andhra Pradesh District Poverty Initiatives Project (APDPIP), a 5 year project (2000-2005) being implemented in the six poorest districts in the state—Adilabad, Mahbubnagar, Anantapur, Chittoor, Srikakulam and Vizianagaram.[9] Given its success in the first phase, the government has rolled out the second phase of *Velugu*—Andhra Pradesh Rural Poverty Reduction Project—APRPRP in the remaining 16 districts of the state. The new phase started in 2003 and is designed to last 5 years, reaching approximately 550 disadvantaged *mandals* in the remaining 16 districts of the state.[10]

Upscaling through Institution Building

The upscaling of SHGs in Andhra Pradesh has been both in terms of numbers as also in terms of structure. GoAP established an independent support organization by the name of—"Society for Elimination of Rural Poverty" (SERP) to implement poverty elimination projects which aim at social mobilization to enhance livelihoods and employment generation opportunities of the poor. This organisation forms a bridge between the government and people and is in the nature of a government NGO (GONGO). It is simultaneously autonomous to oversee *Velugu*, even whilst originating from the government.[11]

Institutional structural building has taken the shape of forming new edifices. The SAPAP project focused upon the creation of self-managed grassroot level institutions of the poor, namely (CIGs), such as Self Help Groups, Village Organisations (VOs), and *Mandal* Samakhyas (MSs). 5,201 SHGs have further been federated into 380 VOs at the village level. The *Mandal* Mahila Samakhya (MMS), the apex body of VOs at the *mandal* level, plays a crucial, supporting role in sustaining the VOs.[12] Federations provide an organizational identity to SHGs that, while crucial for sustainability, is difficult for small organizations such as the SHGs to develop. Federating helps SHGs realize benefits of a larger organization, without losing the advantages of small organization.[13] Federations of SHGs are fast becoming powerful voices expressing the social and economic needs of the poor.[14]

DPIP continued with the three-tier system similar to that in SAPAP. SHGs, are the basic organization entities. The VO comprises the SHGs of a village (8 to 10 groups) and their task is to address their common issues. VOs are also in charge of training SHG members in areas such as book-keeping and management. MMS are the highest federated entity of *Velugu* and gathers the VOs together. Its task is to monitor the VOs, contact the government, VOs and the SHGs in case of a particular need, audit SHGs and also help with micro finance. *Velugu* phase two is expected to cover 548 *mandals*, 2,000,000 families, 187,5000 SHGs,

15,000VOs and 500 MSS. Currently, the project has organized and strengthened about 99,000 self help groups in 316 *Mandals* in the six Districts. It has formed federated organizations of SHGs including 6126 VOs and 201 MSs.

Capacity building is an important component in the upscaling of Andhra Pradesh's poverty alleviation initiatives. RPRP is being implemented in 563 *Mandals* in sixteen districts, covering 25000 habitations. 212 villages in the coastal regions have been taken up for institution building where fishing is the most important livelihood source. Capacity building support has been extended to 77637 SHGs throughout the state. In order to strengthen existing SHGs, the project is promoting the use of animators to provide facilitation support to members and leaders and develop linkages with banks and other institutions. District Resource Teams are to support these animators. 165 District Resource Persons have been selected and trained in participatory training methods, SHG formation and strengthening, book keeping and financial management.[15] The focus in the initial phase has also been on building the capacity of the project staff. The project has conducted training needs assessment for all categories of staff in all districts and conducted many training programmes for District Programme Managers (DPMs), Community Coordinators and trainers of support organizations in seven districts. 292 of the proposed 460 *Mandal Velugu* Training Centres have been set up.

Using the Economic Environment

Just as the political environment of the state of Andhra Pradesh was conducive to the upscaling of SHGs, the overall national economic environment has played a pivotal role in the spread of micro credit to the rural poor. The primary aim of the SHG-Bank linkage programme in India is to integrate informal savings and credit groups with mainstream banking by providing them with credit to enhance their fund base. Once an SHG has demonstrated its capacity to sustain and to absorb outside credit loans are extended to it from the formal banking structure. The state of Andhra Pradesh is at the forefront of the SHG-Bank Linkage Programme with close to 40 per cent of the cumulative bank linkages. A total of 281,338 groups have been linked with banks in Andhra Pradesh until March 2003 with loans for Rs. 9,753 millions, equivalent to U$ 212 millions approximately. In terms of bank participation, in the state of Andhra Pradesh, 62 per cent of the loans were provided by commercial banks during the period 2002-2003, 36 per cent by regional rural banks, and the remaining 2 per cent by cooperative banks.[16]

It is important to understand how at the national level, the wisdom of using existing financial infrastructure to meet the needs of micro credit initiatives has saved on duplication and transaction costs and has also been instrumental in changing perceptions about the credit worthiness of the poor. Even though by 1994 there were 5000 SHGs linked with banks through the National Bank for Agriculture and Rural Development (NABARD) throughout the country, NABARD was not absolutely convinced that SHGs were the main path to follow in the provision of micro finance to the rural poor. Subsequently, one of the reasons why NABARD was finally convinced to support SHGs, was to avoid the creation of a parallel institution to deal with micro finance. There is already a large existing network of commercial, rural and cooperative banks in India of 160,000 retail outlets permitting 99 per cent of the population of in country to have a branch within 5 km of their village.

In 1992, in Andhra Pradesh, NABARD started partnering with SHG promoters (State and NGO) and banks marking the beginnings of the linkage programme in the state. *However, the scale was still small.* DWCRA groups were weak as micro credit users and NABARD along with the GOAP, took the initiative of strengthening these groups along their guidelines to incorporate them into the SHGs-linkage programme. Over time, DWCRA SHGs improved, yet banks, provided only savings accounts and did not see credit as a possible service to them. Organizing the poor into groups has reduced the transaction costs of a very atomized demand. However, the perceived "limited and risky market opportunities in the rural areas clouded bankers' minds" and on that front NABARD played a key role, convincing them that the endeavour was profitable.

From the year 2000, DPIP and RPRP have provided NABARD with a big platform for the expansion of the SHGs-Bank linkage. Even so, conceptually, the SHG promoted by NABARD is slightly different to the one promoted by the APDPIP RPRP. This is because, NABARD is a development agency and it emphasizes rural development treating empowerment and the rest of the social issues as a by-product of the scheme. Again, NABARD seeks providing access to credit to all those that live in the rural areas and not necessarily only to the poor. Instead, DPIP and RPRP are poverty alleviation programmes that use micro finance as a tool to pull out of poverty, which is understood in its various dimensions including economic situation, empowerment, risk, and so on.[17]

The Philosophy behind Social Mobilisation: Including People

Of all the methods of addressing poverty alleviation, Andhra Pradesh has chosen social mobilisation. DWCRA groups brought in savings and credit to compensate for the loss of homogeneity that took place with the Ananthpur modifications. However, the SAPAP rationale was more explicit. It was based on the premise that in Andhra Pradesh there exists an elite, who has appropriated public resources for their private and sectional gain, which has rendered the state machinery to be unaccountable, adversely affecting the poor. As individuals, the poor pay unacceptable socio-political and financial transaction costs for accessing resources from the state. Matters worsen since they are incapable of augmenting their own production capacities and whatever few gains are made, are insecure because of the random risks emanating through ill health, old age, environmental factors, and social and political oppression.[18] SAPAP saw the process of social mobilization as an institutional mechanism to facilitate the poor to interact with government machinery so that public resources and services are better accessed.

Besides mobilizing people through SHGs Andhra Pradesh has used other methods of inclusiveness. One of the most significant contributions of *Velugu* is the use of people's participatory techniques to identify the poor. Attempts at poverty alleviation will fall short if the methods used to identify the "poor' are inadequate, thereby excluding a considerable number of the vulnerable population. Under *Velugu* it was decided that the community itself should prepare a list of the poor people since they knew best who the poor in their midst's were. This method has met with success and now programmes are better directed at target populations. This is in contrast to the usual national method of identifying persons "Below the Poverty Line" (BPL) where a predetermined survey is used. This often causes misidentification and lists are not transparent or authentic. The participatory methodology of identifying the poor has been very effective in creating a transparent and inclusive methodology for community based targeting for programmes. The findings have been ratified by Gram Panchayats at the village level and many targeted development programmes are using the findings to target the poorest households. This method of identification has successively used the principle of inclusion and people's participation to generate information on the basis of which the programme is implemented.

Education, Information and Voice

Often, poverty alleviation programmes receive an impetus from an intervention that has been targeted in another direction. Efforts at augmenting education and literacy have always proved strengthening for development. This has been amply illustrated by the experience of Nellore district. During the late 80s the Government of India started a National Literacy Mission that supported district collectors to undertake a literacy campaign.[19] By the time the campaign developed, of the 2.5 million persons that lived in Nellore, 65 per cent were illiterate. About 70,000 young volunteers, from different villages of Nellore, received training to be in-charge of 10 illiterates thereby reaching a goal of 700,000 illiterates. NGOs, the private sector and political parties, worked simultaneously with the government in spreading the message of the campaign. The methodology used in the campaign made the poor look into their life, understand their situation and question impediments towards poverty alleviation.

The linkages between education, information and empowerment became overtly visible in the way awareness through the literacy campaign snowballed into the anti-*arak*[20] movement in Andhra Pradesh. Through the literacy campaign, people realized that the consumption of *arak* drained family resources and also led to domestic violence. Hence, women who were already organized around literacy decided to fight the sale of *arak*. Soon the movement spread to other villages and was publicized in the press by both communities and the state. SHGs became the channel to carry forward the voice that literacy and information gave to women. There are always forward and backward linkages between positive social change and positive economic progress. This is evident from the fact that the resources that were saved from being drained through the sale and consumption of *arak* were diverted into savings and investment for livelihood generation. The DWCRA groups were enlarged to include a 'Save a Rupee a Day' campaign and new SHGs formed under it were called Podupulakshmi groups. Between 1993 and 1995, 50,000 groups were formed within this district itself. After Nellore, Kurnool was the next district to see positive change.[21] The dynamics unleashed spread through the state and consequently received official government support.[22]

Currently too, the emphasis upon information dissemination is heavy in *Velugu*. Training and sensitization programmes are an important component of the programme. IEC (Information, Education and Communication) is to ensure a continuous dissemination of information across stakeholders. Use is to be made of diverse mediums of communication such as print as well as electronic media, local folk theatre groups and face-to-face interactions, including workshops. The Communication Strategy has two components one being 'Communication for Behavioural Change' (CBC) and the other, 'Information & Documentation' (I&D). The former aims to ensure beneficiaries are empowered and motivated to participate in their own development. It also opens channels for dialogue. The latter's objective is to ensure inter- and intra-information flows within the project and also between the project and the outside world about objectives, vision, components, finances, processes, final outcomes and impact.[23]

Livelihoods, Investment and Risk

The experience of *Velugu* Phase One imparted lessons to the second Phase. It was seen that besides group mobilization it is important to focus on livelihoods, by expanding the assets of the poor and creating economic opportunities. Further, the element of risk is critical for the survival of the poor and determines their coping capacities, hence, new ways have to be found to reduce, mitigate and manage risk.[24] The Community Investment Fund (CIF) is a step taken to incorporate these lessons into the second phase of the programme. This component supports investments in sub-projects and is implemented by the community through

SHGs/VOs etc. As the social mobilization process matures in a village, communities are encouraged to analyse their livelihood situation (both as consumers and as producers/sellers). This analysis throws up options for the community to act wherever they can. Livelihood Enhancement Action Plans (LEAPs), i.e. Village Micro-Plans are developed as sub-projects by the poor. Three types of sub-projects are promoted—Income Generation; Productive physical infrastructure; and Social development. There is a beneficiary contribution for all categories of sub-projects. The CIF share from the *Velugu* project is provided as a loan component to the members through their SHGs. Members and SHGs pay the amount back to the Village Organisation. The VO can utilize the loan repayment for a second installment of finance to the same members or they can finance new members. To augment support the sub-projects, financial support is accessed from banks and private sector and civil society partnerships are also being promoted.

Another innovation in the treatment of problems related to livelihoods is the value chain analysis. LEAP starts with the social and resource maps of the village. An analysis is made of the traded-in and traded-out items, and income and expenditure of the poor. This facilitates an analysis of the value-chain of the critical/significant livelihoods of the poor. With such an analysis, the credit system, risk and uncertainties and best practices in each of these livelihoods are captured. Infrastructure gaps, constraints and structural needs are also identified. In such manner there is an institutionalizing of a mechanism that facilitates expression of voice by the poor.

Provision is also being made to mitigate risk. The Comprehensive Insurance Package (CIP) seeks to develop a community-based delivery of life and health (hospitalization) insurance services. The CIP includes life and health insurance covers for the whole household. The pilot would cover about 15 project *mandals* and it is expected that 50 per cent of the poor households per *mandal* could be enrolled for comprehensive insurance coverage. These would comprise about 30,000 households, including about 140,000 adults and children.[25] The Comprehensive Basic Health Package (CBHP) is supposed to improve the health status of the poor through community managed preventive, promotive and quality ambulatory care and a scoping study of Weather Based Index Insurance, is to serve as an alternative to traditional crop insurance scheme.

Food security is one of the major problems of the poor. The rice credit line is a unique and pioneering programme in India carried out in the pilot phase in select DPIP areas in Andhra Pradesh. The programme came into operation with the GoAP issuing a Government Order (GO) in August 2001 providing ten thousand tonns of grade A rice to DPIP for piloting the food credit line. As per the GO, the programme is for areas declared as drought affected by the state government. In keeping with the underlying philosophy, the repayment model was left to each district to be decided based on local situation and in consultation with their community. Largely, three lending models have come to stay. In the first, rice up to 50 kg is taken and repaid in a month, in the second, rice up to one hundred kg is taken and repaid in two months. In the third, the rice money for up to one hundred kg is repaid in six months or linked to local harvest schedules.

Livelihoods and Land

Poverty and inequity in rural India is centrally linked to land ownership. Approximately 10 per cent of rural households in Andhra Pradesh are landless and another 36 per cent own less than one acre of land. Only 6 per cent of rural households own more than 5 acres of land. Inequity in land ownership reinforces traditional caste and feudal hierarchies and prevents the poor from moving out of the most debilitating poverty.[26] Andhra Pradesh has adopted substantial legislation and introduced numerous government schemes aimed at providing land to poor rural households. The overall experience has been characterized by some success. However, there is also a significant degree of failure, much of it due to incomplete or ineffective implementation. The key point here is that existing laws and programmes still offer significant scope for positive change. APRPRP makes this emphasis through the active convergence of SERP with the relevant state government departments. Attempts are made to effectively implement existing laws and programmes that offer potential for increasing the rural poor's access and rights to land. Further landless households are allowed to purchase land from willing sellers under the project's Community Investment Fund (CIF).

Partnerships: Including NGOs

One branch of evolution of savings groups in Andhra Pradesh can be traced back to the nineteen seventies to the efforts of NGOs. At the time of the IRDP, there were no other agencies in India lending to the poor, hence NGOs had a particularly active role in providing loans and drawing out resources from donors. There was however a limit available resources and hence to the capacity of NGOs to socially mobilize people. Of special significance is the Cooperative Development Foundation (CDF) who at first worked with men in savings and credit agricultural cooperatives. Subsequently, CDF tried to include women into the existing cooperatives, but men strongly opposed this move. Hence special thrift and credit groups for women were created which were called Women Thrift Cooperatives (WTCs).[27] Later, in the early eighties, the Bhagavatula Charitable Trust in Visakhapatnam district had begun mutual savings and credit groups in rural areas, mostly among women. During the late eighties NGOs like MYRADA (Mysore Resettlement and Development Agency)[28] and PRADAN (Professional Agency for Development Action)[29] also created and promoted similar SHGs. By 1990 there were a number of organizations in India, which mobilized the poor around groups which had 15 to 20 women members that met once a month to conduct savings and internal credit activities.

NGOs have had an alternatively waxing and waning relationship with the state, in the context of the formation of SHGs in Andhra Pradesh. With DWCRA, initially, NGO activity was absent since it was a government intervention. With the modifications carried out in Ananthpur, one innovation lay in including NGOs to work with the state. The district government saw the value of NGOs in mobilizing and strengthening groups, and partnered with them, a move that the GoI followed later. SAPAP was also initially implemented through 18 partner voluntary organizations (PVOs) or NGOs. But *Velugu*, has the resources to hire professionals of calibre and does not rely on NGOs.[30] Currently, in Andhra Pradesh there seem to be parallel efforts of state sponsored and NGO facilitated SHGs, since SERP has fitted the role of being a GONGO (Government NGO) eliminating the need for the government to explicitly partner with NGOs.

Converging of State Effort

A consequence of not using NGOs is that it is possible for the government to better co-ordinate diverse state poverty alleviation efforts across Andhra Pradesh. Care is taken to synchronise Velugu's efforts with other schemes, programmes and agencies of the government. Theoretically this allows for optimum utilization of resources and avoids duplication and overlap. SERP aims to proactively converge its work on the one hand with line departments like the Education, Health, Revenue, Disabled etc. and on the other, with many rural development agencies like the DRDA, SC Corporation, ITDAs etc. and also projects like the DPEP. This synergistic linkage between diverse government initiatives is further seen in the way the RPRP programme fits in with the stipulated strategy for poverty eradication of the Swarnandhra Pradesh 'Vision 2020' a policy document committed to poverty eradication through economic growth. According to the document, the GoAP commits to spend the additional resources generated through economic growth on social development, improving education, health, promoting rural and urban development etc.

Partnerships: Including the Private Sector

The project has made rapid progress in exploring partnerships with the private sector to enable SHG groups to get access to new markets. Social Transformation of Economy with Enterprise (STEER) is the one-window contact for partners set up for the DPIP project. The partners for the DPIP have ranged from companies like HLL (Hindustan Levers Ltd.) to institutions like Indian Institute of Managements and IRMA, Banks like ICICI and non-resident Indians. STEER has been extended to APRPRP. Some of the partnerships being explored include paper mills for growing trees, food and drink companies for growing fruit trees, cattle feed companies for growing maize, a large organic food producer for sourcing produce, certification and buy back arrangements, linkage with natural and herbal medicine companies for value addition and procurement of non timber forest produce and setting up e-*chaupals* (internet kiosks) for aqua culture.

Social Issues: Gender

Since women are seen as more credit-worthy than men, SHG formations largely take place around women. But it is found that the process of empowerment and poverty alleviation can be more sustainable when all the members of the family are involved. Hence within DPIP, women's groups are taken as an entry point for the formation of men's groups, youth groups, children groups, groups for physically challenged, etc. Community activists are sensitized on social issues and from among them, several Social Activists are identified as gender focal points.[31] In some districts where the MSs have already emerged, there is a forum created called the Women's Rights Protection Committee, which looks into the injustices and legal issues of the women members.

The presence of women does not necessarily mean that gender issues are addressed. APDPIP endorses that poor communities are able to achieve poverty alleviation through self-managed grassroots institutions by harmonizing the concerns of men and women. At various levels of the project there is a mandate to have a gender specialist who will spearhead the gender initiatives appropriate to the project's vision, mission and goals. The state project management unit and the district project management units have full time Gender Coordinators.

There is an attempt to integrate gender concerns with all the components of DPIP. This is done through consultations and workshops with all the DPMUs. For example, gender sensitive CIF guidelines were drafted and it was mandated that every CIF sub-project would address gender equity. CIF proposals have reflected gender sensitivity by addressing both practical gender needs of women like community bathrooms, smokeless stoves, crèches for children of working mothers, health camps and other strategic gender needs like appointment of legal counsellor, equal wages, land based activities etc.

Gender: Family

When attention is paid to the building of institutions, little attention is paid to the family. It is in the recognition of this truth that SERP undertook an innovative, action research intervention, which used folk theatre and opened up the family for questioning. Plays were performed before entire villages on issues related to gender division of labour in the house, son preference and relationships between mothers-in-law and daughters-in-law.[32] These were followed by discussions, which were intended to raise questions in the minds of the community so that perceptions about gender discrimination would change. Such an experiment is the first of its kind to be attempted.[33] The intervention was named 'Gender Equity in the Family' and was conducted within the APDPIP in the district of Mahbubnagar.

Social Issues: Child Labour, Disability

The literacy rate in Andhra Pradesh is 45.11 per cent, with the male being 56.24 per cent and female 33.71 per cent. As per the State Government's policy, any child out of school is regarded as child labour and the strategy is to get all the children into schools. *Velugu* addresses the twin problems of child labour and high drop-out rates of school children, with a focus on 5-14 age group children. Regular campaigns are conducted to sensitise parents, especially mothers, youth, PRIs, other community members and schoolteachers about the importance of education and its long-term implications for child welfare and poverty reduction. Bridge schools run short and long term remedial courses to prepare child laborers and school drop-outs to enter formal education. There are plans for the establishment of 24 residential schools in Phase-I and 64 in Phase-II exclusively to cover an estimated 1,26,000 girl child labour (36,000 in Phase-I and 90,000 in Phase-II).[34] Many of the youth groups are used in identifying children out of schools, enrolling them into the schools, motivating parents etc.

Velugu also aims to directly address the problems the disabled by organising them into mutual support groups. Plans include promoting of community based rehabilitation programmes and innovative livelihood strategies through sub-projects for the disabled groups.

Social Issues: Health

Effective health care includes promotive, preventive, curative and rehabilitative dimensions. It is with this ethos that the health pilot project in *Velugu* plans a holistic approach to community based primary health care to empower people and communities to take care of their own health and take responsibility for the community's health.[35] The three major principles of this pilot are—(1) Equity, wherein the programme must reach everyone, including the poorest of the poor. (2) Integration, where curative and preventive medicine will be integrated with other factors that enhance life and health, such as agriculture, education, and a safe water supply. (3) Empowerment, with a specific focus on women. Within mature SHGs, health activists will be identified by the communities to become Community Health Development Workers (CHDWs). These are to become the first contact persons for the delivery of simple health services, for which, communities do not have to depend on the medical doctors. This will also give them opportunity to impart health awareness and education. The goal is for health to become part of daily routine, rather than something to attend to during an episode of illness. There will be a base hospital (a charity hospital) to become the epicentre, to provide emergency care round the clock. The outreach activities are organised around this epicentre with the help of the CHDWs. A training centre will become a CHE Centre (Continuous Health Education Centre).

Monitoring and Evaluation

Indicators used to monitor and evaluate a programme are critical in assessing successes and failures of implementation. These have to be chosen wisely. Within *Velugu* some of the quantitative and qualitative performance indicators identified through the monitoring and evaluation system are—the number of new/ strengthened CIGs in marginal communities (desegregated by gender and by tribal groups); Number of groups integrated into Village Organizations (VOs) and Mandal Samakhyas (MSs); Number of CIGs rated and linked to lending institutions; Volume of formal sector credit obtained by CIGs through linkages to banks; Number of sub-project proposals submitted, funded and implemented (by sector); Inclusiveness of VOs and MSs (number of new groups in marginalized communities); Inclusiveness of organizations of the poor in the Gram Sabhas/Panchayats decision making (level of disclosure on budget, frequency and regularity of meetings, level of participation by the poor); Increased diversity in sources of income of the poor (desegregated by gender); Increase in the productive assets held by the poor (by type); Child labour indicators (school enrollment, attendance, attrition rate of girl students in bridge/regular residential schools); Number of girls successful in moving from bridge to regular schools; Household participation in collective action to improve accountability of public officials, in the delivery of services; Changes in household perception of the quality and quantity of public services; and changes in asset composition.

II. IMPACT ANALYSIS

The impact of SHGs can be seen in two dimensions. The first is in poverty alleviation. This impact cannot be captured at one point of time in a conclusive manner. There has to be a sustained upward trend in moving away from poverty for the families of SHG members and the *process* of poverty alleviation should be studied. The second dimension of the impact of SHGs, is the empowerment of the poor and of women in particular. An increase in incomes, livelihoods or assets does not necessarily lead to 'empowerment' in the true sense. Any intervention, such as participation in a SHG and access to micro credit, will shift five spaces in a person's life—economic, physical, socio-cultural, political and mental. Impact will lead to empowerment if the non-mental spaces are instrumental in increasing mental spaces in such a way that action and voice are generated to improve the quality of life. Social inclusion, information and people's participation are significant catalysts that empower people through positive shifts in spaces.

Economic Spaces

There is absolutely no doubt that SHGs have led to an expansion in the economic spaces of members. The poor are eligible to become members in the SHGs of DWCRA and SAPAP models. However the composition of the members according to pre-DWCRA income status of their households, reveals that the coverage of the poorest-of-the-poor is low on the one hand and on the other, the coverage of non-poor is considerable.[36] There are several reasons that explain why this happens—the poor being unsure of their capacity to save, hesitate to join the groups; many a time initial mobilisers are biased and may exclude the poorest to participate in a micro credit programme; and sometimes, the poor are indifferent to programmes such as DWCRA and hence do not join the groups.[37] The second problem of exclusion seems to relate to the method by which the poor are targeted, which does not include them in their self-identification. Income levels of households have increased in all categories of SHG members in the SAPAP model. However, the increase was higher among relatively better off among the poor. As high as 47 per cent of sample households were found to be above the poverty line.[38] The wealth ranking exercise carried out with 83 SHGs suggests that poverty declined among 69 per cent of the members and the proportion of the very poor reduced from 48 per cent to 18 per cent. The reduction in poverty was less among *dalits* and women headed households compared to non-*dalits* and male-headed households.

The members included in SHGs attempt to use the credit to generate livelihood options. The capacity of the household to pull out of poverty depends upon the sustainability of those options as also on the decline in dependency on exploitative sources of availing credit. The positive factor lies in that dependency on moneylenders among members is declining due to the access to credit from SHGs of the DWCRA programme. As high as 61 per cent of members reported that they would have gone to moneylenders had there been no SHGs.[39] Further, access to credit has enabled women to undertake economic activities. These fall under three categories, agriculture, animal husbandry, and industry, service and business sectors.[40] The activities are dominantly production oriented rather than in the nature of services. They are largely continuous activities rather than seasonal. The ownership of DWCRA sponsored activities is equally divided into individual and family ownership. This reveals that the enterprise is actually owned, assisted and managed by other members of the family also, though the financial assistance is provided to the women members of the family. A majority of the women of SHGs, however, reported that the assistance provided under DWCRA is not adequate to meet the initial requirements in case of some activities.[41] Here it is important to consider the effect of DWCRA in enabling traditional artisan occupations to sustain. Large proportions of women, from artisan families become members of the groups to further strengthen and expand their ongoing economic activities. These women are found to continue with their earlier (pre-DWCRA) occupations. As a matter of fact, DWCRA groups that have been formed with a common interest in expanding/strengthening their *existing* traditional activities have been significantly successful.[42] In contrast a smaller proportion of them have taken up new occupations.[43] Women are not able to manage these activities because of the lack of previous experience. Moreover, overcrowding in some of the activities like vegetable vending and fruit vending has forced some to close down their activity[44]. Thus, most of the activities facilitated through DWCRA groups has helped to utilise existing skills of women. On the other hand, attempts of the Government to impart new skills and upgrade existing skills have not reached many areas of the state. As a result, many of the women groups are not able to derive the benefits from the government facilitated DWCRA 'bazaars' as marketing outlets. On the other hand, it has been reported that some of the unemployed and wage employed have become self-employed. The diversification of occupation to non-agricultural activities has enhanced the quality of income of the households since the dependency on risk-based agriculture has reduced. Increases in income have been spent on better nutrition for the children and on health care for the family, kitchen gardens have enhanced the overall nutritional status of children, pregnant and lactating mothers.[45]

In the SAPAP and DPIP groups too, the most important change in the lives of the rural poor was found in the fact that dependency on moneylenders has declined.[46] The financial status of households and savings capacities have improved due to improvement in access to formal credit institutions, since SHGs are linked with banks. Negotiations of SHGs to obtain loans from bank, the initiatives of MMSs to obtain loans from the government and apex lending bodies for onlending to SHGs have together contributed towards enhancing the financial status of households. However, it is also found that the very-poor, who joined groups have not been able to access as much in number and quantum of loans as the poor, or as moderately better-off farmers.[47] Further, the credit accessed was reported to be inadequate.[48] In terms of assets, it was found that households now possessed more livestock rather than land. Yet, there is also a very thin scaling up of extent of land owned after participation in groups.[49] Another positive finding is that land which was mortaged or pledged is being redeemed.[50] In the

Ananthpur district there has been an increase in the possession of consumer durables with households.[51] There is also evidence that the purchase of equipment and setting up of shops is dominant among households.[52] Occupational diversification has taken place among the members. This is evident from the increase in the number of sources of livelihoods of women members and their husbands and larger proportion of member households shifting from agriculture to service and trade. The providing of training in tailoring, embroidery, knitting and word processing has strengthened the skill base of members in a limited way and has helped women to diversify their occupations to some extent. Dependency on migration as a livelihood strategy has also declined. Credit has enabled the poor to make more effective use of skills they *already* possessed. This is contrast to the fact that the demand for credit is not induced by the development of new skills.

The success of micro credit depends to a large extent upon the competence of the SHG to function as a money transaction entity. Just as the government has to be accountable to the people who vote it into power, so also SHGs as units have to be accountable to their members and to the larger financial structure that sustains them. This is achieved through a system of rating that tests SHGs for their financial health. There are several such rating devises in Andhra Pradesh. During 2003 APMAS, an apex NGO, developed a study to assess the quality of the Bank-Linked SHGs in 8 districts covering 40 *mandals* and 400 SHGs. The study considered the size of the groups, proportion of socio-economic characteristics of the members, savings behaviour, revolving funds, etc. and assigned grades to the groups. The preliminary results of the study showed that in an A, B, C grading system, 66 per cent of the groups got an A grade, 26 per cent got a B grade, and the remaining 8 per cent got a C grade. Grading by the government of Andhra Pradesh of DWCRA groups according to their functioning, found that 18, 63, and 19 per cent of the groups are found to be A, B and C categories respectively, a grading that has been confirmed by Andhra Pradesh Mahila Abivrudhi Samithi.[53]

Physical Spaces

Due to the necessity of participation in group activities there has been a mandatory expansion in the physical spaces of women.

Women need to attend meetings at the SHG, mandal and federation levels. There are reports from the field about allegations of infidelity made by husbands about wives who are now mobile. However, there is evidence to indicate that women have better control over their bodies in terms of choices about reproductive behaviour. As a state, Andhra Pradesh has also achieved a reduction in the growth rate of population from 2.42 during 1981 to 1991 to 1.39 per cent during 1991 to 2001.[54] This decline in decadal growth rate of population has been attributed to the phenomenal growth of SHGs in the state.[55] It has been found that DWCRA members have adopted family planning. There has also been an increasing awareness about health related issues. Most of the pregnant women, similarly, had tetanus coverage. The effect is also seen on decisions related to children and a majority of the children of the beneficiaries attend school. However, geographical and social distance has also taken its toll. Groups in the interior villages and scheduled tribes have not been benefited to the extent of the exterior villages and as much as other caste beneficiary households.[56]

Socio-Cultural Spaces

Empowerment can be reached through social inclusion. SHGs can be paradoxically both inclusive and also exclusive. In the necessity for homogeneity of groups and in the targeting of the poor there is horizontal inclusion at various levels. However, vertically there can be demarcations if groups get formed along caste and religion lines. DWCRA groups are formed on the basis of income, caste and neighbourhood and these groups are more homogeneous.[57] In the SAPAP groups, the poor from scheduled castes, scheduled tribes, backward castes and other castes are included and women constitute 90 per cent of the total participants. Caste-homogeneous as well as heterogeneous groups of women are formed. Men groups were also formed, but they are less in number.

It seems as if there have been positive effects of SHGs upon socio-cultural spaces. This is not surprising since models like the SAPAP type is focused on discriminated groups. Also DWCRA groups include all castes of women.[58] However, due to variations in the caste composition of the poor across districts, the composition of coverage varies across districts.[59] However, backward castes, scheduled castes, and scheduled tribes together constitute a significant proportion of the beneficiaries covered. Further the participation of widows, who constitute the poorest of the poor, is 9 per cent.[60]

Gender poverty measured in terms of gender bias with respect to norms of eating, male preference in distribution of food and access to clothing has not declined significantly. Interestingly, to begin with, gender poverty is lower among the *dalits* compared to other communities despite relatively higher levels of overall poverty among the *dalits*.[61] Food security of member households has improved after participation in groups. The practice of cutting down consumption as a coping strategy in the event of food shortage has reduced. Acute malnutrition among children, infant and child mortality/premature adult deaths have declined. Children's school enrolment and regularity in school attendence has improved. Drainage facilities, toilet facilities and access to pucca houses, electricity and gas have improved. Further, when SHGs address issues such as the establishing of "*Ammavadis*' (baby care centres), it has improved opportunities to generate livelihoods and also simultaneously made a positive impact upon the education of girl children. This is so because it facilitates poor women with young children, to work, without pulling their elder daughters out of school.

Political Spaces

The most important dimension to remember is that while SHGs are formed around an economic issue of micro credit and savings, the formation of groups is a political process. This process picks up momentum with the SHGs being federated and also establishing links with local self-governing bodies. The SHGs of DWCRA are federated into Mahila Banks. The SHGs of SAPAP are federated into Village Organisations (VOs) and in turn the VOs are federated into Mahila Samakhyas. The DWCRA model includes linkages of SHGs/mahila banks with the line departments (LDs) of the government, the formal financial institutions and corporate sector. The SAPAP and DPIP model links SHGs and MSs with the state including (line departments, local governance bodies), civil society and the market.

In DWCRA groups, there was poor development and growth

of leadership among members. While the selection of leaders is democratic in 87 per cent of the groups, leadership rotation was absent in 94 per cent of the SHGs.[62] Where leadership was imposed, it was due to the lack of initiative among the members to become leaders. As a result groups become over dependent on the leader. The leader manages all activities regarding accounts, loans and attendance. As a consequence, the member's involvement in mobilizing savings is only 4 per cent.[63] In the absence of the group leader, meetings are not held up to six months or more.[64] It is also found that eighty-four per cent of leaders and 93 per cent of members are not part of any other institutions including local bodies. Such a phenomenon has been referred to as the "island-within-a-lake", where a large following of passive members are apathetic as against a small subgroup of leaders.[65]

The close relationship between political spaces and access to information is seen in Andhra Pradesh. However, if this access get localised among select members of groups on account of their position as leaders, then there emerge new heirarchies and exclusions. Since community coordinators, community volunteers and paraprofessionals were trained under SAPAP and DPIP, members of SHGs have access to specialised information. However, it has been found that since there is no periodical rotation of leadership the increased dependence on the existing leader may create the possibility for exploitation. As in DWCRA groups other members are found to be passive and there is again the "island-within-a-lake" phenomenon.

Mental Spaces

The linkages between shifts in different spaces is evident when one sees how an initiating change in economic spaces due to micro credit has triggered off changes in other spaces and led to positive changes in mental spaces. Findings from the field show that the very processes of group formation and participation in groups are empowering for women. Case studies from *Velegu* have shown how women from marginalized sections are far from being passive victims of poverty and oppression and instead actively try to change their situation. It is evident that there has been an expansion in mental space, which causes them to take action.[66] These women not only negotiate their relations with their husbands and members of their families, but also challenged relations with upper castes in their village.

The improvements in the access to productive assets, improved livelihoods and control over all aspects of life of women have contributed to the decline of disparities.[67] Women members' husbands feel that their wives are more independent. The women of SHGs have improved their control over their lives. More specifically, women have improved access and/or control over their labour/family labour, resources, freedom to move and interact, leadership positions, reproduction, and body. However, there are variations in the different dimensions of improvement. Highest achievements are made with respect to mobility, breaking of gender division of productive labour, access to their own savings, access to friendship outside their family and access to leadership positions in gram panchayats; moderate achievements are made with respect to reproductive rights and body rights (freedom from violence); and lower achievements are made with respect to extent of access of women to husband's labour (productive and reproductive), rights of women to land and house, their ability to control male alcohol consumption and their ability to influence the setting of wages. Women have intervened collectively in several institutions, viz., family, community, markets (labour, commodity and financial), and state including local self-government institutions. Within the family, higher collective achievement has been with respect to girl child education followed by release of bonded labour. At the community level, women groups at various levels are changing attitudes on girl child education and caste-based discrimination. The interventions in labour and commodity markets have to be strengthened, though the interventions in financial market are impressive. Linkages with government departments are stronger with those departments that deal with women's reproductive tasks or women managed productive activities and weaker with those activities which are controlled by men. However, it is felt that women's SHGs have to begin to play their role in making gram panchayats function more transparently.[68]

Through their work with SHGs *Velugu* has succeeded in some measure in altering the economic spaces, physical geographical spaces and public political spaces of women. There is also some success in the alteration of socio-cultural space in the focused treatment of the problems of marginalised groups. However, there is no direct focus upon addressing the *private* political space as is vested within families and households. Conversations with the activists in the field brought to light how in some areas, the hostility within the household because of the importance that women got in the public space through membership in the SHGs in some areas tensions had increased. The intervention 'Gender Equity in the Family' was well received with communities being open to discussing householding practices and issues of justice.

III. DRIVING FACTORS

Commitment and Political Economy for Change

The steady upscaling of the SHG route of poverty alleviation is illustrative of the commitment of the GOAP towards maintaining a sequence of change guided by lessons learned from past experience. It is to the credit of the governments in power and to the implementing actors to, on the one hand maintain consistency in logic and on the other, generate a process marked with imaginative adaptations to change. What is remarkable is the extent of upscaling that has taken place in a relatively short period of time. This has been possible due to state initiative and sponsorship. NGO effort is localized and does not have the machinery available to government bodies.

Accountability

Accountability is a two-way street. There is no doubt of the fact that the state, implementing agencies and service providers have to be accountable to the people. Including people into development processes ensures this, since it makes provision for a system of checks and balances and opens channels of communication. However, while this is true, as soon as peoples' participation is made the route for development, people also have to be accountable. The flip side of accountability is responsibility. It is only when people are also seen as accountable towards their own lives and towards the development of their regions it becomes their responsibility to participate in decision making. Needs have to be voiced and vigilance has to be maintained which rises above people succumbing to short-lived sops. Andhra Pradesh seems to be walking this fine line of balance between making accountability work both from top to down as also from down upwards. The state has opened avenues of people's participation through the use of PIP methods and ground staff who have their roots within the communities they work with. Further, SHGs have the capacity to voice the needs of the communities. There is tremendous potential in this endeavour if the vision of SHGs is expanded beyond transacting money to include local concerns about the quality of life. Under *Velugu*, as the social mobilization process matures in a village, communities are encouraged to analyse their livelihood situations, which in turn reveals options for the community to act. This thread can be traced back to the literacy campaign where people gained the capacity to look into their own life situation took a stand against *arak*.

While there is no doubt of the need for accountability for any programme to succeed, it is difficult to zero in on any fixed list of measures that will ensure accountability. The most obvious relationship of accountability and transparency is between the state and the people. Both have to be accountable to each other. This requires a system of communication where intent, need and impact of programmes can be conveyed both ways. The chain of personnel, drawn from local communities, diverse methods of community participation and SHGs themselves, has the margin to allow for such accountability to exist. However, breaks in communication can take place if there is inadequate training and orientation at each level. The training programmes under *Velugu* are of utmost importance, and much depends on their efficacy to impart the right orientation.

There is also the 'third branch' within which accountability is most paramount. These are persons who implement programmes, such as administrative personnel, bureaucrats etc. This branch connects the state with the people and it has one relation with the state and another with the people. Service delivery mechanisms and programmes often fail when this branch is weak. When questions of accountability arise, it automatically draws attention to what is at stake for the actor who has to be accountable. The state within a democracy has its seat(s) to protect. People have their and their children's lives to protect. The issues at stake for the third branch have to be minutely identified in order to develop a system of motivating factors, which can make this segment transparent and accountable. Within Andhra Pradesh one has witnessed exemplary vision and courage of the third branch which took programmes forward. This has to be intensified through a system of checks, balances and incentives since, if the vision of prosperity remains alive with this segment, it will sustain even if political regimes change.

Social Capital

It is important to account for the social capital that is generated in these processes of social mobilization when SHGs are formed. The chances that groups will be formed along caste and religion lines are strong since these are the groups that are already in place and are those people identify themselves with. Here the issue can also be interpreted as one of identities. SHGs should be able to construct new identities for their members as economically active, aware persons who have been convinced and are motivated to pull out of poverty with the use of micro credit. Inasmuch as existing identities of caste and religion are reinforced, existing pockets of social capital, which is socially divisive, will not be questioned. The social capital, which SHGs should generate, should be democratic in nature and inclusive in content.

Social Inclusion

The other concern is whether micro credit interventions reach the very poor and are these communities bypassed in favour of the poor. There is an inbuilt mandate, which excludes the no-so-poor from interventions in the newer and later models of micro credit. Yet it has been found and argued that credit does not reach the very poor since these have low absorption capacities and the transaction costs of reaching them is too high. Often it is thought that necessarily the very poor will also be those form the very backward castes, such as the *dalits*. In Andhra Pradesh, state effort has gone into including the hitherto excluded social groups such as the *Dalit*. However, focusing on only *Dalit* groups, in the initial stages of the DPIP has led to an excluding inclusion. Such was the experience in the district of Mahbubnagar. The concentration upon the problems of the *Dalits* caused a feeling of being left out on the part of the other backward castes who are also socially discriminated against but are a little higher in the social hierarchy than the *Dalits*.[69] Learning from this experience, RPRP seems to be attempting a synthesis of social and economic inclusion since groups are now formed taking into both kinds of discrimination.

Courage for Flexibility

It can be seen that in the development of the DWCRA *programme* in Andhra Pradesh the government has been simultaneously active in initiating change as also been at the receiving end of people's quest for accountability. The mandate of *Velugu* is impressive. Peoples participation tailored to local and specific needs is central to each component, as against a ready-made model where one size fits all. This embodies flexibility as also courage on the part of the state to deal with unpredictable outcomes. Further, when the doors are opened to accountability, flexibility is automatically required. Andhra Pradesh seems to currently reiterate this ethos through *Velugu*.

Institutional Innovation

The success of the use of SHGs in Andhra Pradesh can be traced very fundamentally to the larger macro environment where at the national level, the Government of India took the initiative in harnessing existing banking structures through the NABARD and linking them with SHGs. A key in the success of the programme has been the commitment of NABARD administration with this programme. Beginning with its top management they have had the vision that SHGs were a good scheme for rural development.[70] This illustrates how by creating new synergies, linkages and relationships between institutions they can be strengthened. The creation of new institutions is also significant in the formation of SHGs, VOs and federations in Andhra Pradesh. SERP has proved to be a bridge between NGO and state. The structure of this organisation is interesting and can be studied. The institutionalising of state effort through GONGOs may well be the model that other regions want to experiment with.

Andhra Pradesh has managed to forge several links at different levels between and across institutional actors. The institutionalising of people's groups through SHGs, VOs, or MMSs is an attempt to construct a structure that can stand up against existing monoliths like the state, the private sector, the banking sector etc. Organising the poor lends them voice and the capacity to deal with institutions they otherwise are intimidated by. It is important to realise that while theoretically these links may seem one-to-one, in reality the size and socio-political strengths of the players are not matched. Hence there will always be the danger of the more powerful using the less powerful for their own ends. Self-interest, which is the prime motivating factor of market behaviour and also of the give-and-take within democracy, is a double-edged sword. It is here that accountability has to be sharp so that gains flow both ways between institutional actors. For example, concern has been expressed about the use of SHGs to sell the products of multinational corporations that too with state consent.[71] In a situation where the corporate sector and the state gains, the benefits to SHGs should also be visible, for there to be a win-win situation.

IV. LEARNING AND EXPERIMENTATION

In Andhra Pradesh, one noteworthy observation relates to the linkages between different approaches towards development, poverty reduction and empowerment. It is not merely enough to address the economic indicators of poverty. While incomes have to be augmented through livelihood generation interventions, for which credit is an important component, attention also has to be paid to the determinants of human poverty in terms of health and education requirements. Likewise, social poverty, which manifests in the presence of corrosive evils like caste taboos, norms of dowry, adherence to vices such as alcohol and drugs, have to be woven into empowerment programmes. Learning and experimentation has been carried out at several times, for example with respect to the rice credit line, emulating the Jamked community health model, and the—'Gender Equity in the Family' project. While credit has to be given to courage for experimentation, it is necessary for successful experiments to be deepened and also expanded.

External Catalysts

When one talks of interventions involving the government, NGOs and the poor, the first significant external catalyst that facilitated positive change in the case of Andhra Pradesh, is the funding agency. These have been the World Bank, UNICEF, UNDP, CARE, UNDP, IFAD, etc. (IFAD has been working with the tribal poor in Andhra Pradesh in the formation of SHGs for forest mangement.) It is evident that the SHG route to development and empowerment is seen as worthwhile to invest large amounts of money and efforts into. The timely assistance offered to programmes has given the impetus to extend and deepen interventions.

The second external catalyst can be identified in the context of the initiative that government officials have taken which are *outside* their job requirements of implementing projects. The capacity to have a vision, to place it before the government and find ways to translate thought into action are 'external' to the given understanding of the role of the administrative services. These have proved critical in the progression of Andhra Pradesh towards pro-poor strategies.

The third external catalyst can be seen in the contribution of organizations from the private and NGO sector. These have proved significant to the upscaling of SHGs. The opening of markets to SHGs by the private sector, training and capacity building inputs by organizations make for significant external catalysts. Equally important is the role that experts, evaluators and consultants have played in assessing the situation on the ground from a perspective different from that of the practitioners. This outside input has proved fruitful in the introduction of ideas that are innovative and experimental in nature.

Lessons Learned

The primary lesson learned from the Andhra experience is that there is value in using SHGs as a conduit for poverty alleviation initiatives. However, one has to understand the limitations of this use and gauge the ways in which these can be surpassed to get more out of such an approach. The need for small homogenous groups to be formed is simultaneously the strength and the weakness of SHGs. It is critical to choose wisely the common denominator that brings people together in a group. When this common feature is poverty, the identification of the poor as also the understanding of poverty is the most important exercise.

Andhra Pradesh's foray into PIP methods has to be further studied to ascertain their success in such understanding and identification.

Second, when micro credit is the pivot around which organisation takes place, its ability to alleviate poverty/empower is limited. In Andhra Pradesh, however, these limitations have been overcome by integrating micro credit with a powerful 'plus' component of social and economic infrastructure. The danger here lies in that while it seems almost Utopian on paper, during implementation, community institutions like SHGs may not be equipped to take on such complex tasks. Again the issue zeroes in on the necessity of adequate capacity building. While dissemination of information, training, sensitization and awareness building are addressed, education, health and the care economy have to receive a more focused thrust statewide.

Third, SHGs should not be seen only in their capacity to route micro credit. Their political potential is powerful. SHGs and federations form the training ground to make leaders and potential political aspirants. This critical mass has tremendous potential to work for the betterment of the regions they represent. Andhra Pradesh has unleashed an extensive wave of mobilization and sharp attention has to be paid to the danger of other vested interests co-opting such a critical mass.

Fourth, the potential of women—only SHGs for women's empowerment depends upon several other supportive measures like education, health, housing and infrastructure. While all five spaces may expand positively, there is a limit to the capacity for credit based SHGs to empower women. Further since gender related discrimination requires interventions that will not alienate men and forming only women groups may well do just that unless other methods of awareness building are used.

Fifth, partnerships are fundamental for development. This kind of inclusiveness where institutions and actors both public and private, work in synergy, has considerable potential for poverty alleviation. It can bear positive results if care is taken to protect the interests of all the participants. Market dynamics are not adequate to allocate costs and benefits. It is however difficult to conclusively say what the effect of excluding NGOs will be. In a larger design of partnerships, it may not be advisable to create rifts between actors working towards similar goals.

Sixth, the Andhra experience has shown how the linkage

between the national, regional and local environment can be made with political will. The political economy within which the upscaling has taken place is a democracy. In any democracy there is a trade-off between the state acting in the interest of the people so as to maintain their own position and protecting their vested interest at the cost of the people. It cannot be taken amiss that the state is seeing SHGs as a method of gaining popularity, if the outcomes reflect the alleviation of poverty that is intended. In the pursuit of numbers, care has to be taken that the subtleties involved in empowerment processes are not lost. Monitoring and evaluation should be conducted with indicators that are able to capture the complex matrix of socio-cultural, economic and political variables that influence empowerment.

Seventh, the Andhra experience has brought to the fore the close nexus between accountability and people's participation. Unless a sense of ownership is infused into any programme, participants will not demand accountability or feel accountable. Involving people at every level of decision making within the programme transforms 'beneficiaries' into participants and ultimately everyone benefits. Such channels of communication can be opened by the political state as has been done in Andhra Pradesh. When a government is not fearful of transparency, it instils confidence and involvement on the part of those who are governed.

Finally, Andhra Pradesh has shown that, to approach a complicated problem such as poverty, a complex mix of methods is required. At one level, use has to be made of existing structures and at the same time new edifices have to be created. What is important, however, is that these two should somewhere be able to synchronize. Again, economic and social issues are equally important if poverty has to be understood. Discriminations at diverse levels criss-cross and often annihilate the positive results of a strategy. The attempt to understand the problem often half wins the battle.

NOTES

1. Internationally such groups have been formed around medical problems and addictions. Self-help is seen as an inexpensive way of providing vital community services.

2. This paper focuses specifically upon SHGs around micro credit.
3. '*Velugu*' means 'light' in Telugu, the language of Andhra Pradesh.
4. A 'mandal' is a sub-district geographical unit unique to Andhra Pradesh which is both a revenue and development planning unit, but smaller in size than a 'block'.
5. This was done with the help of the UNICEF.
6. The cost of the revolving fund was paid 20 per cent by UNICEF, 40 per cent by each state government and 40 per cent by the Central Government. Once UNICEF withdrew from the project in 1996-97, the costs were equally shared between the state and the central government.
7. The credit for the courage to break rules and for the political will in this endeavour has been attributed to Mr. Tucker who came in as District Collector in 1992 and Mr. Chandramouli, Project Director of DRDA in charge of DWCRA. The Commissioner A.K. Goel, and the Rural Development Minister, Ms. Laxmi Devi also offered further support.
8. SAPAP was assisted by the UNDP. It emerged out of the 1993 Dhaka declaration for Eradication of Poverty which was the result of the need for an action plan to study the regional problem of persistent poverty, felt in 1991, when the SAARC heads of the state met at Colombo and established the independent South Asian Commission on Poverty Alleviation.
9. APDPIP was designed with the active participation of Mr. K Raju who included his learning from Nellore, Kurnool and SAPAP into the project.
10. The total cost of the project is estimated in U$ 275.4 millions, of which U$ 157 millions are to be spent in the Community Investment Fund only. Of these U$ 157 millions 75 per cent will be spent on productive activities while the remaining 25 per cent will be directed towards social and infrastructure activities. The project is financed by several stakeholders: the World Bank (IDA) is providing a loan for U$ 150 millions (54 per cent of the total), the communities are investing U$ 13,79 millions, the Community Building/MicroFinance Institutions are providing U$ 51,47 millions and the GOAP is investing U$ 59,93 millions.
11. The Chairperson of SERP is the Chief Minister of Andhra Pradesh and the primary positions including that of Chief Executive Officer are held by senior bureaucrats.
12. UNDP, 2000.
13. Nair http://www.coopdevelopmentcenter.coop/Sector/Microfinance percent20& percent20Finance/federation percent20Report-finaldraft.doc
14. This has happened in a large way in the state-sponsored programme as also at the level of NGO initiatives.

15. Support is provided by APMAS, CARE and OUTREACH.
16. NABARD 2003.
17. Hoe, 2003.
18. UNDP 2000.
19. Mr. K. Raju who was then Collector of Nellore visualized a mandate that was broader than making people literate. He wanted to use the literacy campaign as a means for poverty alleviation and empowerment and not as an end in itself. The idea was to make women understand how within a year, they could become literate and how literacy was instrumental to succeed in the fight against poverty.
20. A kind of locally brewed alcohol.
21. After Nellore, Mr. Raju was transferred to the district of Kurnool, where he promoted the SHG concept.
22. After Mr. Raj, Mr. Sabmasiva Rao, Collector of Nellore, oversaw the SHG movement in Nellore and convinced of its worth, two years later upon being appointed Secretary to the then Chief Minister (CM) convinced the latter of the necessity of state support.
23. The website of *Velugu* is an example.
24. Project Appraisal Document of RPRP World Bank 2003.
25. There are three models to be tried out No cash; cash and community managed. See www.Velugu.org
26. Recent discussions on enhancing employment opportunities in rural areas center around developing nonfarm sector opportunities. While this is a long term solution, it require a lot of effort in terms of skill building, dissemination of market intelligence etc. Immediately, however, land issues need to be addressed.
27. Members save Rs. 20 per month and earn a monthly interest of 1 per cent while a monthly interest of 2 per cent is charged on the loan. The loanable funds are generated from member's savings only. Credit is linked to savings. A maximum of three times of savings of a member is provided as credit.
28. MYRADA is a Non-Governmental Organisation managing rural development programmes in 3 States of South India and providing on-going support including deputations of staff to programmes in 6 other States.
29. PRADAN is a voluntary organization registered under the societies registration act in Delhi. It currently works in selected villages in 26 districts across 7 states through small teams based in the field.
30. According to Mr. Raju, the main reason for the limited role that DPIP has given to NGOs is based on the view that SHGs are people's organizations, and to make them sustainable government and NGOs should have a secondary role to let the people to govern their own institutions.

31. These social activists are identified after taking into consideration their perspectives on human justice, equity and equality.
32. These three issues were identified as the common and prominent gender discriminatory issues.
33. Again here it was the vision, belief in gender equality and support of the then Chief Executive Officer (CEO), Mr. Raju and the current CEO, Mr. Vijay Kumar due to whom such an experimental action research attempt could begin, sustain and be successfully completed.
34. This component is being implemented by the A.P. Social Welfare Residential Educational Institutions Society.
35. The Jamkhed Rural Health *Programme* initiated by Drs. Raj and Mabelle Arole in 1970, also known as the Comprehensive Rural Health Project (CRHP) has been a great influence on the development of this pilot. At Jamkhed, rural Maharashtra, a unique process in community action has resulted as one of the best primary health projects in the world. This project has evidence of bringing down infant mortality and child mortality down drastically. Jamkhed, is located far away from a city and is typically rural, drought-prone and poverty stricken.
36. GoAP 1999, Raju and Ali, 1996.
37. APMAS, 2002.
38. Outreach, 2001.
39. This percentage varies across districts 90 per cent in East Godavari and 69 per cent in Mahbubnagar (ORGMARG 2000).
40. YFA, 1996, Kanchanya, 1998, Raju and Ali, 1996, ICM 1996, Jayalakshmi 1997, Narayanaswamy and Jagannathan, 1999.
41. Raju and Ali, 1996.
42. BASIX 1999.
43. Raju and Ali, 1996.
44. Raju and Ali, 1996, Kanchanya 1998, ICM 1996, Jayalakshmi, 1997, Narayanaswamy and Jagannathan.
45. YFA 1996, Kanchanya, 1998.
46. Outreach 2001, Ranjani *et al.* 2002, and Mahendra Dev *et al.* 2002.
47. Ranjani *et al.*, 2002.
48. Outreach, 2001.
49. Outreach 2001, Ranjani *et al.*, 2002 and Mahendra Dev *et al.*, 2002.
50. Ranjani *et al.*, 2000.
51. Mahendra Dev *et al.*, 2002.
52. Ranjani *et al.*, 2002
53. APMAS, 2000.
54. Economic Survey, 2001.
55. James, 2002.
56. YFA, 1996, Kanchanya, 1998.
57. ORGMARG, 2000.

58. ORGMARG, 2000.
59. ORGMARG, 2000, Raju and Ali, 1996, ICM, 1996, Jayalakshmi, 1997, Narayanaswamy and Jagannathan, 1999, YFA, 1996, Kanchanya, 1998, Mahendra Dev and Rao, 2002.
60. ORGMARG, 2000, Raju and Ali, 1996.
61. Ranjani *et al.*, 2002.
62. APMAS, 2002, ORGMARG, 2000.
63. ORGMARG, 2000.
64. APMAS, 2002.
65. Oka, 2002.
66. See, *Voices of Women, Velugu*, n.d., Society of Elimination of Rural Poverty, Hyderabad, which captures the experiences of twenty, five poor women from the district of Kurnool, who in their participation in SHGs have succeeded in challenging, engaging and negotiating with economic, social and political constraints that oppress their lives.
67. Ranjani *et al.*, 2002.
68. Mahendra Dev *et al.*, 2002.
69. Author's field observation.
70. Particularly Mr. Kotaiah's, (former Chairman of NABARD) commitment has been essential for the achievement of the current state of the movement.
71. Project Shakti ("strength") connects self-help groups with business opportunities. Hindustan Lever offers the groups the chance to become very local, small-scale sellers of the company's products. The groups, typically 15-20 people, buy a small stock of items such as *Lifebuoy* soap, *Wheel* detergent or *Clinic* shampoo, which are then sold direct to consumers in their homes. Working in conjunction with the local district authorities, Project Shakti was piloted in 2002 in 50 villages in the state of Andhra Pradesh.
    http://www.unilever.com/environmentsociety/community/economicdevelopment/Creating_rural_entrepreneurs_in_India.asp
    Also see, Sharma Sudhirendar, 2002, 'Is micro-credit a macro trap?', *Financial Daily, THE HINDU*, Wednesday, Septamber 25.

6

Micro-Pensions in India: Towards Mainstreaming

MUKUL ASHER and SAVITA SHANKAR

I. INTRODUCTION

There is increasing recognition that to meet the needs of 21st century India, the reform of India's complex social security system comprising seven components (Figure 6.1) should proceed along three broad directions (Asher, 2006).

Abbreviations Used

DB	—	Defined Benefit
DC	—	Defined Contribution
EDLI	—	Employees' Deposit Linked Insurance Scheme
EPF	—	Employees' Provident Fund
EPS	—	Employees' Pension Scheme
GPF	—	Government Provident Fund
GS	—	Gratuity Scheme
Coops	—	Cooperatives
CSPS	—	Civil Service Pension Scheme
MFs	—	Mutual Funds
NGO	—	Non-Government Organizations
SHG	—	Self Help Groups

Source: Asher (2007a).

First, provident and pension fund organisations in all seven components need to substantially enhance the professionalism

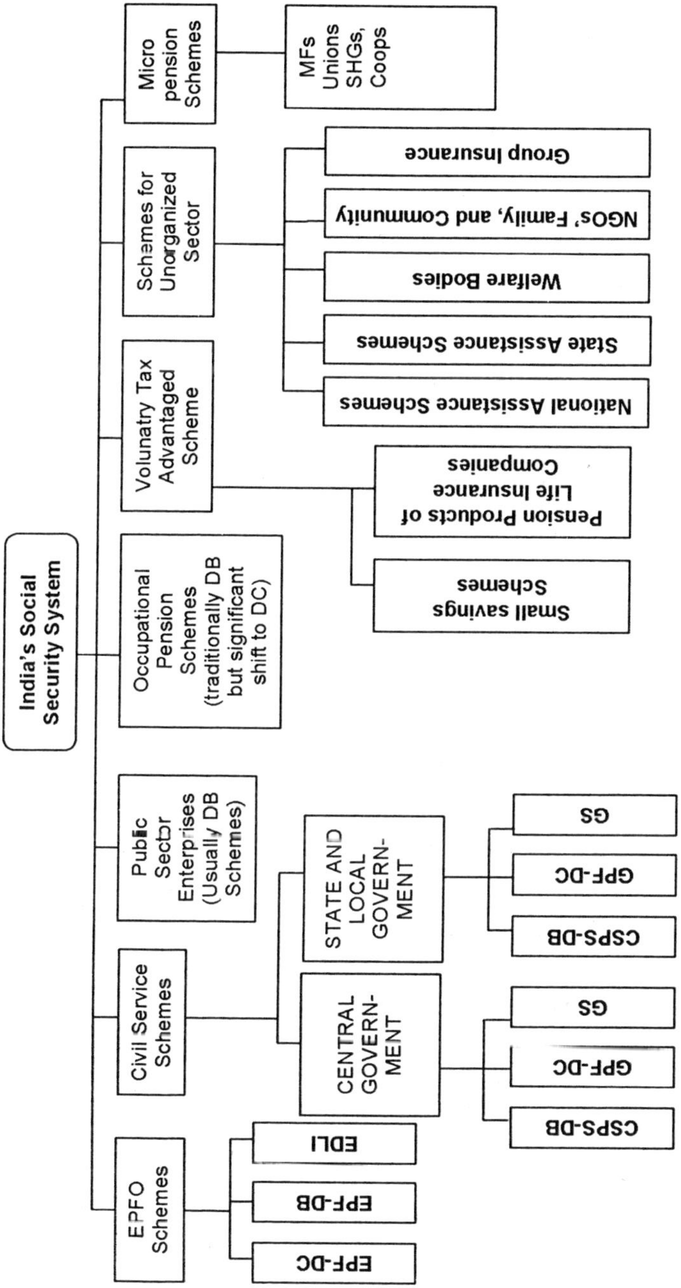

Fig. 6.1: India's Social Security System.

with which they perform the core functions. Ross (2004) has identified five core functions. The first involves reliable collection of contributions, taxes and other receipts, including any loan payments. The second concerns payment of benefits for each of the schemes in a timely and correct way. The third involves securing financial management and productive investment of provident and pension fund assets. The fourth core function is maintaining an effective communication network, including development of accurate data and record keeping mechanisms to support collection, payment and financial activities. The fifth is production of financial statements and reports that are tied to providing effective and reliable governance, fiduciary responsibility, transparency, and accountability.

The second factor concerns systemic perspective. It requires that all components of the social security system are well integrated in meeting the retirement needs of the population. This is consistent with obtaining retirement income security from multiple sources. The role of each component and the schemes within that component should be periodically reviewed to assess their suitability, scalability and sustainability.

The third is the need to enhance financial literacy, particularly concerning long time horizons, need for empirical data based price discovery and tyranny of small numbers relating to insurance and pensions among both policymakers and the general public. Any pension arrangement is a financial contract spanning five to six decades. It should therefore command a high level of trust and confidence from the participants.

Expanding the population with access to financial services, i.e. financial inclusion is one of the priorities of the Reserve Bank of India. The provident and pension fund organizations and the pension regulatory structures should promote financial literacy and financial inclusion. The prevailing tendency of regarding pensions as a welfare measure without due regard for empirical evidence and rigorous economic, financial and fiscal analysis represents a formidable constraint in pension reform. This will require a mindset change among policymakers and governmental organization from current focus on administration to public policy and management will also be essential (Asher, 2007b).

Demographic Trends and Ageing of India's Population

India is experiencing a demographic transition leading to lower total fertility rate, increased life expectancy and greater proportion of the aged in the population. The share of the elderly or persons aged 65 years and above in India's population is expected to rise from 4.6 per cent in 2000 to 9 per cent in 2030. In absolute terms, the number of those above the age of 60 will rise from 87.5 million in 2005 to 100.8 million in 2010. By 2030 this number is projected to be around 200 million, which will increase further to 330 million by 2050. This suggests that lack of pension coverage will affect more persons than ever before. The share of elderly as a proportion of working age population, namely the old age dependency ratio, will also increase.

Increased life expectancy means that each elderly person will require support for a longer period. In 2005, an Indian man reaching 60 years of age can on an average be expected to live for another 17 years and an average woman 18 years. This is expected to increase. Uncertainty about the pace of increase has major implications for annuity markets and for health insurance.

Both the level and the pace of ageing are likely to provide significant challenges as even by 2030, India's per capita income will be relatively low. If the current normal retirement age of 60 is not increased, then the challenge of financing the elderly will be even greater. As women are increasingly living longer than men; greater feminization of the population is taking place (Liebig and Rajan, 2003). Providing secure and sustainable retirement income therefore ranks high in the social priorities. Presently, only about a fifth of India's 460 million strong labour force and about a quarter of its 90 million elderly benefit from atleast one of the components of India's social security system.

It is in the above context that this paper examines the role of micro-pensions in India. This article argues that as one of the seven components of India's social security system, micro-pensions can play a limited but useful role if they are brought into the mainstream of the financial system.

The paper is organized as follows. The nature and design of micro-pensions in India is reviewed in Section II. A brief discussion of channels for expanding coverage of micro-pensions is provided in Section III. This is followed by a brief discussion of reform directions in Section IV. The final section provides concluding observations.

II. THE NATURE AND DESIGN OF MICRO-PENSIONS

A pension scheme may be of defined contribution (DC) or defined benefit (DB) nature. In a DC scheme, while contributions are explicitly defined, benefits are not. This is because the risks associated with investing them, and then converting them to a regular retirement income stream are borne by the individual members. In contrast, in Defined Benefit (DB) scheme, the benefits to be provided are explicitly stated, while contributions are left undefined. In a DB scheme, it is the plan sponsor which bears the investment, mortality, and other risks.

In any Defined Contribution (DC) pension scheme, there is an accumulation phase as well as a pay-out phase.

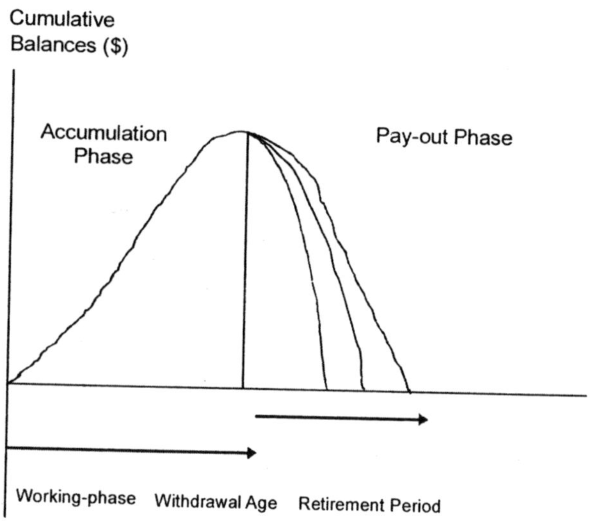

Cumulative Balances = Net contributions (contributions minus withdrawals) *plus* interest credited on accumulated balances.
Payout phase: the funds accumulated can be spent rapidly or slowly. Death may occur before the funds are exhausted or reverse is also a possibility. So need to protect against longevity risk. As it is the purchasing power of the funds that is relevant, protection against the inflation risk is also desirable.

Source: Asher and Nandy, (2006).

Fig. 6.2: Accumulation and Payout Phases of DC Schemes

During the accumulation phase, a member of a DC plan or an annuity purchaser[1] contributes towards accumulating balances. The value of such accumulation depends on the amount of contributions (for a DC plan, covered wage level times the contribution rate) less pre-retirement withdrawals plus returns (net of investment management expenses) obtained from the investment of funds less applicable taxes. It is usual for administrative expenses to be borne by the members collectively. These, however, need to be transparent and benchmarked.

A micro-pension scheme is typically designed as a defined contribution scheme. The scheme essentially operates on the principle of voluntary savings accumulated over a long period. These savings are intermediated through financial and capital markets by a professional fund manager. At an agreed upon withdrawal age (usually 58 or 60 years) the accumulated balances can be withdrawn in a lump sum, a phased withdrawal, annuity or some combination of these methods.

Micro-Pension Schemes in India

Micro-pensions operate as a part of the broader framework of micro-finance institutions (MFIs). In any country, membership in micro-pensions is likely to be a fraction of the membership of MFIs. The key proximate objective is therefore to increase this fraction in a financially sustainable manner.

In India, the insurance companies and two mutual funds have been offering pension plans for individuals for a considerable period. However, only one mutual fund, UTI AMC (Asset Management Company) which is in the public sector began offering plans in 2006 which can be loosely termed as micro-pensions. As on April 1, 2007, there is therefore only one fund manager in the micro-pensions space, though it has teamed with a variety of third-party organizations.

The key characteristic of the UTI AMC micro-pension plans are small sum (ranging from Rs. 50 to Rs. 200 per month); flexibility in payments (monthly or yearly contributions are not mandatory), and presence of a third party, such as cooperative, self help group (SHG) or an NGO[2]. The non-mandatory nature is an important departure from the traditional pension plans.

The role of the third party is to be a locus for generating a large number of members with common characteristics; undertake certain administrative functions; and act as channel of communication. They can therefore assist in reducing transactions costs involved in identifying members, in contributions, and in record-keeping. The third party must therefore command trust and confidence of the members as well as be competent in administration and financial matters. Moreover both the trust and the competence must be sustained over a long period. Increasing supply of such third parties is therefore critical to expanding the reach of micro-pensions.

The role played by the partners is in collection of the monthly contributions from individual members. These savings are pooled and transferred to UTI for funds management. Each member receives a unique account number

The first micro-pension scheme with UTI AMC as the fund manager was launched nearly a year ago. Since then, UTI AMC has partnered with SEWA (Self Employed Women's Association), a micro finance institution based in Ahmedabad; COMPFED, a federation formed by milk producers in Bihar; Paradip Port Trust; and an urban cooperative bank run by women. More such partnerships are expected.

A strategic tie-up between Bank of India (BOI) and UTI Mutual Fund for providing members of self-help groups an investment opportunity through a micro-pension initiative could help address the issue of relatively short life-span of most SGHs. But its impact on transaction costs and financial viability need to be empirically determined.

The schemes involve contributions ranging from Rs. 50 to Rs. 200 per month per member, but they need not be made every month. The contributions must typically be made until age 55 and the pension payments begin after age 58. A maximum of 40 per cent of the corpus can be invested in equity and the balance invested in debt. Actual investment in equity is however around 20 per cent. The target appears to be an annual return of 10 to 12 per cent after all expenses. It is too early to evaluate the extent to which the target is likely to be achieved.

For managing micro-pension funds, UTI AMC has made only minor adjustments in their usual charges levied for managing regular pension funds. The management fees range from 1.75 per cent to 2.5 per cent of assets depending on the assets under management. Unlike in the case of regular pension plans, there is no entry load. But exit load of 1 per cent is levied if amounts are withdrawn before the agreed upon retirement age. The exit load appears to be harsh given the fact that economic and financial uncertainties and liquidity and credit access constraints loom large for the members of micro-pension schemes. Perhaps zero exit load after five to eight year membership could be considered.

The combined membership of the micro-pension schemes is difficult to estimate precisely. But knowledgeable observers put it at around 0.2 million. In contrast, in micro finance schemes membership is around 35 million. This may be regarded as a proxy indicator of the potential coverage of micro pension schemes in India.

The costs charged in the accumulation phase by the UTI AMC have been noted earlier. There are, however, no empirical studies available as yet to estimate such costs as a percentage of contributions and of assets and their behaviour over time. The transaction costs in the case of group micro-credit providers in India however range between 3.2 per cent and 11.3 per cent of the loans provided, depending on the geographical area (Shankar, 2006).

The Pay-Out Phase

In the pay-out phase (usually coinciding with retirement[3]), longevity, investment and inflation risks need to be addressed. In addition, survivors' benefits and disability insurance are also essential. This is particularly the case in India as life-time labour force participation of women is relatively low, and even when they do participate, women as a group earn less than men, and therefore, require more years of support. Uneven property rights and social status of women, particularly of widows, are additional reasons for the need to provide survivors' insurance benefits. More systematic consideration of these issues, informed by international experiences, and analytical insights, is needed.

The longevity risk concerns the fact that while each person is certain to die, the age, the cause, and the place of death are not known. Some may die within a short period after retirement; while others may live for a much longer period. The latter category of persons may find their financial resources exhausted, while those dying early in retirement may not face this challenge

The earlier the age at which final withdrawal is permitted, the longer the period for which the accumulated balances will be required to be used to finance old-age. In 2001, in India, average men and women at age 60 had life expectancy of 16 years and 17 years respectively. This implies that accumulated balance in provident fund at age 55 will on an average need to last for 21 years for men, and 22 years for women. For some groups, such as civil servants, the life expectancy is much higher[4]. Moreover, the dispersion around the mean life expectancy should also be taken into consideration. India's demographic trend therefore suggests that there will be considerable lengthening of the pay-out phase. Regional and group variations will however be considerable.

The structure of the pay-out phase in the UTI AMC's micro-pension plans appears to have received less attention. A phased or systematic withdrawal plan would involve periodic withdrawal after retirement until the amounts are exhausted. Till then, the amount will continue to be invested as in the accumulation phase. This pattern may be too risky given the volatility in the capital markets. Moreover, there are many different ways to structure phased withdrawals.

Greater attention to this design issue is warranted, including the costs to the members of different types of options.

In savings-based micro-pension schemes, investment, macroeconomic and other risks are borne by the individual. Risk-sharing arrangements have therefore been often advocated.

Some have argued for co-contributions by the government at the accumulation stage for participants in micro-pensions. Other options include risk sharing by the society (through government) at the pay-out phase. These could be in the form of special bonds or bank deposits with higher interest rates for senior citizens (with a cap on total investment) which vary according to market interest rates on long-term government bonds. This can be combined with well-targeted and reasonably funded old age assistance schemes financed from general budgetary revenue.

More research is needed in the Indian context before designing risk-sharing options. In particular, political economy considerations, where populist policies often trump financial and economic sustainability, should play an important role in design of such options. It would appear that co-contributions by the government at the accumulation stage may be particularly vulnerable to dysfunctional populist policies.

The issue of who should bear the costs of the services of the third parties needs to be considered. If full costs are charged to members, micro-pension schemes may become financially unviable. Rigorous research efforts are needed to separate accounting and financial costs on the one hand from economic costs, which involve costing all the resources, used in delivering micro-pension services. Once these costs are identified, then cost-sharing arrangements among different stakeholders in both accumulation and pay-out phases can be further investigated.

III. CHANNELS FOR EXPANDING COVERAGE

This section focuses on potential channels for increasing coverage of micro-pensions. The role of micro finance institutions is of particular importance in this regard (Hermes and Lensink, 2007). The core activity of most micro-finance institutions is providing micro-credit. Micro-credit loans essentially are short term in nature and range between one year and three years. While repeat loans are often observed, the time horizon is usually not comparable with those of micro-pension schemes which have a much longer time horizon. Hence there is likely to be timing mismatch which means that the two services may not overlap entirely and to that extent there may not be cost savings.

Group loans account for 93 per cent of the micro finance in India (as per Sa-dhan, Industry association of Community Development Finance Institutions in India's website www.sa-dhan.net). A strong case can be made that if the potential of micro-finance is to be realized, loans should be on an individual basis and savers and borrowers need to be separated. Record keeping in the case of group loans is usually on a group level. Micro-pensions schemes will however require individual record keeping.

Individual members may fear that when the provider of micro-credit is also the administrator of the micro-pension schemes, at the time of default, the savings under the schemes may be adversely affected. This may reduce the attractiveness of the scheme. There is, therefore, a need to separate record keeping and other routine administration, fund management and custodian function of assets.

The linkage of the scheme with a commercial bank such as the collaboration of UTI AMC with Bank of India SHG members may give further credibility to the scheme, but may raise costs.

Only established micro finance institutions having the reputation required to market a scheme involving payouts over a long period of time can effectively market micro-pension schemes. While customers may be willing to avail micro-credit from less established institutions, they may not be willing to place long term savings with them.

However, in spite of these challenges, the case for using micro finance institutions who have passed due diligence process for micro pension services is strong. These institutions have incurred the establishment costs in various locations, not all of them are easily accessible. Many of them also have experienced personnel who can with some basic training market and administer these schemes.

Other Channels for Expanding Coverage

The other channel through which micro-pensions could be spread is by use of the post office network. Post offices have established ready presence in remote areas and hence this presence could be used to service micro-pension schemes.

Being part of the Government machinery, post offices enjoy high degree of credibility. While post office personnel are experienced in handling small savings they need to be trained to service pension schemes. Moreover the post office may need to offer more flexibility in terms of deposit timings and even perhaps doorstep collection services to ensure regularity of savings. An experienced asset management company should handle funds management.

Reverse mortgage arrangements to turn housing equity into retirement consumption schemes are another channel that can be considered. The 2007-08 budget has proposed that the National Housing Bank consider such an instrument.

It appears that if the variety of channels sketched above to expand the coverage of micro-pensions is utilized, there is a scope for enrolling around five million members over the next few years. This is not an insignificant number in the context of total pension coverage in India.

IV. REFORM DIRECTIONS

The analysis in the previous section has demonstrated that the micro-pensions sector is in the early stages of development in India. Relatively minor adjustments to standard individual pension plans been made in offering micro-pension products. The empirical basis of financial and economic sustainability of the schemes as well as risk management practices benefiting the members is still weak.

As Prahalad (2005) has persuasively argued, in offering standard middle and high income products to those at the "bottom of the pyramid", social entrepreneurship (along with social responsibility) which radically reduces transaction costs and results in genuine resource cost savings without compromising on quality is essential. This is the direction which micro-pension reforms should take.

In addition to design changes concerning exit load suggested earlier, the fund management fees will need to be substantially lowered. Aggarwal (2007) noted that the Coal Mines Provident Fund Organisation (CMPFO) recently conducted an auction to pick fund managers for assets of Rs. 20,000 crores (USD 4.6 billion). The lowest bids were for 0.01 per cent of assets under management far lower than the 1.75 to 2.25 per cent charged by the UTI AMF for micro-pensions. Admittedly, the two costs are not directly comparable. Nevertheless, they suggest possibilities for reducing costs which need to be encouraged. However, these will not come about automatically. The financial industry in general and micro-finance institutions in particular will need to be innovative. Minor modifications to existing schemes, while useful as a beginning, would clearly be insufficient to meet the needs.

Micro-pensions represent a long-term financial contract with potential for significant agency problems and systemic risk to the financial system. Due to the sensitivity of the population, the contingent liability is on the Government.

There is therefore a strong case for regulation on micro-pensions. The tabling of the bill of the Microfinancial Sector (Development and Regulation) Bill, 2007 provides for regulation of the microfinance sector by the NABARD. This is a positive step, which will result in mainstreaming of this sector. Similar regulation of micro-pensions is required. It is suggested that Pension Fund Regulatory and Development Authority (PFRDA) when it is formally functioning should consider forming a separate division for micro-pensions[5]. The division should work closely with SEBI, IRDA and NABARD so as to prevent regulatory arbitrage and bring coherence to the micro-pensions sector. The regulator should also play a development role by promoting professionalism and financial literacy.

V. CONCLUDING REMARKS

The current micro-pension arrangements in India are based on relatively minor modifications of the existing pension schemes. Not only the number of fund managers is limited, but the design of micro-pensions is also relatively rigid.

The paper has argued that to expand coverage of micro-pensions, social entrepreneurship (along with social responsibility) will be needed by the financial sector, including the MFIs, insurance companies and mutual funds. Such entrepreneurship should aim to drastically reduce overall transaction costs, including fund management costs. The paper has also argued that micro-pensions sector requires a regulator. The PFRDA as an overall pension regulator is an appropriate agency for regulating micro-pensions. But it must closely co-ordinate with SEBI, IRDA, RBI, and NABARD. The PFRDA should have a separate wing for micro-pensions in recognition of the special requirements. This wing should help develop appropriate products and delivery mechanisms, help instill confidence, promote professionalism and encourage financial literacy and inclusion.

Research on micro-pensions is in its infancy. Implications of alternative designs and delivery systems for micro-pensions need to be rigorously researched for financial sustainability and for their impact on the level of benefits to members. Different risk-sharing arrangements among all the stakeholders also need to be explored. The National Insurance Academy (NIA), NABARD (National Bank for Agriculture and Rural Development), university academics and industry researchers are urged to ensure that further progress of micro-pensions is based on sound empirical and analytical foundations.

There is a potential for micro-pensions to play a limited but useful role as an integral component of India's social security system.

NOTES

1. An annuity provides for a systematic liquidation of a capital sum. It is distinguished by a variety of features such as how the funds are invested, when annuitized payments are scheduled to begin, and how they are paid for (Shapiro and Streiff, 2004, p. 2). The mortality risk is the main risk faced by the life insurer, while investment risk is the main risk in provision of annuities. The increased life expectancy therefore reduces life insurance costs, but increases the annuities cost, i.e. lower annuity benefits for a given capital sum. The risk profile of those voluntarily seeking annuities increases if there is significant adverse selection problem, i.e. those who are especially likely to live longer constitute disproportionately large proportion of the demand for annuities.
2. If the third party uses traditional agent model to obtain members, costs will be higher, impacting the viability of micro-pensions.
3. The age at which final withdrawal is permitted may or may not coincide with the retirement age. In the Employees Provident Fund (EPF) scheme, administered by the Employees Provident Fund Organization (EPFO), the withdrawal age is 55 years, but the retirement age in India is generally higher, ranging from 58 to 60 years. In the pension plans of insurance companies, such as by HDFC Standard Life Insurance, the age at which vesting occurs (i.e. the pay-out phase begins) may vary between the age of 50 and 70 years.
4. According to LIC (1996-98). Occupational Pensioners Mortality, the life expectancy at age 60 was 22.5 years for all occupational pensioners.
5. The PFRDA Bill has been introduced in Parliament since 2004. But the left parties whose claim to speak on behalf of ordinary workers is dubious, have been using their temporary political clout to block the will of the majority by blocking the passage of the PFRDA Bill.

REFERENCES

Aggarwal, A. (2007). "Don't Compare Mutual Funds with Pension Plans", *Business Standard,* March 31.

Asher, M. (2007a). "Pension Reform and Old Age Grants in India" Paper presented at the conference on "Innovative Approaches to Social Security in India, Brazil and South Africa", University of Johannesburg.

Asher, M. (2007b). "India must breed more policy wonks", *Far Eastern Economic Review,* Vol. 170, No. 2, pp. 30-33.

Asher, M. (2006). " Pension Issues and Challenges Facing India", *Economic and Political Weekly*. November 11, 2006. pp. 4638-4641.

Asher, M. and Nandy, A. (2006). "Issues and Options in the Pay-out Phase in Defined Contribution Schemes", *Pravartak*, Vol. 1, Issue, pp. 1-7.

Hermes, N. and Lensink, R. (2007). "Impact of Micro finance: A Critical Survey", *Economic and Political Weekly*, February 10, pp. 462-465.

Liebig, P.S. and Irudaya Rajan, S., (ed.), (2003). "*An Aging India: Perspectives, Prospects and Policies*," USA: Haworth Press.

Prahalad, C.K. (2005). *The Fortune at the Bottom of the Pyramid: Eradicating Poverty through Profits*. Wharton School of Publishing, New Jersey.

Ross, S.G. (2004). "Collection of social contributions: Current practice and Critical Issues". Paper presented at the International Conference on Changes in the Structure and Organization of Social Security Administration, Cracow, Poland, 3-4 June.

Shankar, S. (2006). "Transaction Costs in Group Micro Credit in India: Case Studies of Three Micro Finance Institutions" Working Paper, Institute for Financial Management and Research.

Shapiro, D. and Streiff, T.F. (2004). *Annuities*, 4th edition, Dearborn: Dearborn Financial Publishing, Inc.

7

Clustering for Progress: The Road Travelled and the Way Ahead

KESHAB DAS, MUKESH GULATI,
TAMAL SARKAR and SUKANYA BANERJEE

I. CLUSTERS, THEIR RELEVANCE AND NEED FOR POLICY

The Concept and the Context: Why Promote Clusters?

At least since the mid-1980s, in both policy and academic circles, there is an increasing awareness across the globe regarding the contributions of micro, small and medium enterprises (MSMEs) towards economic development. These MSMEs have been instrumental in generating large scale employment, contributing towards rise in incomes of labour and returns to capital; and promoting regional development[1]. In fact, MSMEs are no longer seen as a transient phenomenon of dwindling importance of enterprises operating at a low scale. On the contrary, the increasing demand for technological and labour-use flexibility, which is the order of the day in many sectors, is more suitable to MSMEs rather than large integrated plants with relatively rigid managerial and production systems[2].

It has also been recognized during the last two decades that, often MSMEs[3] producing a range of similar or same products are found to co-exist in typical geographical locations for decades and even centuries in many countries. This phenomenon is referred to as clustering of MSMEs. Such clusters are found to be in plenty both in developed and transition economies as shown in Table 7.1.

Table 7.1: Clusters in Some Developed and Transition Economies (other than India)

S. No.	*Country*	*No. of Clusters*
	Developed Economies	
1.	Denmark	19
2.	France	95
3.	Germany	31
4.	Italy	199
5.	Japan	18
6.	Switzerland	13
7.	UK	165
8.	USA	152
	Transition Economies	
9.	Bahrain	3
10.	Bangladesh	23
11.	Brazil	4
12.	China	101
13.	Iran	116
14.	Kuwait	3
15.	Mexico	7
16.	Oman	24
17.	Pakistan	43
18.	Qatar	8
19.	Saudi Arabia	21
20.	Sri Lanka	15
21.	Thailand	35
22.	UAE	17

Note: List of clusters for the individual countries is in no way exhaustive and is a function of the extent of data gathered by this study. Again, since data for India is quite exhaustive, we have shown it separately, lest it should bias the table.

Sources: (1) P. Bianchi, *et al.* (1996) (2) http://www.lged-rein.org/solar/solar_sre_clustervill.htm (3) www.smeda.org.pk (4) www.ahan.org.pk (5) www.competitiveness.lk/ceramics.htm (6) Dr. Claas Van Der Linde (2002) (7) OECD 2007.

That clusters could 'fuel' regional industrial growth through productivity rise has been observed in numerous cases (M. Clara, 1995, DTI, 2004, Enright, 1998, World Development Report: 1999). Firms in cluster have shown higher productivity both in national as also international context as compared to their counterpart industries situated isolated and not in clusters. In India, ".... Micro and Small Enterprises (MSEs) have emerged as an important segment, providing resilience... in the post-liberalisation period... Further consolidation of the restructuring process wherein shifting from... non-cluster to cluster units is associated with better productivity and growth. It is likely that these core activities tend to gravitate towards product and/or spatial clusters..." (Awasthi, 2004). Such happenings in clusters were also demonstrated at the international level too. A study by the Bank of Italy to quantify comparative advantages of firms located in clusters, referring to it as a "cluster effect", established higher efficiency of cluster firms as compared to similar firms not located in clusters through an econometric analysis of a sample of firms located in known clusters (Paniccia *et al.*, undated).

In addition, there exist numerous examples to indicate that collective action by clustered firms has not only led to improvement in product quality but also helped them in having access to larger markets (Clara, 1995, Schmitz, 1999, World Development, 1999). It has further been observed that, being clustered, MSMEs choose networking and collective action as a strategy to access market, credit, infrastructure, R&D etc. which are required by individual units but cannot be obtained through individual efforts. Similarly, it will be easier for financial institutions to offer credit at the cluster level in a targeted fashion and with greater assurance of repayment.

Thus, there are strong cases for promotion of firms in a cluster, as a strategy for industrial development. Again, while at the enterprise level, a cluster might seem a place for purely private entrepreneurial activity, but from a policy perspective, various governments (national and sub-national), specialized institutes, service providers, academia and above all the consumers all have their specific role to play. In fact, "...Governments and public authorities can no longer be viewed as impersonal, impartial guarantors of socially optimal outcomes. Like private institutions, they are operated by people who develop and cherish their special skills, interests and attitudes. Public institutions are present in most main areas when it comes to influencing clusters." (The Cluster Policies Whitebook, 2004: 2). Further, the ability of a cluster to relate to and 'operate' across markets and regions has been recognized as special attributes that facilitates flexibility. It is imperative that the policy strategy considers the variety of competencies of a range of stakeholders and their roles that could be relevant for clusters.

Advantage Clusters: Some Basic Principles

In a cluster, MSMEs derive advantages that large firms usually get due to their size, through agglomeration economies that attract transporters, raw material and machinery suppliers, BDS providers etc. to the cluster and also through knowledge spillovers and increased cluster specialization (Marshall, 1890). Clusters also gain due to motivational effects that arise due to demanding customers, inter-firm rivalries and complementarities (Porter, 1990). Firms also gain due to low transaction cost because of the level of trust that is found in a cluster in general (OECD, 2007). However, these are all passive economies of scale and are omnipresent in a cluster (Schmitz: 1999).

What really make a difference between performing and non-performing clusters are active economies of scale, derived through conscious collaboration by consortia of firms, industry associations, vertical linkages, public-private partnerships and delivery of specialized services.

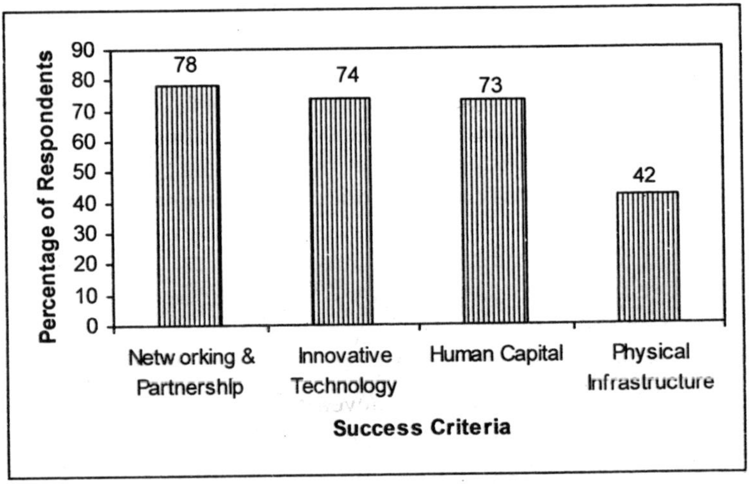

Source: DTI (undated), page no. 6

Fig. 7.1: Some Critical Success Factors in Cluster Development

As has been observed internationally, active economies of scale have complemented the development of successful clusters. A study of cluster development efforts (DTI, undated) shows that some of the important factors that propelled success are promotion of networking and partnerships, infusion of innovative technology, development of strong skills base and creation of infrastructure across the cluster (Figure 7.1).

Importantly, it has been underscored in a massive literature (e.g. World Development Report, 1999) that these collective gains have been obtained in clusters of such traditional goods like textiles, ceramics, furniture, processed food etc. and also in sophisticated products such as precision machine tools, pharmaceuticals, computer parts, surgical instruments etc.

Cluster-Definitional and Related Conceptual Issues

Clusters have been defined/conceptualized differently by different scholars/practitioners. An idea about the variety can be obtained from the compilation of some recent literature (Box 7.1).

Box 7.1: Clusters: Some Definitions

- "Clusters are a geographically proximate group of interconnected companies and associated institutions in a particular field linked by commonalities and complementarities. Clusters encompass a array of linked industries and other entities important to competition...including governmental and other institutions—such as universities, standard setting agencies, think tanks, vocational training providers and trade associations." *Porter (1998).*
- "... geographically bounded concentration of similar, related or complementary businesses, with active channels for business transactions, communications and dialogue, that share specialized infrastructure, labor markets and services, and that are faced with common opportunities and threats." *Rosenfeld (1997).*
- "Regional clustering has been used to describe industrial districts of small crafts firms, high technology centers, agglomerations of financial and business service firms in cities, company towns, and large branch plants and their supply chains." "....clusters at least must be characterized along relevant dimensions if appropriate policies are to be devised...(these include) ...density...breadth...depth...activity base...growth potential ...innovative capacity." *Enright (1998).*

Source: OECD, 2007, Cluster Policies, Whitebook, 2004 & Enright, 1998.

Broadly a cluster of enterprises may be defined as a typical geographical concentration of micro, small, medium and large firms producing same or a similar range of products (goods or services). Units in a cluster face same or similar set of threats (e.g. product obsolescence, lack of markets etc.) and opportunities (e.g. increasing turnover through quality up-gradation or introduction of new products or markets etc.) (MSME, 2006). The firms producing 'the product' by which a cluster is known are called principal firms or principal stakeholders of the cluster.

The principal firms obtain inputs from a range of supporting firms through backward and forward linkages. These include raw material suppliers and manufacturers of parts and machinery; intermediary buyers like traders, exporters and import agents; and technical and financial service providers like banks, technical institutions, private business development service (BDS) providers on quality, environment, design, energy, capital investment etc. Various interest groups such as product and umbrella associations/forums of firms also contribute towards the dynamics of the cluster. All these-principal firms, support firms and service providers, technical and financial institutions and interest groups are a part of the cluster and are called cluster stakeholders. However, there have been wide variances with respect to fixing the number of firms and area covered by a cluster.

The definitional debate: In fact, there is no hard and fast rule either regarding the generality of the product, or regarding the largeness of the area that a cluster covers. For example, in Austria, a successful wood cluster exists with less than a dozen firms, whereas the knitwear cluster of Prato in Italy had 9000 firms at one point of time (MSME, 2006).

Although attempts have been made to recognize a cluster by specifying the minimum number of units in a given measured location, these are difficult to generalize across activities/products. Italy is the cradle for cluster development for global understanding on clusters. It is probably the only country in the world that has a national law[4] for promotion of clusters, yet different regions within Italy have their own criteria for classifying areas as clusters, reflecting the need for diversity under the conceptual framework.

In practice, there exists considerable variety in classifying a cluster, especially with respect to how wide a product range and the geographic area a cluster too wide a should consist of. It has been observed that too wide a product range can make product group meaningless as the common opportunities and threats lose their sharpness or specificity. Similarly, too large a geographical area deprives the units in the cluster to exploit the development potential through proactive joint action. On the other hand, defining a product too narrowly, especially in the context of a transition economy can make the entire process of cluster mapping meaningless, as it becomes difficult to find a sizeable number of similar firms, with commonalities that enable interconnectedness. It may be mentioned here that conglomeration of firms does not necessarily imply a "cluster" (as defined above). Table 7.2 lists down such instances that are not considered as "cluster".

Table 7.2: Conglomerations Not Considered as Cluster

	Not a Cluster	*Reason*
1.	A *"sector"* that is present in various places all over a state or a country	Too large a geographical area deprives the units across the area to exploit advantages of proactive joint action.
2.	An *industrial estate* or an *industrial park having multiple products*	Too wide a product range means no common opportunities and threats. Hence, little scope of joint action.
3.	A *network* (small group) of enterprises producing similar products	Too small a number for enabling significant and variety of joint actions. These are often part of a cluster.
4.	A *cooperative*, which promotes cooperation among a number of enterprises under some norm, rule or a public scheme of assistance.	A central feature of dynamic clusters is "competitive cooperation". In case of a cooperative, competition does not exist. It is often a part of a cluster.
5.	A *group of villages, town or city* consisting of enterprises producing a diverse range of products or services.	These are clusters in a different sense and are not enterprise based clusters, which are being discussed in this paper.

Defining clusters in India: In India a number of agencies have come up with a range of definitions, tailored to suit the typology of clusters, which an agency decides/is mandated to cater to, by specifying a certain minimum number of units in a given measured location.

Table 7.3: Defining Clusters in India

Institution	*Definition*
Integrated Handloom Cluster Development Programme (IHCDP), Ministry of Textiles	A handloom cluster has been defined as one having a minimum of 500 looms.[5]
National Minority Development Finance Corporation (NMDFC)	Handloom cluster, which has more than 75 per cent of the population as "minorities".
Scheme of Fund for Regeneration of Traditional Industries (SFURTI), Ministry of MSME	A micro village industry cluster having 500 beneficiary families of artisans/micro enterprises, suppliers of raw materials, traders, service providers etc., located within one or two revenue sub-divisions in a district (or in contiguous districts).
DC (Handicrafts), Ministry of Textiles	Agglomerations having 100 artisans. In case of North East Region, Jammu & Kashmir and other hilly terrains, the clusters will have a minimum of 50 artisans.
NABARD, Cluster Development Programme	Micro enterprises and household units functioning on SHG mode and having a minimum of 50 beneficiaries upto a maximum of 200. In intensive clusters, the number of beneficiaries may go up to 500-700 and can even extend over a block or taluka.
Government of Gujarat	A minimum of 50 industrial units, indulging in the manufacture of the same or related products and located within a radius of 10 km in a particular location.
Government of Orissa Handicraft cluster	At least 100 traditional artisans practicing the same craft for non-KBK districts and at least 50 traditional artisans in KBK districts and situated within a radius of 3-5 kms.
UNIDO-CDP	At least 100 SME units or 50 handicraft units in a town/city or few villages and their surrounding areas for an industrial (traditional manufacturing) or an artisanal cluster respectively. Further a minimum of 500 handlooms for a handloom cluster.

Given the necessity for regular interaction for active cooperation among the cluster stakeholders, a cluster may be defined as a compact geographical area that can be traversed in 1.5 to 2 hours by local means of transportation and preferably specialized in single or analogous products[6].

It is important, to observe that there is a strong case for not trying to have a common definition of clusters; in fact, depending upon the nature of activity in a cluster and the intervention required, different functional definitions should be relevant subject to the condition that (a) the product range should not be too wide and (b) the area covered provides scope for interaction among stakeholders. Table 7.4 is indicative of the different ways by which a cluster can be distinguished; it is imperative, however, that reliable statistics for these variables are available.

Table 7.4: Common Parameters for Classifying Clusters

Sub-sector/Product/Service			
Geographical Area (in sq. km. for the identifiable meso level locality)			
Name of place: One that is easily identifiable or has a brand value			
Parameters	*Measurable Unit*	*Mature Clusters (Higher cut-off)*	*Potential Clusters (Lower cut-off)*
Enterprises	Number		
Turnover	Value		
Export	Value		
Employment Size	Number		

Clusters in India: Typologies and Status

There exists no single method of typifying a cluster. Localised clusters are concentrated geographically while dispersed clusters are spread across wider geographic areas. The density of a cluster defines its number of firms and or the volume of business handled by it. The breadth of the cluster defines the availability of few (narrow cluster) or more (broad cluster) of its related industries within its geographic range. Depth of the cluster depicts the availability of supply chains in the cluster. A localised, dense, broad and deep cluster are expected to be activity rich and has higher innovative capacity (Enright, 1998). Here again issues related to normal and specialized (Schmitz, 1999) activities come into operation.

These characteristics can help to identify a cluster, but these are cluster neutral at least from a policy view point. Issues that will make a difference from a policy angle are the target and a path that a typical cluster might set for itself. From a policy view point, (Bianchi *et al.*, 1997) a cluster can be typified by its 'current and future' and 'market and production' structure as shown in Figure 7.2, where 'L' stands for local, 'N' for national and 'I' for international. The framework suggests that a cluster, or at least majority of its firms, can at least theoretically have any of these nine combinations.

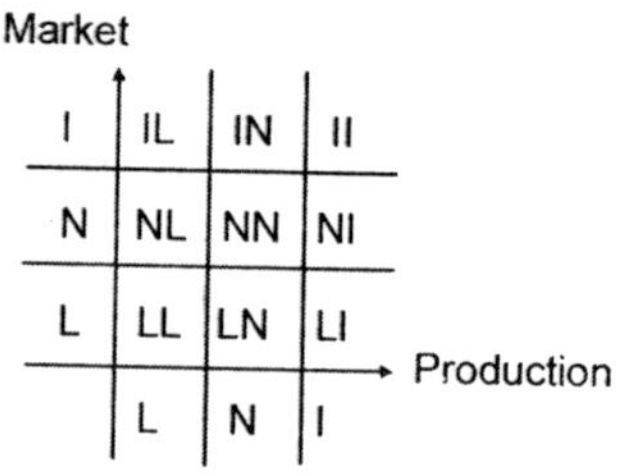

Fig. 7.2: Market-Production Framework

While local, national or international markets are self-explanatory; local production system is based mostly on local resources, whereas national or international production system depends mostly on national and international resources. Such resources include sourcing of raw materials, technology, sub-contracting, HRD etc. The challenges for micro enterprise cluster are often to move from an 'LL' to 'LN' to 'NN' and even an 'NI' framework. This naturally makes the cluster product most efficient. Similarly, the challenge for a traditional manufacturing cluster is to move from an 'LN' to 'NN' to 'NI' and ultimately to 'II' framework respectively. Figure 7.3 and Figure 7.4 depicts a possible path each for such transition for a traditional manufacturing and an micro enterprise cluster respectively, where policy is relevant.

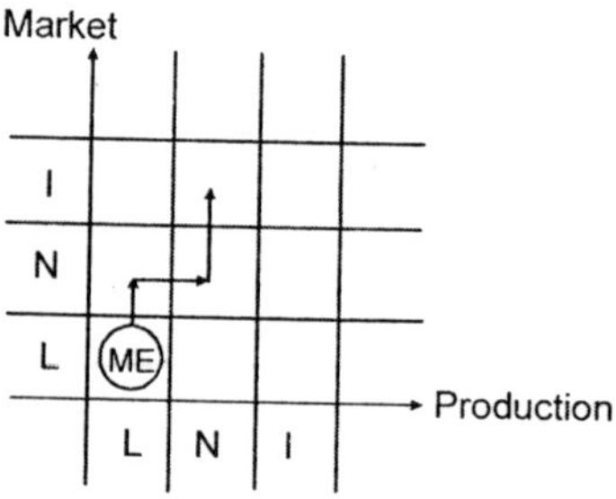

Fig. 7.3: Micro Enterprise (ME) Cluster

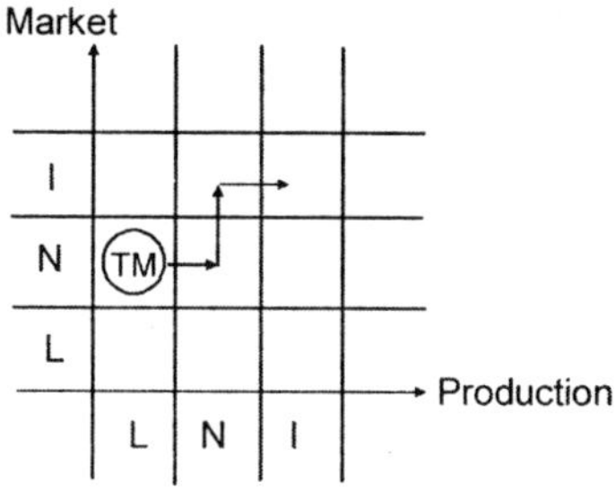

Fig. 7.4: Traditional Manufacturing (TM) Cluster

These are the typologies of clusters which predominates the Indian economy and employ a substantial secondary sector labour force.

Again, while the high growth rate of the Indian economy is heating up the labour market, although selectively, yet the export basket of India continues to be dominated by low-technology goods and services that are highly price sensitive and low value adding. This is a situation for intense stock taking on dual count—(a) current level of competitiveness is fast eroding in high tech industries and (b) a huge basket of industries that are major sources of employment are not known for innovation at all, an issue that is imperative to handle the increasing global challenges of competitiveness. Thus apart from looking into innovation related issues in cluster, we find that another category of clusters, namely those encompassing high profile industries, will require distinct policy support for its ever innovative nature, which conditions its survival/growth or peril.

Typology and distribution of Indian clusters: Hence, from a policy perspective, it would be useful to follow a 3-way classification for clusters, namely high-tech clusters such as those in the IT and IT enabled services, computers, bio technology and related services, precision instrumentation or avionics, etc. traditional manufacturing clusters (non high-tech and non-micro clusters) and low-tech poverty-intensive micro enterprise (handloom, handicraft and other micro enterprises) clusters. The traditional manufacturing and micro enterprises clusters may also be termed as natural enterprises clusters[7].

Based on the above broad classification of clusters in India, the real challenge is to obtain a reliable database for the same. It needs to be noted that no official statistics is yet available, which provides cluster level information. However, independent survey/study (secondary analysis) by various ministries/agencies/ institutes suggest that India has around 6600 (goods based clusters). It would, nevertheless, be safe to estimate that close to 6000 of these clusters would fall in the third category, namely, low-tech micro enterprise clusters (as mostly in the artisanal—handloom & handicraft and micro-enterprise segments). Of the remaining clusters, over 99 per cent are traditional manufacturing cluster and the rest account for high-tech clusters. Though, there exist very few concentrations of IT, bio-technology and other high-tech firms in India such (mostly) policy promoted cluster are on the rise[8] and will require separate policy touch for excelling. There is no database of services clusters (e.g. ITES, tourism, education).

Table 7.5: Typology of Cluster: Significance to the National Economy

Parameters	*Micro-enterprise Clusters*	*Traditional Manufacturing Clusters*	*High-tech Clusters*
Typology of Products (few examples)	Handloom, handicraft, coir, village industries	Leather & leather products, automotive components, ceramics etc.	Information Technology, pharmaceuticals, bio-technology, computers, tourism, education etc.
Number of Clusters	6000 (93.6%)	388 (6.1%)	20 approx. (0.3%)
Estimated Share of Employment (by cluster typology)	80%	14%	6%
Average Wage levels	Low	Medium	High
Likely growth rate (2002-07)	Negative or marginally positive	Positive (10-15%)	Positive (20-30%)

Source: Annual Report of various Ministries, Government of India and UNIDO-CDP cluster database and estimates.

Given the distribution of such clusters, it could be represented through the following pyramid that essentially, indicates the preponderance of micro enterprise clusters (Figure 7.5).

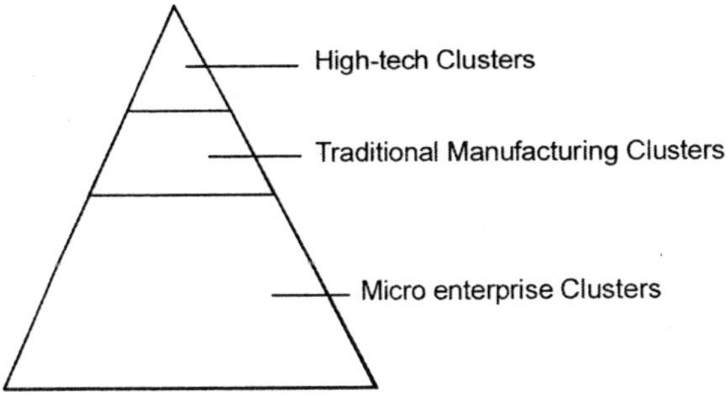

A region-wise distribution of the typology of clusters (other than high-tech) appears in Table 7.6[9].

Table 7.6: Expanse of Indian Clusters

	Traditional Manufacturing		*Micro enterprise*					
			Handicraft		*Handloom*		*Others*	
Region	*No.*	*(%)*	*No.*	*(%)*	*No.*	*(%)*	*No.*	*(%)*
North	123	31.7	716	25.75	140	23.56	698	24.11
East	36	9.28	645	23.19	43	7.24	464	16.02
West	140	36.09	764	27.47	134	22.57	787	27.17
South	89	22.95	502	18.05	214	36.02	858	29.62
North-East	0	0	153	5.51	63	10.61	89	3.08
Total	388	100.00	2780	100.00	594	100.00	2896	100.00

Source: Database of UNIDO-CDP and Third Census of SSI units, 2001-02.

Clustering in India: Scope for Policy

In India a number of approaches to support MSMEs are operational with specific objectives. For instance creation of industrial estates focuses on provision of infrastructure facilities. Business incubators support individual firms in creating new ways of doing business. SHG formation as also microfinance supports micro units in getting credit. Various technology upgradation programmes as well as marketing and credit schemes support individual firms to create or adopt new technology and enhance business scope.

There are also a number of sectoral policies that promote various typical sectors, e.g. leather, textiles, etc. However most such policies are not designed or motivated enough to utilize the benefits of clustering by promoting "proactive joint action" by utilizing a range of internal and external linkages to enhance productivity, move up the value chain and be innovative. Thus a typical cluster policy that will promote "Joint Action" and "Linkages" in clusters along with the usual macroeconomic and other sectoral and regional policies will do well for firms which are in clusters. It is also but natural, that a developed cluster so created, will create better utilization of the scope provided for in sectoral and regional policies too. Similarly, the spirit of cluster policy can also be mainstreamed in sectoral and regional policies. A number of schemes for cluster based development have also become operational (details provided in section 2 of the Report) with varying objectives, methodologies and scope, producing various results and lessons. Thus, it is crucial as well as timely to put in order the parameters that will address the needs of a range of clusters and will deliver through professional implementation mechanism.

II. CLUSTER DEVELOPMENT EXPERIENCE: SIGNIFICANCE IN INDIA AND ABROAD

Although, clusters exist for centuries, comprehensive cluster based support at policy level is rather a recent phenomenon globally as also in India. Interestingly, this approach seems to fit in well with support at policy the paradigm of promotion, internationalization and integration with global economy instead of protection and enterprise level support. However, globally and more so for transition economies, not all clusters are high performance or 'overachiever' clusters. While 'performing' clusters follow 'high road' "...synonymous with innovation, high quality, functional flexibility and good working conditions...", numerous 'non-performing' or 'underachiever' clusters follow a 'low road' "...based on competing with the basis of low prices, cheap materials ... and cheap labour..." (Humphrey and Schmitz, 1995) in their growth pursuits. A turnaround here necessitates a planned cluster development initiative.

International Policy Experience: Major Programmes/ Schemes/Approaches

An OECD Study (2007) suggests that apart from developing clusters, cluster development initiatives can be considered useful for their other merits. For example, trade regulation and competition policy on an international scale may confine a country's ability to provide direct firm subsidies and here cluster policy provides a way out for promoting competitiveness in industry. It also helps to dialogue with the private sector and focus provision of public funds from a demand based paradigm. However, there is a clear difference between programmes that attempt to strengthen existing clusters and those that conceptualise to build on embryonic concentrations by bringing in new activity and then promoting networking. Again, through such policy, one should ensure that no attempts are made to defend products and services, which will definitely not be sustainable in the long run.

A review of cluster development initiatives (policies and programmes) in both developed and transitional economies reveals the following[10]:

- Cluster promotion has become an integral part of the national industrial development in countries at different levels initiatives are of economic development.
- Cluster based initiatives are known to be in operation in more than 50 countries as per available literature. Some of the countries that have clear policy/programme on cluster development are listed in Table 7.7.

Table 7.7: Some Countries have Cluster Development Policies and/or Programmes[11]

	Country	*Cluster Policy*	*Cluster Programmes*
1.	China	×	✓
2.	Finland	✓	✓
3.	France	✓	✓
4.	Germany	×	✓
5.	Italy	✓	✓
6.	Japan	×	✓
7.	Korea	✓	✓
8.	Spain	×	✓
9.	Sweden	×	✓
10.	USA	×	✓
11.	Saudi Arabia	×	✓
12.	UK	✓	✓

Note: Information given in this table is not exhaustive and is just a reflection of the extent of data collected.

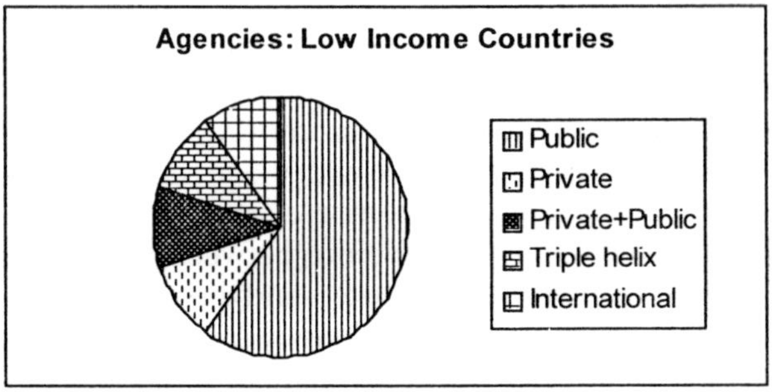

Fig. 7.6A: Agencies Participating in Cluster Initiatives: Low Income Countries

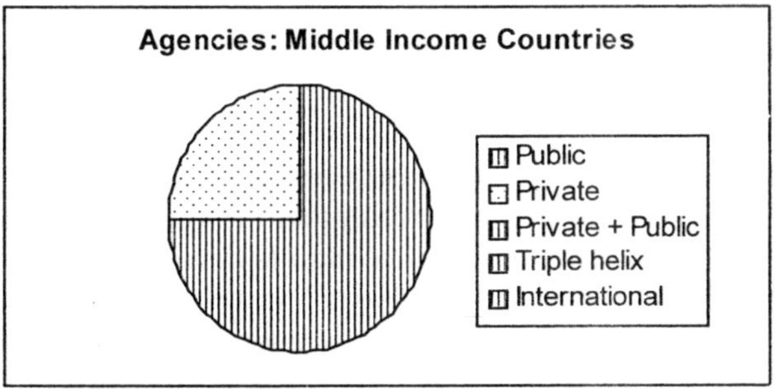

Fig. 7.6B: Agencies Participating in Cluster Initiatives: Middle Income Countries

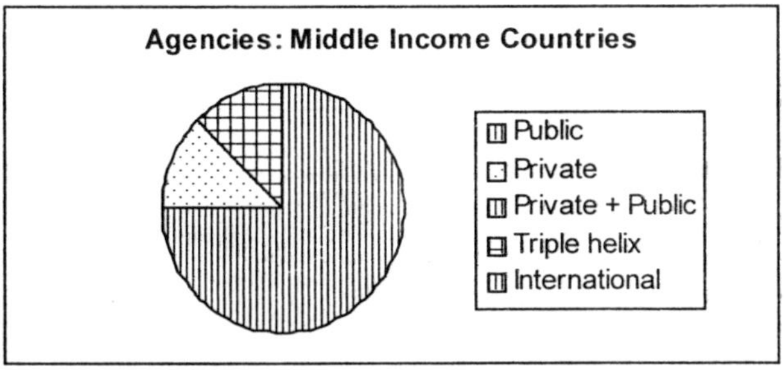

Fig. 7.6C: Agencies Participating in Cluster Initiatives: High Income Countries

Note: In the diagrams above, we should note that the categories are interpenetrating, *i.e.*, some countries have more than one agencies operating to facilitate cluster initiatives. These charts are based on the analysis of 25 country programmes.

- Share of public funding, whether from domestic or international sources is quite high. In a number of instances, governments financed between 75 and 90 per cent, irrespective of the level of development of a country. Private sector has also chipped in, but its share is marginal.
- Cutting across sub-sectors, in many countries (both economically developed and developing), the state has promoted specialized support services through formation of institutions specialized for promoting competitiveness.
- In most developed economies (e.g., France, Italy, Norway, Spain and South Korea) emphasis have been on promoting innovativeness in high-tech knowledge-based clusters through facilitating industry-academia-government networks. In a number of cases, role of the state has been envisaged for the initial period of development.
- In most countries, especially developing ones, product specific (both traditional and modern) cluster programmes have been designed. These often include intervention not only in the production process (through input, finance and technology support) but also in helping enterprises link up with export market and business service provision.
- There is clear time framework of implementing a cluster initiative in most countries, although in many cases such programmes are carried out as a dynamic long-term process.
- In most cases, linkages with global value chain has been emphasized for higher value addition and investments made in key facilities as creating networking platforms for information exchange.
- A notable aspect of cluster initiatives in most countries has been the collaboration between ministries, other external agencies and private sector. In many countries, the regional governments have also taken active interest in these efforts.
- Selection of clusters are done top down (as per priorities and judgement of the funding institution) or bottom up (self-selection through call for proposals) or a combination of both.

- Different approaches are required while supporting a leading or lagging region/dynamic or sinking sectors. Providing a blanket approach to all sectors can be ineffective and dilute available resource and focus.
- In general, three types of interventionary instruments are used—engaging actors (sensitisation and promotion), provide collective services (short run activities) not available from the private domain and facilitating business linkages (long run activities).
- It has also been found prudent to offer a range of instruments so that clusters at various levels of maturity find the support useful and popular instruments need to be upscaled.
- Linking clusters in same industries over different geographic areas but under a common theme helps cross learning.
- Coordination of stakeholders, calls for a specific person—the facilitator with networking skills and abilities. At its most basic form of facilitation an animator is employed to bring firms together for informational or social events.....". Taking the facilitation role further.....network building....." In Denmark there was a broker certification system. "...The concept of facilitator training and certification continues to be used today....." (OECD, 2007).
- At the operational level, disappointment comes often due to insufficient funding and timeframe. Period less than 3 years were found to be highly inadequate. Performance related funding is also practiced. Shared responsibility of centre and region is one vehicle for supporting policy coherence. Administrative boundary issue is also a frequent challenge.

There is also need for—

(a) demand oriented approach,
(b) broad based networking with range of stakeholders,
(c) ownership of project by local stakeholders,
(d) empowering them by providing appropriate skills, and
(e) provide right motivation and incentives.

Box 7.2: International Cluster Development Initiatives of UNIDO

> "..... The case of Hondurus represents a project which evolved from the creation of SME networks into the establishment of a specialized institution (CERTEC) acting as a networking promotion agency. The case of Nicaragua illustrates two main points: how, as a result of its successes with network brokering, a project has achieved significant influence on policy making at the national level and how the principles of scale economies inform the delivery of appropriate support measures. The case of Mexico highlights a case of promoting vertical integration arguing for the direct involvement of large-scale manufacturers into suppliers' upgrading efforts. The case of Jamaica presents an example of entry at the top institutional level (whereby the effort to bring cluster-based development lays at the operational core of the national SME support agency and as a case of creation of specialized service centres (on garments, fashion, furniture etc.)....".

Source: Ceglie, Clara and Dini: UNIDO (1997).

- Ability to measure success is a challenge. There exists a spectrum of methodologies for evaluation of any programme ranging from take up rates of project, number of jobs created, innovations fructified, new business launched, overall cluster economic performance, ability to attract additional funds, etc.

Box 7.3: Measuring Success—Some Case Studies

> - *Finland* Centres programme measure success by the number of jobs created, innovations done, participants and persons trained.
> - *Japan's* Industrial Cluster programme measure the number of collaborative projects and new business launched by firms and universities as yardsticks of success.
> - *Spain's* Basque Country programme focuses on overall cluster economic performance.
> - The *Norway* Programme tracks indicators common to all projects (increased cooperation, innovation and international involvement) and specific goals per individual project (project's own scale, level of development, challenges and potential).
> - The *Georgia* Research Alliance programme, measure success (among others) by their ability to attract additional funds, whose goal was to increase the economic performance for the state via technology, states to have achieved a 5 to 1 leverage, attracting 1 billion USD in federal research dollars and 1 billion USD in private investment for the state's total investment of 400 million USD.

Source: OECD, 2007.

To summarize, we find that, irrespective of the economic status of a nation, the state has always remained an active promoter of inducing cluster-based development of MSMEs. Apart from the ministries that promoted cluster development, there exists a synergy among the promoters, other external agencies and the private sector in such cluster development initiatives. Areas of intervention in a cluster are dependent on the economic status of a nation. In most developed economies, emphasis has been laid on promoting innovativeness. Here, the critical success factors identified in the global context are networking, partnership, innovative technology and strong skills base for high profit yielding products. Whereas, product specific cluster programmes (e.g. for artisanal or industrial clusters), with a mixed basket of typology of support (e.g. marketing, technology, linkages to global value chain, financing etc.) are more prevalent in transition economies.

It is important to note here that impact of cluster development on typical developing country issues such as poverty alleviation or industrial relocation, etc. has not figured prominently in the policy issues *per se*. However, one has a feeling, that it is the beginning of a long churning process, which has just started maturing.

SSI Policy Experience in India Prior to 1991

With almost 60 years of policy experience in India concerning small firm development, there is hardly an aspect of intervention that has not been touched upon. In fact, small scale industry (SSI) policy has included numerous schemes and programmes addressing vital issues such as credit, technology upgradation, skill formation, marketing support, tax rebates, export promotion and infrastructure creation. As in any policy context, these various instruments quintessentially have been either regulatory or promotional in nature. In terms of promotional measures, again, while priority sector lending, variety of fiscal concessions and rebates on inputs were some of the common incentives provided to the SSI sector as a whole, sector-specific and issue (e.g. technology) specific support schemes also formed part of the policy strategy. It would be fair to surmise that these regulatory and promotional measures have contributed both, directly and indirectly, to the growth of the sector.

However, on a closer look, it is easy to comprehend that government remained grossly committed to play the role of protector and/or support provider to whichever unit that came under a certain defined size parameter. In certain cases support was provided to specific industry groups. The example of giving boost to sub-sectoral industrial estates or product-oriented parks sharply brings out the focus of such an approach. In this process of state as benefactor of small enterprises what probably lost sight was the understanding, assessing and addressing the emerging issues from a systemic perspective. Supporting the route of market-based solutions, wherever those would have been possible, was also not deliberated upon.

There was also lack of convergence between various 'stand-alone' schemes. Such convergence is critical as in the growth cycle, while the journey can start at any point, be it technology upgradation, finance, market, organizational structure; at some point there will be necessity for other support too. In the absence of such follow up support in a natural and quick succession, the initial growth path can be a wasted investment.

Further, these policy instruments seem to have paid little attention to the potential of targeting a collective of enterprises with a shared business vision; which is an important vehicle to promote growth in a competitive business environment. Importantly, it seems clear from global experiences of inducing such group approach (Nadvi, 1999, Rosenfeld, 1996, Rabellotti, 1999, Schmitz, 1999) and even somewhat limited Indian experience (1997-2007); that the roles played by BMOs, BDS providers, specialized NGOs and private sector value chain partners (especially for poverty intensive clusters) have been significant in fostering MSME clusters.

Cluster Development Thoughts in India

Thematic issue (e.g. technology) based development in cluster, was initiated as early as 1987 by SBI through their Project UPTECH and soon followed up by SIDBI in 1991. In 1996 a UNIDO study identified a list of 138 traditional manufacturing and micro enterprise clusters. In 1997, the Abid Hussain Committee on Small Scale Industries forcefully brought in the dimension of clusters in SSI promotion. It said: "...this (cluster based approach) is a very practical approach to SME promotion in India since there already exist a large range of small scale industry clusters across the country...". This was immediately simultaneously (1997) taken up by a more integrated cluster development programme by UNIDO-CDP with a special emphasis on social capital as a key strategy for cluster development. Besides UNIDO through its cluster projects also developed a methodology on cluster development. The then DC (SSI) also started a project, UPTECH, in clusters as early as 1998 (MSME, 2006).

Subsequently various Budget Speeches of the Central Government highlighted the importance of cluster based development. The Finance Minister in his budget speech in 1999-2000 on rural industrialization said, "...Accordingly, I propose a National Programme for Rural Industrialisation (NPRI) with the mission to set up 100 rural clusters every year to give a boost to rural industrialization". Similar lines of support were given to the handloom sector in the Union Budget 2005-06, "...The Government proposes to adopt the cluster development approach for the production and marketing of handloom products." The significance of cluster is also well highlighted in the Union Budget 2006-07, "...the Prime Minister has decided to constitute an Empowered Group of Ministers who will lay down the policy for cluster development and oversee the implementation..."

An Approach Paper to the 11th Five Year Plan document states that "...A cluster approach can help increase viability by providing these units with infrastructure, information, credit and support services of better quality at lower costs, while also promoting their capacity for effective management of their own collectives..." (Planning Commission, 2006). Similar emphases on achieving industrial progress through clusters have been expressed in Budget papers and official documents of various state governments.

Cluster Development Schemes/Programmes in India

Though thematic development initiatives in clusters dates back to the late eighties, it was only as late as 2002-03 that holistic cluster development programmes gathered some noticeable momentum at the national level, with the initiation of such a programme by the then Ministry of SSI (now Ministry of MSME).

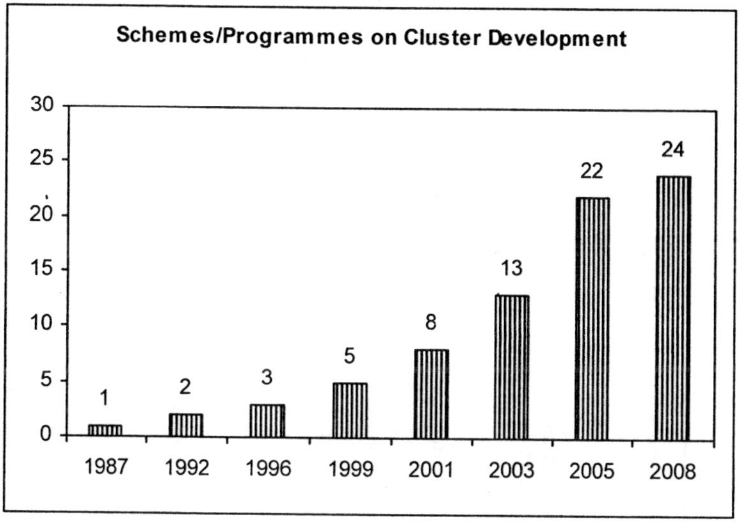

Fig. 7.7: Year-wise Distribution of Schemes/Programmes on Cluster Development in India

During the two decades of cluster development initiatives, around 24 schemes/programmes have supported or continue supporting various forms of cluster development initiatives in India. Out of these listed schemes, 9 have been part of three Ministries of Central Government, namely, the Ministry of Textiles, Ministry of MSME and Ministry of Commerce and Industry. The State Governments of Gujarat, Orissa, Kerala, Rajasthan and Madhya Pradesh have also initiated schemes/programmes at the state level covering clusters across sub-sectors. Additionally, financial and technical institutions such as SBI, SIDBI, NABARD, NMDFC, NEDFi and NMCC have also devised schemes/schemes to support clusters. International institutions like UNIDO and ILO are also implementing various cluster development programmes. Department of Ayush, Government of India has allocated Rs. 500 crores for development of 20-25 clusters in the 11th Five-Year Plan[12]. Some techno-commercial institutions at the national and state level (e.g. CII[13], RUDA[14] etc.) are also involved in several cluster based developmental activities[15]. The year of inception, the typology and the number of clusters supported under each scheme or programme is given in Table 7.8.

Table 7.8: Schemes/Programmes of Cluster Development Institutions in India

	Year of Inception of Scheme	*Typology of Clusters Assisted*	*Clusters Assisted (2006-07)*
Central Government			
1. Ministry of Textiles			
Scheme for Integrated Textile Parks (SITP)	2005-06	Textiles (Handlooms & Powerlooms)	30
Baba Saheb Ambedkar Hastshilp Vikas Yojana Scheme (AHVY)—DC (Handicrafts)	2001-02	Handicraft	684
Integrated Handloom Cluster Development Scheme (IHCDP) DC (Handlooms)	2005-06	Handloom	21
Textiles Committee of India	2002	Textiles (Handlooms and Powerlooms)	23
2. Ministry of MSME			
Micro and Small Enterprises Cluster Development Programme (MSECDP)	1998	Traditional manufacturing & micro enterprise	90
National Small Industries Corporation Ltd. (NSIC)	2002-03	Traditional manufacturing	30
National Programme for Rural Industrialisation (NPRI)	1999-2000	Micro-enterprises	100
Scheme of Fund for Regeneration of Traditional Industries (SFURTI)	2005-06	Micro-enterprises	100
3. Ministry of Commerce and Industry			
Industrial Infrastructure Upgradation Scheme (IIUS)	2004-05	Traditional manufacturing	26
Other Institutions			
4. NMDFC Micro Financing Scheme through the Cluster Development Approach	2005-06	Micro-enterprises	5
5. SBI Project UPTECH	1987-88	Traditional manufacturing & micro enterprise	28
6. SIDBI Technology Upgradation Programme (TUP)	1991	Traditional manufacturing & micro enterprise	45
SIDBI—Financing and Development of SMEs	2006-07	Traditional manufacturing & micro enterprise	3
7. NABARD Cluster Development Programme	2003-04	Micro-enterprises, Handloom and Handicrafts	48
8. NMCC—Project Vikas with Support from Microsoft	2006-07	Traditional manufacturing	7
9. NEDFI Cluster Development Programme	2004-05	Micro-enterprise	9

(*Contd.*)

	Year of Inception of Scheme	Typology of Clusters Assisted	Clusters Assisted (2006-07)
State Government			
10. Margin Money Scheme for Cluster Development Activities (Government of Kerala) Grant assistance to Cluster Development Activity (Government of Kerala)	2003	Traditional manufacturing and micro enterprise	17
11. Gujarat Industrial Policy—2000, Scheme for Assistance to Cluster Development	2000	Traditional manufacturing and micro enterprise	19
12. Integrated Cluster Development Programme (Traditional products of Khadi & Village Industries, Sericulture and Crafts & Handloom Products) (Government of MP)	2004-05	Micro-enterprise, (Handloom, Handicraft)	6
13. Craft Village Scheme (Silpigram Yojana) (Government of Orissa)	2004-05	Handicraft	30
14. Cluster Development Programme (Government of Rajasthan)	2005-06	Handloom and Handicraft	15
International Organisation			
15. UNIDO Cluster Development Programme, Delhi UNIDO Cluster Development Programme, Orissa UNIDO Consolidated Project for SME Development in India	1996 2005 2007	Traditional manufacturing and micro enterprise	20
16. Boosting Employment through Small Enterprise Development (ILO)	2000	Handicraft	2
Total			*1358*

Source: (i) Ministries of Central Government (www.goidirectory.nic.in); (ii) Official websites of the State Government and other institutions (the websites are provided in the bibliography); (iii) Personal meetings.

Analysis of Schemes: Macro Parameters

At a broader level of classification, all cluster schemes can be divided into two broad categories, viz (i) those with holistic cluster promotion focus and (ii) those with a specific area of support such as technology, infrastructure, BDS, etc. in a cluster. In a substantive sense, all Central Government schemes and most state government schemes have adopted a certain variant of a holistic UNIDO cluster development approach, which evolved as a result of intense experience of cluster development across 20 clusters over a wide sectoral and geographical expanse for over 11 years (1996-2007) (for details, see, Annex 3).

The basic functional components such as undertaking diagnostic studies and engaging Cluster Development Agents (also termed as Cluster Development Executives) form part of most of these schemes, e.g., the schemes like AHVY, IHCDP, TC, MSECDP and SFURTI. In certain cases, developing infrastructure has been included as a priority area. The state government schemes are fairly general in nature and aim at encouraging public private participation in areas like cluster level infrastructure (as in Gujarat) or employment creation (as in MP). The financial institutions, however, have emphasized improvement in technology in clusters and the provision to provide credit for the purposes. A list of possible cluster related activities appears in Annex 2.

Individual schemes focus on different types of clusters depending upon their target clientele, e.g. DC (Handlooms) for handloom cluster, Ministry of ARI (now MSME) in rural cluster, Ministry of SSI (now MSME) in industrial clusters set in both rural and urban backdrop, etc. The state governments have typically chosen to support a wide range of clusters, but, expectedly rural and artisanal ones for poverty intensive cluster states, e.g. Madhya Pradesh and Orissa. So far as the financial institutions (for instance, NMDFC, SBIUPTECH, SIDBI) are concerned, the selection of clusters are tilted towards village and micro enterprise clusters for NMDFC and a mix for SBI UPTECH and SIDBI. Details of cluster schemes is provided in Annex 4.

It is estimated that the 24 schemes (operational or completed) have supported around 1358 clusters so far, of which 278 are traditional manufacturing and 1080 are micro enterprise clusters (as shown in Figure 7.8). The inception of AHVY (under DC

(Handicrafts), Ministry of Textiles) in 2001-02 resulted in a remarkable increase in the number of artisanal clusters supported, prior to which focus was mainly laid on traditional manufacturing clusters. No cluster in the area of high tech has been supported so far by the schemes.

The resource allocated for cluster development under the listed schemes of assistance is estimated at Rs. 700 crore till 2006-07. Of the total estimated amount, 91.4 per cent has been contributed by the Central Government, 2.4 per cent by the State and the remaining

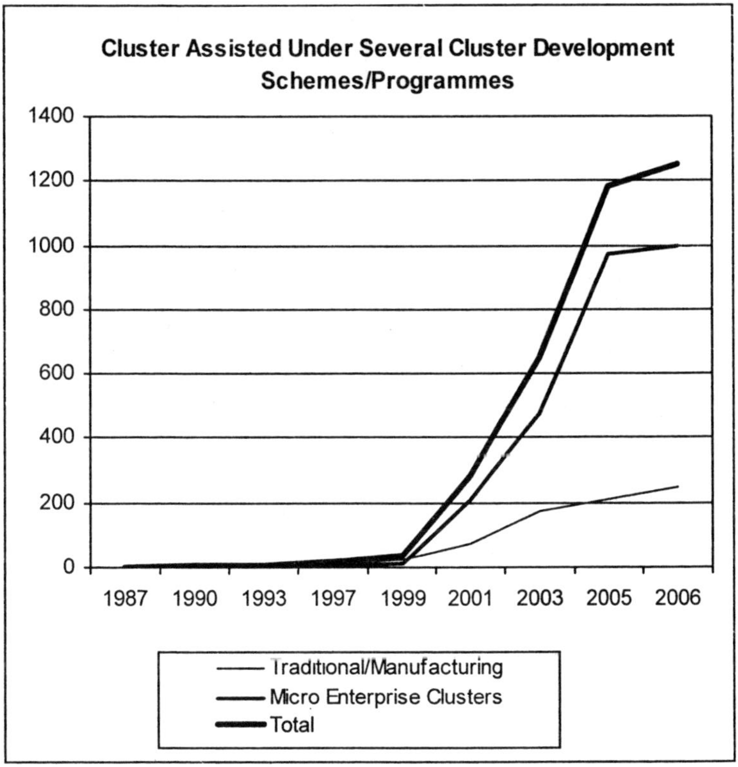

Fig. 7.8: Year wise Cluster Assisted under several Cluster Development Schemes/Programmes

6.2 per cent by the techno-financial institutes and international organisations.

The amount of assistance assigned for cluster development is heavily skewed towards infrastructure[16], amounting to 87 per cent of the total expenditure as shown in Figure 7.9.

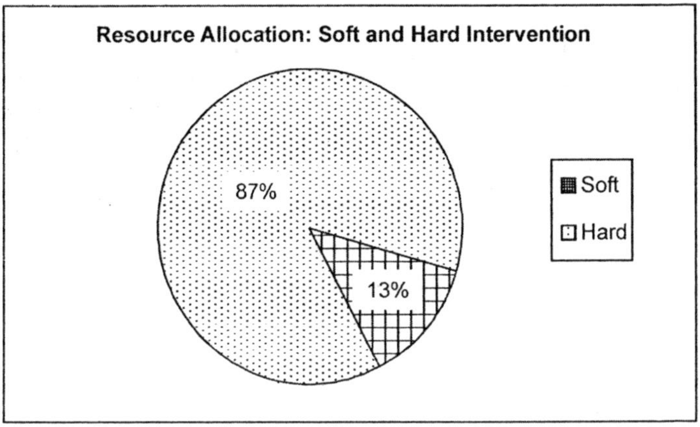

Fig. 7.9: Resource Allocated for Soft and Hard Interventions

It is estimated that during the next five years, resources worth Rs. 4500 crore of development fund are likely to be invested (subject to various clearances) for cluster development. An estimated 80 per cent of this amount is likely to be targeted for cluster infrastructure.

Scheme Support for Typologies of Interventions

The 'typology of interventions' in clusters in India can also be broadly categorized into: (1) market development, (2) enhancing. productivity and competitiveness, and (3) promotion of local governance structures (networks). The 'nature of activities' for each of the above typology can be broadly classified into benchmarking (learning through visits, discussions and understanding of successful models), promotion of joint activities (soft interventions like training, market promotion, technology development), infrastructure creation/promotion specific to the cluster and linkage with value chain partners. Table 7.9 details the 'typology of activities' by combining the 'typology of interventions' and the 'nature of activities' by which these are achieved (Ray and Sarkar, 2007). Another area that commands support is promotion of local innovation, with high risk of failures. These may include innovative marketing arrangement, technology or creation of appropriate institutional organizational structure. This, however, is not focused as a part of CDP in any Scheme.

Table 7.9: Typology of Activities

		Marketing	*Productivity and Competitiveness*	*Sustainable Local Organisations*
		M	**P**	**S**
Benchmarking	**B**	MB	PB	SB
Other "soft" activities	**R**	MR	PR	SR
Infrastructure	**I**	MI	PI	SI
Promoting linkage with lead value chain partners	**L**	ML	PL	SL

A subjective evaluation of 18 schemes (Table 7.10) based on stated areas of support (and ignoring the flexibility provided for inclusion of any other demand driven activity whether mentioned in those 18 schemes) shows that there is hardly any support for promotion of local institutional capacity and promotion of private sector led development.

Table 7.10: Subjective Evaluation of Typology of Activities Supported by Schemes/Programmes

		Marketing	*Productivity and Competitiveness*	*Sustainable Local Organizations*	*Total (Row)*
		M	**P**	**S**	
Benchmarking	**B**	10	9	7	26
Other "soft" activities	**R**	13	10	6	29
Infrastructure	**I**	9	8	3	20
Promoting linkage with lead value chain partners	**L**	5	4	4	13
Total (Column)		37	31	20	

Note: This is for 18 schemes for which sufficient details are available. The maximum score for each cell in the total (column) can be 72 and that for each cell in total (row) can be 54. The maximum score for any other cell can be 18.

Support Institutions for Cluster Development in India

For successful intervention in cluster, apart from CDEs/CDAs at the grassroot level, role of (a) implementing agencies (IAs) who provide support to the CDEs/CDAs and that of (b) resource organizations (ROs) providing technical guidance to the CDEs/CDAs, are significant. To understand the current scenario of the maturity of the implementing agencies and resource organizations in India, we have looked into their cluster experiences. An IA is said to have one cluster-year experience, if it has worked in one cluster for one year. Similarly, an RO is said to have one cluster year experience if it has guided an IA in one cluster for one year.

Outcome of Cluster Development

The process of holistic cluster development started in the year 1997 with the onset of cluster development programme by the United Nations Industrial Development Organization (UNIDO). Cluster development in true spirit was picked up only as late as 2002-03 by the national institutions and results have started flowing in. Published data regarding outcome of the programmes are scarce, excepting for one-off knowledge of a certain cluster at a certain point of time. Since the UNIDO programme started a little early some data is available with respect to 7 clusters where work was initiated. This is presented in Table 7.11 and Table 7.12 below. It may be mentioned here that apart from firm level changes, impact was also noticed at cluster level in the form of creation of number of new networks, associations and linkages that were established with a large number of support organizations during these programmes (UNIDO: 2001, 2003).

This shows that cluster development programme, through the process of creation of networks and linkages, creates outcome in the form of enhanced turnover, exports, quality up-gradation, savings, investment, training etc. A recent Project of UNIDO also shows that cluster development programme also impacts on relatively poor stakeholders, only when it is specially designed to include those stakeholders (UNIDO: 2006).

These were also found to be working for various other cluster development initiatives promoted by a number of agencies across India. A handful of case studies have been carried out for a few institutions for clusters development programmes at various levels of maturity and promoted by different typology of institutions. These include the following clusters along with their level of maturity and implementing organization:

	Name of Cluster	*Implementing Organization*	*Started*	*Ended*
	Interventions in Traditional Manufacturing Clusters			
CS1	Rajkot Diesel Engines and Engineering Cluster	EDI [for DC (MSME)]	2003	2006
CS2	Coimbatore Wet Grinder Cluster	NIMSME as RO [for DC (MSME)]	2003	2006
	Intervention in Micro Enterprise Clusters			
CS3	Bidri Cluster of Bidar, Karnataka	NABARD	2003	2006
CS4	Stone Carving Cluster of Konark, Orissa	UNIDO-CDP Orissa	2005	Continuing

CS: Case Study

Table 7.11: Estimated Results of Intervention at Firm Level

Cluster	*Year of Intervention*	*Additional Domestic Sales*		*Additional Exports*		*Additional Savings Generated*		*Additional Quality Accreditation*
		USD Million	*Number of Firms*	*USD Million (new mkt)*	*Number of Firms*	*USD Million*	*Number of Firms*	*Number of firms*
Jaipur	1997-2000	0.12	75[17]	1.00 (2)	14			
Ludhiana	1997-2000			10.00[18]	26	1.20	55	
Pune	1997-2000					0.02	20	9[19]
Tirupur	1997-2000			10.00[20]	15	0.80	45	16 (24)[21]
Ahmedabad	1999-2002	2.00	21	1.50 (1)	9	0.10	70	32 (60)[22]
Ambur	1999-2002	0.03	30	0.13 (1)	5	0.09	25	6
Bangalore	1999-2002	1.10	50	(1)		0.17	40	
Total		3.25	174	22.63	68	2.34	235	63 (99)[23]

Source: Compiled from End of Project Reports of UNIDO Projects US/GLO/144 and US/IND/97/148.

Table 7.12: Estimated Results of Intervention at Firm Level

Cluster	*Year of Intervention*	*Additional Investment made*		*Additional Credit*	*New Training Programmes*		*Number of firms supported*
		USD Million	*Number of firms*	*Artisanal units*	*Number*	*Number of firms*	*Number of firms*
Jaipur	1997-2000			65	5	50	90
Ludhiana	1997-2000	8.00	22		5	75	75
Pune	1997-2000				1	50	275
Tirupur	1997-2000				13	50	75
Ahmedabad	1999-2002	1.50	41		10	101	120
Ambur	1999-2002	0.30	7	30	4	94	115
Bangalore	1999-2002	1.00	21		4	50	100
		10.8	88	95	42	470	850

Source: Compiled from End of Project Reports of UNIDO Projects US/GLO/144 and US/IND/97/148.

Box 7.4: CS1: Rajkot Diesel Engines and Engineering Cluster

The Diesel Engine and Engineering cluster of Rajkot (Gujarat) has 4170 firms producing 6 major items. Intervention in the cluster was initiated by EDI with the programme support of the Office of DC (MSME) (and ICICI intervened in 2003) for a period of 3 years. Some of the major problems were identified as competition from import of light weight engine, shortage of raw material and fluctuating prices, limited buyer linkages, old technology and limited knowledge about international standards and manufacturing practices.

The strategy for intervention was to demonstrate results in the most critical area, i.e. technology usage. It started off with technology benchmarking with the latest available technologies. A business delegation was taken to 'International Machine Tools Exhibition' in Taiwan for this purpose. Simultaneously, meetings were arranged with the potential buyers to provide an insight on the expectations of the buyers. This was followed by local buyer-seller meets in association with Indian Institute of Machine Tools Manufacturing (IIMM). Demonstrations were also made on use of modern cutting tools through manufacturers like Taegutec, Sandvik Asia. Provisioning of appropriate technology, personal counselling was also undertaken. Over 100 technological implementations were carried out in the cluster resulting in improvement in productivity by about 20 per cent and decrease in rejection rate from 12 per cent to 5 per cent. The raw material problem was taken care of as Rajkot

(*Contd.*)

Engineering Association (REA) started procuring and distributing pig iron in bulk. Use of precision machines increased. Diversification into new and higher value added products has also started. Both national and international BDS providers like CMTI, NSIC and Indian Oil are now linked to the cluster. The local industry association—REA is now publishing News bulletin, procuring required raw materials in bulk, facilitating participation in international fairs. For the future, there is a need to establish a testing laboratories in the cluster. The cluster also requires to se cutting edge technology which requires high value investment. This can be done by establishing a CFC. Joint efforts are also required in marketing and exports.

Source: EDI, Ahmedabad.

Box 7.5: CS2: Wet-grinder Cluster, Coimbatore

The wet grinder cluster is situated in and around Coimbatore (Tamil Nadu). The 52 year old cluster comprises of 500 components suppliers, 150 assemblers, 50 composite firms. The major problems faced by the cluster include inadequate raw material supplies and financial resources, poor design and development, lack of direct exports and uniform product standards, poor institutional linkages and disorganized functioning. MSME-DI, Chennai intervened in the cluster in the year 2003 with technical support of NIMSME, Hyderabad. The implementation strategy was strengthening of the dormant Association, viz. Coimbatore Wet Grinders and Accessories Manufacturers Association (COWMA), promotion of joint action through formation of consortia.

As a result of the intervention firms established linkages with dealers in Indore, Ahmedabad, Bhubaneshwar and Behrampur and realized on the spot sales of Rs. 50 lakhs. 30 members of three Consortia availed credit under MCGF Scheme of SIDBI. A CFC is being set up with grant-in-aid of Rs. 99 lakhs by DC (MSME) and Rs. 16.54 lakhs by the Government of Tamil Nadu. A strengthened COWMA reduced VAT on wet-grinders from 12.5 per cent to 4 per cent. "Coimbatore Wet-grinder" was registered under GI Act. It is the first industrial product registered under GI Act in India. The future challenges include taking advantages under GI Registration and standardization of the product under GI and BIS, implementation of VAT by the cluster enterprises, continuing and adoption of design and development activities, creation of more consortia under MCGFS Scheme, enhancing exports, etc.

Source: NIMSME, Hyderabad.

Box 7.6: CS3: Bidri Cluster at Bidar in Karnataka

> The Bidri cluster of Bidar is situated in the state of Karnataka. The cluster is spread around Janata Colony and the old city. It has 216 artisans, producing flower vase and products of metal and silver. The cluster is about 5 years old. The major problems of the cluster were old and dated designs and machinery, lack of working capital as well as direct access to markets. NABARD intervened in the cluster in the year 2003-04. The implementation strategy was to provide exposure for learning and development with the support of a local NGO. The major turning points were visits to urban markets and artisan product fairs and interaction with customers. The exposure visit provided the necessary stimulus and insight into the process of change. As a result of the intervention the artisans were organized into 15 SHGs and then federated to solve the long term capacity issues (on both market and procurement front). The artisans started getting work for full year compared to just 3 months of work earlier, resulting in increase in income by over 4 times. New designs were introduced through agencies like NIFT/NID and over Rs. 1 million was disbursed to the artisans as credit for the first time in the cluster. Active support of the local bank and the office of DC (Handicrafts) also helped a lot. The traditional art form got registered under the Geographical Indication (GI) Act. Future challenges include new machine, specialized electric furnace and raw material under CSR for zinc. They also feel the need for long term effective computer education.

Source: NABARD, Mumbai.

Box 7.7: CS4: Stone Carving Cluster at Konark, Orissa

> The stone carving cluster of Konark, is situated in the State of Orissa. The cluster is spread over 15 villages. It has 750 artisans employed in 66 firms producing handcrafted stone products. The cluster is about 50 years old. The major problems identified in the cluster were low margins, low capacity utilization, limited mechanization, lack of availability of raw stones and innovation. UNIDO intervened in the cluster in October 2005. The implementation strategy was to introduce modern tools, ensure regular supply of stones and to provide new design inputs, provide access to new markets and strengthen the supply chain. The major turning points were formation of 4 cooperatives and 4 sales outlets and setting up of 2 CFC, provision of direct linkage with the foreign buyers, and participation in Stone Mart.
>
> As a result of the intervention 245 artisans have been organized into 16 associations. 150 artisans from the cluster have availed credit

(Contd.)

of Rs. 37 Lakh from MFI/Bank. 35 artisans have received artisan Credit Card. New business worth Rs. 17 million has been generated. 35 cooperative and 17 household units have bought new tools worth Rs. 400,000. 2 CFCs have been established. 112 artisans have been trained to produce new products. Capacity building of 8 associations has been done. One group has obtained mining rights to have direct access to raw materials. 90 new products have been developed. 250 artisans have received artisan I-cards and over100 artisans have been covered under Rajiv Gandhi health insurance. The future challenges of the cluster are to ensure good supply of labor and raw materials, introduction of new designs on a continuous basis and develop standardization.

Source: UNIDO-CDP, Orissa.

Networks are the integral part of cluster development. The activities undertaken by the networks in a cluster vary with the maturity of the network, moving from activities that demands low investment and shows quick result to activities with high investment and longer gestation period. The continued existence of networks in a cluster depends on the past successful experience of working together. Even after a formal CDP is over, the network continues to deliver results for the cluster. We describe below 2 case studies of different vintage and by different institutions.

	Network	*Implementing Agency*	*Started*	*Ended*
CS5	Suvarnakar CFC	NIFT for Government of Gujarat	2001	2005
CS6	CORE	UNIDO—CDP, Orissa	2005	Continuing

Box 7.8: CS5: Suvarnakar CFC, Ahmedabad

At the Jewellary cluster of Ahmedabad, a CFC (namely 'Suvarnakar CFC') has been established in Oct 2006 under the aegis of Suvarnakar Auyodogic Utpadak Mandali Ltd. Out of total budget of Rs. 1 crore, contribution of the beneficiary was Rs. 60 lacs. The remaining amount was provided by the Government of Gujarat. The main machine installed under CFC are bangle making machine, gold testing machine (imported from Germany), chain making machine. Total cost of these 3 machines was 26 lacs. The basic objective was to introduce latest technology, get better finish etc. The machines installed in CFC are

(*Contd.*)

properly utilised and a revenue of Rs. 3000 is generated per day (50 units are taking CFC machine services per day). The association is presently working out a proposal to establish hall marking centre wherein people can get their jewelry hall marked locally and at a cheaper rate (other hall marking centres are located on private initiative at a distant place). This could be a potent source of income generation for the association and which could be further used for developmental activities.

Source: Survey Report.

Box 7.9: CS6: CORE, Rourkella

The Engineering cluster at Rourkela is situated in the state of Orissa. The cluster has 145 units. The total turnover of the cluster is Rs. 75 crores. UNIDO has been implementing a cluster Development Programme in Rourkela since 2005. The major problems of the cluster were high manufacturing cost compared to other similar clusters. The implementation strategy was to benchmark the cluster with some good cluster and use the best practices to achieve cost efficiency. Consequently eight young entrepreneurs visited Trichy engineering cluster, saw the common procurement center of BHEL industrial Development and Service Society (BIDASS) and interacted with the firms. They also saw the working of common oxygen plant set up by BIDASS. The results showed that efficient procurement was the basis of competitiveness for Trichy. On returning they formed the Cluster of Rourkela Engineering Enterprise (CORE)—a consortium (network) of 15 units with a seed capital of Rs. 1.5 lakhs. Negotiations by CORE fetched a discount of 12 per cent on flexible billing terms. The effort was then extended to other consumables resulting in a saving of 10 per cent instantly. Due to the extensive cost reduction the consortium could also bag a large order.

Source: UNIDO-CDP, Orissa.

III. POLICY CHALLENGES—VIEWPOINTS OF STAKEHOLDERS

Policy Challenges

While promoting the basic cluster specialty of joint action, policy challenges can be broadly classified into (1) optimum targeting and initiating development, (2) managing development and (3) monitoring and learning from development supported by divergent thematic needs of different typologies of clusters[24].

(1) *Targeting and initiating development*: To start with one needs to have a broad understanding of defining a cluster. Again, it is argued that, once a cluster qualifies a definition, what practical factors need to be considered for selection?

(2) *Managing development*: With cluster level interventions picking up, what are the critical issues for satisfactory implementation? Issues related to policy support for private sector and BDS providers are also being debated. Again, implementation at the ground level will require a flexible and efficient system that suits the cluster. Role of a dedicated non-stakeholder cluster development agent/ executive (CDA/CDE) has also come up strongly. Also of critical importance are components, value and duration of support with special reference to relatively less endowed/poor stakeholders and ensuring their inclusiveness. Not the least is an enabling environment that is capable and supportive of such promotion, leading towards sustainable development.

(3) *Monitoring Development:* It is also essential to have effective outcome and creating a system for learning.

While many of these issues will be gauged later (in Section 4) based on available literature (e.g. schemes, reports, etc.), a decade old experience of CDPs in India provides a repository of knowledge at various levels which also needs to be tapped. Accordingly the above issues were discussed informally with a range of (i) policy makers, (ii) practitioners—public and private as well as implementing and resource agencies and (iii) cluster stakeholders where CDP is ongoing/completed (Table 7.13). Their views along with emerging suggestions on various issues related to policy challenges appear subsequently.

Table 7.13: Stakeholder Discussants

Number of		*Number of*	
Policy level Institutions	7	BDS/Technical and Financial Institutions	5
Resource Agencies	3	CDEs	3
Implementing Agencies	11	Associations/Networks	5
Firms/Artisans	10	*Total*	*44*

Defining a Cluster

Discussants felt that a cluster should have a minimum of 100 units. For north-east and hilly areas such number can be smaller. However, contiguity is important for promoting joint action. While some suggested that a cluster should be within a maximum radius of 25 kms, others felt that it should be a distance which can be covered within two hours of time by local transportation by a stakeholder. However, village based clusters or clusters in the north east/hilly India will be naturally dispersed.

Some felt that largeness of a cluster is not an issue as majority of the stakeholders does not take interest to start with; in contrast, restricting cluster size artificially might close the door to a group of interested firms and can be a tactical mistake. On the contrary, if there is genuine contiguity, then it will be a political mess to define a cluster, to suit implementation, based on highest concentration.

On product range it was suggested that strict industrial classification will not be able to capture all clusters and at times such efforts may come up with irrelevant or too narrow a classification. Many a times multiple related products are made by firms in a cluster and describing them as different clusters will become an operational mess. Hence local knowledge/intelligence should be combined with product classification to define the product range of a cluster.

While the above views hold good for existing clusters, some felt that from a totally different perspective, wherein a cluster (or a concentration of units to start with) is being created, the size of services clusters cluster can be small (e.g. a textiles park) or big (e.g. a food processing cluster with its backward and forward linkage). Again there is no database of services clusters. Even, the existing database of 388 traditional manufacturing clusters is inadequate as already work is going on in many more clusters. The quality of data is also inadequate to promote interest of related agencies to select the clusters.

Selection of Clusters

While some institutions have multi-institution committees for selection, for most it is an internal exercise. At times some institutions use the norm for equal geographic distribution. Some institutions, especially those which cater to the needs of the poverty intensive clusters, are also using the norm for presence of Scheduled Caste and Scheduled Tribe population. It was suggested that selection should be preceded by an input-output framework. Here clusters of varied levels of maturity and different typologies need to be selected, although level of maturity of a cluster is sector dependent.

Implementation Technique

There is need for holistic planning up to marketing and not piecemeal disjointed approach for any cluster. Business development service (BDS) providers and private sector value chain partners provide maximum benefit in the areas of marketing, quality, infrastructure creation, etc. There is need to support these stakeholders as per their capability. Many a time services of good BDS providers cannot be utilized due to high fees. In the absence (or difficulty) for creating any fixed norm, high service charges cannot be supported.

Again, different schemes define cooperation structure in different ways, while some look for 'society', others ask for 'consortium'. Hence the definition should be uniform across the scheme of assistance. Local technical institutions should also provide services to the cluster. Improved industry-institute linkage to create awareness about the requirements of industry and orientation of course curriculum of local ITI and colleges, as per cluster need (to some extent and wherever possible) is also required.

For some clusters there may be even need for perspective planning with support for enterprise development as well as general (as opposed to cluster specific) infrastructure development. For clusters requiring support of multiple agencies, the secretary industry of the state should coordinate the issues at the ground level. Programmes should be projected with tripartite agreements.

Choice of Implementing Agency and Resource Organization

It was unanimously felt that there is a huge dearth of trained implementing agencies. Similarly, there is absence of trained resource organization too. It was suggested that be it a resource implementing organization or an implementing agency, it should have at least two trained persons and have an organization culture that promotes delegation, accountability and transparency. Implementing agency has to be based in the cluster; resource agencies should also be agency has to be preferably stationed in the State with long run commitments.

Some suggested that apart from institutions District Industries Centres (DICs) can become implementing agencies, provided appropriate manpower planning is done. Some felt that banks can also become implementing agency but being a profit initiative they would look for tax sops for such promotional activity. Majority should also be felt that it is very difficult to have industry associations as coordinating cluster initiative as an "implementing agency". Firstly, there are very few associations which have such capacity and secondly, an association has relative comparative advantage in promoting broader policy level issues, infrastructure, etc., as compared to business issues, the latter being an important aspect for cluster development. See Annex 5 for selection criterion of an implementing agency.

Flexible and Efficient Support Framework

Most of the cluster initiatives are public sector driven. There is more need for involvement of the private sector both as a CSR and even a profit initiative. Cluster stakeholder patience has very short gestation period and in ordinary circumstances, they prefer no change rather than uncertainty, hence decisions should be quick with pre-defined limits. Again, due to natural partial knowledge of cluster reality (which only evolves with time) to start with, action plan also goes under revision multiple times. Hence, approval for action plan, at a higher level leads to delays. At times activities planned do not adhere to time schedule as the stakeholders do not work on planned expectations due to multiple reasons. It was suggested that there should be adequate flexibility in altering an annual action plan both with respect to items and timings. There is also need for tools that can balance need for accountability with need for flexibility to match the cluster requirements.

Role of CDA/CDE

There is a near unanimity on the fact that there should be a dedicated person for managing development (CDA/CDE) in each cluster. CDA should be trained and be of the right attitude. CDA must continue for at least three years in a given cluster so that their contribution will be substantive. CDAs taken from government organizations should not be given any other dedicated person responsibility. CDA can also be appointed from the private sector. CDA must be stationed in the cluster. Well qualified CDAs are not willing to work at village level. Hence we need two types of CDAs networking CDAs, who create trust and technical CDAs who give vital linkages, e.g. technical, market, etc. The CDA should be properly remunerated. For large clusters one can even have a team of CDEs with horizontal functional groups.

Value and Duration of Support

A cluster should be supported both for infrastructure as well as soft support in the areas of network creation, marketing, support is of little technology, quality, etc. The degree of support for infrastructure (hard) and other "soft" support varies from 20 per cent for soft use, unless the inputs for SME clusters to even 80 per cent of soft support for micro unit clusters. Although a couple of respondents were not for supporting soft intervention at all. However, it was unanimously among suggested that only infrastructure support is of little use, unless the necessary trust has been created among stakeholders through support in 'soft' activities. It is also imperative to first provide support for the 'soft' issues and thereafter provide 'hard' support.

The duration of support is suggested for maximum cases between 4 to 5 years of full-fledged holistic support. Support less than that many a times eludes inclusion of less endowed units. The nature of support has also been suggested in tapered form that increases suggested for during the first 3 years and decreases during the next 2 years for maximum cases a 5-year intervention. The percentage support overall has been between 4 to 5 suggested at a maximum of 70 per cent. Many a time support is not given or less than optimum support is given for cluster management (e.g. professional fees of the implementing agency or the CDA). This leads to slow or non-serious starter of the programme. Hence, appropriate cluster management cost should be an integral part of cluster development fund.

Innovation is and will increasingly be a challenge in the near future as the Indian economy keeps on maturing. More fund should be allocated for R&D initiatives in cluster as this involve risk. It was suggested that government should bear 90 per cent of such cost, 10 per cent should be borne by the cluster stakeholder as this will lead to involvement of the stakeholders. Innovation is also warranted in artisan clusters, which are facing the burnt of low mechanization and are all geared up to absorb small lot mechanization.

Inclusiveness

It was unanimously felt that less endowed firms get fewer benefits and the more endowed firms get the maximum benefits. This happens due to less risk taking capacity of the relatively smaller units. Hence, one should make special efforts to identify and support the relatively smaller units. However, there should not be any pre-fixed generalized cut off ratio for identifying the poorest units. This will vary for clusters and should be worked out locally. In an artisan cluster, the local PRI system can be involved to identify the poorest units. However, providing different levels of support for all activities will bring in divisions in togetherness in a situation where an oneness in industrial mindset is being pursued across the cluster.

Enabling Environment

There is also need for capacity building of the local technical and financial institutions as well as line departments to understand the cluster concept and also the need as well as typology of support required for cluster development. There is also need for constant orientation and sensitization of top management of all concerned government departments, especially given the fact that transfers are a regular feature and without a wider coverage, continuity might be lost. Given the newness of this approach, there is also need for orientation of political leadership.

Sustainability

Sustainability should be measured both in terms of new economic opportunities created as well as new institutional capacity in the form of associations/networks created/revived or technical measured both in institutions that have become proactive and are doing additional/new roles for the promotion of the cluster. One also need to look into activities that have been initiated and have been picked up on a regular basis by the local association/networks/SPV. Instead if the units go back to exactly the same style of functioning, then the programme will not be termed sustainable. For associations, now the percentage of developmental as against lobbying work being done by an association should be considered as an index of long term programme sustainability. This is an area, which the associations have not picked-up as of now.

Monitoring, Evaluation and Learning

At one extreme, it was suggested that for a CDP promoting institution, M&E should be the only activity. All other activities should be hired out to professional agencies. It was pointed out that often there does not exist enough resources including trained manpower to monitor development. Internal monitoring systems of institutions were suggested as having limited capacity and at times too small to capture the vastness of development process initiated by a scheme. This leads to fall in efficiency of the implementing agency and weakens the entire process. At times there is lack of appropriate tools for efficient and continuous evaluation. Learning that emanates from monitoring are also not captured. Need was also felt for professional monitoring mechanism that ensures attainment of broad objective and also ensures continuous learning. It was also suggested that the process of monitoring can be done better if the initiative is looked after as a 'Project Mode' with customized deliverables.

Since most of the cluster schemes are promoted by Central Government Institutions, cost of follow up and regular field level monitoring will be high. It was suggested that here the DICs can be trained to do field level monitoring and provide vital feedback as a professional agency. While overall programme monitoring can be done by an independent agency, the cluster level development should be monitored by a committee of local learning should be stakeholder and support institutions' group. However, support fund should be given directly to the cluster stakeholders through the implementing agency. It was also suggested that monitoring and evaluation process can be naturally strengthened through capacity building of implementers at the local level. There is also need for appropriate project designing with quantified deliverables. Cross scheme/programme, learning should be institutionalized at an appropriate level.

IV. POLICY AGENDA FOR WAY FORWARD

Backdrop

Over the last few decades, clusters as a tool for industrial development has gained ground globally. In less than a decade's cluster based time, India has 24 independently funded initiatives. Thanks to probably the largest number of documented clusters India has and the wide variety they exhibit with respect to typology based on technology usage (micro, traditional manufacturing and high tech) and achievements (underachiever, overachiever); that led several types of public institutions in adopting this approach, suited to the new mantra of liberalisation and privatisation signifying a greater role for the private sector and partnership based development approach. Despite a robust cluster based initiative in India, challenges remain in terms of:

- Inclusivity in terms of the objectives of the cluster initiatives, selection of certain geographical regions and type of clusters chosen,
- Coordination that enables convergence and leveraging in terms of financial support from different public and private institutions and thematic areas of support such as environmental considerations, social welfare, credit inputs and infrastructure,
- Knowledge about what works and what does not—methodological challenges, and
- Institutional ability at all levels to ensure effectiveness and efficiency of the initiatives.

This Section attempts to address these key issues based on global literature review on clusters (Section 1), analysis emanating from secondary and field based assessment (Section 2) and key policy challenges based on a range of discussions with a number of policy makers and practitioners engaged in cluster development (Section 3).

The way forward provides actionable agenda for the policy makers, implanting institutions, private sector and other knowledge based institutions that have a role in the overall development arena. While this Section does draw upon international experiences, the way forward is specifically meant for India in light of her unique conditions and steps already initiated.

Vision for a Cluster Based Development Policy

The guiding vision for cluster policies should be:

(i) Coherent with macro policy agenda of inclusive growth,
(ii) Compatible with current national enterprise structure, and
(iii) Strategic to address the critical gaps.

Coherence with macro policy agenda: Clusters as local socio-economic systems are essentially a part of the global and national socio-economic space. They not only draw from the wider context but also contribute towards it. Within the national socio-economic policy arena, there are specific sectoral policies that have a direct bearing on the clusters. Industrial development being a 'state subject' clusters also fall under the state policy domain. However, there are several areas where the national policy framework has an important role to play to address cross cutting gaps and ensure coordination. Therefore a national policy framework on clusters should complement the state's cluster based development policies.

An important choice that cluster policies need to make is whether to choose potential winner or loser clusters and if both, in what proportion. Internationally there are examples of all kinds. Some of the countries like Italy and regions like European Union chose to work on both, whereas most of the OECD countries have concentrated on promoting innovation among the high technology areas such as aviation, medical electronics, bio-technology, nano-technology and advanced research based pharmaceutical products. The lagging clusters in the current Indian domain largely comprise of micro-enterprise (including artisanal) clusters, which provide opportunity to either grow or diversify into different areas as per the potential and local aspirations. These are highly employment intensive and are an important source of non-farm income in a multi-livelihood space. Thus they deserve special attention and inclusion of social and environmental aspects in cluster initiatives need to become integral with the economic agenda.

Compatibility with current national enterprise structure: As seen above, India has 3 types of MSME clusters—high-tech or knowledge intensive, traditional manufacturing clusters and micro (including artisanal). The micro enterprise clusters are culturally and socially important from the view point of employment generation and poverty alleviation. Baring a few star clusters, typical characteristic of micro clusters is that they tend to cater to the local and regional markets[25]. The traditional manufacturing clusters are relatively technologically more advanced and contribute very significantly in terms of manufactured output and employment generation. The high-tech clusters are rather a recent phenomenon and seem to have come in existence over the last 10-25 years. These clusters are internationally well-linked clusters mainly for their markets and not in terms of production outsourcing. These clusters are relatively few in number and have not been documented so far.

Strategic to address the critical gaps: A country's future competitiveness depends on the progress on two dimensions, viz., (a) individual cluster and (b) cross-cutting issues affecting several clusters at the sectoral and regional level and thus the whole economy. While a number of initiatives have been taken for development of individual clusters, the cross-cluster issues affecting an entire sector in a 'joint action' mode have been largely ignored. The cross-cutting issues need to be examined at the levels of funding, knowledge and implementation capacities. The deterrents included herein relate to lack of proper information base on clusters, inadequate institutional capacities in the public and private sector for implementation and knowledge support, lack of operational synergy across different public schemes of assistance among others. There is also a need for a relevant monitoring and evaluation system to ensure effectiveness and efficiency of the initiatives, where there seems to be a major gap.

Accordingly, the suggested *Vision for the Cluster Policy Framework* is as follows:

> The Indian industrial and services sector economy develops into an inter-connected array of clusters with a strong and

enabling all round environment around them to achieve higher levels of global competitiveness with inclusiveness and equity. Inclusiveness will be ensured by including the lagging clusters and supporting initiatives that not only ensure greater economic growth but also address adequately the social and environmental concerns.

The clusters will be developed with one of the following set of objectives for the 3 different set of clusters that characterise the Indian enterprise based economy:

- Ensuring dignified survival for the unemployed or under-employed people in the micro enterprise clusters and protecting them from further decline as long as it is viable to do so;
- Sustain growth for furthering the socio-economic development of production or service clusters in the traditional manufacturing sectors; and
- Help build clusters in high-tech areas through diversification and support for emerging clusters in new areas of knowledge and innovation.

Achievability of Vision—Key Challenges and their Status

Achievability of the potential needs to be assessed on the basis of

(i) Adequacy of financial resources,
(ii) Appropriate information and knowledge base for implementation, and
(iii) Matching coordination, monitoring and evaluation capacities at institutional level.

Adequate financial resources: Given the higher 'public good' nature, most of the cluster initiatives are substantively financed through public resources, whether in India or abroad. Judging from the current schemes and likely funds to be placed in the 11th Five Year Plan as deliberated in various documents of the National Ministries (to be approved), availability of finance does not seem to be a constraint. Moreover a number of potentially on-going schemes of assistance that can be harnessed to augment the resources for cluster based initiatives are being ignored at present.

Broadly the financial support is required for two types of inputs viz.:

- *Soft Inputs*: such as marketing, training, network creation, research and development, design inputs, BDS provision, benchmarking, quality up-gradation, productivity improvement etc.
- *Hard Inputs*: relating to cluster specific infrastructure creation.

In case of infrastructure, the amount of financial support varies on a case by case basis, whereas for soft interventions require a support of Rs. 10-15 lakhs per cluster per year and also additional cost of implementation coordination. In both these cases level of support needs to be linked to the degree of socio-economic viability of the proposed development interventions. Given the nature of local interventions characterising the multi-stakeholder participation and local empowerment, financial support that does not ensure proper implementation coordination at the cluster level, the efficiency and effectiveness of initiatives suffers.

Appropriate information and knowledge base for implementation: Effective cluster development initiatives call for integration of private sector efforts along with technical institutions. An assessment of the current scenario reflects a deep disconnect between the need (from private) and delivery currently (from public) at cluster level due to lack of adequate and relevant knowledge, poor inter-connectivity across institutions and lack of internal systems that enable the flow of information and knowledge. In fact there is a high degree of mistrust and lack of enough positive experience to facilitate flow of knowledge and best practices in some of the illustrated areas of research, technology, vocational training, design, social welfare, credit into the clusters, thus harnessing the available potential.

This calls for trials to be undertaken to develop relevant tools for mutual engagement at various levels. National and state level initiatives are required to push the public institutions to reach out to the clusters and customise knowledge and information delivery that can meet the required needs. However, the only source of inputs need not be public institutions. With increasing linkages between the national and international large enterprises both as buyers and mother enterprises in the private or public sector with a strong sub-contract SME base, scope for provision of relevant information and knowledge through this channel is very high. Cluster initiatives can harness this potential through fostering of linkages between the large and small enterprises across the value chains and enable knowledge transfer.

Matching Coordination, Monitoring and Evaluation Capacities at Institutional Level

While there are 24 independently funded cluster initiatives both at the national and state level, the capacities for coordination, monitoring and evaluation within the public institutions that have initiated cluster programmes is a cause of serious concern. A significant amount of funding support through a range of schemes has been earmarked for implementation through industry associations, consortiums, public-private partnership based special purpose vehicles (SPVs), NGOs and public institutions for this purpose and this calls for a good degree of analytical capacities relating to financial and management appraisals, regular process based monitoring, coordination with different type of stakeholders and flexibility on the cluster initiative designs to ensure compatibility with the changing requirements. This is a significant departure from the old school of thought, from being providers to facilitators.

A significant number of multi-stakeholder based cluster development initiatives will need to be implemented by the private sector institutions, particularly the industry associations, export promotion councils, networks and chambers of commerce. According to one estimate by Federation of Indian Small and Medium Enterprises (FISME), there are 3500 industry associations in the MSME sector primarily in the traditional manufacturing sector. Yet, a very few of them (probably less than 5%)[26] have any development activity implementation initiative record with an internal professional secretariat to implement. The operationally weak industry associations are inadequately capacitated to design and undertake relevant development initiatives for themselves. This is a major challenge as well as an opportunity for cluster development policy. There is no national or regional initiative to specifically undertake development of industry associations to promote selective micro development initiatives across the cluster, at least in their areas of comparative advantage. In the 'micro' clusters, the level of organisation is still poorer with hardly any presence of such association *per se*.

The efficacy of cluster development process calls for awareness and training of public officials, particularly at the middle level about new practices on appraisal of initiatives, re-deployment of internal human resources and consequential development of appropriate internal monitoring and evaluation systems.

An assessment of the additional funds requirements to undertake initiatives suggested above is made separately at Annex 6. Most of these resources are likely to be drawn from the national public funds, considering the current support percentage between the national (91.4%) and state (2.4%) level institutions for various cluster initiatives. Private sector support will come only in specific activities that have a greater 'private good'. The gross additional public financing requirements excluding the individual cluster based initiatives is assessed to be Rs. 250 crores over a 5-year period under the 11th Five-Year plan. These sources could be augmented through existing channels of schematic assistance relating to cluster development.

Role of public, private and knowledge based institutions under the proposed national policy agenda: The proposed agenda is discussed around the roles of national government, state governments and the private sector. The inputs provided herein are expected to enable synergy across various initiatives through information building, knowledge sharing, implementing centrally and regionally coordinated initiatives in the clusters.

National and State Government: It is proposed that a *national cluster policy* be framed to integrate with the macro economic policies and social development policy should be objectives. In specific, the national government should undertake the following:

- *Strengthen cluster information base*: Build up new database on clusters for sectors where it does not exist, strengthen the policies and social existing database where it is deficient, particularly in terms of social and environmental parameters and classify the existing database of clusters to identify common areas of assistance and with options for synergy across various ministries and knowledge institutions

- *Funding of cluster initiatives and their management:* Make available adequate funds to the implementing agencies (public or private institutions) through various schemes of assistance administered through different ministries and help up-grade their capacities to manage the initiatives.
- *Enable knowledge sharing across states* and institutions on best practices and methodologies relating to cluster development based initiatives.
- *Coordinate common programmes of technical assistance to clusters* that cut across different states and draw upon common sources of knowledge, institutional framework and best practices. The initiatives in this regard relate to BDS provision, international linkages and investment promotion from abroad.
- *Initiate common programmes for thematic inter-linkages:* Undertake initiatives around specific thematic areas around common needs of clusters. Such initiatives help to build an interface between specific union ministries and state departments and their practical application in clusters. These areas relate to interfacing clusters with R&D institutions, social welfare departments, environment management, vocation training and technical colleges to illustrate a few.
- *Undertake capacity building initiatives* for local development institutions, industry/micro-enterprise based associations and regional resource institutions through largely public funding.
- *Ensure that public development schemes focus on inclusivity* of growth and accordingly relevant monitoring and evaluation frameworks to ensure greater effectiveness of expected outputs.

State Government: The state level governments should essentially be responsible for coordinating implementation of clusters initiatives in their respective states through national and state level funding, leveraged by private sector pooling of fund.

The state governments should be expected to draw state policy coordinating framework on clusters that in specific should ensure:

- *Provision of funding support to supplement the national resources* to support cluster initiatives, implemented significantly through local industry associations and other fora knowledge for upscaling.
- *Enable knowledge sharing within the state* across clusters on best practices and methodologies and also promote cluster to cluster learning.
- Draw *state level policy framework on clusters* that integrates with the overall macro economic and social development policy and objectives at the national level.
- Provide *funding and policy support for capacity building* to the nationally funded and coordinated initiatives for local development institutions and industry/micro-enterprise based associations.
- Set up a *separate cluster cell in the department* and designate a nodal resource organisation to coordinate, support and monitor cluster initiatives in the state.
- The specific stages for any *state government to take up cluster initiatives* are detailed as under:

    - Understand relevance of clusters through identification of local clusters and compile basic information about them.
    - Decide on the key objectives for cluster based development and select clusters for intervention over more than one phases. The first phase is usually the pilot phase meant for clusters where chances of success are higher.
    - Undertake initial cluster analysis of the chosen clusters for intervention in the pilot phase and developing vision for them.
    - Draw up specific activity framework in the short, medium and long term with stakeholders.
    - Coordinate the execution of the collaborative action plan in the clusters.
    - Undertake a process review of initiatives and assessing the gaps therein.

- Based on the learnings drawn from the pilot initiatives, expand the scale and scope of interventions

Private sector: Cluster development cannot be expected to succeed without an active participation and sharing of responsibility by the private sector in terms development of conceptualisation on development initiatives, partial funding and significant role in implementation. Accordingly, policy instruments need cannot succeed to promote these institutions as follows:

- *Strengthen capacity of* macro level chambers of commerce and industry to initiate cluster based initiatives as implementing agencies: Ideally, such agencies should not be cluster (product) based associations.
- *Strengthen MSME associations to initiate development initiatives in clusters:* The industry associations have to play an active role to increasingly undertake development initiatives in partnership with pubic institutions, knowledge partners, R&D institutions and value chain partners. Smaller groups of enterprises need to join hands as networks and consortia to undertake initiatives for their limited private interests.
- *Roles of other private agencies:* Promote and facilitate private sector enterprises which are natural value chain partner to cluster enterprises.
- *Promote creation and facilitate existing BDS providers* through training and also by supporting their important role in cluster development. There is also need to recognise the various levels of BDS providers for ensuring their services through appropriate remuneration for the benefit of the cluster.
- *Major areas of private sector initiatives:* The major areas of their work will involve:

  - Development and management of local cluster specific infrastructure,
  - Contributing private investment to select "public goods" for social development through philanthropy and compliance,

- Nurturing of local suppliers,
- Undertake and fund collaborative research and development,
- Provision of information to the industry members through directories, setting up of information exchanges, coordination of BDS providers,
- Benchmark with better clusters within India and abroad,
- Disseminate best practices learnt,
- Undertake joint procurement,
- Undertake demonstration projects,
- Organise joint fairs and delegations,
- Develop curricula with local technical and educational institutions,
- Undertake liasoning with specialised infrastructure providers,
- Attract investments,
- Work with the government to streamline regulations, and
- Establish testing and standards organisations.

Knowledge Institutions: Technical institutions, research organisation, vocational training centres have an important role to play by:

- *Undertake joint research with cluster stakeholders* including machinery suppliers, speciality input suppliers and major customers.
- *Undertake assessment of emerging skill requirements,* develop suitable joint (along with industry) training curricula along with local industry and run training programmes jointly funded with the government and the industry.

Policy Agenda for Action

Cluster based development policy provides an opportunity for focused attention to the diverse sectoral and socio-economic local environments as also to integrate, coordinate, synergise the efforts of pubic, private and knowledge based institutions, both vertically and horizontally. The cluster policy, therefore, has seemingly contrasting tasks to balance the need for flexibility to meet diverse requirements and yet coordinate among those diverse efforts for ensuring synergy. This section details a list of specific policy measures expected to lead to effectiveness of the cluster based development approach by ensuring an enabling environment, to be put in place. Thus it goes a step forward from the existing stage of multiple cluster development initiatives undertaken by different ministries, institutions, departments and the private sector as per their individual area of focus.

1. *Avoid a common definition except for statistical enumeration of clusters:* Several countries have spent enormous amount of time and resources debating what is a cluster. It is suggested that while a framework[27] for drawing up the definition of a cluster be placed as a part of the cluster policy, any attempt to provide a single definition should be avoided. Further more, state governments and institutions with specific areas of focus may draw up their own criteria to define clusters depending on the suitability in their context. Local knowledge/intelligence should be combined with product classification to define the product range of a cluster and the distance that enables approachability among cluster actors.
2. *Undertake a national cluster mapping for targeted policy focus:* For an effective cluster policy formulation, drawing up of schemes of assistance, allocation of resources, setting up programme implementation coordination and their monitoring over time, it is important to identify the common areas that relate to different clusters. Aggregation of significant issues across states and sectors will help to build synergy among and between public, private and knowledge institutions. For example, Union Ministry of Environment and Forest and related knowledge institutions will need a listing of clusters across pollution intensive sectors where they have a significant role to play. Similarly, Union Ministry of Science and Technology along with their state counterparts and other knowledge institutions will find it useful to assess the clusters that call for significant S&T related inputs. Such information on all India basis is not available today and will need to be built.

Second, enumeration of clusters across services and knowledge intensive industries are not available that should be mapped in order to direct specific attention around fast growing sectors of tourism, health, information technology, research, education, among others. Third, an enumeration of clusters around specific agriculture products and horticulture products also need to be mapped to encourage food processing industries and procurement. Fourth, an integrated framework to benchmark the clusters based on the diverse areas of their performance will enable various relevant public and private institutions to focus their attention where and when their focus is most desired. For example, a rating of all the electroplating clusters on environment standards and the extent of their compliance can be extremely helpful for public and private stakeholders.

3. *Establish an Inter-ministerial Coordination Focal Point:* A permanent inter-ministerial coordination focal point should target the review of all ongoing development initiatives, identify areas of synergy, suggest necessary institutional arrangements for implementation, get studies organised, draw upon international best practices and finally evolve a communication strategy to disseminate them.
4. *Develop a cadre of human resources to initiative cluster development:* Cluster based approaches are significantly process based and therefore, more intensive in terms of quality human resources to be deployed for development coordination. The role of a local facilitator, called either as 'cluster development agent/executive' (CDA/CDE) as in India or 'cluster broker' as is internationally better known, becomes critical to mobilise local resources and leverage public and private funding around select key critical areas.

   The hard bit of knowledge about clusters in terms of skills, infrastructure and technology can be acquired based on education, training and investment, but the know-how of the process involved and the know-who (people and institutions willing to engage themselves into collaborative forms of working) can be developed only based on work experiences and personal connections. This knowledge of local social capital requires a process of intense engagement with the local actors and institution. The ability of the CDA/CDE to learn from enterprises, institutions and buyers outside the cluster which s/he can link up with is also important. Yet the human resources available in this domain of expertise is scarce and need to be augmented.

5. *Prefer cluster activation to new cluster creation:* A very important aspect that policy makers have to deal with is whether to create or support clusters. In this light, policy makers and practitioners alike have reached the conclusion that activation of existing cluster be preferred over cluster creation, unless the conditions warrant otherwise. It is because cluster activation leverages upon what already exists in terms of production systems, market linkages, institutional framework and value chain linkages and therefore are less resource intensive, low risk development venture, provides quick returns and draws upon a coalition of private and public sector stakeholders.

   On the other hand, cluster creation requires to develop a production system that requires huge mobilisation of public and private investment and hence highly resource intensive, driven by the public sector intervention, requires sustained finances, is fraught with high failure rate and provides returns in long term.

   Yet cluster creation may be required in conditions where the local economy does not have any significantly important areas of economic activity, or the existing economy is dangerously linked to one or two sectors which may have an endangered future.

6. *All states with clusters should be encouraged to initiate cluster based development:* Currently there are only six states that have undertaken cluster based development, while the scope is immense. This will call for initial sensitisation of the public representatives and top management of the concerned state government departments through short-term programmes that can be undertaken by some of the premium institutions like Entrepreneurship Development Institute of India, NIMSME, etc. with adequate

background, understanding and experience on cluster based local development.

7. *Set up cluster development cells within the funding agencies and state government departments:* In each state, a cluster development cell with adequate quality human resources be established for management of cluster based development, preferably within the pubic funding institutions where process based monitoring is an integral component of all the initiatives. The cells should be provided necessary room for flexibility, development of qualitative indicators, room for internal learning and correction and yet be accountable. The states should undertake training and orientation of all the relevant department officials (e.g. fisheries, handlooms, handicrafts, industries, food processing, labour and employment, vocational training etc.) on cluster development approach, methodology and how to integrate their departmental activity in line with specific cluster based requirements.
8. *Strengthen some of the existing development agencies to become resource centres:* In order to ensure quality of cluster initiatives, it is suggested that at least 8-10 national and 25-30 regional institutions be groomed to support the implementation of cluster based development initiatives. Such institutions need not be created afresh, but should ideally be drawn from among those that have a previous track record in development initiative, whether from the public or private sector. Currently, there are only 3-4 national institutions with good standing and only 3-4 regional institutions undertaking such a work. Moreover, research studies should be instituted with support from some of the leading think-tanks, management institutions and other research institutions to develop cutting edge methodologies, tools of assistance, evaluation techniques, undertake external evaluations, benchmark clusters and suggest policy measures on a regular basis.
9. *Undertake a national initiative on export promotion* across specific clusters that have a high potential to grow. This should be undertaken by the National Government through Ministry of Industry and Commerce with support

drawn from specialised agencies to help clusters link up with international value chains and investment promotion to plug the gaps therein.

10. *Undertake a national initiative to achieve environmental compliance* across specific clusters to ensure environmental compliances. This initiative should also be nationally coordinated through Ministry of Environment with support drawn from specialised agencies and implemented by a range of public and private institutions.
11. *Undertake a nationally coordinated initiative on select social issues* such as working conditions, provision of micro-credit needs of workers community, living conditions and safety aspects around specific clusters with scope for significant improvement. Such initiatives may be coordinated by the relevant ministries such as Ministry of Social Welfare, Ministry of Labour, Ministry of Tribal Affairs with linkages drawn from NABARD, Micro-Finance Institutions, National Minority Development Finance Corporation among others. Initial efforts in integrating micro-credit provision through micro-finance institutions (MFIs) across select handloom and handicraft clusters in Orissa have demonstrated the potential to alleviate poverty. Similarly, initiative by a local industry association to ensure improved social compliance in Jalandhar is a case in point (*See* box below).

Box 7.10: Sports Goods Manufacturers at Jallandhar take Social Responsibility Seriously

Thirty soccer ball manufacturers and exporters at Jalandhar in Punjab set up Sports Goods Foundation of India (SGFI), constituting 80 per cent of the export turnover of the cluster in 1998. This came about in the face of international media allegations about child labour being used in the industry. They set up a self-monitoring transparent mechanism across 3000 stitching centres in rural areas of Jalandhar where 15000 artisans hand-stitched inflatable balls for the exporters. Encouraged by the success of the initiative, the Foundation has since ventured into education for the children of their stitchers through 27 special schools and 30 free tuition centres. Besides 4 schools are being run successfully with funding

(*Contd.*)

support through the local government. On the health front, the busines community has undertaken 25 free medical checkup camps that have helped about 9000 workers. In the year 2006, it was felt that some of the stitchers could be displaced by the onset of machine stitching. Accordingly, under a cluster initiative by UNIDO, the Foundation has organized several SHGs to help them find alternate livelihoods and link up credit provision through banks.

12. *Establish cluster-oriented free trade zones,* industrial parks and other common facilities that can help clusters realise their growth potential and upgrade facilities that individual enterprises may find difficult to achieve. Such initiatives need to be taken by respective ministries such as Ministry of MSME, Ministry of Textiles, Ministry of Industry and Commerce, Ministry of Food Processing and relevant departments in the respective state governments.
13. *Undertake initiatives to develop specific financial products suited for clusters:* Different sectors and clusters have specific credit needs that are not fulfilled by the limited number of financial products that the various banks currently have in their domain. One of the positive measures that can help augment credit flow to the micro and small enterprises is to develop specialised financial products that cater to the specific needs of sectors and clusters. Some of the banks particularly in the private sector have designed 'downscaled' products in the last few years with success. Reserve Bank of India had also identified 60 clusters with high success potential to link credit to SMEs. Small Industries Development Bank of India (SIDBI) has initiated a project in this regard with support drawn from multi-donor funded facility in the year 2007.

Box 7.11: Mutual Credit Guarantee Scheme—The Italian Experience

The Italian Mutual Guarantee Associations (Confidi) are solidarity groups established, in the form of non-profit consortia or co-operatives, by small firms without access to credit. They have strong local ties and are promoted by the active assistance of artisan associations and local chambers of commerce. A Confidi has a large member base, implying a

(Contd.)

> vast amount of funds for back guarantees. The small firms directly contribute to create a risk fund, which provides mutual guarantees to their members for borrowing finance from the banking system. Additional funds are contributed by external support entities, such as Local Authorities, Chamber of Commerce and Industrial Associations. Through their capacity to reduce asymmetric information, these associations are able to achieve considerable financial and economic advantages.
>
> Confidi evaluate their members' request of loan and recommend them to the lenders, provide guarantees and pursue defaulting borrowers for loss recovery. They do not extend credit directly to their members. The decisive characteristic of Confidi is that they are based on social capital in addition to financial capital. Confidi have a competitive advantage in screening and monitoring borrowers as well as in post-claim loss recovery over other forms of guarantee organizations and banks due to their social proximity to borrowers. Confidi have extensive knowledge of the operating sector of a member and are thus aware of factors such as competition within the sector, market trends or production techniques.
>
> Additionally, they assess the viability of an applicant's project by taking the entrepreneur's background, business performance and reputation into account and are able to make better-informed decisions than banks. Since defaults of Confidi members are about 10 per cent lower than in the case of non-guaranteed loans (in the case of well structured clusters like those in Marche the default percentage is less than 1%), banks actually compete with each other to work with the local Confidi.

14. *Draw up initiatives that help select clusters to undertake innovation* by linking them up with international value chains and international benchmark clusters. Most of the currently established technology development institutions tend to focus their initiatives for the upper end of the clients in SME sector, thus benefiting only a handful few. Ministry of Science and Technology through its several affiliated organisations and National Manufacturing Competitiveness Council (NMCC) with support from Ministry of MSME may take lead to evolve the level of technology and innovation across select sectors and clusters. This can be enabled by:

- Provision of financial support and knowledge linkages to early innovators to help them develop new products, services and processes.
- Sponsoring independent testing, producer certification and rating services for cluster products/services.
- Linking up with high-end buyers of cluster's products and services.
- Drawing up specific multi-stakeholder initiatives for research to commercialisation of new ideas translated into beneficial products, processes and practices.
- Linking up research and development programmes of the publicly funded laboratories with private sector participation and steering (See Box below).

Box 7.12: Rajkot Diesel Engine Cluster: Network for Common R&D

The Diesel Engine Cluster Rajkot, Gujarat was facing competition from imported light weight Diesel Engine (DE). Because of the light weight characteristics people could carry it in cycles and other rural transport system. Thus it could penetrate the rural diesel engine market within a short time span. The local manufacturers of relatively heavy weight DE started experiencing slow down in market sales. Moreover, sales realization also declined in export market especially in African countries. 7 firms manufacturing DE in Rajkot joined hands and formed an informal network under a cluster initiative by Entrepreneurship Development Institute of India (EDII), funded by Ministry of MSME. The objective of the network was to develop a light weight DE which has a potent demand in the local and abroad market. Moreover, it was also believed that the light weight DE could reduce material cost and enhance cost competitiveness. Thus the consortium engaged itself in R&D work. Apart from utilizing in-house expertise, experienced technical persons from outside were also engaged in this endeavour. After a number of trials and error they could finally develop a light weight DE as per the market requirements. Being a new initiative, no one was quite sure of the success, yet the members thought it prudent to take a calculated risk and invest on R&D work. It is quite likely that the new product will be launched in the market by January 2008.

15. *Draw up national and regional initiatives to augment the supply of skilled human resources* to the clusters that are facing acute shortages in the wake of emerging high demand supply gap. These initiatives should be nationally coordinated but implemented at the National and State level depending on the domain). There are successful pilot examples available such as shoe manufacturers up-gradation programme undertaken at Agra for 60,000 workers by CLRI in the year 2005-06 (see box below), 100 workers for protective equipment stitchers at Jalandhar by Department of Science and Technology (DST), 400 workers for garment stitching in Ludhiana, Welders training programmes at Tiruchirapalli with support from DST. This would require:

    - Reorientation of the curricula of the existing educational and technical institutions (State Government and private sector).
    - Training of the existing faculty by providing them with necessary exposure to the small enterprises and augmenting the faculty resources by getting entrepreneurs, BDS providers and supervisors to also become special faculty members (State Government and private sector).
    - Involvement of the local and sectoral industry associations along with machinery suppliers to work with existing institutions (State Government and private sector).
    - Undertake workers' certification programmes with grading to help them undertake jobs suitable to their potential (Nationally coordinated, State Government implemented).

National Ministry of Labour and Employment in collaboration with International Labour Organisation has in the year 2007 begun to assess the potential of scaling up skill development and formalisation of the same while targeting them on specific clusters.

Box 7.13: Standardisation of Training for Shoe Workers in Agra

> Agra is home to shoes in India. More than 100,000 artisans earn their livelihood from shoe making. The workers were only able to get work in 4 months in a year. In the meantime, around 30 large firms in the organised sector needed skilled operators (new entrants) in the areas of stitching, cutting, lasting, pasting and sole attaching. The total number of formally trained operators available in entire India is estimated not to exceed 1000 per annum. Younger generation in Agra is not inclined to take up the same vocation. Central Leather Research Institute (CLRI) with support from DIPP under Human Resource Development Mission undertook an initiative in the year 2006 to target 60,000 artisans. During the now concluded initiative, 40,000 artisans have been assessed as per their skills and certified as A, B and C grade operators in different type of operations. In the next phase short-term modular curriculum varying from 1-3 months will have to be developed to upgrade the assessed artisans.

16. *Leading chambers of commerce and sectoral associations to initiate cluster development initiatives:* The national, state level and sectoral industry associations must initiate their own cluster development initiatives with or without support from the public funds. This would not only enable to build private sector capacities to design and implement their development initiatives but also set new benchmarks among the public and other knowledge based development agencies to augment the quality of such initiatives. 'Confederation of Indian Industry' (CII), 'Federation of Indian Chamber of Commerce and Industry' (FICCI) and 'Indian Machine Tool Industry Association' (IMTMA) have undertaken successful initiatives in certain sectors, with some good successes to emulate. These need to be up-scaled significantly.

Box 7.14: Indian Machine Tools Industry Sets New Benchmark

> The machine tools cluster in Bangalore is the largest concentration of machine tool enterprises in India with 400 enterprises and total revenue of Rs. 300 crores in the year 2004. Under a cluster development initiative by UNIDO (1999-2003), it was identified that common procurement, joint

(*Contd.*)

marketing, skill development and setting up of common facility for exhibitions could help the enterprises grow significantly. While the initial start was provided by dynamic external facilitator under the development initiative, the local chapter of Indian Machine Tools Industry Association (IMTMA) took upon itself to not only continue the development initiatives in Bangalore, but also extend to other machine tool clusters in Ludhiana, Ghaziabad, Pune and Rajkot. Once the trust among members was strong enough, a total of 71 different activities were undertaken during May 2003 to March 2005 that cost the association and its members Rs. 70.55 lakh, but led to gross quantitative return of Rs. 298.08 lakh thus reflecting an output-input ratio of 4.2:1. Besides the measurable outcomes, the association members have felt a closer bonding among themselves, stronger association, increased linkages between public and private institutions and generated confidence to undertake increased investments for new markets, including the one of China.

17. *Support initiatives for cluster development by large private/ public sector enterprises:* It is in the business interest of the large private sector enterprises to build up capacities of their SME supplier firms. Direct interest taken up by the mother enterprises will only induce positive response among the supplier enterprises and therefore, most of the initiatives will be self-funded. However, certain specific initiatives where direct business profits are low, especially in the small to medium term, public funding may be called upon in areas such as capacity building, setting up of common facility centres, augmenting local industrial infrastructure and social initiatives meant for the benefit of local communities and labour welfare. Aggregation of sufficient quantify of supplies especially from the unorganised sectors such as handicrafts and handlooms calls for financial stakes and capacity building to be taken up by large buyers. One initiative in this regard taken up by Fab India, a handloom and Khadi garments/furnishing retail chain has based on a successful model in Chanderi (see box below), decided to upscale the initiative across several more clusters in the country through private equity shared along with the artisans and ICICI Bank.

Box 7.15: Up-End Marketing by Private Sector

> Fab India is an established handicraft retail outlet with branches all over India. In July 2004, at the linkage support provided by the local MP, after several rounds of discussion, the core buying team of Fab India visited Chanderi to explore the possibilities of bulk Purchase. After initial discussions and assessment of Bunkar Vikas Sansthan (BVS), an organization comprising of the SHGs of local artisans, Fab India decided to open its own office in Chanderi and also signed an MOU with BVS. The MOU with Fab India ensured BVS an order of Rs. 50 lakhs in the first year with a likely increase of Rs. 25 lakhs every year. BVS was given the responsibility of managing the production of its SHG and through them with other SHGs in the cluster. The CEO of BVS was entrusted withthe responsibility of managing the entire business. Actual sales to Fab India are estimated at Rs. 27 lakhs in 2004 and Rs. 42.4 lakhs in 2005. The figure is likely to reach Rs. 70 lakhs in the year 2006. While the CEO of BVS was the chief manager to start with, soon a number of weavers rose from the ranks to deal directly with Fab India. The activities with Fab India trained the weavers in timely and quality production.

18. *Support cluster-specific transportation, communication and other infrastructure* as per the cluster requirements where needed. These initiatives should be implemented preferably on PPP basis but it need not necessarily be the only way. Cluster stakeholders stake in terms of financing and management should be ensured with safeguards to ensure wider participation and higher support for weaker clusters.

Box 7.16: Kalady Rice Millers Consortium Pvt. Ltd.

> Kalady Rice Millers Consortium (KRMC) is a special purpose vehicle (SPV) that was formed in October 2003, as a private limited company. It is situated in the Kalady Rice Mill cluster of Ernakulum District, Kerala. The consortium has 44 members. The cluster firms were losing large sums as they were unable to sell or use the rice bran (which is a high value yielding by product) as their yield was low. The cost of bran is normally inbuilt into the sale price of rice and thus even their rice was becoming overpriced. This triggered the need for setting up

(*Contd.*)

> the bran extraction plant by firms that were otherwise competing. A bran extraction plant worth Rs. 50 million with a capacity of 3000 MT was set up by the network by availing a loan of Rs. 15 million, own fund of Rs. 35 million and an assistance of Rs. 500,000 from Government of Kerala under public-private partnership. Subsequently it has set up a testing laboratory, weigh bridge, mill store, training Institute and a high yield rice cultivation project spread in 4 acres. The consortium is in the process of setting up a rice bran oil refining plant with the support of DC (MSME), under MSECDP (Government of India). The consortium has initiated product innovation with research support of CFTRI and looks for higher project support for the risk involved.

19. *Support cluster specific information compilation in the areas of* BDS providers listing, subcontract exchanges, product and process standards, technical and other support institutional listing, raw material and machinery supplier listing, bulk tender requirements etc. and dissemination mechanisms across clusters. This can be done by sectoral industry/artisan associations to implement failing which state agencies can coordinate.
20. *Undertake a national initiative to strengthen capacities of the industry associations:* to increasingly undertake collaborative development initiatives in contrast to provision of only lobbying services to their members. These initiatives should lead to rating of industry associations and other business membership organisations (BMOs). The BMOs should be horizontally linked with one another within each distinct sector as also geographically across diverse sectors, duly federated at the national level to address issues that need to be dealt with at different levels. Such initiatives may be nationally coordinated, implemented by sectoral/regional associations and other sectoral agencies with support also drawn from the state government. Chambers of commerce and apex industry associations have a significant role to play in providing knowledge inputs, training to the secretariats of cluster specific associations and linking them up with national and state level policy.

21. *Undertake national and regional initiatives to augment the supply of key business development services (BDS):* There are five key areas that require augmentation for providing suitable BDS for the clusters. These are international marketing, technology, financial services, designing and management inputs. One can draw lessons from the some of the successful initiatives in the past that have helped to augment both from the supply and demand side of BDS.
22. *Follow an appropriate framework for monitoring and evaluation (M&E):* M&E framework for cluster initiatives should ideally enable corrective action during the ongoing process and provide policy lessons to re-work strategies at the cluster level and across the clusters for policy makers. For this purpose both quantitative and qualitative information needs to be accounted for since both have their significance that complements each other. New tools need to be evolved that balance accountability with flexibility. Excessive focus on standardisation and uniformity for administrative convenience leads to loss of focus on process based local strengthening and customisation as per specific local needs. There are three broad levels at which M&E needs to capture information to undertake corrective measures when they can be undertaken. The lowest level is at the *cluster level*, second one at the *scheme/ programme level* and the third is at the *policy level.*

At the cluster level, the results to be measured should be:

- Economic benefits by counting the increased profits, improved turnover, expanded capacities, increased credit off-take, local infrastructure set up.
- Social changes including the extent of collaborative behaviour improvement measured through number of collaborative initiatives, strengthening of local associations, forging of new public-private partnerships, employment levels, working conditions and safety.
- Environment sustenance by counting the extent to which environment damage could be reduced, recycling of natural resources undertaken etc. At the scheme/ programme level, the results to be monitored should be:

- Impact on programme objective.
- Contribution by other agencies and private sector.
- Cluster based M&E at the Ministry level.
- Documentation and dissemination of learning
- Upscaling.

At the policy level M&E may be done based on the following criteria:

- ➢ What is the extent of synergy enhancement among various cluster initiatives both in terms of funding, information and knowledge flows among public and private institutions?
- ➢ What is the extent to which institutional capacity gap has been bridged?
- ➢ What is the extent to which cluster initiatives have become private sector driven in terms of their management as well as funding of local development initiatives that may be motivated either based on business potential and/or social responsibility factors.
- ➢ How have the cluster initiatives met the diversity of objectives within the overall vision of inclusive development and growth? Regular ratings of clusters on various factors over a 3-year time frame can help assess the progress or otherwise.

Annexures

ANNEXURE 1: LAW ON CLUSTERS IN ITALY (LAW 317)

The original measure that gave an institutional framework for policymaking targeting regional clusters was the Law 317 which was approved on 25 September 1991. The main innovation of this law was its focus on SMEs and, in particular, the scope that it gave for providing support to groups of small firms rather than concentrating only on single, usually large firms. This was an admission of the crucial importance of the industrial district model in the Italian economy and recognized that such districts had, or potentially had, different policy needs. Article 4 of the law was particularly significant because it formalizes the concept of "consortia" between small firms and gave prominence to the provisions of collective services for groups of firms (often known as "real service"). In general, the legislative framework has been overtaken by decentralization, with regions now in change of increasingly broad areas of innovation and enterprise policy. While this law seems to have had only a limited impact in practice for a variety of reasons, the objective of promoting structural relations among firms and between firms and other economic actors in a region remains a high priority and has emerged in other forms in more recent national programmes.

ANNEXURE 2: TYPOLOGY OF CLUSTER ACTIVITIES— AN INDICATIVE LIST

Trust Building	*Market Development*
1. Awareness programme	1. Market survey
	2. Product development and value addition
2. Demonstration workshop	3. Product line extension
	4. Brochure development/product catalogue
3. Special purpose meeting	5. Development of common website/portal
4. Cluster visit	6. Product Directory/Manufacturers' Directory
5. Joint Pilot initiative	7. Marketing consortium and joint marketing
6. Association formation	8. Establishment of common showroom
7. Networking	9. Distribution channel planning
8. Formation of Consortium	10. Design development
	11. Diversification
	12. Fashion forecasting
	13. Market targeting (domestic/export)
	14. Organising trade fair/trade fair participation (domestic, international)
	15. Buyer-seller meeting
	16. Common branding
	17. Catalogue show
	18. Marketing seminar
	19. Export development programme
	20. Delegation visit abroad
	21. Common warehousing
	22. Visual merchandising
	23. Virtual exhibition
	24. Niche marketing
	25. Cluster twining
	26. Intervention on packaging
	27. Sub contraction exchange programme
	28. Vendor development programme
	29. Corporate linkage programme
	30. Organising fashion show/jewelry show (for RMG/Jewellery cluster)
	31. BDS for Marketing

Technology Upgradation	*Capacity Building and Skill Development*
1. Technology mapping	1. Strengthening of the local industry association
2. Process demonstration	2. Training for the association secretariat
3. Technology Upgradation Programme (TUP)	3. Newsletter
4. Adoption of appropriate technology/installation of new machines	4. BDS data bank
5. Technological implementations	5. FAQ
6. Technology counselling	6. Training/seminar for the cluster stakeholders
7. Energy conservation programme/energy audit	7. On the job training/skill development training
8. Technology sourcing/hunting	8. Benchmarking
9. Technology transfer	9. Documenting best practices
10. ISO 9000/14000/FPO/HACCP/ CE mark/WHO-GMP etc. implementation	10. Creating a knowledge bank
11. Sharing best practices	11. Information/knowledge dissemination
12. Reverse engineering	12. Provisioning of handholding services
13. Technology benchmarking	13. CDE programme
14. Indigenisation	14. Research and knowledge sharing
15. Technology incubation	15. GI/patent
16. Technology tie up	16. Creating an ICT enabling environment
17. Hiring technical BDS jointly	17. Engaging NDA
18. Factory improvement programme (FIP)	18. Social capital development
19. Quality audit and quality circle	19. Networking with support institutions
20. Adopting quality control measures	20. Creating informal knowledge bank in clusters
21. TQM/TPM	21. Shop Floor Management
22. Just in Time manufacturing	22. Establishing/strengthening BDS-enterprise linkages
23. Waste minimization	23. Training of Trainers (ToT) Programme
24. R&D under PPP initiative	24. Organising Growth programme
25. Calibration workshop	25. Establishing training centre for skill formation (PPP mode).
26. Linkages with technical institutions/CSIRs/ICAR/IITs etc.	

Strengthening Backward Linkages	*Finance Related*
1. Ensuring smooth supply of quality raw material	1. Training on project report preparation/project appraisal
2. Formation of Input Purchase Network (IPN)	2. Liasoning with banks
3. Raw material bank	3. MCGF
4. Buyer-seller meet	4. SHG formation
5. Ensuring smooth supply of quality inputs	5. Micro credit and micro finance
6. Quality awareness programme for suppliers and users.	6. Promotion of CLCSS/TUFS schemes
7. Quality audit	7. Training on working capital management
8. Inventory management	8. Cost audit
	9. NGO Banker interface
	10. Credit facilitation
	11. Sick Industry Revival Programme (SIRP)/Industrial Rehabilitation Programme (IRP)
	12. Artisan credit card

Social Compliance Initiative	*Infrastructure Related*
1. Adoption of H&S measures	1. Technology incubation centre
2. Group insurance for workers/artisans	2. Common testing laboratory
3. Group mediclaim	3. Liasoning with schemes like IIUS etc.
4. ESI	4. Technology Park/Food Processing Park/Bio Technology Park/Science and Technology Entrepreneurs Park (STEP)
5. Adoption of welfare measures like proper lighting, ventilation. drinking water, canteen, recreation facilities	
6. CSR initiatives/SA 8000	5. Establishment of common captive power plant
7. BSCI (Business Social Compliance Initiative)	6. Design Centre
8. Pollution audit & adoption of pollution control measures	7. Common Raw Material Depot
9. Common RO plant/CETP	

Policy Sensitization
1. Research and policy advocacy
2. Facilitating development of cluster specific schemes (demand driven)
3. Imbibing cluster competitiveness through suitable policy measures

ANNEXURE 3: UNIDO CLUSTER DEVELOPMENT APPROACH

1. Fundamental Principles

- Micro or SME development is an interlinked phenomenon that cuts across several themes (Technology, Skills, Marketing, Financial etc.)—*Remember Holistic.*
- Efficiency and effectiveness of cluster initiatives for enterprises is enhanced significantly by promoting 'targeted' (planned) Joint Action, at the core of which lies mutual trust *Remember Social Capital.*
- Every cluster resembles a live organic entity and thus requires customized support *Remember non-Schematic.*
- A cluster can respond to the future challenges if the ability of its key stakeholders with private sector in the lead, is enhanced significantly to undertake collective action. *Remember Local Governance Framework and Sustainability*
- Fostering a competitive market for Business Development Services (BDS) is essential to develop dynamic clusters but requires a strong thrust on stimulation of articulated demand among the MSMEs—*Remember Demand Articulation.*

2. Unique Objectives

- Stimulate collective efficiency among enterprises.
- Build Culture of competitive Cooperation among key cluster stakeholders.
- Build Local Governance framework (Enabling a local system of interconnected private and public institutions with private sector in the lead to respond to cluster needs)
- Create competitive market of BDS.

3. Unique Methodology

- Target every cluster activity simultaneously at Micro (enterprise) and Meso (network, associations and local institutional) level.
- Deploy full time empowered Cluster Development Agent(s), i.e. CDA(s) with no business stake in the cluster (to diagnose, plan activities, respond fast, resolve conflicts, get activities implemented and monitor development.

- Invest a minimum of 3-4 years time frame for a cluster.
- Prioritise Issues of focus (what needs to be done and when).
- Integrate BDS from outside.
- Rarely, if ever, support individual firms.
- Articulate demand by groups.
- Provide linkages with multiple government schemes/ support programme.
- Cluster stakeholders.

4. Expected End of Project Result

- Culture of competitive cooperation built to solve collective problems.
- Significant investment of financial resources shared by private sector for developmental initiatives.
- Vibrancy and capacity of key industry associations/ networks ensured.
- Entire value chain representative groups and institutional framework agreeable to a common articulated or unarticulated cluster vision.

5. Policy Level

- Create an acceptance of the approach at the policy level.
- Train and prepare local institutions to widespread this approach.

Cluster Facilitators (CDAs): Three Key Roles

Most clustering initiatives around the world have a facilitator (or a facilitating team) in place, usually resourced in part by a public agency. Typically, the role of the facilitator includes:

1. *Communicator and boundary crosser:* Connecting stakeholders and opening up communications across the cluster. Providing a neutral voice to facilitate linkages.
2. *Strategist:* Strategically understanding the cluster, its competitive position, its culture and its development options.

3. *Change agent:* Facilitating the establishment of collaborative initiatives to upgrade the cluster's competitiveness, ideally *acting as the lubricant rather than the engine.*

ANNEXURE 4: SELECT CLUSTER SCHEMES IN INDIA

1. Ministry of Textiles

Scheme for Integrated Textile Parks (SITP)

Objective: Provide the textiles industry with world-class infrastructure facilities.
Implementation: At each cluster a special purpose vehicle (SPV) will be formed with representatives of local industry, financial institutions, State and Central Government. Ministry of Textiles (MoT) will sign an MoU with IL&FS or a similar professional agency, which has considerable experience in infrastructure development, as Project Management Consultant (PMC) for implementing the Scheme. PMC will report to MoT, who will directly supervise the implementation of projects under the superintendence and control of Secretary (Textiles). The role of the State government is to provide all the requisite clearances, assist in land identification, providing flexible and conducive labour environment, exemption of stamp duty, dovetailing other related schemes etc. The ongoing projects sanctioned under the TCID/APE Schemes will be given an option to switchover to the proposed Scheme.

Source: Ministry of Textiles, Government of India—http://texmin.nic.in

Baba Saheb Ambedkar Hastshilp Vikas Yojana (AHVY)

Objective: Organise artisan's clusters into SHG's/Cooperatives to take up economic activities, make artisans active entrepreneurs cum primary stakeholders for easy access to domestic and oversees market., upgrade skill through appropriate design and technology intervention, provide infrastructure support, ensure effective participation of all members involved in production and marketing, process and create centres of excellence with well integrated forward and backward linkages.

(*Contd.*)

Implementation: AHVY scheme devised as an integrated approach for sustainable development and promotion of identified handicrafts clusters, envisages external intervention of four types—social, technological, marketing and financial. The schemes may be implemented by any of the following implementing agencies (IAs)—reputed NGOs/ Cooperatives/apex Cooperative Societies/Trusts/COHANDS/ EPCH/CEPC/MHSC/IICT/NCDPD/NIFT/NID/University Department, DRDA/NIMSME, EDI, Central/State Handloom and Handicrafts Development Corporations/Agencies, federation of NGOs/SHGs Consortium etc.

The process start with diagnostic survey of the identified clusters in the form of detailed project report indicating the needed interventions in order of priority, sequencing of the implementation of the interventions and concurrent activities etc. Mobilisation of the beneficiaries shall be undertaken in the clusters where diagnostic survey has been completed. Technological, marketing, financing activities will follow as per cluster need. As the Implementing Agencies, specially the smaller ones do not have enough exposure of current developments in the field of design, technology and management, Guiding and Monitoring Agencies may be involved for monitoring and supervision as per the requirement, guiding IAs in terms of market intelligence, technology and design input as per the cluster's need, linking with other developmental partners both Government and Non-Government, including banks and financial institutions and putting in place a reliable and sustainable supply chain mechanism.

Source: DC (Handicrafts), Ministry of Textiles, Government of India, http://handicrafts.nic.in/ ahvyscheme.htm

Integrated Handloom Cluster Development Programme (IHCDP)

Objective: Empower and build capacity of handloom weavers to meet the challenges of the market and global competition, facilitate collectivization of handloom weavers and service providers, provide common infrastructure, encourage convergence of schematic assistance and support service

(Contd.)

from various schemes and programmes of government and other agencies. IHCDP is an attempt to facilitate the sustainable development of handloom weavers located in identified clusters into a cohesive, self-managing and competitive socio-economic unit.

Implementation: Development Commissioner (Handlooms) is the nodal agency responsible for holding and disbursement of funds to the identified implementing agencies (IAs). Overall monitoring of the project is under the supervision of an Apex Committee. The IAs can be institutions of the Central and State Governments, semi-Government institutions, NABARD, EDI, NHDC and NGOs with suitable expertise and experience to undertake a scheme. IA shall identify and support a CDA exclusively for each cluster, who will be responsible for conducting diagnostic study, preparation and implementation of cluster action plan, promoting linkages with institutions, building the local governance framework, etc. The Apex committee will identify and engage the National Resource Agency (NRA) in identification of clusters, conducting training of CDAs and other officials of the NA, validation of cluster action plans and monitoring and evaluation. The role of the Apex Committee is to provide overall strategic directions to the project, approval of the projects, budgets and action plan submitted by the implementing agencies, periodical review and monitoring of the progress made by various cluster-developing agencies etc. The State Government can assist by constituting necessary provision for allotment of land free of cost/subsidized cost to the cluster for construction of common facility centre/dye centre etc.

Source: DC (Handlooms), Ministry of Textiles, Government of India, http://handlooms.nic.in/ hl_comp_scheme_main.htm.

Cluster Development Programme, Textiles Committee of India

Objective: Capacity building of SMEs, through a cluster based approach, by way of fostering the collective efficiency of SMEs and improving the support systems, so that the emerging opportunities on account of globalization and liberalization are exploited.

(*Contd.*)

Implementation: The Scheme will be implemented by the Textiles Committee itself. A Diagnostic Study will be conduced in selected clusters to identify gaps and support initiatives required to be provided by various organisations. An Action Plan will be drawn up based on such Diagnostic Study, to fill the identified gaps, within a time period of 3 years. While the regional offices of the Textiles Committee will act as nodal offices for the concerned clusters, an experienced officer within the concerned office is designated as Cluster Development Agent (CDA) exclusively, for implementation of the programme. The local industry and the Support Service Institutions will be involved through Cluster Co-ordination Development Group (CCDG). The impact of the programme will be assessed periodically by adopting scientific methodology.

Source: Ministry of Textiles, Government of India.

2. Ministry of MSME

Micro and Small Enterprises Cluster Development Programme (MSECDP)

Objective: Enhancing productivity/competitiveness of small enterprises, facilitate economies of scale in terms of deployment of resources, integrated and focused development of micro and small enterprises and gainfully link them to value chains with higher gains at lower cost.

Process of Implementation: A lead Government institution to be the prime mover of a proposal for cluster development in the initial stages of its conceptualisation, design, determination of technical parameters, project preparation and documentation, etc., in consultation with the cluster beneficiaries. It will, however, be necessary to constitute the SPV at the earliest possible, with clear indication of the time frame for completion of this essential requirement while submitting the proposal for Government assistance.

An officer/executive of the cluster-based SPV or the implementing agency (other than the SPV) has to be selected

(*Contd.*)

and trained to act as the Cluster Development Executive (CDE). The CDE is required to conduct the Diagnostic Study, prepare the Action Plan based on the former and get the Plan implemented with full participation of the Cluster Actors, so as to build up the collective capacity of the units in the Cluster to sustain and carry on the promotional as well as commercial activities in the long run even after the project comes to an end. The main steps for cluster development programme will be selection of cluster(s), selection of Cluster Development Executive(s), trust building, diagnostic study, preparation of action plan, approval of budget and leveraging of funds from various institutions, implementation of the action plan, monitoring and evaluation, handing over and exit, self-management phase. Funds will be released by the Office of DC (MSME) directly to SPV/IA, under intimation to the govt. Monitoring and evaluation is done by State Government if implemented by State or by Ministry of SSI if not implemented by State Government.

Source: DC (MSME), Ministry of Micro Small and Medium Enterprises.

Scheme of Fund for Regeneration of Traditional Industries (SFURTI)

Objective: To develop clusters of traditional industries in various parts of the country, make them more competitive, strengthen the local governance systems, and build up innovative traditional skills, improved technologies, advanced processes, market intelligence and new models of public-private partnerships.

Process of Implementation: KVIC and the Coir Board will be the Nodal Agencies (NAs), driving the scheme. The cluster development proposals received from the NAs will be considered by the Scheme Steering Committee (SSC). The SSC is entrusted to see that the selected clusters are spread over the country reasonably evenly, with at least 10 per cent located in North-Eastern Region. The SSC will identify Technical Agencies (TAs) having expertise in cluster development methodology for providing technical support to the Nodal Agencies and the Implementing Agencies (IAs) undertaking cluster development activities. With the help of the TAs, the

(*Contd.*)

Nodal Agencies will identify the clusters and IA for each cluster. Each IA will identify and appoint a Cluster Development Agent (CDA), exclusively for each cluster, who will be located in the cluster full time and will be responsible for implementing the Scheme in the assigned cluster. The CDAs will conduct the diagnostic studies in the clusters and prepare annual action plans which, after validation, will form the basis for the development of the cluster.

Source: Ministry of Micro Small and Medium Enterprises, http://msme.gov.in/msme_sfurti.htm)

3. Ministry of Commerce and Industry

Industrial Infrastructure Upgradation Scheme (IIUS)

Objective: To enhance international competitiveness of the domestic industry by providing quality infrastructure through public-private partnership approach in selected functional clusters/locations which have greater potential to become globally competitive. The improvements in performance will be secured in selected competitiveness indicators to be developed in consultation with each industrial group.

Process of Implementation: The development of the cluster will be through a Special Purpose Vehicle (SPV) which will carry out the business of developing, operating and maintaining the infrastructure facility created in the industrial locations. SPV will be a Corporate Body/Association registered under the Companies/Societies Act. The structure of SPV will be approved by an APEX Committee which will also decide and approve the cluster/industrial locations for development under the scheme. Financial Institutions (FIs) will help DIPP (Secretary to Apex Committee) in project structuring, implementation and leverage of funds. For projects where costs are borne by FIs, the appraisal done by FIs is accepted by DIPP. For projects not funded by FIs is appraised by DIPP through an independent agency. Monitoring and Evaluation will be carried out by DIPP.

Source: DIPP, Ministry of Commerce and Industry, http://dipp.nic.in/iius/iius_index.htm

4. Other Techno-Financial Institutes

Schemes on Microfinance, NMDFC

Objective: Help artisans to seize opportunities and meet the challenges of a rapidly globalising world, dovetail with various government schemes, strengthen network, policy focus on employment generation, fuelling growth through creation of new craft based enterprises and revitalising them. Other specific goals include increasing the availability of financial services, social security and create a conducive and pro-poor environment within developmental institutes and governmental agencies operating locally.

Process of Implementation: NMDFC is the financing institution. It has dovetailed with the existing scheme of DC (Handloom) and DC (Handicraft) on cluster development to work jointly and effectively on development of Minority Craft Cluster. The implementation of the cluster is done through Local Implementing Agencies, which can be identified by DC (Handloom), DC (Handicraft) or NMDFC. The local agency is responsible for identification of target groups and assessing the requirement of each member with regard to credit and related needs. Certain activities like infrastructure support (CFC, process house, effluent treatment plant etc.) and marketing support (marketing information, guidance, participation in various fairs and exhibitions, etc.) will be provided under the schemes of DC (Handicrafts) and DC (Handlooms). However, NMDFC through its regular programme of marketing exhibitions would give preference to such clusters. The monitoring and evaluation will be done by an Apex level committee constituting NMDFC (MD), DC (Handicraft) or representatives, DC (Handloom) or representatives and representatives of UNIDO and NABARD.

Source: NMDFC.

Financing and Development of SMEs, SIDBI

Objective: Making SME lending an attractive and viable financing option as also facilitate increased turnover and

(*Contd.*)

employment in the sector. One of the component of the project is Technical Assistance (include clusters), which aims at strengthening the policy/legal/regulatory framework and its enforcement, improve credit information of SMEs, build institutional capacity of the banks to reduce transaction cost, provide BDS and institutional support to Project Management Division and M&E.

Process of Implementation: This is a World Bank-led multi-agency/multi-activity project, where SIDBI has been assigned with the responsibility of implementing it and the Banking Division, Ministry of Finance, Government of India is the nodal agency. The IBRD, DFID, UK, KfW Germany and GTZ Germany are the international partners in the Project.

Source: SIDBI, New Delhi.

Cluster Development Scheme, NABARD

Objective: Strengthening of existing clusters and development of new clusters in exceptional cases towards sustainable competitive advantage through technology upgradation and transfer, raw material access, skill development, managerial inputs, credit support and marketing assistance.

Process of Implementation: Identification of clusters, conduct diagnostic study and preparation of cluster status and action plan, identification of solutions to problems/issues, of NGOs/VAs/Developmental Agencies, constitution of Cluster Development Committee, assignment of clear roles to various partner agencies, approval of Action Plan/Launching of the Programme, sensitisation for the partners of the programme, awareness/Skill development of artisans, increasing product range and improving quality and productivity, supporting technology upgradation/transfer, implementation of credit linked promotional programmes through NGOs/VAs/Developmental Agencies, monitoring the progress closely through the Cluster Development Committee at regular intervals, development of Management Information System.

Source: Website of NABARD http://www.nabard.org/nonfarm_sector/pp_ad_cluster.asp and personal meetings.

Project Vikas, NMCC

Objective: To stimulate manufacturing competitiveness of SMEs across clusters in the country, demonstrating Microsoft's commitment to IT innovation by facilitating knowledge based business and skill environment.
Process of Implementation: The intervention will take place in three phases:

Phase I—Understanding cluster needs and preparing a cluster action plan, improving local participation in cluster level activities.

Phase II—Improving skill sets of the cluster based on the action plan with an aim to increase the level of ICT in the business process.

Phase III—This phase will see actual increase in the productivity due to ICT usage in different firms and organizations in the cluster.

Source: Website of NMCC, http://nmcc-vikas.in/Pages/default.aspx

5. State Government

Marginal Money Loan and Grant Assistance for Cluster Development Activities, Government of Kerala

Objective: To serve the needs of cluster and their development.
Process of Implementation: Common Corporate Entity (CCE) shall form a consortium registered as a Private Ltd. company under the Companies Act and approved by the Director of Industries and Commerce. The application shall be given to the General Manager, District Industries Centre by CCE, who will forward it with due recommendation to the DI&C. Recommendation of the financial institution/bank shall be obtained before the loan is sanctioned. Director of Industries shall have sanctioning powers for margin money loans to any entity including MML for both working capital and term loan. MML will be disbursed to the entity only through the financing institution concerned. The CCE shall be bond to pay the interest (9% p.a) from the date of withdrawal of DD. The Financing agency shall advise the Director, along with its recommendation, the schedule of repayment of the loan

(*Contd.*)

so as to enable the Director to prepare the repayment schedule for the MML. Margin Money loan granted under this scheme is to be repaid by the borrower in 16 equal quarterly instalments. No collateral security or charge on assets of the CCE during the pendency of loan by the CCE to the financial institutions or banks is required for the MML. But the Government shall have a charge on the assets of the CCE once the term loan liabilities are serviced.

Source: Department of Industries, Government of Kerala, http://www.keralaindustry.org/cluster_mml.htm

Scheme for Assistance to Cluster Development, Government of Gujarat

Objective: Strengthening existing clusters by providing necessary support to improve competitiveness and meet the global challenges ahead. As part of these initiatives, the State Government intends to encourage Industries Associations for creating necessary common infrastructure facilities at lower cost. *Process of Implementation:* The project proposal should preferably be prepared by a recognized institution and should ensure that it contains essential features of a project document. The State Level Approval Committee will grant the approval to the proposals received for cluster development and decide the quantum of assistance for each proposal. The Committee will also prescribe the terms and conditions for implementation of the project and monitor the progress. Applications under the Scheme for various proposals/projects from Clusters of industries at various locations will be received and processed by the Industries Commissionerate, Gandhinagar.

Source: Office of Industries Commissionerate, Government of Gujarat, http://ic.gujarat.gov.in/promo-sch/cluster-state-gr.htm

Integrated Cluster Development Programme, Government of MP

Objective: The main aim of this scheme is to develop important clusters of traditional products of KVI & tourism centres to attract tourists in coordination with various departments of

(*Contd.*)

the State and Government of India. Provide facilities to sericulture activities as per scheme directives. To take up comprehensive development of living heritage clusters to increase employment opportunities.
Process of Implementation: Under this scheme, on the basis of Cluster's requirement, special project proposal can be entertained and assistance can be granted at a time for total development. Power of assistance approval will be with the State Level Approval Authority.

Source: Department of Rural Industries, Government of MP.

Craft Village Scheme, Government of Orissa

Objective: To create sustainable self-employment opportunities for craft persons, higher level of production and design efficiencies in the cluster, market oriented development of major craft clusters of Orissa, building capacities of SHGs so that they sustain on their own and create synergies between the various stakeholders for promotion of craft clusters.
Process of Implementation: (i) Each cluster picked up for intervention will be diagnosed in details. An action plan based upon the gaps identified would be prepared for intervention. (ii) Promoting the concept of collective efficiencies, joint action and self-reliance through SHG or other modes of cooperation. (iii) Dissemination of best practices from other clusters and awareness building programmes such as exposure visit, workshop, seminars etc. (iv) Market led and need based interventions in skill upgradation, technology, design and product development. (v) Joint efforts of crafts persons to link with the markets through multiple channels like NGOs, exporters, marketers, entrepreneurs etc. (vi) Synergy of all support institutions. (vii) Effective usage of Business Development Service providers for collective efficiency of the cluster. (viii) Building of local capacities for sustenance of the developmental efforts in the cluster. SIDAC would be the apex monitoring and coordinating agency responsible for selection of CDA and would deploy need-based mechanisms of actual implementation, monitoring and review of the programme.

Source: UNIDO, Orissa.

ANNEXURE 5: SUGGESTED SELECTION CRITERIA FOR IMPLEMENTING AGENCIES

	Criteria	*Scoring Criteria*	*Reasoning*	*Score*
1.	Specialized technical employees	Number and experience of employees	Higher the institutional capacities better the performance.	5
2.	Experience of involvement in sector	Prior experience in sector	Prior experience will benefit in terms of immediate results.	5
3	Location of the organization	Geographical presence /spread of the agency	Close proximity to the cluster will help networking and liaisoning.	10
4	Facilitate BDS	Ability to deliver BDS internally	Higher access and flexibility to provide services.	5
5	Potential to tie up Public Private Partnership	Prior experience	Need for sustainable development	10
6.	Prior experience in similar initiatives/ cluster development	Years of experience in cluster development	Better understanding of the activities to be undertaken.	10
7.	Record of Liaisoning with financial institutions/technical institutes	Ability to network with financial/technical institutions	Potential to bring in such initiatives in the cluster.	5
8.	Management related inputs to CDEs	Ability to guide	Better performance of implementing stakeholders.	10
9.	Similarity in objective with the scheme	Nearness of views in socio-economic/ sector/entrepreneurship development	Whole hearted involvement of the organisation.	10
10.	Understanding of the cluster development methodology	Exposure to cluster development methodology and number of employees trained	Can provide guidance with confidence.	10
11.	Market related interventions	Ability to take up market related interventions	This is the score of all understanding, which will shape the rest.	10
12.	Prior experience in social development	Years of experience	Building blocks for CDP.	10
	TOTAL			*100*

The maximum score is 100. The selection for implementing agencies will be depending on the relative scoring of the organisations.

Source: EDI, Ahmedabad.

ANNEXURE 6: ADDITIONAL RESOURCE REQUIREMENT ASSESSMENT

Five Year Framework (2007-2012)

Three levels of financial resources: There are three levels of programmes, viz. national, regional and local. The national programmes tend to address cross-cutting issues around sectors and across regions. Within a region, programmes can be developed that combine aspects related to multi-clusters within a district and across contiguous districts. Such programmes are referred to as regional development initiatives. At the local level, there are essentially three basic categories of cluster based initiatives. The three levels are not mutually exclusive, but reflect the primary focus as per details below:

(1) *Ensuring service delivery and providing technical support for collaborative projects:* It focuses on delivery of services in one or more pre-identified areas such as skills, technology, design, working conditions, credit delivery, investment promotion, quality development, market development as per the mandate of the funding institution. These projects are generally short-term in nature and can be for periods ranging from 6 months to 3 years. The core expertise of the implementing agency is to deliver or get delivered the specified areas of support and may cost the public exchequer between Rs. 10 lakh to Rs. 2 crores depending upon the scale and scope of the project, averaging at Rs. 50 lakh per cluster.

(2) *Engagement of local cluster stakeholder actors* to link and leverage upon the available resources and strengths. This is meant for a medium term horizon over a period of 3-5 years and generally costs the public exchequer Rs. 60 lakh to Rs. 1 crore over the entire duration. The focus of projects is to address some of the systemic issues seen from the perspective of linkages, relationships and synergies. The core expertise of the implementing agency is its ability to diagnose the critical issues and engage multi-stakeholders for collaborative initiatives.

(3) *Development of capital intensive projects around heavy R&D or infrastructure:* Typically such projects have a long term

horizon of 5-10 years and try to address long term bottlenecks. While there have so far not been any R&D focused cluster initiatives, there are several infrastructure based initiatives, already detailed out in Chapter 2. The cost of infrastructure per cluster could vary from Rs. 10 lakh for a small cluster to Rs. 50 crores for a big cluster.

There are already several initiatives that are ongoing through a number of schemes by different ministries, either through new budget provisions or by using dovetailing existing options. This component of the budget is not calculated here, considering that the provision already exists. It is only the additional support that may be required for the following initiatives that are considered important to ensure effectiveness of the ongoing initiatives.

Capacity building for creation of cluster related institutional infrastructure and undertaking of initiatives that promote synergy across various initiatives may cost a total of Rs. 250 crores over 5-year period for the following specific measures:

(a) BDS development across 10 main areas such as designs, export promotion, technology across various sectors, management, finance: @ Rs. 5 crore each will lead to Rs. 50 crore;
(b) Skills assessment across various sectors (20) and instituting initiatives to plug the gaps: @ Rs. 5 crore each will lead to Rs. 100 crores;
(c) Industry association capacity building: Rs. 50 crores;
(d) Implementing agencies and resource institutional strengthening: Rs. 50 crores;
(e) Other programmes such as building of information database, creation of new knowledge around cluster development frameworks, development of monitoring and evaluation frameworks etc. can be supported from existing funding options.

NOTES

1. Piore *et al.*: 1984, Pyke *et al*: 1990, Pyke: 1992 and Sengenberger *et al.*: 1990.

2. Becattini: 1990, Best: 1990, Bianchi *et al.*: 1997 and Porter: 1990.
3. Along with/without large firms.
4. Law 317: A brief explanation of the law given in Annex 1.
5. This is a revised definition (being considered) from the previous minimum of 5000 looms.
6. As stated by Mr. Jawahar Sircar, Additional Secretary and Development Commissioner (MSME), at the Workshop on "Policy and Status Paper on Cluster Development in India" held on July 10, 2007 in New Delhi (organized by Foundation for MSME Clusters).
7. As stated by Mr. Jawahar Sircar, Additional Secretary and Development Commissioner (MSME), at the second Workshop on "Policy and Status Paper on Cluster Development in India" held on October 5, 2007 in New Delhi (organized by Foundation for MSME Clusters).
8. Software Technology Park of India (STPI) is set up by the Department of Communication and Information Technology, Government of India in 1991, with the objective of encouraging, promoting and boosting the software exports from India. STPI Centres have come up across the country in as many as 21 locations, the major industry concentrations is at Bangalore, Noida, Chennai, Hyderabad and Pune, reflecting the natural technology clustering effect.
9. While the handloom and handicraft clusters are well defined and validated at the primary level, the figures for other micro enterprise clusters is based on secondary data with wider product category and need to be further worked upon.
10. This section draws heavily from OECD 2007, The Cluster Policies White Book, IKED 2004, The Cluster Initiative Greenbook, 2003 and A Practical Guide to Cluster Development, DTI (undated).
11. Data collected from (1) www.ktm.fi/index.phtml?l=en&s=1971, (2) Industrial Development Report, UNIDO 2005. (3) www.janbo.gr.jp/relation/data/pdf/Cluster_Kenkyu_houkoku_english.pdf, (4) OECD: 2007.
12. Subject to various clearances.
13. CII has been continuously charting a Road map to enhance competitiveness of its dominant SME membership. A cluster is formed by voluntarily coming together of a group of 10-12 companies to work together towards a focused goal. Till date 75 clusters network/consortia as they better knows in internationally accepted terminology are formed impacting 297 companies.
14. RUDA follows a sub-sectoral as well as integrated and cluster based approach for promoting rural micro enterprises. Till date, 12 clusters have been supported by RUDA in Rajasthan in cooperation with several institutions like UNIDO, CLRI, CGCRI etc. RUDA is now officially the nodal agency for cluster development in Rajasthan.

15. Though they do not have any cluster development scheme *per se*.
16. Broadly investment in infrastructure is referred to as hard intervention. Investment in capacity building (e.g. training), market promotion, technology development, network promotion etc. are referred to as soft interventions.
17. Over 100 artisans.
18. Estimated at USD 10 million by end 2002.
19. By 2002.
20. Estimated at USD 10 million by 2002-03.
21. Including 8 units which are under process and 36 with those that started the programme on their own based on the work done in the 24 units.
22. Including 25 units which are under process at the time of writing the End of Project Report.
23. Including 28 units where work is in progress at the time of writing the End of Project Report.
24. Many of these issues were raised during the First Workshop on "Policy and Status Paper on Cluster Development in India" held on 10th July 2007.
25. There are only a few isolated star clusters in India. For example, only one cluster of Moradabad (Uttar Pradesh) brassware among 3000 handicraft clusters contributes to around one-third of all handicraft goods. Similarly, in the coir sector, almost 80 per cent of all exports originate from Allapuzha in Kerala.
26. Based on estimate of working with several industry associations in a number of clusters and also discussions with experts working in this field.
27. *See* Section 2.

REFERENCES

A Practical Guide to Cluster Development. A Report to the Department of Trade and Industry and the English RDAs by Ecotec Research & Consulting.

Andersson, Thomas, Sylvia Schwaag Serger, Jens Sorvik and Emily Wise Hansson (2004). The Cluster Policies White Book, International Organisation for Knowledge Economy and Enterprise Development (IKED).

Awasthi, D. (2004). Labour Process and Productivity in Micro and Small Enterprises (MSEs): The Indian Experience, presented at the 46th Annual Labour Economics Conference organised by Institute of Development Studies, Jaipur.

Becattini, G. (1990). The Re-emergence of Small Enterprises in Italy, Sengenberger, Loveman & Piore.

Best, Michael H. (1990). Cluster Dynamics in Theory and Practice with Application to Penang, UNIDO Report.

Bianchi, P. and Tommaso (1997). The role of Small & Medium Enterprises in a changing global scenario: Towards a new Policy approach, Consorzio Ferrare Ricerche.

Bianchi, P. *et al.* (1996). The Italian SME Experience and Possible Lessons for Emerging Countries. Nomisma. UNIDO.

Ceglie G., Clara Michele & Dini Marco (1997). SME Cluster and Network Development in Developing Countries: The experience of UNIDO.

Clara, M. (1995). Real Service Centres In Italian Industrial Districts Lessons Learned From a Comparative Analysis. UNIDO. Case Study Prepared for project US/GLO/95/144/UNIDO/Italy Programme for SME Development.

DTI, (2004). A Practical Guide to Cluster Development.: Report to DTI and English RDAs by Ecotec Research and Consulting.

Enright, M.S. (1998). The Globalization of Competition and the Localization of Competitive Advantage: Policies Toward Regional Clustering. School of Business. Hong Kong.

Humphrey, J. and Hubert Schmitz (1995). Principles for promoting clusters & networks of SMEs, Small and Medium Enterprises Branch, UNIDO.

Industrial Development Report, UNIDO, 2005.

Linde, Dr. Class van der (2002). The Cluster meta-study-List of clusters, Institute for Strategy and Competitiveness, Harvard Business School. October 3, 2002.

Marshall, A. 1974 (1890). Principals of Economics. 8th Edition. ELBS and Macmillan. London.

Nadvi, K. (1999). Collective Efficiency and Collective Failure: The Response of the Sialkot Surgical Instrument Cluster to Global Quality Pressure. World Development. Vol 27. No. 9. Pergemon N.W. September 1999, 1605—1626.

OECD, Reviews of Regional Innovation, Competitive Regional Clusters, National Policy Approaches, OECD, 2007.

Paniccia, I. and G. Luiss (undated), Italian Industrial Districts: Evolution And Performance.

Piore, M. & Sabel, C. (1984). The Second Industrial Divide: Possibilities for Prosperity. New York. Basic Books.

Planning Commission (2006). Towards Faster and More Inclusive Growth: An Approach to the 11th Five Year Plan, Government of India, New Delhi, p. 35.

Porter, Michael (1990). The Competitive Advantage of Nations, Harvard Business Review.

Pyke, F. (1992). Industrial development through small-firm Cooperation. International Institute for Labour Studies. ILO., Geneva.

Pyke, F., G. Becattini and W. Sengenberger (1990), Industrial Districts and Inter-firm Cooperation in Italy, Geneva: International Institute for Labour Studies.

Rabellotti R. (1999). Recovery of a Mexican Cluster: Devaluation Bonanza or Collective Efficiency?, University of Piemonte Orientale, Italy.

Ray, Dr. Shovan and Dr. Tamal Sarkar (2007). Cluster Development and Poverty. *Alleviation: Policy Suggestions*, UNIDO, unpublished.

Report of the Workshop on 'Policy and Status Paper on Cluster Development in India', July 10, 2007, New Delhi, organised by Foundation for MSME Cluster.

Rosenfeld, Stuart A. (1996). Does Cooperation enhance competitiveness? Assessing the impacts of inter-firm collaboration, Elsevier Research Policy.

Schmitz, H. & K. Nadvi, (1999). Clustering and Industrialisation: Introduction. World Development. Vol. 27, No. 9. Pergemon N.W. September 1999, 1503-1515.

Schmitz, Hubert (1999). Collective efficiency and increasing returns. *Cambridge Journal of Economics*. 1999, 23, 465-483.

Sengenberger, W., G.W. Loveman and M.J. Piore (1990). The Re-emergence of Small Enterprises: Industrial Restructuring in Industrialised Countries, Geneva: ILO.

Solvell, O., G. Lindqvist & Christian Ketels (2003), The Cluster initiative Greenbook. Third Census of SSI units, 2001-02.

UNIDO (2004) Approaches to Cluster Mapping.

UNIDO Methodology—Making Clusters Work (2006), Foundation for MSME Clusters World Development Report (Special Issue). 1999. Industrial Clusters in Developing Countries. Vol. 27. No. 9. Pergemon N.W.

Websites

www.ahan.org.pk {Rural Enterprise Modernization initiative of the Government of Pakistan (AHAN)} www.competitiveness.lk/ceramics.htm

www.goidirectory.nic.in

www.janbo.gr.jp/relation/data/pdf/Cluster_Kenkyu_houkoku_english.pdf

www.janbo.gr.jp/relation/data/pdf/Cluster_Kenkyu_houkoku_english.pdf

(Japan Association of New Business Incubation Organizations)

www.ktm.fi/index.phtml?l=en&s=1971

www.ktm.fi/index.phtml?l=en&s=1971 (Ministry of Trade and Industry, China)

www.smeda.org.pk (Small and Medium Enterprise Development Authority)

www.wikipedia.org/wiki/Massachusetts_Route_128
http://www.blr.stpi.in/about_background.htm
http://www.indiabudget.nic.in/
http://www.lged-rein.org/solar/solar_sre_clustervill.htm (Solar Energy Programme under Sustainable Rural Energy, LGED)
http://www.nmcc.nic.in/NMCP.aspx

8

Entrepreneurial Capacity-Building: A Model for Inclusive Growth in an Era of Globalisation

VANITA VISWANATH and
AMIT KUMAR BURMAN

I. INTRODUCTION

The economy of India now has been declared as the third largest in the world as measured by purchasing power parity (PPP). When measured in US dollar exchange rate terms, it is the twelfth largest in the world, with a GDP of US $ 1.0 trillion (2007). India is the second fastest growing major economy in the world, with a GDP growth rate of 9.4 per cent for the fiscal year 2006–2007. However, India's high population results in a per capita income of $ 4,031 at PPP and $ 885 at nominal (2007 estimate). India's economy is diverse and encompasses agriculture, handicrafts, textiles, manufacturing, and a multitude of services. Although two-thirds of the Indian workforce still earns its livelihood directly or indirectly through agriculture, services are a growing sector and are playing an increasingly important role in India's economy. The reduction of controls on private enterprise, the digital era, and the large number of young and educated people fluent in English, is gradually transforming India into an important 'back office' destination for global companies for the outsourcing of their customer services and technical support. India is a major exporter of highly-skilled workers in software and financial services, and software engineering. Other sectors like manufacturing, pharmaceuticals, biotechnology, nano technology, telecommunication, ship-building, aviation and tourism, are showing strong potentials with higher growth rates. There are job opportunities thrown up by the private sector and to cater those positions the educational institutions and the private sector are working in partnership to create a skilled cadre to enter the flourishing job market.

However, economic growth has failed to address the wealth distribution in India, which has been fairly uneven, with the top 10 per cent of income groups earning 33 per cent of the income. While poverty in India has reduced significantly, 17.59 per cent (over 230 million) of Indians still live below the national poverty line. A 2007 report by the state-run National Commission for Enterprises in the Unorganized Sector (NCEUS) found that 77 per cent of Indians, or 836 million people, lived on less than 20 rupees per day (USD 0.50), with most working in informal labour sector with no job or social security and living in abject poverty.

Simple growth theory tells us that the proximate determinants of growth are (a) the share of investment in GDP (to capture the effort being made to build up the capital stock), (b) the rate of population growth (to capture how much of investment effort has to be devoted to simply equipping a larger population with the infrastructure and other capital needed to maintain the current level of productivity, and (c) the gap between output per worker and the world's best practice (to capture the gap between the country's current status and its steady growth path, and also to capture the magnitude of the productivity gains possible through acquisition of the world's best-practice technologies). However, none of this addresses the barriers 'at entry' for the many which are substantial. The traditional trickle-down perspective relegated the poor to recipients or beneficiaries of growth driven by those with means and already in positions of advantage.

The poor in India have lagged behind in reaping the benefits of the growing economy as they lack capacity to understand the market. The awareness of those at the 'bottom of the pyramid' about market forces is limited and, unfortunately, only those who can understand and adjust to it survive. The problem is especially acute for those in the informal sector (home-based) as well as those working on land and dependent on natural resources like forests. Even where employment has increased, the status of poor people in value-added manufacturing remains low. Their skill levels have not substantially increased. In India, scale is important so large numbers need to be benefited for any intervention, especially in the scenario of deprivation amongst plenty. Since majority of the poor depend on natural resources, it is imperative not to overlook their productivity and the gainful employment in such areas. The tribal people in India, for example, depend on forest resources for meeting their energy needs, income, and for employment. Benefits derived by such people are reflected as a percentage of the total income of the household (Vinod Kumar Bahuguna).

The experience of countries that succeeded in reducing poverty significantly indicates the importance of high rates of economic growth in achieving this. High growth, however, is not a sufficient condition for poverty reduction; the pattern and sources of growth, the manner in which its benefits are distributed, and safeguarding resources and entitlements of the poor to reduce the incidence and likelihood of deprivation, are equally important. Overall, a human development understanding combining, inter alia, *welfare, opportunities, capabilities, and choice has to be built into programmes and policy to sustain overall poverty reduction efforts.*

II. GROWTH WITH EQUITY: KEY CHALLENGES

Globalization processes have thrown up varied challenges. With the growth of the market, one of the emerging challenges is keeping pace with rapidly expanding market opportunities and changing market dynamics. New sectors are opening up in India such as construction and agribusiness in addition to information technology that fuelled the growth of the economy. In response to C.K. Prahalad's widely celebrated view that there is money to be made at the "bottom of the pyramid", corporates are entering rural markets with fast moving consumer goods priced and packaged for those with modest purchasing power. Recent initiatives of corporates to set up small retail stores and rural "malls" for products needed by poor people, are classic examples of such tapping of the potential of the hitherto untapped consumer base. Where earlier a complex supply chain from producer to consumer would exist, corporates have identified and organized procurement mechanisms almost at the village level, such as E-choupal of ITC Ltd., to buy directly from the producers of agriculture, forest and other products. The big players in the market are clearly approaching the rural catchments with altogether new and very unconventional strategies.

However, there are concerns over the consequences of unfettered growth. Apart from concern with environmental damage and depletion of natural resources due to over-exploitation, there is much angst about growth sans equity. The neglect of the focus on equity has given rise to concerns of increasing disparity in the society and thus a sense of dissatisfaction and unrest among various sections of the poor. For the poor to take advantage of opportunities and thus be able to demonstrate their capabilities as informed, skilled and market savvy producers, there are investments to be made in skill and overall capacity development as well as in building their collective strength and leadership. Market opportunities are widespread but only those who have developed their skills to harness that potential are able to survive in such a milieu. These investments should come not just from government programmes but also corporate resources since companies are obtaining profits from a widening consumer base at the bottom of the pyramid.

Another big challenge is the continuing low economic status of women, which is half the population. Patriarchy and seclusion in addition to poor health and low literacy characterize the condition of women. Women have been characterized variously as marginalized, powerless, exploited, ignorant, and unskilled. The reason for such characterization is basically their lack of education, exposure to the outer world, decision making power and most significantly, their largely invisible and unremunerated labour in the household and key economic activities, e.g. agriculture. It is a general perception that women's economic contribution to the household is not significant so it impacts their power within the family. With increased returns from their income-generating activities, not only will there be more income for the family, but women's economic role would get recognized. This issue is particularly salient in India because statistics generally show a very low level of female participation in the labour force since the reference is to their participation in the organized industry whereas they actually have a high participation but in the informal labour force. Working women are invisible to most of the population. If all activities—including maintenance of kitchen gardens and poultry, grinding food grains, collecting water and firewood, etc.—

are taken into account, then 88 per cent of rural homeworkers and 66 per cent of urban homeworkers can be considered as economically productive. It is widely acknowledged that there is greater informalization of the workforce as opportunities in the market have grown[1] and in India, much of this workforce consists of women. This is another reason why women's workforce participation rates are not accurately documented.

Great strides have been made for women in India through political changes at the base of the pyramid, such as greater representation of women in elected local bodies as well rapid spread of the phenomena of self-help groups (SHGs)[2] who have been able to better their economic and social condition through access to microfinance. There is widespread evidence that SHGs have become the major vehicles of economic, social and political empowerment for women and the success of this mechanism, unique to India, has been widely noted in studies all over the world (Satish, Aniket, 2005, CGAP, 2007).

As with most large countries, growth is not uniform in all parts of India and even efforts at empowerment at the bottom of the pyramid for inclusiveness, particularly of women, is uneven. It depends on a variety of local and regional factors such as history, social structure, politics, geography, leadership, and support networks including local civil society institutions.

III. ENTREPRENEURSHIP FOR INCLUSIVE GROWTH: UDYOGINI'S EXPERIENCE

The Role of Civil Society in Building Inclusiveness and Capabilities

Much of the work of empowering the poor, especially women, has been the domain of non-governmental organizations (NGOs). NGOs work in difficult and often remote areas with lack of basic infrastructure like roads, electricity, communication, and information. They work for a population largely dependent on natural resources and traditional skills for their livelihood. Their strength lies in mobilization of the rural communities and the challenge is to build market, financial and technical linkages and help these communities to make use of such linkages.

NGOs have been acknowledged for the initiatives for the development of the underprivileged section of the society because of certain strengths, especially their capacity to work in difficult conditions and focus on the poor. They have a real challenge now to build the capacities of the poor and marginalized to take advantage of market opportunities. These challenges are more acute in backward states in India clustered, for the most part, in NW, NE and Central India. Udyogini (meaning woman in industry) is an NGO that is working to promote inclusive growth with a focus on empowering women through enterprise in the backward states of NW and Central India.

Udyogini is based in New Delhi but with field programmes in the three states of Rajasthan, Madhya Pradesh and Uttar Pradesh. Udyogini's vision is to be a premier micro enterprise development agency that will enable women to pull themselves out of poverty by continually improving their incomes and capacities to control their income and productive resources. Its mission is to provide quality, appropriate and timely business development services for training and promotion of poor women as entrepreneurs. Udyogini's focus is to enable poor women to become entrepreneurs by being able to access the market, understand market dynamics, establish and operate their enterprise (individually or collectively), negotiate with market players to get the best price for her products, plan for the money they earn and have a strong voice in the household. Some of the steps taken by Udyogini towards such a development have been in the areas of micro-planning, micro-credit, micro-enterprise and business development service provision.

Phases of 'Inclusive' Growth for Poor Women: A Perspective

Capacity building for women especially for greater market access and control should be seen in terms of two phases of livelihood security and enterprise growth (Viswanath, 2003, p. 236).

- *Livelihood security:* The attributes of this phase are: women are involved in rudimentary income-generating activities; with training, they begin to understand market channels and operations and the requirements for undertaking sustainable micro-enterprises; coping mechanisms are in place in generally non transparent and changing market relationships.

- *Enterprise growth:* The attributes of this stage are: there is demonstrable capacity of women to act entrepreneurial; they have understanding of markets beyond the local; enterprises are yielding enough income for them to have become primary sources of income for the women with reduced dependence on intermittent wage labour.

These stages are useful for situational assessments and for developing strategies for enterprise development for women although it is surely conceivable to have certain enterprise related elements included even in the stage of livelihood security. Movement towards the second stage will likely take longer for women with a combination of disadvantage. These include: low literacy; those dependent mainly on wage labour and without a marketable skill; those with poor health status (including trauma resulting from domestic violence) and with children in poor health that affects their productivity; women with very small children that affects their mobility; women without control over critical decisions or incomes, especially in highly patriarchal societies; women displaced by conflict or other crises and who have to start afresh in a new place without support or infrastructure.

These categories also serve as a reminder that strategies for women's livelihood promotion have to focus on movement—towards a trajectory of building on women's strengths and potential and enabling them to take greater control over their lives so that they can become 'capable' ala Amartya Sen. Hence, critical disadvantages that women face must be identified and strategies devised to overcome them. Udyogini views women' capacity development as helping businesses move from initiation to survival and then growth, i.e., from ensuring subsistence but regular wages during the survival phase to systems development and some surplus in the growth phase. Capacity building of the women includes their presence in the market to negotiate for their products and work smartly with intermediaries in the value chain who have a better market reach then themselves. Udyogini endeavours to consolidate women's position in existing value chains.

It is in the nature of entrepreneurship that all those needing increased income are not going to take risks and invest their human and financial resources to make enterprises work. Most poor producers prefer activities that provide a regular wage. However, there is lack of qualified and employable labour, especially of women, and barriers to investment by large enterprises in hard-to-reach areas that can employ large numbers, even in the current high growth scenario. This calls for a strategy that will help at least a few producers become managers/owners of small and micro enterprises making value-added products. They can then employ and manage local labour.

Udyogini's experience in building the capacity of women for enterprise (entrepreneur development) is the subject of this paper and is analyzed in the context of its work in one field location in the state of Madhya Pradesh in Central India.

The Project Location and Key Interventions

To take advantage of the expanded market opportunities and meet its challenges, it is necessary to build and scale-up models of inclusive growth for the poor. Udyogini decided that its model-building would be useful if its work is focused on key sectors of the economy in which women are overrepresented. Agriculture and Non-Timber Forest Produce (NTFP) is one such. Mandla district is located in the east-central part of the Madhya Pradesh. A district with a glorious history, Mandla comprises numerous rivers and endowed with rich forests. The world's famous Tiger Sanctuary, Kanha National Park located in the district, has the richest biodiversity of all the national parks in India and attracts both domestic as well as foreign tourists.

Mandla is a predominantly tribal district. Agriculture is dependent on rainfall since the poor do not have irrigated land. The soil in the district is not very fertile and the topography of the area is undulating. The poor here generally practiced subsistence agriculture with meagre land. Sex ratio in the district is positive. Literacy rate is above 70 per cent. But employment opportunities in the area are scarce. For their livelihood, people depend on subsistence farming, products of forest and earnings from labour work (they migrate for labour work outside the district after Diwali[3] festival in November and return before Holi[4] in March).

The non-timber forest resources (consisting of a vast variety of herbs and medicinal plants) of Mandla have a demand in the growing cosmetic and medicine market of India and abroad. This has attracted a variety of market players eager to exploit the resources of the area to the detriment of the tribal population that has been traditionally dependent on the sale of NTFP for their income requirements. Access and rights to tribals to manage and use these resources have gradually been reduced in favour of market players. This had affected women more than men since women, in the main, gather NTFP in the area as also the ecology due to the over-exploitation of resources.

Udyogini's interventions in the area cover both agriculture and non-timber forest produce enterprises. Udyogini promotes this through business training, business counselling, research and development and building links for market, finance and technical support. At present Udyogini has managed to reach about 1500 tribal families in 75 villages of Mandla District. The major activities undertaken in the area are:

- Mobilizing women from these families into self-help groups (SHGs),
- Micro credit operations at the SHG level and linking them with financial institutions,
- Market assessments for enterprise identification and market links;
- Establishment and support to women producers for operation of the selected enterprises (trading and processing of agricultural and forest commodities, vermi-composting, production of organic vegetables);
- Training of women on pricing, market dynamics, feasibility, business planning, systems development;
- Identification of business development service providers (BDSPs) from among the community who can go on to become entrepreneurs;
- Aggregation of produce from village to intermediary levels, i.e. supply chain management;
- Operation of aggregation centres (trading centres) where buying and selling takes place at market prices that are ascertained daily from the district level market centre
- Operation of processing centres for certain commodities (oil, paddy and wheat); and
- Creation of a producers' business association led by BDSPs with a product and institutional brand identity (named UJAS).

Capacity-building initiatives are intended to help women make the transition from livelihood security/subsistence to enterprise growth. To prepare the women to understand enterprise, establish and operate enterprises, Udyogini is preparing business development service providers who can undertake their own operations as well as teach others.

Business Development Service Providers: Concept, Rationale, Roles, Selection and Training

Business development service providers (BDSPs) are those women who exhibit potential to become entrepreneurs and who can move from survival to the growth phase. They are expected to lead enterprise initiatives at the grassroots level, take charge of enterprise operations and motivate other women to participate in value-added tasks for surplus generation. Effective BDSPs are the first step in transfer of ownership and initiative for enterprise to the grassroots. BDSPs undertaking enterprise functions are important to building local capacity in a context where the majority of women will be wage earners due to their generally risk-averse social and market behavior and only few are likely to want to move ahead.

In remote and hard-to-reach locations where local interests are entrenched due to their social, not just economic, distance from the market, a facilitating, service-providing professional NGO which is not 'home-grown' will find it difficult to build long-term links with the community in a way that will be acceptable to them. A tribal community which has its own unique culture and local relations is even more difficult to 'externalise.' Hence, it is necessary that some routine core functions from at least the supply side of enterprise operations be handled by an institution of local producers, even if the demand-side interventions is supported by an external institution, at least in the medium-term.

BDSPs belong to the tribal community and essentially are a part of the SHGs formed. They were engaged in activities like forest produce collection and worked alongside their husbands in agriculture. They are generally socially constrained and are not widely mobile. Udyogini organizes women into SHGs for both savings and credit operations and enterprise operations. It has rechristened SHGs as WEGs (Women Enterprise Groups) to reflect the enterprise work they do in addition to savings and credit.

There are certain activities which all BDSPs are expected to perform and there are certain specialized activities which they are assigned. Common activities include conducting training, help the field staff in strengthening group processes, mobilizing women around specific economic activities, managing their own enterprise etc. These BDSPs further teach the group members on how to select an enterprise, doing feasibility, market survey, determining the selling price for their products, anticipating the right time to sell their products etc. In addition, for sustainability of 'inclusive growth' efforts at the grassroots level, BDSPs have a key role in local institution building and strengthening. In MP, a producer's institution called UJAS (meaning light/flame) has been registered for running enterprises. BDSPs have to take on the leadership and governance of these institutions. For these and the earlier mentioned enterprise functions, BDSPs are 'specialised'.

The process of the BDSP preparation consists of General Orientation, Selection, Function-focused training, Certification and Mentoring.

In *General Orientation,* trained Udyogini staff conducts Grassroots Management Trainings (GMT)[5] which orient members of the WEGs on the facets of enterprise promotion and management over several months. This orientation is for both motivation towards undertaking enterprise operations and basic knowledge about those operations. In selection, few women among the trainees who show extraordinary potential in terms of understanding the context and thus actualizing the concept of entrepreneurship are identified for further training. The common traits sought for selection of BDSPs are as follows:

- Understanding of the enterprise/business concept;
- The motivation level to take the work further;
- Their pro-activeness and attitude towards helping other women;
- Functional literacy with fundamental calculation skills;
- Their freedom and confidence to work out of the home;
- Leadership; and
- The articulation in conveying messages to women and the market players.

Those selected include women who, after the GMTs, conducted market survey for their products, responded to market appropriately for selling and/or purchasing, or proactively started their own enterprises. Some helped other group members in the WEG to build their understanding on enterprise and motivated them to take up some enterprise. Others have convinced their husbands to support the enterprise by undertaking long-distance market-related visits that they themselves are not able to undertake. To ensure rigour and objectivity in the selection process a selection format of these BDSPs that contains 16 parameters is being used. There are ranks for each parameter.

In *Function-focused* training, each of the selected BDSPs is then further groomed in monthly training based on their interest area and aptitude. There are certain qualities which these BDSPs essentially need in order to serve under such a role. For example, being vocal so that they can convey their message to the other women; having the capacity to negotiate with the market they in order to get a right price for their products; having a fundamental calculation skill so that they can fix prices for their products; having a proper understanding of the process of entrepreneurship and the process of enterprise establishment to guide the women to take up such activity. The BDSPs are trained principally in market assessments, feasibility, business planning, market negotiations, costing and pricing, production planning. They are also trained in and made responsible for specific field operations, e.g. trade centre operations, oil mill operations, crèches for children, mobilization, grassroots management trainings, and village level aggregation centres. The idea is to help women to take a business, like professional approach to all tasks (both core enterprise/profit-making work as well as capacity-building and business support operations). Women vary in terms of *capacity and ability, however, which requires some standardisation.*

Certification: Certification is given to BDSPs on functional roles. They have to clear tests administered by the field staff.

Mentoring: Finally, certified BDSPs are put under the mentorship of the Udyogini field assistants who supervise their performance accordingly and report through feedback forms to the training executive. The training person then works on the feedback received and the BDSP is mentored in that role to make her more effective in delivery.

Capacity Building of BDSPs: Key Successes and Key Constraints

Udyogini in its MP project has came a long way from just two BDSPs in the first year of initiative (2003) to a cadre of 75 BDSPs after 4 years of the project to build their capacity on various tasks/ functions of enterprise management and operations.

As with all capacity-building efforts, BDSPs have been able to perform certain functions well and have still some ways to go to perform others. The required activities are clubbed into four principal aspects, namely, motivating, strengthening and training women in the WEGs; conducting assessments and studies; enterprise management and promotion functions; and governance and leadership of UJAS. An additional key quality is acumen, i.e. being able to make good judgements that will lead to growth of both the enterprise and the entrepreneur. This acumen is a cross-cutting issue that is required in the other four aspects. These are analysed below.

Motivating, Strengthening and Training Women in the WEG: BDSPs encourage and motivate the community women towards formation of WEGs, enterprise promotion and other productive activities. This role is performed through conducting GMTs where the BDSPs get a proper platform for such endeavors; A BDSP, Devki said "In spite of the fact that we work more these traders earn more; can't we do something which helps us too to earn more?" The articulation of this feeling of frustration and need to find a solution before a whole group suggests a leap forward for motivation and drive that is uncommon in that area. It took a BDSP like Devki 6-7 months to get to this point. Devki and BDSPs like her have motivated not less than 10 groups (approximately 150 women) in their area to take up enterprise. There are about 25 BDSPs in the project area who are exclusively involved in motivating women. Where Devki and others like her have been successful in motivating the women of the WEGs to take up enterprises like *mahua* (a forest herb) trading, vermi composting (organic fertiliser) and vegetable cultivation, others have not been so effective. The reason for this difference is that successful motivation for enterprise requires BDSPs to build rapport with the local women. Rapport is necessary for ensuring that women are willing to go forward with being trained for enterprise.

This rapport-building is successful with BDSPs who are able to envision progress and that itself is a function of their exposure outside their village. Successful rapport-building is also a function of their previous contacts, own personality and interest and communication skills. Post-rapport building, BDSPs have to train women for enterprise. Successful BDSPs are those that can communicate using innovative explanatory methods such as case studies and role-plays. In addition, demonstration of functional skills in enterprise is a necessary condition for women to absorb training inputs from a BDSP. It has been observed that BDSPs who have proved their skills in running enterprise and making them grow have more recognition and acceptance among the women rather than a BDSP who is just delivering training without having proved the application. There are few BDSPs like Sumantra who are proactive enough to devise certain tools through which they make their messages more contextual using local dialects and resources.

Conducting assessments and studies: Key functions here are market and resource assessments at the present time. Prior to interventions in capacity-building, BDSPs went to the local market to sell the produce they collected but did not observe the market with the intention of getting educated or talk to the buyer/trader to understand market dynamics, including pricing. The result was that women sold the products without negotiation as they were not informed about market prices for commodities. Capacity-building of BDSPs has resulted in them being able to conduct market surveys, seek out additional information from Udyogini staff, study the data and determine cost-benefit and then build relevant linkages with buyers/traders. BDSPs in charge of the village-level aggregation sub-centres were able to also assist the WEGs in determining cost-benefit by providing market information. Vimla, a BDSP who takes care of one of the trading centres now phones the traders at the nearest large market centre in the city of Jabalpur, and obtains information on current prices on a daily basis. BDSPs like Sumantra do market surveys before each season to analyse the trends before suggesting to the group to undertake an activity.

Enterprise Management and Promotion functions: The BDSPs handle operations of processing centre for which they receive function-based training. The operations of the processing centres involve activities like collection of raw material, production, packaging, processing, sale, record maintenance, etc. These BDSPs also handle the Commodity Trade Centre which is an aggregation point where procurement, sale and purchase of commodities take place. They build linkages and implement the trading operations for which they receive commission. In order to do this job well, BDSPs need to be able to not just negotiate deals with buyers but close the deals as well.

Increased access to information and operations in the market has given rise to confidence. Now BDSPs Vimla and Kanti proactively reach out to women producers in the villages to make them aware of the benefits of association with UJAS by explaining to them about the unfair trade practices in the market and the advantages of fair trade through UJAS. Women's understanding of this (and partially because it came from a BDSP) has increased the procurement in the centre substantially as many women now understand the difference that UJAS promises. Both the trade and processing centres work in tandem as the idea is to add value through processing to the commodities coming to the trade centre (especially oilseeds and grains) which could generate some premium to the producers and also push women up another rung of the business chain. Some BDSPs have been reasonably successful in repairing the machines and do not require frequent assistance of the technician any more. They have a came a long way from hesitant women to start the lever of the processing machine to boldly unscrewing the nuts and fixing the minor problems themselves.

Record-maintenance is another key enterprise function that is required. This is a challenge because of the illiteracy or low level of education. The record maintenance done by Vimla who has only 10 years of schooling can make any educated feel embarrassed. Careful and intensive mentoring by Udyogini staff was a key element in building the capacity of Vimla to manage record maintenance of a standard required by the trading centre. However, her capacity to handle records when there are a large number of customers in the centre all at once, is still problematic.

Governance and Leadership of UJAS: "If we adopt the traders' way to do our business in the local market, we will learn more about trading and earn more as well." This was said by the producers of UJAS in a group meeting. Similarly, two BDSPs, Katro and Gangotri Bai were annoyed about why villagers sold their collected *Mahua*[6] to the local traders and why their enterprise group was not functioning as a mobile shop for *Mahua* operations. These questions were then raised by them in the group meetings. Articulation of these issues in group meetings is the starting point for a collective feeling and development of leadership for UJAS. These were also ideas that were built on further between Udyogini and UJAS as the strategy for enterprise development in the area was being debated, including the establishment of aggregation centres at various levels (village, cluster and district).

The parameters of leadership to be demonstrated in UJAS include: capacity to promote the growth of an enterprise (e.g. increased turnover); confidence to address a gathering; clarity of thinking and capacity to articulate those views; commitment as demonstrated by capacity to manage both home and work without compromising the work. Governance elements are key functions for the institution such as conducting regular meetings, sharing the progress, renewing and receiving memberships. BDSPs like Kanti, Narmadiya and Patiya being the office bearers are involved in the management and governance of UJAS. Leadership and governance capacity are both needed to strengthen an institution. However, a good leader is not always a good manager. Hence, there is some functional differentiation. Kanti is the President of UJAS. She is a good leader because she is a visionary with the capacity to give UJAS a direction. But she is a good leader also because she *understands the functional differentiation between leadership and management*. Since vision and clarity in purpose are continuously required the leader of UJAS needs more support on an ongoing basis to be able to help UJAS grow.

Acumen: Acumen is a key element that can determine whether a BDSP can perform routine functions or can take on higher order management tasks. Acumen includes good judgement and capacity to detect market demand, i.e. sensing a business opportunity. Tulsi, a BDSP, detected a high demand for salt in the local area but had a low supply. She went to the wholesale market and bought it in bulk and exchanged it for the local herb '*mahua*' which women had collected in abundance, recognizing also that payment in produce was necessary because cash was hard to come by locally. Tulsi then stored the '*mahua*' and sold it for a profit when the prices were high. Rajkumari, a BDSP, sensed a business opportunity after learning about this critical aspect of entrepreneurship. In her area, the poor did not generally practice vegetable cultivation in the summers due to the lack of irrigation facilities and there was a danger of cattle grazing destroying the crops. During this period the major portion of vegetables came from the nearby cities. Rajkumari sensed an opportunity to produce vegetables by taking a few smart steps. She approached Udyogini for a loan of Rs. 1000 for purchase of seeds and saplings along with the low-cost drip irrigation kit for low water needs that she had learnt about in the Udyogini training. With her husband, she prepared the plot and also installed the drip irrigation kit in her field. She cultivated vegetables like tomato, potato and onion in her plot. She also made a temporary hut in the plot to keep a watch on the animals. She got a good harvest of vegetables in the season. She sold those vegetables in the market keeping a part of it for self consumption. Rajkumari earned money in a season in which hardly anyone earned from vegetable cultivation. Rajkumari set an example for others in the area which would enable new options for the households that would otherwise migrate for better income. This success was discussed in the group which inspired the members too where they decided to go for vegetable cultivation in the next season.

Acumen is also the confidence to 'think on one's feet' and make sound decisions. Vimla, another BDSP, was working in the UJAS trading centre when a farmer came in with a truckload of maize. Normally, UJAS would not purchase a whole truckload and such a decision would be taken by Udyogini professionals providing services to UJAS and not by a BDSP. However, since there were no professionals around on the particular day in which a key business decision needed to be taken, Vimla decided to purchase the whole truckload, making an agreement with the farmer to pay him later but at the rate prevailing on the day he brought the maize to UJAS. Vimla calculated that with so much quantity, she could sell in a bigger market and get profit for UJAS.

BDSPs: The Growth Trajectory

BDSPs are entrepreneurs in a dual sense—they have helped create UJAS as a business institution that they manage and build for greater wealth creation for the poor and they develop their expertise individually as consultants for microenterprises for the poor. Today their involvement is vital in the market; the traders in the local market now consider them a part of the competition. Their marketing activities have enabled many villagers become less dependent on exploitative intermediaries.

Consistent with Udyogini's vision to be an expert service-providing institution, these BDSPs are already hired as consultants for Udyogini's outreach to new WEGs in and outside the district. A key feature of this quality BDSP concept is "Deliver better to earn better", i.e. these BDSPs are hired for their services by Udyogini on consultant basis for whatever services they deliver. The more they deliver and the greater the demand for their services, the better they earn. This mode of return for developing and providing expertise has motivated BDSPs. They understand also that the more they deliver the more practice they get leading to increased quality and confidence in service delivery. Udyogini's training department keeps a close watch on the quality of the training and mentors them to function better. These BDSPs are now being used a resource group by the Business Development Services Centres (the consulting arm of Udyogini) which provides them exposure and opportunities to work as consultants in other agencies. This conscious decision has been made only after acknowledging the success and effectiveness in the services delivered by them.'

BDSPs have a growth trajectory. The trajectory has been formulated in such a way that BDSPs move from being enterprise educators/trainers (subject-matter specialists) to enterprise developers and institution-builders. Certified grassroots BDSPs (the *educators/trainers*) can build themselves as supervisors at the operational level and the *supervisors* can be promoted as *managers* depending upon the capacity they build and the performance they demonstrate. One may add a fourth level, that of enterprise *leaders*, In UJAS, BDSPs at the manager level are those who are being mentored as leaders as well. A system exists that ensures the execution of roles and responsibilities as well as up to the mark performance at every level. All the three level BDSPs have their own set of functions, roles, responsibilities, and domain. The development of these three levels of business providers requires different set of capacity building programmes/inputs to take up their respective assignments together with adequate support from the facilitators of Udyogini.

Capacity-building for Entrepreneurship: Challenges and new opportunities for improving skills at the bottom of the pyramid

The key challenges for capacity-building of potential entrepreneurs from among women at the bottom of the pyramid are: limited mobility, double burden of household and enterprise; literacy; economic risks. These challenges are not limited to the district of Mandla alone. These are evident in other areas of the country in which Udyogini works. Indeed, these are broadly the challenges facing poor women all over India and other countries in the region which are socio-economically similar.

Limited mobility occurs mainly because, traditionally, women are viewed as having responsibility for household and child care. This has prevented them from getting the education and exposure they need for other tasks that would have helped them grow in their work at the workplace. Even when they are able to involve themselves in non-household tasks their household responsibilities remain, imposing a double burden on them. This is a challenge to their growth as entrepreneurs which requires them to invest more of their time in their enterprise to obtain higher returns. Some of these challenges exist for women who are not necessarily poor and these relate to patriarchal constraints and the expectation that women have to maintain primacy of household and children over their other tasks.

In the rural areas, women cannot always neatly organize their time because they are subject to risks and efficiency problems that throw schedules off gear. When they have to identify their priorities in such a situation, they will generally choose household tasks over enterprise tasks. Hence, choosing women whose household requirements are not daunting is important for the promotion of entrepreneurship. Alternatively, there are rare cases of women who give primary importance to enterprise despite the constraints. Kanti Bai is one of them and hence being mentored as leader. For her boldness, she is now on the national governing board of Udyogini. Some women have found a remarkable way around their double burden to move the enterprise forward. They have convinced their husbands now to run the oil processing machine in the UJAS centre in a second shift (since they can give time for only one shift) which would help in utilising the machine productively.

The concept of entrepreneurship is, in itself, complex and more so for a tribal women living in a remote region. Illiteracy is an additional barrier in enterprise tasks. These tasks include stock keeping and accounting as well as noting down market rates. Other challenges for the illiterate include inability to enforce the right to be heard by public officials and getting services to which they are entitled because public officials and market players see illiteracy as a class issue and reinforce the barriers by their patronizing behaviour towards the poor. In UJAS, women who have at least completed middle school have to be hired to undertake the required tasks. Kesar, a BDSP, despite being quite capable in understanding enterprise, feels unsure about her ability to manage the trading centre independently in the absence of BDSP called Phuliya who has had 10 years of schooling. Many of those who perform functional tasks requiring basic education are actually young girls since schooling has been given value only in the current generation and access has improved. Illiteracy does not have to be a barrier for the determined entrepreneur/leader who can, with knowledge and sharpness, move the enterprise forward. In Udyogini, Kanti Bai is a shining example of a woman who, though illiterate, is determined to succeed. A successful enterprise or entrepreneur can always outsource work that requires education provided the enterprise is making profits and can pay for it. However, in Udyogini's field location, so far, women like Kanti Bai are few.

Economic risks are important challenges in areas where poor people live. These risks are associated with environmental and weather problems, infrastructure gaps, resource depletion, and decreasing land productivity. The poor have coping strategies—which mainly take the form of migration to other areas in search of work. They also go into deep debt to moneylenders who charge usurious rates of interest. Poor infrastructure reduces quality market access and increases the length of the value chain reducing the margins for the poor. Although enterprises for the poor are supposed to reduce economic risks by providing a stable source of income, the enterprise-building process is very knowledge and skill intensive requiring women to invest much time and energy in the learning process. It also requires women to have determination to overcome patriarchal and social obstacles. Economic risks usually interfere in this resulting in their uneven involvement and attention in enterprise promotion.

The capabilities and entitlements approach, as this paper has suggested, is useful for moving towards inclusive growth. Opportunities for market development and access have never been as great in India as they are now and can increase incomes of those at the bottom of the pyramid to a level where men recognize it as significant and then allow women to move outside for still greater contributions. However, for the capabilities approach to be put into practice and to take advantage of new opportunities requires investment, political will and social energy from a variety of public, private and civil society institutions to improve the conditions and maintain the balance for sustainability so that the poor can meaningfully contribute. That is, large-scale market access and safeguards are needed to ensure that unfettered market activities do not deplete natural resources and destroy the environment necessary for the poor to thrive. The work of civil society institutions like Udyogini in building capacity is not always matched by improvements in other ways needed to make capacity-building more effective in promoting enterprises, such as roads and transportation from villages to markets. Public-private partnerships (government, business and civil society) are much advocated for closing the gaps that prevent the realization of capabilities and entitlements. With a high growth rate, and stellar corporate performance that has resulted from decontrols and tax incentives from government, it is not an unreasonable expectation that corporate India will play a bigger role in investment in underserved areas to develop skills and create employment for the poor.

Corporations draw heavily on societal resources and profits will eventually erode as resources on which profits depend become scarce. Therefore, it is in the enlightened self-interest of business to engage constructively in enlarging its contribution to the broader social and environmental agenda. Very rightly while we can justifiably be proud of India's stellar performance in GDP growth, the inequity in the economy is hampering India's true potential.

NOTES

1. Companies are outsourcing basic production to avoid adhering to labour laws (particularly minimum wages and working conditions) and to prevent unionization.

2. SHGs are similar to rotating savings and loan associations or ROSCAs which operate in Africa and Latin America. ROSCAs are generally traditional groupings while SHGs are mobilized by NGOs and similar external agents.
3. Diwali is festival of lights celebrated by the followers of Hindu religion in the month of October or November.
4. Holi is a festival of colors celebrated the followers of Hindu religion in the month of March.
5. GMT referred to Grassroots Management Trainings is an innovative and participatory approach of training the rural women by inculcating the knowledge and skills of managing an enterprise. It is delivered through posters, placards, role-play, skits, training kit etc.
6. A minor-forest produce mainly used to prepare country liquor

REFERENCES

Aniket, K. (16 November, 2005). Self Help Groups: Use of Modified ROSCAs in Microfinance, University of Edinburgh.

Bahuguna, Vinod Kumar, Forests in the Economy of the Rural Poor: An Estimation of the Dependency Level.

Consultative Group to Assist the Poorest (CGAP), (August 2007). "Sustainability of Self-Help Groups in India: Two Analysis", Occasional Paper No. 12.

Prahalad, C.K. (2005). *Fortune at the Bottom of the Pyramid*, Wharton School Publishing.

Satish, P. "Institutional Alternatives for the Promotion of Microfinance Self-Help Groups in India," *Journal of Microfinance*, 3(2): 49-74.

Sen, Amartya (1999). Development as Freedom, Oxford University Press.

Viswanath, Vanita (September 2005). "Entrepreneurship and Rural Women: Capacity-building for Market Reach and Poverty Alleviation in a Remote Region of Western India" Paper presented at the International Conference on Entrepreneurship: Employment and Beyond, Stockholm, Sweden.

9

Integrating Microenterprises into Markets through BDS: SEEP Network/USAID Case Study

MELISSA NUSSBAUM, ASHOK KUMAR,
and ALEXANDRA MIEHLBRADT

I. INTRODUCTION

Over the past several years, non-governmental organizations (NGOs), donors, and development practitioners have been grappling with methods to develop sustainable business service markets that will help small enterprises increase their profits and integrate on beneficial terms into local, regional, and global markets. Although it remains clear that micro-enterprises need services beyond training and access to credit, practitioners struggle to develop sustainable service markets that include microenterprises, particularly in environments where product and business service markets are weak. In June 2002, the SEEP Network's Practitioner Learning Programme (PLP) provided 10 organizations with grants to undertake market research in weak markets, and then pilot interventions to develop commercial and sustainable business service markets that would help microenterprises increase their profits. EDA Rural Systems Pvt. Ltd., a private consulting company in Gurgaon, India that provides management support to development programmes/organisations received a grant to research the leather footwear subsector in Rajasthan and pilot interventions to help artisan micro-entrepreneurs in this subsector increase their incomes.

As a central objective of the SEEP PLP, the purpose of this case study is to understand EDA's challenges and lessons learned in its leather sub-sector project and share them with the practitioner community. Although this case study is by no means exhaustive, it offers key insights into the process by which EDA gathered and analyzed market information and developed and promoted pilot business models for the delivery of services to microentrepreneurs and other market players in the leather subsector in Rajasthan.

The focus of this case study is the decision-making process that led EDA from pages of information on the leather subsector and supply and demand for related business development services (BDS) to identifying and supporting the creation of service business models that help leather microentrepreneurs access new markets and enhance incomes and profits. The case study describes the links between the market assessment (MA) findings, the project design, the pilot implementation, subsequent adjustments, and continuing challenges. This case study illustrates the deep involvement of the EDA staff, from the field personnel to the executive director, in continuously evaluating the project and making changes to improve the models. It presents the choices and decisions EDA made and the strategies used, both those that have worked well and those that have been, or may need to be, adjusted.

At the time of the case study, EDA had finished its MA and had completed approximately six months of pilot interventions. Although EDA is several years away from being able to evaluate the success of the project, its story provides useful lessons for practitioners and donors on how to carry out an effective and integrated process of market research, project design, and pilot implementation.

The case study covers the following topics:

- Section 1, along with Introduction, provides an overview of EDA's market research process, its findings on the leather subsector and supporting BDS markets, and its subsequent project design. The section describes EDA's objectives and rationale for undertaking the project.
- Section 2 describes EDA's intervention strategies—the activities aimed at stimulating specific business service

markets. These activities are common across the three BDS markets on which EDA is focusing.

- Section 3 provides in-depth information on each of the three business service provision models that EDA is promoting for the supply of BDS. For each type of service, this section describes EDA's findings on the market, the service providers EDA chose to work with, the services they deliver, the business model for delivering those services, EDA's experiences in piloting the business model, the challenges encountered, and subsequent project adjustments.
- Section 4 highlights the lessons learned from the project thus far and describes how EDA's continuous efforts to gather feedback and make improvements have impacted its project. This section also describes how the services are bundled together and the benefit of linking different types of services and providers. Section 4 also outlines some of EDA's achievements to date in the project and its challenges going forward.

EDA's Market Research

EDA decided to start a BDS project in the leather subsector in Rajastan while working on a Rural Industries Programme of the Small Industries Development Bank of India focused on credit linkages for enterprises. EDA found that leather microentrepreneurs were interested in receiving and being linked to services beyond credit. EDA believed that additional services might help these low-income micro-entrepreneurs substantially increase their profits.

EDA undertook two studies of the market before designing interventions. The first study was designed to verify EDA's decision to develop a BDS related programme in the leather subsector. The second study aimed to gather in-depth information that would help EDA choose appropriate services and design programme interventions.

Preliminary Study: EDA's preliminary study focused on understanding the leather sandal subsector—the stakeholders, opportunities, and constraints—and determining if both a role and a demand for BDS existed. The study relied on secondary source research and interviews with a range of market players and key informants. EDA gathered information on the market for leather sandals and other leather goods, the scale of the leather subsector and number of microenterprises in it, the inputs required for production and where these inputs could be purchased, the production process and microentrepreneurs' constraints, and demand for business services.

The study showed that many microentrepreneurs were involved in the leather subsector in Rajasthan and other parts of the country. It also showed that although the market for *jootis*—traditional leather sandals—was declining, the market for more modern sandals and other leather products was increasing, particularly in urban areas and export markets. The study showed that although appropriate inputs were available, most microentrepreneurs were not able to reach growing domestic and export markets due to the outdated designs of their products. The study also indicated that BDS markets in the leather subsector were weak, and most artisans had weak and limited links with market players outside their villages. A demand for business services came not only from microentrepreneurs, but also from other market players.

These findings confirmed for EDA that enabling artisans to produce sandals with more modern designs and other leather goods that would appeal to higher value markets could be an appropriate strategy for increasing returns to artisans. The findings indicated that BDS for microentrepreneurs and other players in the market chain could help artisans start producing modern sandals with appealing designs and also a variety of other leather goods that would meet the growing demand in domestic and export markets. EDA thought that it would be possible to improve the capacity of private suppliers who could provide quality BDS to leather artisans and other market players. Lastly, the scale of the subsector and the demand for BDS appeared to justify the investment in a project.

Secondary Study: The preliminary study provided EDA with an overall picture of the leather subsector and showed that demand for business services existed. EDA lacked detail on the demand and supply of various BDS in the leather sub-sector, however, it also lacked some information about the leather sub-sector itself and the relationships among various market players. The secondary study focused primarily on BDS in the leather subsector but also gathered additional information on the subsector itself, particularly the relationships among market players in the subsector.

In the secondary study, EDA explored in depth the relationship between the leather artisans and all the other market players and stakeholders in the subsector. EDA gathered detailed information on the provision of BDS in these relationships, the demand levels for various BDS, and the perception of the artisans about the quality and availability of the BDS. EDA also gathered specific information on BDS providers—the market players who offered embedded services and private and government/NGO providers who were offering stand-alone services. This information helped EDA assess the potential for providing various BDS to artisans on a commercial basis. EDA also gathered additional information on the market for leather sandals and other leather goods and the weekly markets, wholesalers, retailers, exporters, middlemen, and institutions supporting the subsector.

EDA's second study consisted of in-depth interviews, focus group discussions (FGDs), and direct observation of business transactions. EDA staff individually interviewed 134 microentrepreneurs living in 12 rural villages and sponsored an FGD in each village with a group of 7 to 10 microentrepreneurs involved in traditional sandal production. EDA also interviewed a total of 50 BDS providers, both public and private, including input suppliers, exporters, and wholesalers who offer embedded BDS.[1] EDA staff visited local haats—small village markets, usually organized on a weekly basis—to observe artisans purchasing inputs and selling finished sandals to buyers. The second MA was carried out by one field staff member on a full-time basis and a team leader devoting approximately 30 to 40 per cent of his time to the MA over four months. EDA's director also provided guidance on the design of the MA and reviewed the findings.

Overview of the Leather Sub-sector and Supporting BDS

Overall, the Indian leather industry has grown tremendously over the past several decades. Since 1990, leather exports have grown at a nominal rate of 13 per cent per annum (equal to a real growth rate of 4% annum). Today, the industry ranks eighth in the country's exports. Over the past three decades, India has shied from exporting raw materials to finished products, which now constitute

81 per cent of the total leather exports of the country. The exports include leather footwear and garments, footwear components (for example, soles), and other leather goods. Although relevant data is not available specifically for sandals, major stakeholders, including exporters and wholesalers, believe that the domestic and export demand for leather sandals with modern designs is increasing. Similarly, the demand for leather goods and leather garments is increasing in domestic and export markets. Figure 9.1 shows a basic diagram of the leather subsector.

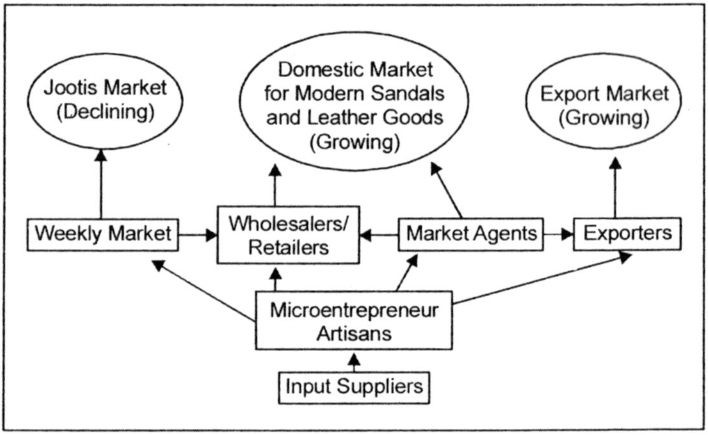

Fig. 9.1: Simplified Leather Subsector Diagram

Market Players

Leather artisans work in family microenterprises, usually with two to three workers, in peri-urban and rural villages. Traditionally, they make basic leather sandals, called *jootis,* mainly for the rural market. These artisans are considered to belong to the lowest level of the caste structure, and their incomes are approximately US$ 30–40 per month. The areas where they live and work are drought-prone and lack many basic services, such as health care and education as well as good infrastructure.

Input suppliers are small shops, producers, or vendors in Jaipur and sometimes peri-urban towns that sell raw materials (such as leather and material for sandal soles), accessories for decorating the sandals, machines for stitching and bufing, and spare parts and lasts, which are wooden or plastic molds to shape the shoes.

Some specialized raw materials, such as particular types of leather, are made in modern, medium-sized enterprises and are not widely available.

Retailers are shops or vendors in Jaipur and other urban centres, such as Delhi, that sell sandals or leather goods directly to consumers.

Wholesalers are enterprises that purchase sandals and/or leather goods at weekly markets or from market agents and sell them to retailers or exporters.

Market agents are traders who purchase shoes from leather artisans and sell them in markets or to wholesalers, retailers, and exporters. Some of them are microentrepreneur artisans themselves and purchase from other leather artisans in their villages. Others operate from urban-based weekly markets.

Exporters are larger enterprises that export a variety of goods from India to other countries. Some specialize in leather; others sell a wider range of items.

Weekly markets, called haats, operate in Jaipur and other small and large urban centers, including Delhi. They host a wide variety of products.

Market Channels

The predominant market channel is the micro-entrepreneur artisans who sell traditional *jootis* to the rural market through the weekly Jaipur haat and other similar smaller haats and purchase their needed inputs at the same time. At the market, their products are purchased by consumers and also market agents, wholesalers, and retailers. To a lesser extent, leather microentrepreneurs sell directly to wholesalers, retailers, market agents, or exporters who supply the urban and export markets.

Key Opportunities and Constraints

Demand for *jootis* in rural areas is declining in favor of substitutes, such as plastic sandals. Demand for modern sandals and other leather goods, however, is increasing in urban markets (such as Delhi), export markets, and, increasingly, in rural markets as well. Rural leather artisans lack new designs appropriate for these markets, the technical skills to produce products that appeal to these markets, and links to the growing markets.

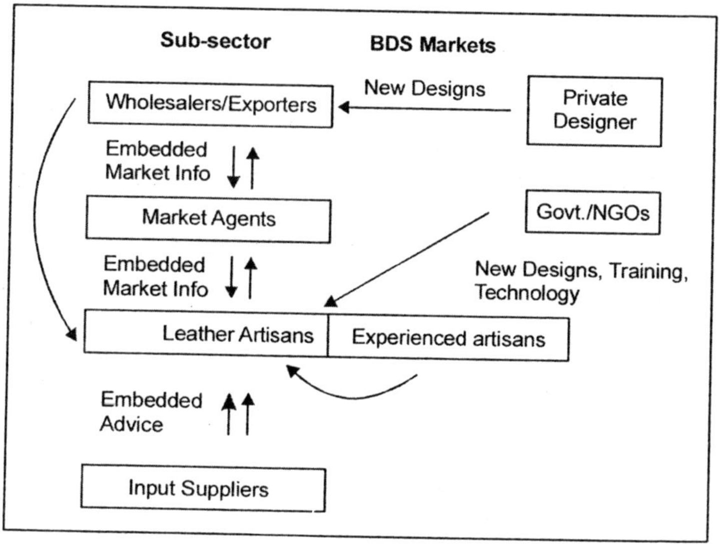

Fig. 9.2: Flow of Key Business Services in the Leather Sandal Subsector

Supporting Business Service Markets

BDS Demand: EDA found that, in general, artisans are aware of new market opportunities. Those artisans who have some contact with exporters, urban wholesalers, or government/NGO programmes in the subsector are more aware of new market opportunities and what they need to reach them than are artisans who have no contacts outside rural markets. EDA found that microentrepreneurs, particularly those with greater market exposure, have an understanding of and value BDS and are willing to pay for quality services. Because of the prevalence of government and NGO programmes offering free or highly subsidized services, however, the artisans are not accustomed to paying for BDS. The services in highest demand are training, market links and information, technology for beer designs, and new products. The microentrepreneurs need new designs, the technical skills to produce the designs, and access to markets to sell their products. Together, these services enable microentrepreneurs to reach new markets.

BDS Supply: The MA indicated that subsidized (government/

donor-funded) and commercial BDS (although in a very limited way) currently exist in the subsector. Figure 9.2 summarizes the flow of key business services in the subsector. EDA found that for most leather artisans, their strongest links are with other artisans. Most business services to artisans, particularly training and market information, are provided from other artisans informally and for free. A very few artisans have managed to develop links with market agents, wholesalers, retailers, or exporters and receive embedded services, including market information, new designs, and sometimes training from these enterprises. In addition, a small number of artisans travel to urban centers beyond Jaipur to sell their products to wholesalers or retailers and gather market information and ideas for new designs. To a very limited extent, some artisans receive basic advice from input suppliers on what types of materials and accessories are most popular or appropriate for specific types of sandals.

The MA indicated that the existing BDS and government programmes are not consistently enabling entrepreneurs to gain the expected benefits, including increased revenue from creating market-demanded designs, connecting the entrepreneurs with exporters and wholesalers, and upgrading their skills. They are not meeting the demanded quality, have limited outreach, and are predominantly provided by the government programs. Table 1 summarizes the supply of services.

Table 9.1: Summary of BDS Supply in the Leather Sandal Sub-sector

Who?	*How?*	*Scale*	*Satisfaction*
Government and NGOs	Free; stand-alone	Limited	Low
Exporters, wholesalers, input suppliers	Embedded; bundled	Limited	Good
Fellow artisans	Informal	High	Mixed

At least four government agencies and a number of NGOs operate programmes to help microentrepreneur artisans. Most, if not all, services from government and NGOs are free or highly subsidized. Banks and financial institutions also specifically target microentrepreneurs with credit and other financial services.

The most prominent government programme is the National Leather Development Programme (NLDP) sponsored by the

United Nations Development Programme in association with the Government of India. NLDP operates in a number of states, including Rajasthan. To widen the market base for leather sandals, the program has taken on a number of initiatives, including introducing new patterns and mechanizing the production process by introducing machines for leather stitching, buffing, punching, and dyeing. In addition, the NLDP offers some BDS, including skill development training, market links, and design inputs. The programme has been able to make positive changes at some of the places it reaches. Leather artisans in these communities generally place greater value on services such as design inputs and marketing. Some leather artisans who received training through NLDP are making better designed, modern sandals. The programme has relatively limited outreach, however, in terms of the numbers of artisans receiving their services. Furthermore, a good number of artisans receiving the services are not able to use them effciently and effectively in the absence of complementary services. Similarly, the skill development training programmes in shoe production by Khadi and Village Industry Commissions, another government programme, have had little impact because the instructors are not invested, the training is not particularly relevant, and the trainees do not receive other services, such as links to new buyers and information on sources for appropriate raw materials and accessories.

Leather Sub-sector Programme Summary

EDA's goal for its project in the leather subsector is to increase the incomes of leather artisans by enabling them to increase their business profits. EDA aims to achieve this goal by promoting the development of a commercial BDS market in the leather subsector that helps microentrepreneurs access new, more lucrative markets and/or decrease costs.

The project is being implemented in Jaipur and Dausa districts of Rajasthan in northern India. In Jaipur district, EDA's project includes nine villages with 2,250 small enterprises, of which 815 are involved in sandal making. In Dausa district, EDA's programme includes three villages with 315 small enterprises, of which 155 are involved in sandal making. Three staff members are devoted to this project: a team leader who oversees the project and two field staff members. The project budget for the MA and pilot interventions over two years is US$ 66,597.

EDA decided which services to pilot based on the following criteria:

- Microentrepreneurs' demand for services;
- Potential for services to help microentrepreneurs reach new markets;
- Potential for reaching significant scale; and
- Existence of service providers and potential for commercial service provision.

The services EDA chose to pilot are training, design services and market linkages, and information on consumer markets.

The overall strategy for the interventions includes initial demand stimulation, supply through local service providers, building on existing supply, and increasing service outreach. The interventions include identifying and building the capacity of providers, developing business models for the supply of services, stimulating demand, and linking providers with each other and the leather artisans. The interventions are described in detail in Section 2.

II. EDA'S INTERVENTIONS

Based on the findings from its market research, its project goals, and the social, cultural, and economic context of the leather artisans and relevant markets, EDA Rural Development Pvt. Ltd. (EDA) developed the following intervention strategies for the three business service markets on which it is focusing:

1. Identify business development services (BDS) providers who could add or intensify BDS provision in their existing businesses and who live in and/or understand the communities in which the leather artisans live.
2. Develop business models for the provision of services together with the identified providers.
3. Build the capacity of the identified providers to understand and meet demand for services and manage their BDS activities profitably.

4. Assist BDS providers in promoting their services among leather microentrepreneurs and other potential customers in the leather subsector.
5. Promote links among market players to get the market moving and so that BDS providers can offer microentrepreneurs a bundle of services to help them reach new markets.
6. Conduct some direct demand stimulation among leather artisans.

For all three services–training, design services and market linkages, and information–EDA has played a large role in stimulating demand for and supply of services with the aim of integrating micro-entrepreneurs into markets. Initially, EDA was intensively involved with market players to stimulate transactions and ensure that the links between artisans and providers were forming. Already, EDA has been able to reduce this involvement somewhat. As EDA observes key market activities occurring with less help from its staff, it will continue to gradually decrease its involvement.

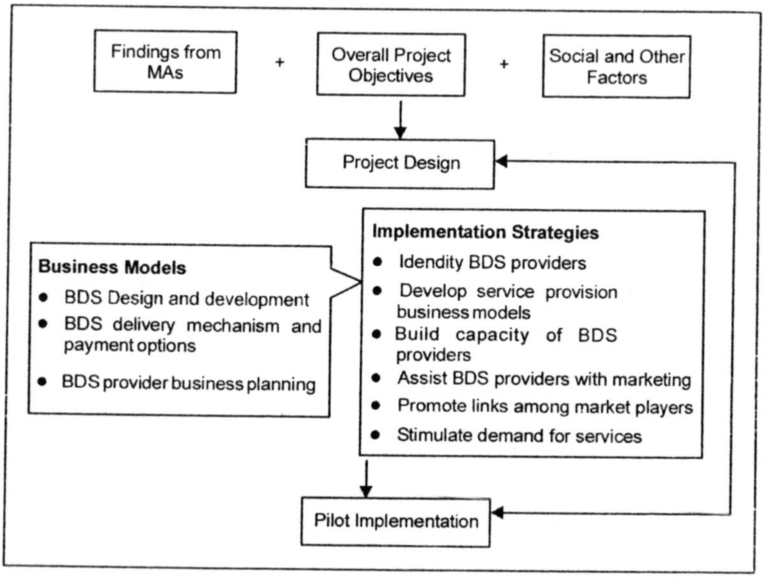

Fig. 9.3: EDA's Framework to Develop a BDS Market

EDA's experience in piloting illustrates that market interventions are a continuous learning cycle that requires the staff to consistently gather feedback and implement changes while at the same time teaching the providers how to do the same independently. This section describes the activities across all the service markets that EDA is implementing to reach its objectives.

Identify Service Providers

The BDS market assessment (MA) provided a detailed analysis of the existing and potential providers of different services. While interviewing the existing BDS providers, EDA discovered their views on how BDS markets in the leather subsector could be made more vibrant and include leather micro-entrepreneurs. While interviewing leather artisans, EDA gained some understanding on how these microentrepreneurs wanted to receive particular BDS.

EDA learned that most of the leather artisans prefer interacting with service providers from the leather artisan community because these entrepreneurs are accessible, approachable, and understand the artisans' businesses. Therefore, EDA decided to try to identify and work with service providers from the leather artisan community when possible. Promoting providers from the leather artisan community would avoid discrimination because the leather microentrepreneurs belong to the lowest level of the Indian caste structure. Local providers are comfortable interacting with those who belong to their own community and speak the local language.

Further, EDA determined that staff from institutions and larger private sector providers, who tend to have their operating base in cities, would not want to stay in villages to provide training and to collect and/or buy finished products from artisans while providing market-related services. Providers from the cities would incur higher costs because they would have to recruit trainers and personnel to visit villages, which would increase the price of these services, making the services less attractive and accessible to microentrepreneurs. On the other hand, providers from the leather artisan community would tend to price services lower because they would have to invest less initially, and they would not have very high expectations in terms of profit. They would be glad to generate incomes on par with or a little higher than their present earnings from making sandals. EDA also thought that the providers from the community would have more accountability to the leather artisans because of the peer pressure and local goodwill that might not apply to providers from cities. Only when local service providers could not be identified would EDA consider promoting larger service providers from the cities.

During the MA, EDA gained information on the other skills and activities of individual artisans. It found some leather artisans with greater exposure to markets and some with experience in training fellow artisans. EDA developed an idea of the characteristics of microentrepreneurs who might be able to take on particular service delivery roles and identified specific artisans with these characteristics. For example, a few microentrepreneurs were skilled in making modern sandals and leather goods and had previously acted as government trainers but had never thought of selling training services on a commercial basis. As EDA explained the market potential for the training service to these artisans, they showed great interest in becoming commercial trainers.

For each service, EDA identifies service providers that are either already offering a modified version of the service or have a suffcient revenue stream from other business activities to be able to add service provision to their existing businesses. Particularly when considering leather artisans as service providers, EDA consciously chooses entrepreneurs with the potential to increase their income incrementally by gradually adding service provision. EDA does not want the microentrepreneurs to abandon their production activities; rather, they can slowly build the additional service provision into their existing businesses and eventually, if their income from the new services exceeds their normal income, focus completely on delivery of the new services.

Based on its market research and regular interaction with artisans' communities, EDA identifies leather artisans who can offer training or market linkage services. Field staff discuss the possibility of providing services with each artisan individually. If the artisan agrees, EDA staff develop a plan with the artisan to help him or her start offering services, initially on a trial basis. Much time is spent at first clarifying expectations and discussing how EDA will assist the artisan. EDA makes sure that the artisans understand that the service provision will be their business, and that EDA will help them but neither subsidize their costs nor guarantee customers. At the time of writing, five or six service providers for training services and five or six providers for market linkages had been identified from the leather artisan community. EDA decided to work with formal institutions or larger private providers for design services because greater skill and interaction with markets is required. At the time of writing, EDA had started working with one institution in Jaipur, the Indian Institute for Crafts and Design (IICD), as a provider of design services. EDA is continuing to identify more service providers.

Develop Service Provision Business Models

EDA works with identified providers to develop service provision business models. Field staff start by discussing with each provider the market information related to the service they will offer. For example, EDA told potential training service providers that leather artisans wanted training in their villages and at times that allowed them to keep their businesses going during the training. Then, staff discuss the three following aspects of service provision with each provider.

BDS Design and Development: EDA staff discuss with each provider what the service will include and help design the service components and features. For example, EDA discussed with IICD what would be included in the designs it would sell, such as templates and information on raw materials.

BDS Delivery and Payment Options: Staff discuss with providers how services can be delivered. For example, EDA discussed with potential market agents how they could embed market information in their relationships with their artisan suppliers. EDA staff explained the benefits of various delivery mechanisms. For example, EDA staff explained to potential market agents that providing artisan suppliers with market information would help them produce sandals that would meet market demand. This would benefit the artisan suppliers and the market agents. EDA staff also talk about payment options with providers. For example, EDA discussed with potential providers of exhibition information and linkage services that they could receive fees in several ways for arranging artisans' participation in trade fairs—commissions from the trade fair organizers, fees from artisans, or both.

BDS Business Planning: Typically, the providers that EDA works with try out service provision on a small scale first before they do any business planning. The providers want proof that customers exist for their services, and that they can make money. After they have started service provisioning, EDA helps some providers develop business plans. For example, EDA helped IICD develop a business plan to expand provision of its design services.

The service provision business models and how they were developed and tested are discussed in detail in Section 3.

EDA found that it had to work intensively with the first few providers to develop viable business models. Helping the first few providers to start service provision took three to four months. After a few providers had started offering services, however, the process became less intense. New providers see how existing providers operate and adopt the existing business model. The process has now become one of adaptation rather than developing models from scratch.

Build Capacity of Service Providers to Meet Demand

Despite the leather artisans' general understanding of business concepts, EDA spends a good deal of time working with them and other providers to understand a commercialized approach to offering services. For the training and market linkage services, EDA focuses on educating the providers on product development, pricing, marketing, and service delivery. EDA helps the providers improve and/or create services that are tailored to meet the demands of the market through appropriate payment mechanisms, fiexible scheduling, and tailored offerings.

The MA, to a great extent, generated information about the areas of capacity building required by potential artisan providers. For example, the existence of different categories of artisans in different villages prompted EDA to help service providers develop differentiated products to meet the requirements of different sets of microentrepreneurs. Because most of the service providers being promoted are new to service provision on a commercial basis, EDA uses its own understanding of the functioning of the service market to develop the providers' capacities.

EDA also helps the service providers to increase their professionalism through their appearance and the marketing of their services. For example, some of the areas that EDA covers with new market agents include the following:

- How to interact in a professional manner with wholesalers and exporters;
- How to dress for business meetings; and
- In what packaging they should carry samples to wholesalers and exporters.
- Some of the areas that EDA covers with new trainers are as follow:
  - How to promote their services; and
  - How to choose the appropriate training course to market according to the level of potential micro-entrepreneur customers.

After they have started service provision, EDA helps the providers translate feedback on their services into actions to improve their services. EDA also helps the providers address a range of business problems as they arise (see Box 9.1). Additional specifics on EDA's capacity building for each service are provided in Section 3.

Box 9.1: EDA Helps a New Market Agent with Legal and Banking Issues

Prakash, a new market agent working with EDA, perceives government regulations as the largest obstacle for his business endeavour. To avoid being stopped by the police while transporting large orders, Prakash must pay US$ 50 to register his business, which still does not guarantee that he will not be harassed on the road. In addition, he must open a bank account because the exporters prefer to pay using checks or through bank transfers. EDA helped Prakash find information on how to register his business and open a bank account and assisted him to manage these procedures. EDA also offers Prakash support by trying to foresee what other obstacles he might encounter and helping him to develop a plan to overcome them.

Assist Service Providers to Market Services

The MA indicated that although leather artisans are willing to pay for services, many of them are unaware of services, including the different offerings, the benefits, and the existence of markets outside their region. Furthermore, the MA indicated that while the artisans identified as service providers had a relatively good level of overall business understanding, they had minimal knowledge of developing appropriate services (in particular, training services) that can meet the demand of different sets of clients, their costing and pricing, and how to promote and market their services.

EDA works with the service providers in marketing their services in the following ways:

- Assistance in developing the design and contents of promotional materials, including pamphlets, business cards and catalogues, and links to printers;
- Teaching them how to present their services when meeting with clients;
- Linking them with potential clients through visits to villages and markets; and
- Educating them on marketing concepts, including pricing and negotiating to ensure that their services are in line with market expectations.

Link Market Players

A major role of EDA is linking service providers with clients and each other. EDA brings the providers and clients together to convince both parties that the service is worthwhile. For example, if artisans in a village show some interest in buying a service, this information is passed on to the respective BDS providers. If needed, the EDA team accompanies the BDS providers to meet the potential clients and facilitates the discussions between them.

EDA introduces and builds business relationships between the BDS providers. This makes it easier for artisans to get a bundle of services that they need to access new markets. For example, when IICD held a reception to introduce its designs, EDA ensured that the trainers and market agents were invited. The objective was to have the trainers and market agents purchase the designs and teach them to other artisans.

EDA also facilitates links between market players when significant gaps are identified. EDA locates suppliers for selected inputs and materials that the service providers and the artisans need to produce new products. For example, EDA is working with a local last maker to ensure that all artisans can access this input. Previously, the government had provided lasts in a sporadic fashion, leaving some microentrepreneurs with a plethora of lasts while others had none. Lastly, EDA introduces market agents to wholesalers and exporters who might purchase their products.

Stimulate Demand for Services

EDA started its demand stimulation during the MA, through which, EDA was able to introduce and contextualize the value of paying for BDS rather than receiving free services. Through simple analogies, EDA explained to the producers the idea of paying for improved quality and relevant services and the impact these services would have on the microentrepreneurs' incomes and businesses. Two examples of the analogies follow:

- "To ensure quality education for your children, where would you prefer to send them: a government school that is cheaper but the quality of education is perceived to be below average or a more expensive private school with a perceived higher quality of education?" Most of the artisans responded that they would like to send their children to a private school.
- "When you or your family members become sick, where do you prefer to go for treatment: a government hospital with cheaper fees but poorer medical service or a more expensive private hospital with higher quality of treatment?" Most of the artisans responded that they would prefer a private hospital.

After EDA had an artisan respondent following this line of thinking, it applied this rationale in the context of services for his or her business. For example, EDA would ask the microentrepreneurs this question: *"In the same way, if a supplier provided training, design inputs, or marketing support of higher quality that would yield results, would you be willing to pay a fee for this service?"* In most cases, respondents said that they would be willing to pay a fee for such services because they would expect an increase in their incomes as a result.

Several of the microentrepreneurs had received subsidized training services through the government and thought that the quality was subpar, and the content was not relevant to their specific needs. Therefore, through the microentrepreneurs' previous experiences with subsidized services and EDA's ability to explain the benefit of paying for services, EDA planted the seeds for developing a commercial BDS market.

EDA continues to stimulate demand for services informally through discussions with microentrepreneurs during its regular visits to villages and in meetings with other market players. EDA also encourages leather artisans who are thinking about purchasing a service to talk with those who already have. EDA plans to decrease its active demand stimulation as more artisans acquire services and demand begins to grow through word of mouth referrals.

Monitoring the Programme

EDA has found no substitute for continuous interactions in the field to monitor the programme. During the pilot phase, staff intensively monitors progress by making daily trips to the villages and local markets. EDA anticipates that aer the pilot phase, it will continue to check on the progress of the market but on a less frequent basis. EDA recognizes, however, that it currently plays a vital role in the development of the market by acting as the link and the method of communication between providers, artisans, and other market players. It anticipates spending two to three additional years focused on promoting additional providers and services and addressing additional areas for improvement identified in the MA that it did not decide to pursue initially.

The field staff and team leader regularly visit the villages and markets to gather feedback on the program. The staff use this feedback to improve their interventions and determine how to expand service provision. They are constantly sharing ideas with the providers and working to facilitate relationships between market players. For example, during some training sessions on sandal production, the trainer orally provided the participants with information on materials suppliers. The information was delivered on an *ad hoc* basis, however, and the trainees did not have paper and pens to record the information. The participating artisans

Box 9.2: EDA Links a new Trainer with Artisan Customers

> During a visit to Bishunpura village in Dausa district by the EDA staff members, some of the leather artisans showed a keen interest in obtaining training in modern sandals with new designs but did not know who could provide this service. This information was passed on to the training service provider, Kailash. Kailash had a brief discussion in the Jaipur haat with a few of the microentrepreneurs from Bishunpura who visited the haat to sell their products. Subsequently, Kailash requested EDA to accompany him to the village for further discussions with the artisans, and EDA complied. EDA helped to facilitate the discussions between Kailash and the Bishunpura artisans. After some time, the deal was finalized. Ten microentrepreneurs received training, paying fees that allowed Kailash to make a profit.

requested an improved method of receiving this valuable information. EDA helped the trainers to print the information on paper, and the trainers agreed to offer this information on a regular basis, thus providing the trainees with tangible information that they can refer to when needed.

Through regular interactions with providers and microentrepreneurs, EDA is constantly trying to understand how many BDS providers have emerged and are offering commercial services. It also tries to understand how many artisans and other market players are buying the services, and why they decided to purchase them. EDA follows up with the providers and service buyers to understand how the services can be improved and how EDA can help the providers to implement the suggested improvements. EDA also attempts to understand the additional initiative the providers are making to develop their services and their business on their own. Understanding how much the providers are willing to do on their own helps EDA to gauge the sustainability of the model.

Quantitatively, EDA gathers information on the following issues:

- Number of service providers in the market;
- Total number of buyers of the services;
- Perceived quality of the services;
- Development of new service products by the providers based on feedback from the buyers; and
- Number of new villages and markets receiving services.

As for the broader vision of the project, EDA revisits its objectives and their progress every three to four months. With a finger on the pulse of its project through regular interactions and monitoring, the quarterly review allows EDA to think broadly about the project and to ensure that it is continuing to move towards its overall goals.

III. SERVICE PROVISION BUSINESS MODELS

The development, testing, and refining of appropriate business models for the delivery of services to artisans and other market players is one of the most challenging parts of market development programmes in weak markets. EDA Rural Systems Pvt. Ltd. (EDA) worked with providers to pilot three main business models through the interventions outlined above. This section shows how the business development services market assessment (MA) findings led to the design of each model. Each model is described and outlined in a diagram. This section discusses EDA's role in facilitating the development of each business model, the challenges faced, and the adjustments made. It also provides examples of actual service providers and microentrepreneurs who have purchased each service.

Design-Related Services Business Model: The urban and export markets constantly demand new designs catering to consumers' changing tastes. Design-related services help artisans and the entire subsector meet this demand.

EDA's Findings on the Market: EDA found no formal, commercialized design service for microentrepreneurs. Artisans received information on designs from government agencies or fellow artisans. Some microentrepreneurs learned basic design skills from the government-subsidized training courses but, given the limited outreach of the government programmes, most microentrepreneurs used traditional designs or copied their neighbours. The more sophisticated microentrepreneurs copied designs they saw in the marketplaces or from information they received from wholesalers and exporters. Information on new designs did not have wide outreach in the market and failed to provide microentrepreneurs with the progressive designs demanded outside local markets. Without information and instructions on the latest designs, the majority of the microentrepreneurs were limited to supplying basic designs to local markets.

As for design information providers, EDA found that most of the information on designs came from government-subsidized training courses. According to the artisans, the training was very basic and did not provide information or technical skills on the styles in demand.

The Service Provider: EDA found that the leather artisans lacked market information on trends and were not sophisticated enough to conceive new designs that met consumer demand. The EDA staff felt that experts in design should be involved in the subsector because meeting consumers' changing demand for new product styles requires design talent, continuous innovation, and a strong level of market understanding. These considerations led EDA to contact the Indian Institute of Design and Crafts (IICD) as a possible design service provider.

IICD is located in Jaipur town, approximately one to two hours from the villages where the artisans live. IICD offers design degree programmes focused on developing the skills and improving the livelihoods of local microentrepreneurs and handi-craft producers. EDA chose to work with IICD as a design services provider because it believed that the overall objective of IICD to aid low-income crafts workers matched with EDA's project objective. IICD had organizational goals to provide students with marketable technical skills and was looking for ways to become financially self-sustainable. In addition, IICD had relationships with exporters and wholesalers in the market who were willing to share information on the designs in demand. EDA recognized that IICD could have greater outreach than only exporters and wholesalers offering designs as an embedded service because IICD could interact with multiple types of market players. By creating and selling new designs for sandals and leather goods commercially, IICD could expand its students' skills, build on existing services, and create a new revenue stream for itself.

The Service and the Business Model: IICD receives market information on consumer preferences from exporters and wholesalers and uses its students to develop prototypes. The prototypes are then made into saleable design packages. Each design package includes a finished prototype, a pattern and descriptions of the raw materials needed, and the production process. IICD catalogues the new designs in a "design bank" for the leather subsector. Fees for the designs are determined based on the level of exclusivity. For example, an exporter who wants exclusive rights to a design will pay a higher fee than an artisan who purchases a design that is available to others as well.

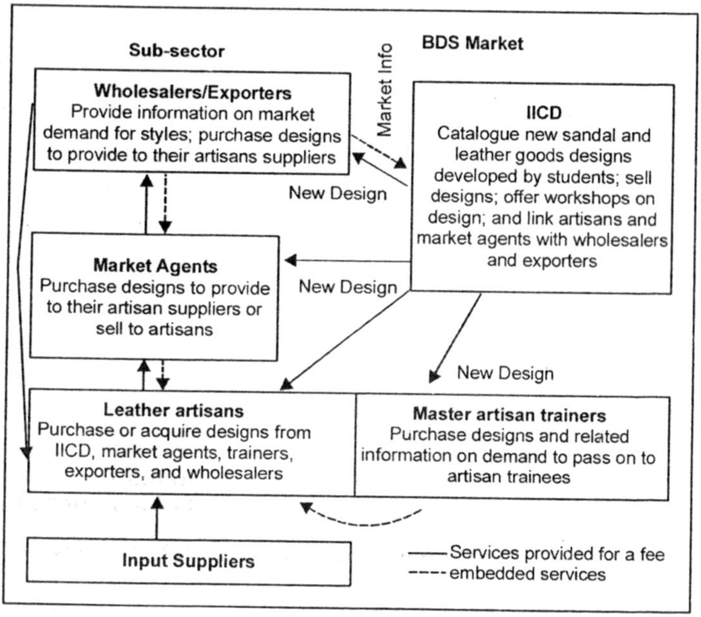

Fig. 9.4: Design-Related Services Business Model

IICD sells the design packages to microentrepreneurs, market agents, trainers, exporters, and wholesalers. IICD markets its services through workshops and training sessions. Initially, IICD is reaching its target groups through introductions and promotions by EDA. In the future, IICD plans to visit local villages and markets to explain its services and distribute promotional materials.

Piloting the Business Model: Having no prior experience selling designs commercially, IICD required evidence of market potential before it piloted its services. EDA provided IICD with US$ 500 to conduct its own MA, which included the students designing 25 different sandal designs. After the designs were complete, EDA invited artisans, trainers, market agents, exporters, and wholesalers to a reception for IICD to introduce its designs and services. The reception resulted in one artisan purchasing a design and an exporter buying two designs. Another benefit of the reception was that it brought together artisans, wholesalers, and exporters who may not have interacted with each other before. For example, a wholesaler told an artisan that he would pay more for modern sandals made from new designs. The interaction between the market players allowed all parties to see the value of the design services.

IICD needed a variety of new skills and capabilities to succeed in its new venture. To date, EDA had built capacity of the IICD through the following actions:

- Assisting IICD in understanding how to commercialize its service in a profitable and sustainable manner;
- Providing assistance in organizing a work-shop—attended by artisans, wholesalers, and offcials from two government projects operating in the leather subsector—to disseminate the new designs developed by IICD and promote the design service; and
- Assisting IICD in developing a business plan to promote the service and increase the outreach.

Challenges and Adjustments: As Bhagirath notes in Box 9.3, a significant problem with the sale of designs is that many of the skilled artisans can see a design, memorize the pattern, and make their own version. Therefore, some of the microentrepreneurs who attended the IICD reception, such as Suraj, an artisan from Sawardha, did not purchase the designs but memorized them, replicated them, and created the sandals themselves. Suraj claims that he would pay a fee for the designs if he were required to pay to view the designs; otherwise, he sees no reason to pay a fee. Many of the microentrepreneurs live in the same villages and keeping information like designs secret can be difficult. In many cases, after a sandal hits the market, other artisans immediately copy the design. Therefore, for a microentrepreneur to benefit from purchasing a design from IICD, he or she must receive an initial order for that design large enough to cover the price of the design. Furthermore, IICD will have to create new designs faster (the 25 designs in the design bank took one and a half months to create) to keep the artisans who purchase its services ahead of those who do not.

The current outreach of this service poses problems of saturation of specific markets. For example, many of the microentrepreneurs invited to the IICD reception were from the village Udaipuria because this village has greater market connections, and its artisans understand the value of design inputs. Therefore, a possibility exists that these micro-entrepreneurs will purchase or copy similar designs, thus making it dificult for each artisan to maximize his or her return on investment.

Although microentrepreneurs clearly value design services, the subsidized service environment poses obstacles for this business model. The artisans targeted by EDA are accustomed to receiving government and NGO services free and are slow to recognize how an improved service will positively impact their business. Therefore, both EDA and IICD will continue to illustrate the benefits of design services by introducing the microentrepreneurs to embroiderers, input suppliers, wholesalers, and exporters who can testify to the demand for improved designs.

Based on the pilot implementation, EDA and IICD found that the market agents, exporters and wholesalers, and to a lesser extent, artisan trainers appear to be a more promising market than selling directly to microentrepreneurs because of the larger product volumes that they deal with as well as their greater capacity to pay. The market agents, exporters, and wholesalers pass designs onto a handful of microentrepreneurs to fill specific orders. The artisan trainers include training in making specific new designs, as well as the patterns and information on where to get raw materials for the new designs, as part of their training courses, increasing the value of the training to microentrepreneurs. Therefore, IICD and EDA are developing strategies to increase their focus on selling to these market players.

In summary, IICD is making the following key changes to handle challenges identified during its first few months as a design service provider:

- Developing new designs at a faster pace to lessen the impact of copying and keep up with consumer trends;
- Encouraging those who purchase designs to make slight modifications (by using different raw materials and accessories) in the main designs, thereby remaining ahead of others; and

- Increasing its focus on selling designs to exporters, wholesalers, market agents, and artisan trainers.

Box 9.3: An Artisan Tries Purchasing New Sandal Designs

> Bhagirath, an artisan from Udaipuria, attended the IICD reception and bought one design. From his interactions with wholesalers and exporters from Delhi at the reception, Bhagirath received an order for 500 sandals. He invested US$4 in the design and will receive US$4 per pair of sandals. The higher price will result in an additional US$0.50 per pair of sandals net profit for Bhagirath. In the future, Bhagirath is interested in purchasing additional designs for sandals as well as for other leather products. One of his main concerns, however, is that all designs are prone to being copied by other artisans. Therefore, he believes that IICD needs to attract the cutting-edge artisans who can quickly bring the new designs to market.

Market Linkage and Information Business Model

To reach new markets, artisans need information on what consumers want and new designs to meet those preferences. They also need links to new buyers and new ways to showcase and sell their products. The market linkage and information services provide these benefits.

EDA's Findings on the Market: EDA learned that the majority of the information on exhibitions and market opportunities received by leather artisans came from government organizations, non-governmental organizations (NGOs), or other artisans/family members. The information was free, and microentrepreneurs usually paid a subsidized fee to attend exhibitions or trade fairs. As for linking the microentrepreneurs with buyers and/or new markets, EDA discovered that approximately 20 market agents in Jaipur district outsourced production and sold the sandals either in the Jaipur haat or supplied them to retailers and/or wholesalers in the Jaipur and Delhi markets. In addition, a few larger, more sophisticated artisans had started to sell sandals with modern designs to more lucrative markets, such as exporters and retailers in Delhi. Some of these artisans had started to outsource to other microenterprises to fill big orders.

EDA found that microentrepreneurs are willing to pay for information and admission to exhibitions and fairs. They also ascertained that the existing traditional sandals needed to be upgraded and improved to increase market agents' interest in the products. Furthermore, the performance of the existing market agents suggested that promotion by agents in other villages would be productive.

Service Providers: EDA chose to build on what exists. It decided to help local artisans start or expand outsourcing production to other microenterprises as well as provide a variety of useful market information to other microentrepreneurs. Eventually, these entrepreneurs would become wholly or mostly traders or market agents, purchasing leather products from microentrepreneurs and selling them to wholesalers, retailers, and exporters as well as arranging micro-entrepreneurs' participation in exhibitions and trade fairs. Not only did this business model exist in a few cases, but local artisans with good market connections were in a strong position to help other microentrepreneurs meet demand from more lucrative urban and export markets.

The Services and the Business Model: The market agents receive their market information from artisans, trainers, exporters and wholesalers, IICD, and exhibition organizers and by making visits to potential markets in and outside Jaipur. Based on this information, each market agent interacts with local artisans in some or all the following ways:

- Buys artisans' products and sells them to wholesalers, retailers, and exporters and/or at markets.

Box 9.4: A market Agent uses IICD Design Services

Ramesh, an artisan and market agent, fills orders through his own production and outsourcing. Because Ramesh was unable to attend the IICD reception, EDA provided him with seven IICD design samples for meetings with wholesalers and exporters in Delhi. During the meetings, Ramesh received orders for 50 to 100 samples of the seven designs from IICD. With the IICD designs, he will earn US$ 0.55 net per pair of sandals: he will keep US$ 0.35 and give US$ 0.20 to the microentrepreneurs from whom he buys the sandals. The IICD samples were made of materials that Ramesh does not know where to find, however, EDA has located a supplier for the material for him so that he can meet the requirements of the orders. Although he does not need to hire additional labour to fill the existing order, he will hire more local microentrepreneurs as his orders increase, thus increasing employment in the village.

- Embeds market information in the above transaction. For example, a market agent might place an order with a microentrepreneur and provide him or her with specific information on the design of the product. Or, a market agent might provide microentrepreneurs he or she buys from with general market information on trends in the colors, decorations, and other design details that are popular in the market.
- Provides sandal or leather products designs (from IICD or exporters) to microentrepreneurs as an embedded service related to specific orders or for a fee.
- Arranges artisans' attendance at exhibitions and trade fairs and rents them display stalls on commission from the exhibition organizers and/or for a fee from the artisans.
- Provides artisans with information on exhibitions and trade fairs as an embedded service and promotional tool for the above service.

Piloting the Business Model: EDA identified a few artisans serving more lucrative export and/or urban markets mainly with their own products as potential market agents because these artisans had both better market connections and were more "market savvy" than others. It also identified artisans who were already outsourcing some production to other microentrepreneurs and selling their products in the markets or who had been trainers for government programmes and recognized the potential for commercialized market linkage services. Currently, the market agents are artisans with another primary source of income. For example, in the village of Udaipuria, Kailash Chand produces sandals, acts as a trainer for government training programmes, provides market-related information for free during his training programmes, and sells information and registration for exhibitions. Those artisans with strong existing revenue streams were less risk-averse to experimenting with trading products than others. EDA is also encouraging skilled market agents who are already involved in buying and selling sandals to increase their outreach by covering more microentrepreneurs in more villages.

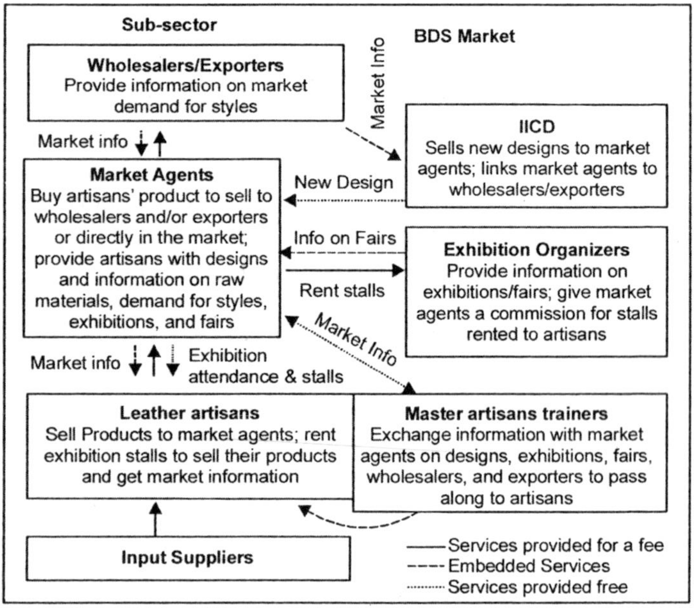

Fig. 9.5: Market Linkage and Information Business Model

EDA is building the capacity of the market agents by taking the following steps:

- Connecting the market agents with potential artisan suppliers in different villages by arranging meetings and/ or introducing the market agents to various microentrepreneurs individually.
- Providing technical assistance on an individual basis to increase the market agents' professionalism, including improving their skills in pricing, negotiation, and effective communication, which helps them to interact with more sophisticated exporters and wholesalers.
- Helping them to develop the design and contents of print materials, including brochures, business cards, and catalogues to promote their products and services, and linking them to business that can print the materials for a fee.
- Assisting them with opening bank accounts.
- Helping them to develop relationships with wholesalers,

retailers, and exporters by introducing them and accompanying them to visit these market players in Jaipur and Delhi.

- Providing information on private sector exhibitions in different places on a frequent basis.
- Introducing and helping them to develop business relationships with exhibition organizers.

EDA also shares its MA findings on a regular basis with market agents, gathers feedback on their trading and market information activities, and seeks their input on the design and implementation of EDA's interventions.

Challenges and Adjustments: The new market agents with whom EDA is working seem to be doing fairly well. They are gradually increasing their outreach by covering more villages. EDA is identifying and promoting more market agents to further expand the number of microenterprises with access to more lucrative markets.

Box 9.5: From Artisan Only to Artisan/Market Agent

EDA approached Prakash to act as a act as a market agent for the microentrepreneurs in Udaipuria. Before his interaction with EDA, Prakash sold his own products in the local markets and to wholesalers. To illustrate the benefits of becoming a market agent, EDA arranged for Prakash to meet with five different exporters in Delhi. Prakash paid all his own expenses for the trip (US$ 30). During these meetings, Prakash realized that a demand existed for his products in Delhi and that the profit margin would be much higher than if he sold to the local markets. Therefore, Prakash decided to sell his own products to the exporters and also outsource larger orders to microentrepreneurs in his village. Regular assistance from EDA was another factor in Prakash's decision to try selling to exporters and outsourcing production. EDA provides Prakash with information and guidance on obstacles that arise. For example, EDA provides Prakash with information on raw material suppliers and embroiderers.

In December 2003, Prakash received an order from an exporter for 25 pairs of sandals with modern designs. Even with outsourced labour, he will net US$ 0.50 per pair. Prakash is also in the process of making a deal for a repeat order of 1,000 to 5,000 sandals with another exporter. Although he currently employs 15 workers, Prakash does not anticipate hiring additional labour. He prefers to outsource to microenterprises in his village because he avoids having to provide food and materials required for the full-time workers.

The outreach for exhibition services has thus far been relatively low. A few microentrepreneurs have purchased this service, and more have expressed interest in aending the exhibitions but do not have the money to pay the fees. EDA hopes that market agents who provide information on fairs and exhibitions will start to offer other value-added services, including information on the types of leather products to be made for a specific exhibition and more options for group renting of exhibition stalls. As more microentrepreneurs get access to new buyers through market agents, however, their demand for exhibitions and fairs may actually decrease rather than increase.

Box 9.6: Market Agent Tries Selling Exhibition Information

At the time of writing, only one market agent had made a commission by arranging artisans' participation in fairs and exhibitions. EDA introduced Kailash to several exhibition organizers and helped him to understand how he could provide information on exhibitions to local microentrepreneurs. Kailash receives the information free from the exhibition organizers and arranges for microentrepreneurs to rent stalls at exhibitions. He receives a commission from the exhibition organizers based on the number of stalls that he rents out. Whenever he gets new information, he visits microentrepreneurs and passes on the information—the dates and locations of the fairs, details on the organization, and the total fee for participating—and indicates that he will receive a fee to reserve a stall. Several microentrepreneurs have now starting coming to him to find out when and where the exhibitions will be held. He had been offering this service for two months at the time of writing and had rented one stall to two microentrepreneurs together, relatives from his village. The microentrepreneurs paid US$160 for one stall, and Kailash's commission was US$16. In the future, he has arranged that the exhibition organizers will pay him 10 per cent of the fees for the total number of stalls he rents.

Training Services Business Model

The traditional sandals that artisans make are not suitable for urban and export markets, but the artisans do not know how to make other products. Training helps the microentrepreneurs learn how to produce new designs and products that are demanded by urban and export markets.

EDA's Findings on the Market: EDA did not find any fee for service, commercial training available to leather artisans. Government agencies provide free or subsidized training. The government training is perceived as having low outreach and little relevance to the market. Many of the microentrepreneurs who attend government training believe that their time is wasted because the skills they learn are outdated and no follow-up on how to use their new skills and market their products is provided. A few exporters and wholesalers provide embedded training and technical assistance to their artisan suppliers. The training is limited, however, and geared towards meeting specific orders. The trainers, whether sponsored by the government or through exporters, are sandal producers who typically have a higher level of skill than other producers. Some artisans with large orders provide training and technical assistance to other microentrepreneurs in their villages to whom they outsource production. Although artisans with training skills and experience existed in the market, none of them had offered their services on a commercial basis.

Demand exists for more frequent and higher quality training courses. From its MA, EDA learned that the microentrepreneurs who have not received government training demand basic training, while those who have attended the government training demand training on more sophisticated and market-relevant products.

Box 9.7: An Artisan Starts Supplying Market Agents

Kalu Ram, a sandal producer from Hastera village in Jaipur district, has been selling sandals at the weekly Jaipur haat for many years. At the haat, he met two market agents promoted by EDA (Omprakash and Mahaveer of Udaipuria village in Jaipur). Kalu Ram told them about his skills, products, and interest in supplying them with sandals. After observing his products and skills, the market agents gave him a small order of 25 pairs of sandals deliverable in a week. Kalu Ram delivered the sandals on time, and the market agents were happy with his skill and the quality of the sandals. Gradually, Kalu Ram got more and bigger orders from the market agents, and they also provided him with leather, accessories, and new designs for the orders. Presently, Kalu Ram supplies around 70 to 100 pairs of sandals every week to the two market agents. He likes supplying to the two market agents because he gets money on time, does not have to sit in the weekly haat to sell his sandals, and also learns new designs from them.

Service Providers: EDA decided to build on existing skills and encourage capable artisans to offer training com-mercially to their fellow microentreprerieurs. Many microentrepreneurs said that they would prefer fellow artisans as trainers, and a number of artisans had experience as trainers for government—or exporter-sponsored training courses. The trainers are all producers themselves and, therefore, like the market agents, have an existing revenue stream and can offer training as a side business.

The Service and the Business Model

In the business model illustrated in Figure 9.6, accomplished artisans provide other microentrepreneurs with skills training on how to make specific types of sandals, specific designs, and/or various leather products. The length of training ranges from one to eight weeks on a part-time basis. The courses range from basic to advanced depending on the level of skill and experience of the trainees. For example, less skilled artisans who previously have not attended training, receive basic training on an upgraded version of a traditional or modern sandal (a new design or technique). More skilled artisans who have attended some training and have greater market exposure receive training on leather goods such as handbags and wallets. The trainers also provide the microentrepreneurs with information on markets, exhibitions, buyers, and raw material and accessories suppliers. The trainers receive technical skills, design information, and information on market demand for products from IICD, market agents, and wholesalers and exporters.

The microentrepreneurs pay a fee in installments for training. Typically, the microentrepreneurs pay one-third up front, one-third halfway through the training, and the remainder at the end of the training. This ensures that the trainers maintain high-quality sessions and enables the microentrepreneurs to earn income between sessions to pay for the fee.

Rather than the artisans having to travel far to receive training, courses are organized per village. The trainer travels to a village and provides training for artisans in that village in a local venue, usually a local artisan's workshop. The advantages of this approach are that the local artisans can work during the day and attend training in the evenings or any time convenient to both the trainer and trainees. Therefore, the artisans do not forfeit their regular

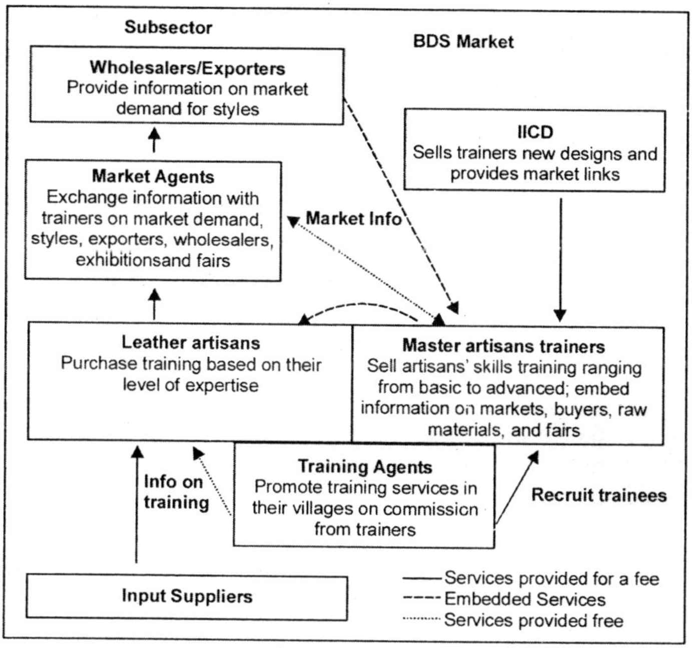

Fig. 9.6: Training Services Business Model

earnings to attend a training course. In addition, the trainer can observe the artisans at work and help them to improve and perfect the skills they have just learned.

To reach more artisans, trainers usually work with "training agents," local artisans who promote the training services, mobilize and enroll microentrepreneurs, and organize the training courses in their local villages. Trainers pay a commission of 10 to 15 per cent of total revenue generated to the training agents.

Piloting the Business Model: EDA obtained a database of artisans who had attended or taught at the government-subsidized training programmes. To develop a business model for training services, EDA approached a few skilled microentrepreneurs who had participated in past government training courses as trainers or participants. EDA asked these microentrepreneurs about their experience with government-sponsored training, particularly how they would improve it to gain more benefit. EDA worked with the microentrepreneurs to use their ideas to develop a commercial training offer. EDA then found potential artisan clients and brought the trainers to meet with them and arrange a training session. The overall objective was to use microentrepreneurs with prior experience as trainers to jump-start the market.

EDA works closely with the trainers to develop their capacity. Currently, EDA provides support in the following ways:

- Encouraging microentrepreneurs to purchase training and helping them form training groups. EDA is gradually reducing this activity, and the trainers are taking up this responsibility; wherever trainers work with training agents, the latter undertake these activities.
- Providing assistance in developing pamphlets to promote training courses, linking trainers with suitable printers, and offering advice on the location for distributing these pamphlets. This enables trainers to promote their services and generate business on their own, thus reducing dependency on EDA.
- Identifying and encouraging artisans to become training agents, and then developing their links with trainers.
- Assisting trainers to develop appropriate training courses, improve training methodologies, determine training costs and prices, and design payment mechanisms.
- Providing trainers with information on new designs, growing markets, sources of quality inputs, and organizations arranging trade fairs and exhibitions.

Box 9.8. From Government to Commercial Trainer

> One of the trainers, Kailash from Udaipuria, started as a trainer for the government Rural Non-Farm Development Agency (RUDA). In his experience with RUDA, Kailash found that most of the RUDA training participants are not interested in learning because the training is free to them. Kailash feels greater satisfaction from offering commercial services because the trainees are more invested and participatory. Currently, less financial gain is available in the commercial model, but Kailash believes that the RUDA training is risky because RUDA is a donor agency, and the funding can dry up. To make up for the difference in revenue, Kailash foresees offering commercial training courses more frequently than the RUDA courses are offered.

(*Contd.*)

	Type of Training	
	RUDA	Commercial
Fee received by trainer	US$ 80	US$ 60
Fee received for food and lodging	US$ 30	Free (provided by participants)
Frequency (on average)	2-3 courses per year	6 courses per year

- Monitoring the training courses to ensure the provision of quality services and effective learning and providing feedback whenever required.
- Sharing findings from the MA and feedback from participants with trainers to help them improve their services.
- Addressing any significant issues of concern to both trainers and trainees (such as negotiation of training prices).

As one initiative to promote competition and improve pricing, EDA took several different pricing quotes from trainers and created a competition in which the winner was the trainer offering the best price. They developed this exercise to show trainers how to negotiate fairly. EDA also illustrated to the trainers that initially having a lower profit margin might be necessary as the market develops to stimulate demand, and when high demand exists, they can raise their prices.

Challenges and Adjustments: The training services business model has been successful in providing improved courses, reaching new clients, and bringing new skills and techniques to the microentrepreneurs. Three issues that require addressing, however, have become evident during the pilot phase:

- *Outreach:* EDA has been able to link some of the trainers with new villages. Although a gradual increase in the number of training agents will expand the outreach of the service, existing trainers find it diffcult to travel frequently to distant villages because they also have their own production businesses to manage. Therefore, EDA plans to help new trainers in more distant villages to offer training in surrounding villages with the aim of slowly expanding the geographical reach of the service. EDA hopes some trainees with required capabilities will become trainers for their own villages. In addition, some training agents may also become trainers developing required experience while working along side trainers. In the future, new local trainers could offer more basic training to supplement their incomes, while the original trainers could continue to evolve their own services by offering more sophisticated training. This service growth would deepen and expand the training market.

- *Timing*: Through piloting, it has become apparent that trainers should take the production cycle and calendar into consideration when offering their services. For example, Kailash provided leather goods training for six artisans in the village of Manpuri Mancheri. After the training course, some of the microentrepreneurs received small orders for bags but were unable to fill the orders because they were in the peak sandal production season. EDA is planning to work with the trainers to develop a calendar of training courses that incorporates production seasons.
- *Subsidization*: Willingness to pay for training is still low because of the availability of free training from government agencies and NGOs. During Kailash's initial visit to Manpuri Mancheri, 20 microentrepreneurs expressed interest in his training course. Only six came to the training, however, the artisans who attended the course reported that many of the microentrepreneurs are reluctant to pay for courses when they have previously received training for free. To address the weak demand due to subsidized training, Kailash explains to prospective trainees that the subsidized training may end soon. He is also honing his service features. He provides trainees with links to buyers and exhibitions for free. He hopes that this approach will aid the microentrepreneurs in seeing increased revenues in the short term from the products they have learned to make with him. This tactic will also improve word of mouth referral.

Bundling the Services

During the MA and pilot implementation, EDA realized that leather microentrepreneurs demand a business benefit, reaching more and better markets, rather than individual services *per se.*

Addressing this demand is also in concert with EDA's overall objective of integrating microentrepreneurs into markets in a way that is more beneficial to them and also contributes to local and regional economies.

To realize this benefit, microentrepreneurs need a bundle of services: information on new designs that are in demand, training on how to produce the new designs, and marketing services to reach the new markets where the designs are in demand. One service alone may not enable the microentrepreneurs to reach more lucrative markets.

To meet this demand, EDA recognized that it had to promote linkages among the services and integrate them into each other. Some of the providers have realized on their own that it makes sense to offer more than one of the services demanded. EDA has been encouraging them along this path. Trainers like Prakash (see Boxes 9.1 and 9.5) use IICD designs during their training courses and provide names of wholesalers and exporters to ensure that training participants can reach new markets. Some market agents purchase designs from IICD and train their artisan suppliers on the design techniques, resulting in a higher profit margin for both the market agent and the artisans. Figure 9.7 illustrates how service providers are connected to provide bundled services.

Box 9.9: Aristans' Experiences with New Training Courses

Nanuram and Omprakash, two microentrepreneurs from Bhadouli village in Dausa district, have been making *jootis* for a long time. They met Kailash, a trainer, who told them about his training course for modern sandals, the embedded services that will be provided to them, and the price for the training. Both of them bought the training course with two other microentrepreneurs from their village. They attended 15 days of training in modern sandal production in their village. After the training, Nanuram and Omprakash made some samples and, with the assistance of the trainer and EDA, they were able to get some orders. Gradually, they started making some modifications in their designs and were able to derive some new designs. Although the market for traditional jootis has dropped off, they both are able to earn good money by making modern sandals. Both of them invested money to buy required lasts for making modern sandals and are in the process of shifting completely from traditional to modern sandal making.

(*Contd.*)

Both Nanuram and Omprakash said, "If we hadn't paid for the training, we would not have made modern sandals. In the past, we were provided free training, and so no one paid any attention. But when one pays a fee, he or she takes interest and finds ways to get the return from the money paid. "Both artisans are now acting as training agents, trying to motivate other microentrepreneurs to purchase training courses.

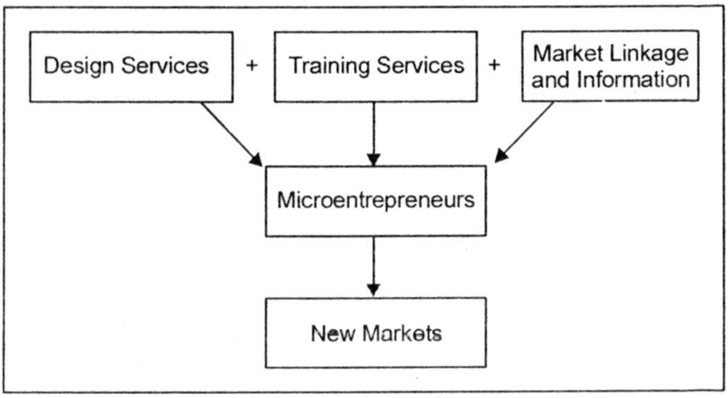

In Bishanpura village in Dausa district, Ramswaroop and Tarachand recently bought a training course along with eight other microentrepreneurs who have been producing jootis for a long time. Kailash offered a training course on modern sandal making in their village for 15 days. After the training, these two artisans approached some wholesalers in Bandikui and Dausa city. In Bandikui, they sold 19 pairs of modern sandals at US$ 2.60 per pair when the price offered for traditional *jootis* is just US$ 1.20 per pair. In addition, the wholesaler in Bandikui has promised them some more orders soon. Wholesalers in Dausa and Jaipur have promised them regular orders in the range of 100 to 500 pairs every month. They both are optimistic that they will get good returns from these orders. Now, both of them plan to buy lasts so that they can deliver the bigger orders. They also plan to encourage other microentrepreneurs to buy such training courses because the training is customized according the their requirements and includes free information useful for the growth of their enterprises.

Furthermore, EDA is also linking the providers together. EDA introduces them to each other and encourages them to refer their clients to each other and purchase each other's services. For example, some trainers sell through market agents or introduce their trainees to market agents. Some market agents purchase training, and then pass on skills through embedded service provision to their artisan suppliers.

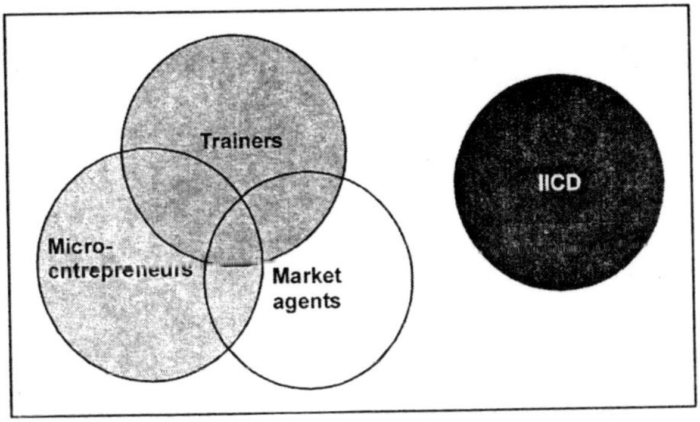

Fig. 9.7: Connecting Service Providers to Deliver Bundles of Services

During the piloting, EDA realized that a need exists to organize small workshops at the village level so that different types of service providers can interact directly with artisans in groups. In these workshops, artisans learn about the services available and visualize all aspects related to them before buying them. At the workshops, service providers discuss with artisans the individual benefits of each service, the combined benefits of bundled services, and how the services will help artisans earn more in their businesses. Thus, artisans are more willing to buy training courses because, for example, they realize that market agents are available to buy the products they will make using the new skills. These workshops also provide an opportunity for artisans to seek clarifications from providers about various services. Collaboration between trainers and market agents on conducting workshops and other marketing initiatives is a win-win proposition for both—each creating demand for the other's services.

IV. LESSONS LEARNED AND THE WAY FORWARD

Although the leather subsector project is still young, EDA is already actively looking back to identify lessons learned and looking forward to pinpoint and develop strategies to address future challenges.

The Essential Feedback Loop

EDA's pilot implementation suggests that market development is a process and should be viewed in this way. Market assessment (MA) is an important part of that process, enabling the design of intervention strategies and the development of models. But other factors, including project objectives and social and cultural factors, are equally important for determining project design and intervention strategies. Although some design decisions developed from the business development services (BDS) MA findings may be final (such as the selection of services to be promoted and the identification of suppliers for respective BDS), the same cannot be said of the methodologies visualized for implementing them. Visualizing in advance all the issues and external factors that could influence implementation is impossible. Therefore, EDA has found that keeping implementation strategies as flexible as possible is helpful so that they can be modified on the basis of experience and learning emerging from the pilot phase.

Gathering more market information once the pilot implementation has started is also often helpful. Gaps in knowledge become more obvious during implementation, and focused market research can help managers adjust strategies to be more effective. For example, EDA realized at a relatively late stage in the pilot implementation that to develop the capacity of market agents, a database of buyers of modern sandals and leather goods would be helpful. Therefore, a small student project was commissioned for this purpose, which has resulted in the development of a good database of such buyers. The study also revealed that making small leather goods, such as leather key rings and small wallets with unique designs, is more profitable than larger products because they require less material and are faster to produce but still sell for a reasonable price. EDA plans to encourage artisans to emboss images of local tourist sites in the leather for these products. This design will provide a unique stamp to local products and increase demand. The information from this small study is helpful not only for the market agents, but also for the trainers. EDA envisions that these roles—identifying designs and buyers—will progressively be taken over by market agents.

The pilot phase has enabled the EDA implementation team to learn what works and what does not. This learning provides the basis for adjusting implementation as the project moves forward. Monitoring the pilot implementation closely is helping EDA to maximize this learning and make strategy adjustments quickly.

This feedback process is envisioned to continue, although perhaps less intensively, throughout implementation. EDA has found that this feedback loop is critical to achieving the objectives of the project.

Achievements to Date

After six months of piloting, positive indications that EDA's interventions can achieve its goal of increasing the incomes of the leather microentrepreneurs by enabling them to access customized, commercial BDS from local providers. Thus far, EDA has seen several encouraging signs that its strategies are working, including the following:

- Microentrepreneurs have purchased the new commercial BDS at full cost from local providers and applied new skills in their businesses. For example, in Gudeliya village in Dausa district, a few microentrepreneurs purchased a training course on modern sandal making. They have now almost completely shied to modern sandal production.
- When trainees immediately use their new skills in their businesses, a demonstration effect among other artisans occurs in the village as they realize the utility and effectiveness of the training. The demand for training increases faster if artisans are able to immediately use the new skills acquired. This evidence supports the importance of integrating services to enable microentrepreneurs to reach more profitable markets.
- New BDS providers have started taking more initiative on their own. For example, trainers have invested their own money in pamphlet development and market agents for product catalogue development. These providers are trying to develop the market for their services by visiting different villages in not only the two project districts but also other areas.
- Anecdotal evidence suggests that EDA's interventions are having a positive impact on the local economies of rural villages where the artisans live. More income is being generated in the communities, and the links between these communities and urban markets is increasing. Anecdotal

evidence also indicates that the interventions are having a positive impact on the leather subsector. More market information is fiowing from retailers, wholesalers, and exporters to product designers and artisans. Wholesalers and exporters have greater access to products that meet the demand from urban and export markets. Although the impact is still small, the trends are encouraging.

The Challenges Ahead

Although EDA's pilot project is promising, the implementation team faces a number of challenges moving forward, particularly to increase outreach and ensure the sustainable growth and development of commercial BDS markets that enable artisans to reach new markets and respond to changing consumer demand. Key obstacles that EDA must overcome to ensure the success of their project follow:

- EDA has commied substantial time and effort to develop the capacity of service providers—work that is essential to ensure the sustainability of pilot efforts and develop vibrant BDS markets. The amount of effort required is related to the low level of market exposure of the service providers and artisans outside cities and the villages near them. The time required is a constraint to achieving wide outreach. EDA hopes that the demonstration effect will reduce the capacity building needed for additional new providers. EDA is also looking for ways to shorten the process and use existing service providers to teach new providers.
- EDA is currently performing multiple roles in the market, particularly related to collecting and giving information to providers and linking market players. These roles will need to be taken over gradually by the market players themselves. EDA must develop a systematic plan to ensure that this transition occurs by the end of the project. Although the flow of information in the sub-sector, particularly to new service providers, has greatly improved, EDA may need to develop additional, sustainable information delivery mechanisms. In addition,

EDA may need to develop some other secondary BDS markets, such as master artisans or expert designers who can train artisan trainers.

- BDS market development is a slow process because it involves a paradigm shift among BDS providers and consumers from a subsidized environment to a commercial one. Artisans are reluctant to spend money on services that are also available free. Potential commercial service providers are also more risk averse when they know they will have to compete against subsidized providers. Indeed, a multilateral donor-funded project is currently being implemented in Rajasthan in which training services to microenterprises, including leather artisans, are offered almost free of cost. This situation poses a real challenge to EDA's project. Nevertheless, a commercial approach seems to EDA to be the most appropriate strategy for creating long-term impact and ensuring sustainability. EDA will continue to work with providers to ensure that commercial services provide suffcient added value over what free services offer to make the cost worth it. EDA will also continue to work with providers to help them learn to market their services effectively.
- The efforts of various donor agencies and government agencies need to be coordinated, however, regarding BDS provision subsidizing. Because of different approaches used by different agencies, the commercial approach to developing BDS markets is more diffcult, at least in a short time frame. Market development will be more rapid if all donors reach a consensus on limiting or eliminating transactional subsidies in BDS markets.

How successful EDA's project will ultimately be cannot be concluded yet. Although the pilot implementation has been encouraging, more work and creativity will be required to scale the project up and reach thousands of leather artisans. From its experience, EDA realizes that ensuring the success of the market interventions is a multiyear project that will fully engage its staff. EDA's strength lies in its ability to remain flexible and agile throughout the process, gathering feedback and making changes along the way.

NOTES

1. For more information on EDA's market assessment methodology, see Ashok Kumar, "Methodology to Interview Respondents to Assess the BDS Market for the Leather Sub-Sector, Rajasthan, India," 2004, http://www.bdsknowledge.org/dyn/bds/docs/131/EDA%20India%20BDS%20MA%20Methodology.pdf, accessed on 16 February 2005.
2. **Definitions**

   The following terms are defined as they are used in this case study. The definitions may vary from those used in other publications:

   Artisan: A microentrepreneur producer. In this case study, artisan refers to a producer who makes and sells leather sandals and other leather products and is used interchangeably with microentrepreneur.

   Business development services (BDS): Any non-financial service provided to businesses on a formal or an informal basis.

   BDS market: BDS providers and enterprises and the exchange of business services among them. This exchange may be formal or informal and may include fee-based transactions for services and/or services provided as part of other commercial transactions.

   BDS provider: A firm or institution that provides BDS directly to enterprises.

   Bundled services: Several business services provided together as part of a package, which may be offered independently or as part of another commercial transaction-for example, a transaction between a wholesaler and a producer.

   Embedded services: Business services provided as part of another commercial transaction; for example, when a trader provides market information and product design advice to a producer when the trader purchases the producer's products. Both the service provider and the service customer usually think of the services as a value-added feature of another product or part of their business relationships.

   Jootis: Traditional leather sandals made and sold in rural areas of India.

   Facilitator: International or local institutions, usually funded by governments or donors, that aim to expand and improve a particular market or markets for the benefit of specific target groups.

   Fee-based services: Services offered for a fee that generally are independent of any other transaction; also called stand-alone services. Fee-based services are usually offered by a provider as one of his or her core products rather than as a value-added feature of another product or service.

Haat: Small village markets, usually organized on a weekly basis.

Last: Wooden or plastic mold of a foot used to shape leather sandals and shoes.

Market agent: A middleman or trader who purchases sandals and other leather products from artisans and sells them in markets or to wholesalers, retailers, and/or exporters. Market agents also provide embedded market information and sometimes other services.

Market assessment: Market research and/or information gathering on markets and their context used to assist in programme design, implementation, monitoring, and/or evaluation.

Microentrepreneur: A small business owner with fewer than 10 workers. In this case study, microentrepreneur refers to the producers, generally working in family-based businesses, who make and seil sandals and other leather goods. Microentrepreneur is used interchangeably with artisan in this case study.

Subsector: A network of related firms that transform raw materials into finished products and transmit them through vertical supply channels to consumers; the transactions among the firms.

Training agent: An artisan who promotes training courses to others, recruits trainees, and arranges the courses in his or her own village and surrounding villages for a commission from the trainer.

Value chain: An individual channel through which raw materials are transformed into finished products and transmied to consumers; the enterprises in that channel and the transactions among enterprises and between enterprises and consumers in that channel.

10

Microfinance/Microenterprise Programmes and Women's Empowerment*

V. PRAMEELA and SMITA PREMCHANDER

I. INTRODUCTION

A broad based understanding of poverty has emerged over the last several years, which recognises poverty as much more than mere economic deprivation. This recognition, which links poverty as much with social and political deprivation has led to the placement of empowerment and human development at the centre of all development dialogue. Intra-community and intra-household inequities amongst the poor have pointed to the feminisation of poverty, which in turn has underscored the need for due attention and focus on women's empowerment.

Women's empowerment encompasses their enhanced status in social, political and economic spheres. In looking specifically at economic empowerment, important policy debates continue about whether economic empowerment, often seen in terms of women's increased access to credit, is an end in itself that unleashes other aspects of women's empowerment, or whether it must occur alongside deliberate strategies for women's broader social and political empowerment. The latter are often seen to enable the full realisation of women's economic empowerment. This debate has come to the forefront with the striking growth of micro-credit within India in an environment that places micro-credit at the centre of empowerment interventions.

---

* Abridged and updated version of the study originally sponsored by CARE India (New Delhi)

The Indian government has paid special attention to women's empowerment, and both a national policy, as well as a Tenth Five-Year plan document, illustrate its commitment to women's empowerment and welfare. Within the different strategies aimed at addressing empowerment, the centrality of economic empowerment has manifested in the various programmes focused around the provision of micro credit to women.

In the context of debates around the existing and potential role of micro-credit in both economic, as also broader, empowerment, an analysis of the degree to, and manner in which programmes related to microcredit policy goals, becomes not only a valid, but necessary analysis, which has formed the motivation for this study, which undertakes to review Indian microfinance policy and selected programmes with a women's empowerment perspective.

This part of the report outlines the background of development of microcredit as a means of poverty alleviation, which later was attributed with empowerment effects and claimed as a means of women's empowerment. It develops the rationale for the study, describes the research questions and the study methodology.

Microcredit for poverty reduction has had acceptance at the national policy level since pre-independence, when the Reserve Bank of India took cognizance of the need to supply rural credit at reasonable interest rates to prevent landless and the poor from extreme indebtedness. Post independence, cheap credit to agricultural sector, especially through the cooperative sector, has been aimed at boosting rural agricultural production and reaching those with low access to formal sector financing. The expansion of the cooperative sector was supplemented by the nationalization of banks in 1969 with an intention to provide credit to 'priority sectors', including agriculture and the rural poor. With the introduction of the Integrated Rural Development Programme in 1980s, the government combined grants with credit provided by the banking sector, with an intention to build assets for the poor.

Prior to the 1980s, the trickle down theory was accepted, which held that, at the household level, higher incomes for men translated into higher incomes for the family. This was questioned in early 1980s in India, when researchers like Jain (1997) pointed that women's income goes towards family food and basic needs, while the man's income goes for assets, relative luxuries and liquor.

This realisation led to the development—world's initial strategy of promoting income-generating activities (IGAs) for women on a large scale. The strategy did not fully succeed, however, as poor women are faced with fewer and poorer opportunities to work. Bhatt *et al.* (1988) suggest that they face under-employment and a casual nature of work; lack of skills and education; lesser mobility, heavy responsibilities; a systematic social practice of under-rating women's work, and lack of access to better technologies, tools and productive assets. This report, known as the Shramashakti Report (1988), highlighted the gap between the needs of women for productive resources, and their access to it. The need for credit was especially highlighted. This led to official recognition of the problem. As there are not enough employment opportunities for women, support for self-employment and women's enterprise came to be recognised as being required for releasing women's economic potential (Kraus-Harper, 1998).

Many NGOs have subsequently taken on the task of women's empowerment through microenterprise in recognition of the impact it can have on women, their families, and poverty alleviation. In doing so, however, these NGOs and the women they support often find themselves confronting a reality where attitudinal biases, lack of collateral security with women and women's lack of awareness and reluctance to approach banks for facilities create lack of access to credit, raw material, and markets. It is against this backdrop that micro credit for women, routed through self help groups (SHGs) of women, came to be recognised as a viable strategy; not only for promotion of women's enterprises, but as a strategy for poverty reduction and women's empowerment in general (Premchander, 2003).

From April 1, 1999, the self-employment programmes of the Integrated Rural Development Programmes (IRDP) of the Ministry of Rural Development, Government of India were merged into one programme. These programmes included Training of Rural Youth for Self Employment (TRYSEM), Development of Women and Children in Rural Areas (DWCRA), Ganga Kalyan Yojana (GKY) and the Million Wells Scheme (MWS). They became part of a single self-employment programme called the Swarnjayanti Gram Swarozgar Yojana (SGSY). According to the Ministry of Rural Development in 1999, the new scheme seeks to focus on the formation of SHGs. SGSY seeks to cover 30 per cent of all rural poor families in the next five years. Thus the success of SHG financing has led to the biggest poverty alleviation programme in India becoming group-based. Women's self-help groups have become effective channels of credit for enterprise. Thus government, banks and wholesale financing organisations now work with NGOs who promote groups and/or provide finance to them.

The Rashtriya Mahila Kosh (RMK) was registered in 1993 as the government's micro-credit agency with its focus on women and their economic empowerment through the provision of credit to poor and asset less women in the informal sector. RMK managed to reach 5.35 lakh women with cumulative credit of Rs. 130 crores by the end of the Ninth Plan in 2001.

Development agencies initiated several programmes involving a microcredit component. Some of these were "microfinance only" and some were "microfinance plus" programmes Microcredit grew to expand to microfinance involving a range of financial products including savings, credit and insurance. The proliferation of microcredit at first, and then microfinance for women across the world as a means of poverty alleviation also brought several international collaborative projects to India. Some of these included the Trade Related Entrepreneurship Assistance and Development (TREAD) programme of UNDP, IFAD supported programmes with NGOs, government, banks and development related bank financial programmes like DPIP and Swashakti. Organizations like LIC, ICICI, Citi Bank, HDFC and other banks, have also started schemes covering microcredit as well as insurance services, through partnerships with intermediary organizations like the Friends of Women's World Banking, SEWA Bank and SewaBimo, based in Ahmedabad. CARE India has had several collaborative projects with international agencies (e.g. CREDIT in Jharkhand, CASHE in Orissa, West Bengal, Madhya Pradesh and Andhra Pradesh, STEP in Andhra Pradesh and disaster mitigation projects in Gujarat), which have components of microfinance services. These programmes are just a few of the many international collaborative programmes in the sector, reaching women through microfinance services. The sector now has a range of private and public organizations offering a wide range of microfinancial products offered through these projects and programmes.

As of March 31, 2005, the National Bank of Agriculture and Rural Development (NABARD) had provided refinance for

16,18,476 groups (cumulative figure since inception of refinance programme for SHGs, in 1991) (NABARD, 2005). The SGSY programme claimed that it had covered 31,19,077 women's SHGs since its inception from 1999, to March 31, 2005.

The above paragraphs outline trajectory of developments through which provision of microfinance services for women have become a mainstream strategy claiming both poverty reduction and women's empowerment. However, impact studies on microcredit and microfinance programmes are few and do not conclusively prove either the poverty reduction or empowerment impacts. This raises the question of where the gaps in policy intent and final empowerment impact may exist, and how these can be understood and overcome.

This paper examines four large GoI programmes with microfinance as a component, and asks how these perform on empowerment impact. It does this on the basis of officially commissioned impact studies. It then proceeds to analyse NGO experiences in microfinance, enterprise promotion and women's leadership development. On the basis of the practical experiences cited, the paper makes recommendations for design of microcredit programmes that empower women. It is concised and updated from a study done by the authors for CARE-India in 2006[1].

II. EMPOWERMENT OBJECTIVE IN FOUR WOMEN'S MICROCREDIT/MICROENTERPRISE PROGRAMMES

Many government programmes of the government and schemes have some component of microcredit. The study reviewed four programmes of the government which have a microcredit component: Swashakti, Swayamsidha, SGSY and RMK.

The largest among these was the SGSY programme which was an amalgamation of several earlier Integrated Rural Development Programmes. The SGSY was included by virtue of being the flagship programme of the Indian government. Similarly RMK was the only official women's credit fund. Swashakti was a World Bank programme which included capacity building components and was specifically aimed at women's empowerment. Finally, Swayamsidha was included because it had the same objectives as Swashakti but was completely resourced through domestic funds. The programme selection thus offered a range of objectives (from credit delivery to women's empowerment) a range of partnerships and implementation structures and processes. The distinguishing features of the four selected programmes are depicted in the graphic below and explained subsequently.

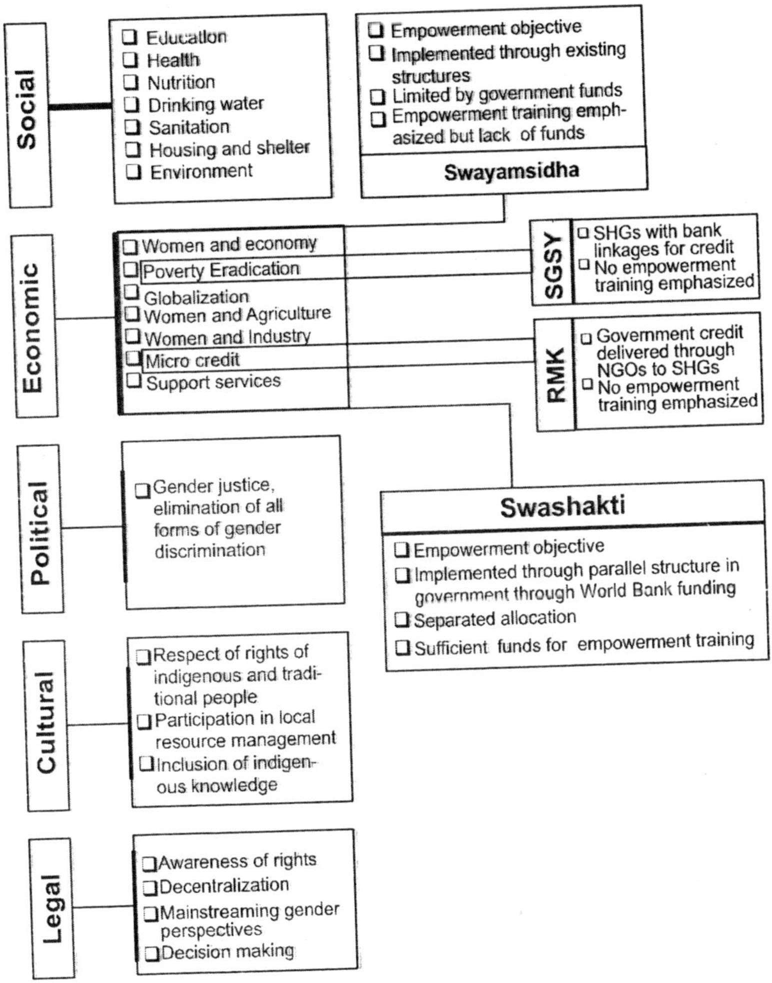

Fig. 10.1: Distinguishing Features of Four Programmes

Table 10.1: Analysis for Four Programmes with Microcredit Component

Aspect	Swashakti (Women's Empowerment)	Swayamsidha (Women's Empowerment)	SGSY (Poverty Reduction)	RMK (Credit Programme)
Programme partner	World Bank (Donor) and GoI	Government of India	Government of India	Government of India
Programme Duration	April 1999 and ended December 2005	February 2001 and going to end in March 2007	September 2001 merging JGSY and EAS and continuing	1993 and continuing
Prgramme objective	Empowerment of women through improving their socio-economic conditions.		Bringing poor families above poverty line by providing them with income generating opportunities through a mix of bank credit and government subsidy.	To provide credit as an instrument for socio-economic change and women's development.
Programme Activities	Baseline Survey Training of trainers for implementing partners. Formation of women SHGs Inculcate savings and credit habits Upgrade skills for IGAs Linkages for credit and marketing Convergence for health, education, sanitation services Set up of MIS Monitoring and Evaluation exercises Impact evaluation	Formation of women SHGs Community-oriented interventions Convergence of related schemes from state or Central Government	Organization of poor into SHGs (SGSY reimburses NGO costs) Skill training Bank credit with SGSY subsidy Support for technology and marketing Development of infrastructure at community level	Selection of NGOs and sanction of loans for SHGs Training of trainers for NGOs
Area coverage	Nine states	650 blocks in 31 states	33 states and UT	Twenty-four states/UTs
Targets reached (since inception)	17,642 women SHGs formed and completed	65,000 women SHGs planned and will be completed in March 2007	31 lakh SHGs and 30,06,046 individuals reached	5,35,000 individual women

This part first describes the distinguishing features of the four programmes. It then analyses inputs and the consequent outcomes of each programme, based on selected impact studies. These lead to several lessons from official programmes, which are then discussed.

Four Official Programmes with Microcredit Component

The analysis of the four official programmes covered an understanding of the inception and objectives of the programme, and the strategy for implementation, including the activities, or inputs, and the structure for implementation and monitoring. A comparison of the programme partners, objectives, activities, implementation structure and coverage is presented in Table 10.1.

Programme Partnership and Inception

SGSY is a (GoI) programme, which was launched in April 1999 through an amalgamation of several IRDP programmes. As IRDP, it has existed since the 1980s, and has been implemented through the government's machinery for rural development, with an active linkage with banks. RMK is also a scheme of the GoI, set up as an independent body with a Governing Board, for sanction and disbursement of microcredit. The Department of Women and Child Development implemented Swashakti with World Bank funds; it was launched in April 1999 and ended in December 2005. Swayamsidha's objectives are similar to those of Swashakti, but it is completely funded by the GoI. It was launched in February 2001 and will end in March 2007. SGSY, Swayamsidha and RMK are funded with contributions from Central and State government funds.

Programme Objectives, Geographical Spread and Scale

Swashakti and Swayamsidha have women's empowerment as their major objective, whereas SGSY's objective is reduction of poverty through improving livelihoods SGSY claims building rural infrastructure for increasing rural production and reducing rural poverty as one its main objectives. Although it does not aim for 'empowerment' of women *per se*, its guidelines require that women should be at least 40 per cent of the beneficiaries. RMK is government scheme with an objective of women's economic empowerment through microcredit and not much emphasized capacity building inputs.

SGSY has all-India coverage, with 33 States and Union Territories (UTs). Its cumulative coverage from April 1999 to December 2005 has been 31 lakh SHGs (3.1 million). The programme claims to have reached 29 lakh women swarozgaris, but it is not clear whether these are apart from the group members mentioned earlier or the same beneficiaries. The second largest outreach is of Swayamsidha, which has been implemented in 31 states covering 650 blocks, and plans an outreach of 65,000 SHGs. RMK has so far reached 24 States/UTs and 5,35,000 individual women. The Swashakti programme was implemented in nine states and had formed 17,642 SHGs during its implementation.

Activities

Inputs for capacity building are high in the case of Swashakti, but not in the case of Swayamsidha and SGSY (which are mainly loan and subsidy components). 70 per cent of the total budget of Swashakti has been spent on training of the SHGs. The capacity building inputs in the case of Swashakti and Swayamsidha are individual (woman) oriented.

SGSY and RMK both are primarily microcredit-providing schemes. SGSY provides credit for individuals and groups with a subsidy component, while RMK provides loans, through NGOs, and only to SHGs and not individuals. SGSY loan is only for IGA activities where as RMK has loan products for IGA, consumption and housing too.

Structures for Implementation

Swashakti has separate offices at both state and district level and have separate staff appointed to form and monitor SHGs, whereas in the case of Swayamsidha, Anganwadi workers are involved in formation and strengthening of SHGs. The SGSY and RMK programmes select SHGs already formed by local NGOs, to whom it provides credit with subsidy. Unlike Swashakti, Anganwadi workers are already over-burdened with different activities and are unable to train the SHGs in a sufficient manner.

Swashakti generates detailed quarterly reports and monthly physical progress reports providing information on number of SHGs formed, their savings and loans, number of clusters registered and number of trainings completed, and details on convergence of SHGs to other schemes and departments. It also gives information on type of community assets created, their total value, and the contribution from project and external funds.

Swayamsidha had quarterly meetings to assess the progress in terms of reaching targets. The programme has set up vigilance and monitoring committees at the district level, and has assigned the task to Block Development Officers and Panchayats at the block and village levels.

The field level reporting task was with Anganwadi workers, who were known to be overburdened with several other tasks SGSY reports at the headquarters in Delhi, were spreadsheets giving information on financial and physical progress of the programme i.e. total allocation and utilization of funds by the groups and individual beneficiaries (women, SC/ST, disabled assisted) and percentage of SHGs that had taken up IGA activities. RMK monitors its programmes through officers, NGOs and consultants appointed for the purpose.

Programme monitoring is better in Swashakti due to the separate set up of state and district level Project Monitoring Units. They have also planned a set of indicators right from the planning stage of the project.

Programme Inputs and Outcomes

The study asked how each programme was assessed for outcomes and impact, if at all, and what the findings have been about impact in general, and especially about impact related to women's empowerment.

The main indicators used by these four programmes to study impacts of the programmes are highlighted below:

Table 10.2: Indicators Used in the Impact Studies

Swashakti	*Swayamsidha*	*SGSY*	*RMK*
• Income and expenditure patterns • Group savings and other group management indicators • Decision making index, • Infant Mortality Rate (IMR) details • Ownership of assets • Control over income • Women members able to visit bank • Access to credit • Access to better health, education • Number of training sessions provided • IGAs started • Households crossing poverty line	• Awareness on legal aspects and marriage age of girl • Savings and group management indicators • Trainings and exposure visits provided • Income Generating Activities (IGAs) started • Community asset creation • Extent of convergence	• Percentage of women covered • Creation of self employment • Community based assets • Problems in getting loan • Other sources of credit	• Families providing respect to women • Family taking women's suggestions • Start of new economic activity and expand existing IGA • Acquisition of economic and other assets • Reduced indebtedness from unreliable and exploitative sources of loan • Status and respect • Self-worth • Mobility • Control over income

The methodology of these four studies was different, with different variables and indicators. For instance, the objective of SGSY was to reach at least 40 per cent of women and create self-employment among them, therefore the impact study covered these two variables. The RMK and Swayamsidha studies did not cover variables like income and expenditure pattern, decision making index, IMR details and ownership of assets and voice of women for demanding basic amenities, but Swashakti impact study covered them. On the other hand, RMK study adopted indicators about families giving respect to women, family taking women's suggestions, but these did not feature in the Swashakti impact study. Awareness about legal aspects, legal age of marriage of girls was studied in both Swayamsidha and Swashakti. The differences in variables and indicators made it difficult to compare the overall impact of these programmes.

Further, the Swashakti programme outlined the impact indicators during the planning of the programme itself. The RMK programme, being supply oriented, did not envisage these indicators earlier, but adopted those of the Swashakti programme later, and even began to monitor them regularly through its partners.

Inputs and Outcomes: Swashakti Programme

The Swashakti programme was the most comprehensive among the four studied, with inputs covering a range of capacity building inputs to women and their SHGs. The following tables show its inputs and outcomes/impacts:

Table 10.3: Swashakti—Inputs and Economic Empowerment

Inputs	*Outcomes/Impacts*
Trainings on NGOs, SHGs and women on: • Economic empowerment related trainings: • Skill training (on farm and non-farm) • Water anagement • IGA • Animal husbandry and dairying	• 38 per cent women reported to have initiated IGAs after availing training. • The increase in proportion of women deriving income from agricultural activities has changed from 26 per cent at the time of baseline to 34 per cent at the time of assessment. • The percentage of women engaged in gainful activities has increased from 77 per cent to 83 per cent at impact stage. • The average annual income of the women households increased from Rs 4,399 to Rs. 8,766. • The percentage share of women's income in the total household income increased from12-16. • The average monthly expenditure increased from Rs. 1122 to Rs. 1989 per month per household. • The percentage of women who had control over their income increased from 63 per cent to 91 per cent. • Ownership of assets:—The percentage of houseless people has come down to 17 per cent from 35 per cent.

The trainings were related to improvement in skills in the farm and non-farm sectors, including animal husbandry, and effects were positive in terms of women initiating IGAs, resulting in increased incomes, especially the share of income contributed by women and controlled by them. Homelessness reduced as a result of the project, and monthly expenditure increased. The existence of the baseline study provided greater validity to before-after comparisons and therefore indicates a more reliable link between the change to project inputs and effects, though a mapping of other external factors which could have contributed to the change has not been made in the study.

The trainings related to social empowerment included a range of topics, especially those related to group management, confidence building, health and hygiene, gender sensitization, and legal literacy. The effects, as elaborated in the following table, showed increased savings,, loan use, women's ability to manage group meetings. They also had better say in decision making at the household level, improved their mobility, and learnt to visit banks and represent their issues in public forums.

Table 10.4: Swashakti—Inputs and Social Empowerment Impacts

Inputs	*Outcomes/Impacts*
Trainings on NGOs, SHGs and women on: • Social empowerment related trainings • SHG concept and group management, credit management, book keeping, leadership, cluster formation and strengthening, group dynamics, (accounting, book keeping,) • Confidence building • Health and hygiene • Gender sensitization • Legal literacy	• Sixty four per cent of groups showed increase in savings amount from Rs. 10 to Rs. 100 per member per month. • The volume of savings increased among the groups indicating regularity among members towards savings and group stability. • Prior to the project 67 per cent of women saved and after joining Swashakti 98 per cent women formed the savings habit. • After formation of SHGs, around 88 per cent are availing loan from the SHGs. • 95 per cent of the group members were able to visit a bank and conduct financial transactions. • 91 per cent study sample groups stated that they held meetings on their own even in the absence of an NGO worker. • More than 91 per cent members were found to be vocal and were able to interact boldly. More than 36 per cent groups began to voice their demands for basic amenities. • On a Decision Index it was observed that around 80 per cent women could be ranked 'Very good/good' with regard to their having a "say" in the decision taken at household level • 60 per cent of women were able to travel alone to all places. • The IMR decreased from 96 per thousand live births to 42 during the project period.

Swashakti programme provided inputs for greater political empowerment of women, including training in leadership, conflict resolution and on Panchayati Raj system. The effects of these trainings, as elaborated in the following table, were greater awareness about legal age of girls for marriage, and clear decisions about whom women should vote for. These indicators are not directly relevant to the variables studied, and better indicators would have been more appropriate, e.g. participation in elections, conflicts and their resolutions within groups and at village level, and access to public benefits through the Panchayati Raj system.

Table 10.5: Swashakti—Inputs and Political Empowerment Impacts

Inputs	*Outcomes/Impacts*
Trainings on NGOs, SHGs and women on: • Political empowerment related trainings • Leadership • Conflict resolution • Panchayati Raj	• 79 per cent of the households said that they could decide who they should vote for • 81 per cent women are aware about the legal age of marriage of girls.

Thus the impact study of Swashakti (AFC, 2005) showed that significant impacts of three types, economic, social and political. The impact study took empowerment perspectives into account by assessing women's access and control over loans, increased incomes, asset ownership, decision making and political participation, on all of which the programme showed positive impacts.

Inputs and Outcomes: Swayamsidha Programme

The Swayamsidha programme had the same objectives as Swashakti, yet the programme had lack of funds for trainings, and depended on convergence with other official programmes for these inputs. The inputs and effects for economic empowerment are reflected in Table 10.6.

The economic inputs related to training in a range of vocational skills and bank linkages. The effects were first assessed in terms of group operations, reflected in regularity of group meetings and record maintenance, which were good only in 15 to 19 of the 62 sample blocks studies. The groups fared better on savings regularity, use of savings as loans, and their repayment was better, being positive in more than 50 per cent of the blocks studied. IGA training was conducted in more than half of the sample blocks, but even those who did not attend skill trainings took IGA loans. However, no comparative information is available to assess the performance of IGAs with and without training. The study reported increased incomes of target group, but did not measure this increase. Further, the study collated the groups per block, whereas it would have been more effective to show the findings consolidated based on the number of groups studied.

Table 10.6: Swayamsidha—Inputs and Economic Impacts

Inputs	*Outcomes/Impacts*
Provides training on bank linkage, IGAs	• In 15 sample blocks (out of 62), 76 to 99 per cent of the SHGs attend meetings regularly. • In 19 sample blocks, all the SHGs were maintaining records. • In 32 sample blocks, all the SHGs were regular in savings and in 7 blocks it was 76-99 per cent. • In 37 sample blocks (out of 62), all the SHGs rotated savings as loans among group members, which were used for IGA and domestic expenditure. • In 3 out of 62 blocks, all SHGs had taken loans from the banks. In 30 sample blocks, all the SHGs repaid loans, in 7 blocks; it was less than 50 per cent. • In 30 sample blocks, all the SHGs opened the accounts in banks. In 10 sample blocks, only 76-99 per cent SHGs did so. • Out of 62 blocks, IGA training was conducted in 35 blocks. In all the States a good number of members initiated IGA even who did not receive training IGA. • Increased their economic status

The social and empowerment inputs included explaining the concept of Swayamsidha, group management, leadership and dynamics, and awareness about legal rights, marriageable age and HIV/AIDS. The impacts are detailed in the following table:

Table 10.7: Swayamsidha—Inputs and Social Impacts

Inputs	*Outcomes/Impacts*
Provides training on concept of Swayamsidha, management and organisation of SHGs, leadership qualities, group dynamics, also SHGs were exposed to issues like marriageable age, legal rights, literacy, dowry, HIV/AIDS etc.	Social Impact: • There was 100 per cent leadership rotation in 7 out of 62 blocks studied in all others, rotation of leaders ranged between 50 and 99 per cent. • Increased awareness of legal rights and laws, social evils like alcoholism, child marriage, dowry and female foeticide. • Increased participation in family decisions. • No gender discrimination is practiced in bringing up their children. • Increased number of women at Panchayats levels and some of them have been elected to the Panchayats.

The study showed increased awareness, participation in family decisions, reduced gender discrimination among children, and increased participation at panchayat level.

The basic principle of Swayamsidha is convergence of all inputs, schemes for women's development and empowerment from different ministries/departments. But the study showed that there was no convergence of not even MWCD central schemes for women's empowerment, which was mainly because, Anganwadi workers who involved in implementation of the scheme were busy with several other tasks and they also lacked training, and therefore, a basic understanding of, the concepts of SHGs, empowerment and gender.

Inputs and Outcomes: RMK Programme

RMK is a programme and fund for provision of credit to NGOs for on-lending to women's SHGs. The programmes focuses on sanctioning, disbursing and monitoring credit repayments, with some trainings for NGOs, in order to better administer the programme. The inputs and effects of the RMK programme are detailed in Table 10.8.

The impact study of RMK showed that most borrowers did not have a difficulty in accessing loans, which gave women the choice to start new, expand or diversify existing activities, and to shift from agriculture to non-farm sector occupations. Women reported increased confidence in managing their businesses, and increased savings. However, only 20 per cent said they had access and control over the increased incomes, and the men also dominated decisions about purchase of assets. The study did, however, show an improvement in nutrition and education, increased self-confidence, improved position within the family and increased participation at the community level.

Table 10.8: RMK—Inputs and Economic and Social Impacts

Inputs	*Outcomes/Impacts*
Trainings to NGOs on loan disbursement and monitoring	• 91.9 per cent of the borrowers reported no difficulty in accessing RMK loans. • SHG formulation and stabilization is not adequately facilitated by the RMK's NGO partners • Availability of RMK micro credit gave women the choice and resource to start new economic activities, expand their existing activities and shift in occupation from e.g. casual wage worker to a producer • 60 per cent of the borrowers expressed that they had gained confidence in running their enterprises. • 83.4 per cent reported that they were saving before taking RMK loans and 92.7 per cent reported that they were saving after taking RMK loans. • Borrowers reported that RMK loans inadequate to meet the credit needs for consumption and production. • The borrower forced to look elsewhere for funds as the number and size of RMK loans remain small. • 60 per cent of borrowers showed a positive shift with respect to improvement in nutrition of the family members. • There was no significant change in the borrowers' access to medical facilities but there was a significant improvement in children's education (62.7%) after taking RMK loan. • 88 per cent of the borrowers reported that they travelled alone for taking loan/advice from NGOs. • RMK borrowers reported that they and their husbands took decisions about purchase of radio/TV, children's education and vaccination and about the loan together. • About 20 per cent of borrowers have control over income and a sizeable percentage of borrowers handed it over to their spouse. • 89 per cent of borrowers (77% non-borrowers) said that their families accepted their advice/suggestions. • 51 per cent of the borrowers reported that they commanded respect due to the activities relating to RMK loan. • All borrowers said that they were active participants in Gram Panchayats and their committees and simple participants in the gram sabhas.

With regard to microcredit, the study showed the RMK loan was inadequate to meet the credit needs for consumption and production and the need to provide larger size loans, and multiple loans together. This suggestion has since been taken on board, and currently RMK has a range of loan products which enables each woman to take loans totalling up to Rs. 85,000.

Inputs and Outcomes: SGSY Programme

The SGSY programme was recast from the combination of the programmes formerly under IRDP, and is the largest poverty alleviation programme in the country. In 2001, the decision to route credit-cum-grants through women's SHGs provided improved access to women to bank credit and government subsidies. The programme envisages skill training through convergence with other departments, in the same way as Swayamsidha, but has additionally the provision for community assets (e.g. construction of meeting halls), and allots a one-time grant to the facilitating NGO to meet group formation expenses. The impacts of SGSY programme are detailed in the following table:

Table 10.9: SGSY—Inputs and Social and Economic Impacts

Inputs	*Outcomes/Impacts*
Provides vocational trainings to SHGs and swarozgaris through the convergence of line departments	• More than 90 per cent of SHGs assisted under the scheme are women groups. • The awareness among them is inadequate. Some of the SHGs have been dormant after getting revolving fund. • Beneficiaries have not taken economic assistance despite receiving skill training. Non-availability of market was stated as a cause for this. Only 10 per cent of SHGs were engaged in group activities.

The study of Ramanathapuram district of Tamil Nadu (IIHRD, 2003) showed that ninety per cent of the assisted groups were women's SHGs. SGSY participants showed increased incomes, higher involvement in micro-enterprises, asset creation, independent marketing of their products and increased participation in group management. The constraints included lack of family support, inadequate loan and training, wrong choice of income generating activity and difficulties in accessing bank loans.

However, most women did not understand the concept of a group, and most groups were dormant after taking the revolving loan fund; only 10 per cent were engaged in group-based economic activities. Women had not received adequate loans, and those obtained skill training had not started economic activities, which was attributed to lack of markets.

Lessons from the Official Programmes

As stated earlier, comparisons across programmes cannot be made on the basis of the data given in the impact studies reviewed. The impact studies of the four programmes all illustrated benefits to women, including financial and non-financial aspects of empowerment. However, differing methodologies and a lack of information about how studies were conducted decrease the confidence with which findings can be understood and compared across programmes.

Impact studies of the four programmes varied, and are not directly comparable due to variations across regions, objectives, parameters and indicators and time periods. With measurement across different indicators, the difficulties of assessing the contribution of different strategies to the overall policy goal of empowerment become exacerbated. However, within the scope of each study all programmes reflected varying conditional changes relating to increase in savings, assets, improvement in nutrition and education; as well as and positional changes such as increased self-confidence and improved position within the family and increased participation at the community level. Importantly however, it is unclear how impact studies disentangled the potential benefit of external support provided to SHGs, especially that of supporting NGOs, from those provided directly by the programme.

The analysis shows that all the four programmes have positive impacts. It is not possible to make reliable cross-progamme comparisons possible, nor unequivocally relate inputs with outcomes based on the limited information and data available in the reports, but some lessons can be derived based on the qualitative analysis provided, these are now discussed.

- *Focus on Women's Empowerment Changes Programme Inputs:* Swashakti and Swayamsidha articulate empowerment objectives, while the other two give primacy to poverty reduction through provision of credit/grants. In line with the empowerment objective, Swashakti has the greatest emphasis on capacity building of group members as well as implementing partners, with a wide range of training programmes scheduled as part of the project. Swayamsidha aims to provide training through convergence with other line departments. By contract, SGSY's training inputs are limited to a component of skill training, while RMK is largely limited to credit provision. The lesson deriving from this is that the objectives of a programme clearly dictate the activity set, and those programmes that do not include women's empowerment as their major objective, may provide credit, but are likely to stop short of creating empowering inputs to individual women or their groups.

- *Empowerment Inputs and Effects:* Swashakti provided skill training on farm and non-farm income generating activities including water management, animal husbandry and dairying. SGSY provided some vocational training, but none on social or political empowerment. Similarly, RMK left it to the mediating NGOs to build capacities of women and their groups.

  As Swashakti had the highest budgets for capacity building of women, it was better able to provide non-deterministic capacity building, e.g. health and hygiene, gender sensitization, legal literacy, and Panchayati Raj. The Swashakti impact study showed that 92 per cent of the beneficiaries received formal training, of which 42 per cent stated that it was good and 51 per cent expressed that the training was average. In this study, 91 per cent of women interviewed indicated that they had control over their income. RMK did not provide empowerment training, nor did any of the other programmes. The RMK study used the same indicator as the Swashakti programme, and found that only 20 per cent of women had control over their income, while others handed over income to their spouses, and although the credit was taken on women's names, the assets made through credit was not in their names. The SGSY and Swayamsidha studies did not address this variable, therefore, comparable findings were not available.

These preliminary findings indicate not only a need for training enabling women to have better access and control over their incomes and assets, but also including a condition in the programme design that assets created through programme credit must be in the names of women, at least as joint owners. Such measures become necessary to ensure that women are empowered and not disempowered by the process of credit delivery. Another recommendation arising from these experiences is that gender sensitisation training for both women and men must be an integral part of microcredit programmes.

➢ *Enabling Enterprise Start-ups:* Swashakti and SGSY provided skill training; in the former, 38 per cent of the women trained initiated IGAs, and in SGSY, too, only 10 per cent of groups were able to start IGAs, reportedly due to lack of market avenues. Swayamsidha has provision for vocational training, but through convergence with programmes of other departments. RMK has no provision for any training, is completely focused on release of loans. Further, SGSY promoted marketing through trade fairs conducted by DRDAs, and ZP but many groups did not utilise this facility. The concurrent evaluation (CMD, 2003) study showed that 62 per cent of the individual beneficiaries did market assessment before starting their IGAs, 88 per cent of them marketed their products on their own and 66 per cent of them did not participate in any trade fairs and exhibitions organised by the government. The SHGs expressed that 28 per cent of them conducted market assessments, 41 per cent of them marketed their own products and only 5 per cent of total groups participated in trade fairs and exhibitions. The evaluation of Swayamsidha showed that all the members who started IGAs faced marketing problems. Though there was a need to link skill training with businesses with marketing potential, officially organized trade fairs and marketing support was not the route preferred by the women.

The lesson from this experience is that budgets or convergence for skill training needs to be ensured, as well as the link with markets and credit. The confluence of all three factors is needed for successful enterprise start-ups. Further, skill training must always be in sectors where demand for products or services exists, e.g. petty shops, trading, weaving, tailoring, data entry, machine repairs, beauty parlours, etc. Further, regular enterprise counselling must be provided to women to increase success rate of individual and group enterprises.

- *Unmet Credit Needs Persist:* Desk studies highlight that credit demand of SHGs is not fully met by SGSY (AFC 2005), and even RMK has too little corpus funding to meet the prevalent demand (Tenth Five Year Plan). Banks also apply the criteria that no group member should have prior loan defaults, thereby disqualifying many groups for SGSY linkage. The dependence on moneylenders for larger amounts of loans and emergency needs continues to exist (AFC, 2005).
- *SHGs Need Further Support for Their Sustainability:* Swashakti provided training on SHG concept, group management (accounting, book keeping,) and confidence building for group operations. The impact study showed that 91 per cent of groups were able to conduct meetings in the absence of NGOs.

  The concurrent evaluation of SGSY (CMD, 2003) showed that a large number of SHGs were formed without any conceptual clarity and awareness, knowledge or understanding of the SGSY programme, hence their grading was poor. They were not able to conduct meetings regularly, or manage their accounts, and their sustainability was low. Loan repayments were poor as the beneficiaries expected government money to be written off without any action against them. SHGs were not properly guided or trained under this programme.

  The RMK impact study (Buch, 2002) showed that 42 per cent of the concerned field staff received training in handling micro loan scheme. The main subjects included formation of SHGs, and their management. No other training or capacity building for women was built into RMK, which is primarily a scheme for credit provision. The impact study showed that 313 of 370 NGOs that were extended credit found existing at the time of study and many of these did not adequately facilitate SHG formulation and stabilization. The SGSY study also found many NGOs and SHGs missing, little follow up on SHGs linked to banks, resulting in many groups having disintegrated within a few months after the official assistance. The impact studies of SGSY, Swayamsidha and RMK showed that more follow up and training was needed for SHGs to become sustainable.

SGSY and RMK are focused on credit and have one-time transactions with the SHGs. As a result, the impact study of SGSY found that many of the SHGs disappeared after taking the loan and did not understood the concept of SHG. In case of RMK many of the NGOs that helped deliver the credit were non-existent, those who existed did not always follow up on the SHGs, and consequently, many groups had disintegrated and were no longer existing at the time of impact assessment, a few months after the official assistance. In case of Swayamsidha the groups were active and conducting meetings regularly only in places where the NGOs were following up, while the Anganwadi workers who facilitated group needed further training themselves before they could make groups active and sustainable.

- *Inadequate Convergence with Line Departments:* None of the four programmes studied could achieve significant convergence with official schemes, beyond linking the SHGs with banks. The Swayamsidha study showed that there was no convergence, not even with MWCD central schemes for women's empowerment. The main reason stated for this was that Anganwadi workers who implemented the scheme were occupied with several other tasks, and did not understand concepts of SHGs, empowerment and gender. The SGSY impact study (CMD, 2003) showed that majority (58%) of the groups did not undergo any skill training, which was expected to be done through convergence with relevant skill training institutions. Only 25 per cent of the groups received the training (the remaining 17% did not respond to the question).

- *Administration of Official Programmes:* An analysis of the implementing structures of the programmes highlights that Swashakti had an independent and parallel structure that enabled exclusive administration of the programme, including staff trainings for working with partner organisations. By contrast, Swayamsidha had few staff devoted solely to the project and worked solely through ICDS structures at the field level, often overburdening Anganwadi workers and the Block Development Officers. A lack of human resources created pressure for local staff to form SHGs, without being able to provide meaningful levels of continued support.
- *NGOs Role is Critical for Sustainability and Impact:* The concurrent evaluation of SGSY states clearly that NGOs play an important role and their presence and intervention are essential for the success and sustainability of the scheme. Their role in building capacities of SHGs is of prime importance in guiding and monitoring the groups even after bank linkages, in setting up and managing the enterprises and becoming self-sustainable. It also points out the need for increased professionalism in NGOs, and setting up a self-regulatory system to increase their accountability (CMD, 2003).

The Swashakti study revealed that the major sources of credit were group savings, followed by the loans provided by banks. Five per cent of groups accessed loan from other sources, i.e. agriculture department, RMK, FWWB, Mahila Vikas etc. Overall NGOs played an important role in channelising credit to the groups. The CREDIT programme of CARE, Jharkhand, and the CASHE programme of CARE, AP and Orissa highlight the positive role of NGOs in creating intermediary organizations that are women-owned and women-managed. These programmes have also utilized NGOs as intermediaries for creating women's empowerment.

The study now turns to experiences of NGOs engaged in providing or facilitating credit linkages for women's SHGs, and draw lessons for women's empowerment.

III. LESSONS FROM NGO MICROFINANCE/ MICROENTERPRISE EXPERIENCES

India is replete with microfinance programmes implemented by NGOs in several states based on different models of microfinance delivery and a mix of services and products. These have been researched and evaluated and offer valuable lessons for microfinance policy and programme design.

Lessons from Experience of NGOs

This section outlines case studies of different donor and implementation agencies, highlighting experiences in microfinance and microenterprises, from which lessons can be derived for the design of such programmes at the national level. Both positive and negative experiences are included, and relate to microfinance programme design (inputs, products and services), leadership and organization building (number of tiers, women-owned or NGO owned), and partnerships for enterprise or livelihoods support.

Flexible Savings: ILO's Southern Regional Office (SRO) implemented a project for Prevention and Elimination of Bonded Labour in South Asia (PEBLISA), in Tamil Nadu and Andhra Pradesh, India. The grassroots projects in Tamil Nadu and Andhra Pradesh were implemented through NGO partners, using microfinance as a strategy for prevention of bonded labour.

The Andhra Pradesh project covered 8 villages, with 93 women SHGs. Lalitha was a member of a one-year old group, Sivajyothi SHG, which met and saved Rs. 10 per week. Along with this regular savings, the project gave a dump box to all the members of SHG to save depending upon their capacity. All the group members kept these boxes at their homes, saving change that remained after purchase of provisions. Lalitha said that she had collected about Rs. 1000 over a period of one year and used this to purchase clothes for her children and herself during festivals. She said that *"I have a lot of freedom about how to use this money. We put in a half or one rupee at a time so we do not feel the burden of saving such small amounts"*. Other SHG members also confirmed that they were able to save between Rs. 500 to 1500 per year. Most often, this money was used for emergency purposes within the family, and when deposited as group's savings, was used for taking loan for starting small businesses (Premchander *et al.*, 2006[2]).

The flexibility of savings, and the freedom to retain it for family use or deposit in the SHG, helped women to meet their emergency needs and they felt in control of the usage of this money. A comparative study between compulsory and mandated savings showed that women who participated in the flexible savings scheme saved more than the latter.

The lesson emerging from this is that a strategy of flexible savings allows the poorest women and households to sustain their participation in a programme. This would prevent drop-outs and exclusion of the most vulnerable, who have uncertain and irregular cash flows as seen from other research (Premchander, 2005). Thus flexible savings, with control over savings, create socially and financially empowering impacts for poor women.

Innovative Credit Products: Activists for Social Action (ASA) an NGO working for empowerment of poor women started microfinance activity in Tamil Nadu in 1993. Its microfinance methodology was based on Bangladesh Grameen model of forming SHGs with five members and federating into centres (20 SHGs), clusters (20 centres), branches (5 clusters), and franchisees (six branches).

ASA developed several credit products; one of these was a separate credit fund for poor women to contest elections in local self-governance institutions. Unlike women from well-off families, the poor could not rely on the financial support from their husbands for campaigning. The fund helped two poor women, both of them belonging to SC/ST castes, to contest and participate in local elections (Sankar, 2005).

Another NGO, Sampark working with poor women had a demand for education loans. Women wanted to borrow Rs. 1200 at the beginning of the academic year, return it over 12 months at the rate of Rs. 100 each, and re-borrow the amount the next year. When approached, the bank considered this risky and refused to sanction a non-business loan. Sampark then assigned a fund from its own resources, deeming it an investment in augmenting human capital of poor households.

This case study highlights the view that microcredit for women should not only be aimed at creating self-employment but also be used for development of credit products, with different norms and repayment schedules, suited for a wide range of purposes according to their needs.

Social Security Services

ASA, an NGO working for empowerment of poor women provided insurance and social security facilities for the women who had taken credit. All borrowing members of SHGs facilitated by the NGO were insured under the official social welfare security scheme, wherein they paid a one-time fee of Rs. 700 for life, or an annual premium of Rs. 150. The borrowers were also insured under the Janashree Bima Yojana (JBY) of the Life Insurance Corporation of India where the annual premium is Rs. 125. In case of natural death of the member, the household was paid Rs. 20,000; and on accidental death, Rs. 50,000. In case of partial or total permanent disability due to accident, the benefit to the member ranged from Rs. 25,000 (loss of one eye or one limb) to Rs. 50,000 (total disability, or two eyes, or one eye and one limb). Forty-four per cent of members could be linked under the JBY scheme. Other insurance schemes that ASA considered was the Oriental and General Insurance for the poor (premium only Rs. 15 per year) and the Raja Rajeshwari Mahila Kalyana Bima Yojana. Loans for livestock were insured to provide risk cover in case of unforeseen eventualities. However, members who had taken agricultural loans had not taken crop insurance (Ranadive and Murthy, 2005).

In accordance with the strategies outlined in the RBI credit policy, many Indian MFIs and NGOs, e.g. SEWA (Gujarat), ASA, MSSS, IRCDS (Tamil Nadu), provide insurance and other social security services along with microcredit, which helped women to withstand crisis situations.

The lesson of this case is that the strategy of including insurance along with other microfinancial services serves several purposes. To begin with, it helps the MFIs to recover loan repayments in crisis situation, more importantly; it helps women to recover from shocks of different types, including death/sickness/accidents in the family, or the loss of assets (e.g. crops, house, machines, and animals) due to accidents or disasters. Thus insurance services have an increasing role to play in microfinance to women.

Credit and Enterprise Support

CARE India's Sustainable Tribal Empowerment Project (STEP)

aimed to empower tribal people, and specifically works towards strengthening Self-help Groups with the help of partner NGOs in four north-coastal districts of Andhra Pradesh. STEP enhanced the capacities of SHGs by focusing on good SHG practices; and linking the SHGs with formal credit institutions. A study was conducted in February 2006, to review the improvement in the quality of SHG-functioning through STEP's programme initiatives, and offer recommendations for CARE's capacity building programmes to further strengthen the SHGs. This case is based on the findings of the study (Sampark, 2006).

Microcredit and Enterprise Interventions: Velugu, a programme of the AP State government, had formed three SHGs in Mamidipalli village, Pathapatnam Mandal, five years ago. The STEP programme enabled a local NGO and partner of STEP, to supervise these groups, which had 30 women members. Two of these groups (Sundramma and Rani SHGs) received CARE revolving loan funds of Rs. 20,000 each. Four members from each group took the loan for the purpose of purchasing bulls and goats by adding their own savings to the loan. Bulls were very useful to them since most of the people cultivated paddy, sunflowers and vegetables. Earlier, they used to hire bulls for Rs. 100 a day for agricultural work, which totalled up to a high sum over the year. Thus, the RLF loan proved to be very useful to them, and bulls turned out to be good investment as the market was local.

Ten years ago, the Integrated Tribal Development Agency (ITDA) of the government provided all the 42 households in this village with one kilo of cashew nut seeds for the purpose of cultivation and also provided support and guidance for fertilizer use and maintenance. Velugu also provided all the households with 30 saplings of trees bearing fruits, like mango, sappota, etc. In time, the cashew nuts provided rich yields and each household had a collection of 50-200 kilos during harvest time. They sold these nuts to the middlemen at a low rate of Rs. 50-80 per kg as they had taken a loan from them for agricultural purposes. More recently, such distress sale has reduced as women can avail of group loans. However, they have still not been able to get good terms of trade for the cashew nuts. Many families sell a large amount of cashew nuts for salt, oil, onions and other household needs. Children exchanged the nuts for chocolates and sweets when the vendors came to their village. The second official assistance of cashew nut production, suffered from the lack of strategy for collection, storage and marketing of the cashew nuts. None of the agencies involved in the project, the NGO partner and the state government planned the post-harvest strategy.

This part of the case study shows that mere credit and general enterprise trainings are not sufficient for the development of the poor. In this case SHGs took loan to market their produce; cashew nuts, but they were not able to make a collective marketing strategy. They needed help with, storage facilities, techniques for value addition, packaging, costing, transportation plans and devising the overall marketing strategy.

Empowerment Action: Despite the problems they faced with loan repayments and marketing of cashew nut produce, all the three groups together had several social mobilization activities in the village to their credit. By having approached the Panchayat, they had got cement roads laid in their villages and had even ensured the construction of a school in their village. The group members approached Velugu office and got them to set up a pond, which would serve as a place to wash clothes and provide drinking water for cattle. The group was successful in getting a hospital constructed in their village. They arranged ration cards for some of their SHG members and procured old age pension for two women. The groups approached the ITDA office and applied for proper housing facilities on behalf of the villagers who didn't have proper houses.

The case study further shows that an NGO partner that was not able to provide inputs for income generating activities, was however, able to support empowerment activities. Thus NGOs may have skills in some areas, but may need to build their own capacities in others.

Planning Enterprise Partnerships

GRAM, an NGO based in Nizamabad district, works with the Dalits (women and men from the lowest social and economic strata) for the past 27 years. Its mission is to empower them through creation of sustainable financial and social organisations owned by the Dalit women and to enhance their livelihoods (Premchander, 2005[3]).

In the initial years of its work in the villages, 1988-89, GRAM worked with the poorest households, who could not bring money as savings, and established grain banks instead. After 1997, to benefit from the new SHG bank linkage methodology, the earlier *sanghas* reformed into SHGs, with 19 Mutually Aided Cooperative Societies (MACS) as second tier organisations, further federated into other MACS at the district level. Enterprise support activities to individuals and SHGs were extended through the Federation and the MACS. The idea of home marketing through SHGs envisaged common purchase of provisions, in order to gain advantage of wholesale prices, and the benefits to be shared by group members. GRAM also encouraged entrepreneurship and offered rewards of up to Rs. 10,000 for innovative enterprise ideas to SHGs. SHGs encouraged a range of local businesses at this time.

Meanwhile, the DRDA (District Rural Development Agency) offered a scheme of Apna Bazar to the Mandal MACS. GRAM and the MACS were informed that they would be supported to start Supermarkets for provisions, and the government would extend full support for this. The public-private partnership envisaged that the government would provide two rooms to the women in a market, loans to invest in working and fixed capital, and links for supply of the materials. Six MACS were brought under this scheme.

In reality, the scheme worked as follows: the government allotted two rooms, which were rent free for the first few months, but then the MACS were to pay rent to the government. The government would give a loan of Rs. 100,000 to the MACS, for provisions, billing machines, storage racks, and other furniture. These items were, however, sourced through a supplier already contracted by the government, so the amount would be released to him and not to the MACS. The MACS were given a week to make commitments of money, and to remit amounts to pay for the materials, because the total investment in fixed and working capital was Rs. 300,000 and not Rs. 100,000. To begin with, the women had to spend more than one lakh (Rs. 100,000) of own money, they had to keep the Apna Bazar in a building made by the government, renting two rooms and paying the rent to the government.

The provisions and other items to be sold were to be provided through one supplier, again contracted out by the government, to supply provisions to all Apna Bazars of women all over the State. The supplier sent goods that were of bad quality, close to expiry date, and items according to his whims, not those ordered by the women's groups, and with delays in supply. Due to these reasons, the Apna Bazar made losses. The government had moved on to other schemes, lost interest in Apna Bazar scheme, the private contractor was in Hyderabad, the capital of the State, which was over 400 miles from the district, and there was no possibility of holding either the government or the private contractor accountable. The MACS stopped paying the monthly rent to the government, and the government asked them to vacate the rooms, so they could rent them out to private businesses. Women did not know what to do with the provisions, and even though they got rid of most of these, there was still the fixed capital: the racks, glass windows, shutters, furniture and billing machines, which were of no use and could not be sold to recover their capital.

Women lost their capital by joining the government scheme, following their advice in investing their own capital and trusting the partnerships that the government had made on their behalf. After this experience, MACS have become very wary of provision shops and have not engaged in the business. At the SHG level too, women find it wise to purchase their provisions on a household basis, and do not find it worthwhile to engage with home marketing any more.

The lesson for the GRAM and MACS was to plan and implement businesses that they would directly have control on, not trust the government blindly and not invest own money into businesses controlled by other external organizations.

Livelihoods Support Partnerships

GRAM, an NGO in AP, engaged in microfinance, had formed SHGs, federated into MACS at block lever, further federated into a MACS at district level. GRAM was located in a semi-arid region, with few livelihoods options, therefore identified milk production and sale as a viable activity that could benefit a large number of women. It forged a partnership for livelihoods support for dairy development, with an MFI and livelihoods support organisation headquartered in Hyderabad, the capital of the State of Andhra Pradesh (Premchander, 2005).

In October 2003, the MFI extended loans of Rs. 10 lakhs (Rs. 1 million) each to three MACS, totalling Rs. 30,00,000

(Rs. 3 million, $ 66,667), for 324 women to buy buffaloes. Each borrower got about Rs. 10,000. The MFI collected an amount of Rs. 600 per animal towards animal insurance, and Rs. 100 from each beneficiary to provide extension support during the period October 2003—September 2004. The MFI discouraged members from private selling, and encouraged them to pour milk to the Andhra Pradesh Dairy Development Cooperative Federation (APDDCF), promising to take care of the marketing with APDDCF Ltd., but this did not happen. The fat testing method was not transparent and was manipulated by the APDDCF, and there was also adulteration of milk during transportation. APDDCF paid less than market rate to the milk suppliers.

The MFI made the arrangements with a specific agent for insurance of the animals, and insisted that the members pay the premium. Yet, when some animals died, the members were not trained in the procedures and could not collect their claims. After a few months, workers of the MFI left the area, so members could not approach anyone with their demands. On account of this, 200 out of 324 borrowers did not repay their loans on time, and the overdue was 39 per cent of the total loans extended. In order not to be defaulters, and to be eligible for the next loan from the MFI, the MACS absorbed the delinquency and repaid its loan to the MFI. Neither the MACS nor GRAM challenged the MFI and its ineffectiveness in the role that it had promised in terms of providing business development services.

After two years, GRAM and Federation realised that as this was a supply-led initiative, wherein the promises of support had not been met to the borrower women, the organisation would not find it easy to recover these loans. On the basis of the recommendation from the advisors and potential lenders to the Federation, the loan-loss was finally written-off by the above MACS in September 2005.

The lesson from the experience was that support organizations need to be held accountable for their actions, and if all the risk is borne only by women, then it erodes their capital when the proposed income-generating scheme fails. Once again, the control of women over productive resources and enterprise decisions must not be taken away; else it increases their vulnerability to external agencies.

Challenging Convergence Practices

In a northern district of Karnataka, Sampark, an NGO engaged with women's empowerment, and sustainable development through microfinance, micro enterprise, craft development and child education, has organised 186 women's SHGs. The first 50 of these groups were organised under the Mahila Arthik Samvrudhi Yojane a KSWDC supported programme that closed in 2002. Another 50 SHGs were organised under the KSWDC-World Bank supported Swashakti project, on which Sampark's partnership ended in May 2004. The other 86 groups were promoted at the initiative of women themselves, and Sampark continued to support all 186, building women's capacities to monitor the groups, make linkages with government programmes, and manage other externally obtained funding for educational grants and loans.

Even though Sampark made its best effort for convergence with official schemes, especially SGSY, it had to contend with two difficult issues. The first one was that groups covered by these schemes tended not to be genuine. One of the groups facilitated by Sampark in 2000, comprising 13 SC women, applied for an SGSY loan and grant in 2003, but was turned down.

Instead, another local NGO, Mediator[4] formed another group, comprising of 12 women below 18 years of age and therefore ineligible to be members, and nine of them later got married and left the village. Within three months of its formation, the new group received a sanction of Rs. 3,00,000 under SGSY. The SC/ST Corporation retained the subsidy of Rs. 1,20,000, which was released by the Taluk Panchayat, and released the loan amount of Rs. 1,80,000 (Rs. 15,000 × 12) to Mediator, who passed on Rs. 90,000 to the women first, and then another Rs. 10,000, retaining the rest of the loan amount. The SHG has fully repaid the loan of Rs. 1,00,000 that they have received so far. They have not yet received the subsidy, or the balance loan of Rs. 80,000, which Mediator has retained. This Mediator gained in two ways, first by ignoring old groups in the village, and forming new ones, so that they could claim the Rs. 10,000 that SGSY grants to NGOs, and secondly, to be able to benefit from the loan and subsidy that should go to the women's groups.

In 2004, older SHGs who had faced this type of discrimination and not received government money, protested and made a representation to the District Level Credit Committee, questioning the decisions about granting SGSY to new groups, while older groups and more stable groups existed and wanted the linkage. Following this representation, 11 of the older groups facilitated by the former NGO were linked. However, the linkage was always made on the signature of the Mediator, which was a 'broker' NGO to the government.

This highlights another problematic practice that the government follows in Koppal district: that of assigning the entire quota for the taluk to one particular NGO, which then presents all applications of SHGs to the government, and claims the money for group formation. This has been the practice in Koppal taluk for several years. The SHGs promoted by all NGOs in Koppal district were linked with SGSY only through this 'broker' NGO, wherein the group sends its application to this NGO, and the government accepts the application only after the 'broker' NGO has signed and forwarded it. As a result, it is Mediator that claims the money for group formation, which is Rs. 10,000 per group, and other NGOs never receive the support of Rs. 10,000, assigned under SGSY for group formation. By routing all the SGSY linkages through one NGO, and given a target of about 10 SHGs per year for a block/taluk, the government ensures that this NGO earns at least Rs. 100,000 per year. If Mediator is appointed as an agent for a larger area, say the whole district, it ensures that it earns at least Rs. 400,000 per year. The question about why the government officers insist on appointing and retaining only one particular agent as a broker for the SGSY linkages is not difficult to guess. Many accredited NGOs in the district have not succeeded in changing this practice, and in fact have shied away from coming together to challenge it openly, in the belief that a confrontation would deny groups formed by them, access to government funds. Many of these NGOs are partners of Swashakti, and there is a Project Officer of Swashakti stationed in Koppal district, but not even Swashakti has not taken up such issues. Thus even when convergence between different programmes is mentioned and sought, there are processes happening at the ground level which defeat the very purpose of a government intervention programme. This highlights the need not only for capacity building of groups, but also networking of NGOs and greater confidence to be imparted to them in demanding better implementation of grant-based programmes.

The lesson from this experience is that the local implementing NGOs, along with the donor funded project mangers could evolve strategies to create greater transparency and accountability in local government operations.

IV. DESIGNING MICROFINANCE PROGRAMMES THAT EMPOWER WOMEN

The recommendations address the question: If microfinance programmes are to empower women, what needs to change at policy and programme level?

The first acknowledgement has to be that the goal of empowerment is central to development, and applies to any marginalized group, of which women are only one. Thus empowerment has to be viewed as a larger development issue, of which one important aspect relates to women's empowerment.

The next critical question is about the clarity of the policy goal. If the goal of a microfinance programme is to empower women, the path to take would be quite different from one where the explicit goal is poverty reduction or credit provision alone. The latter orientation leads to a supply orientation, whereby the effort is to provide microcredit to women. This can lead to empowering effects, but can also lead women into more indebtedness, without giving them improved access to cash and other productive resources. Thus microfinance can lead to empowering effects, but can also lead to disempowering ones, as seen in cases where they were subject to corrupt systems or practices losing the capital invested. Disempowerment also arises from the dominance of leaders who may appropriate the benefits of official assistance, or indeed NGOs who may do the same. The only way to ensure that microfinance empowers rather than disempowers, is to ensure that programme design builds women's knowledge base and decision making abilities, and also to monitor results continuously to guard against positive effects and maximize the positive ones.

Recommendations for Microfinance Policy and Programme Design

The range of policy recommendations already indicate several aspects of programme design, similarly design of programmes is clearly indicative of its policy foundation. The set of recommendations presented here derived from according a clear priority to women's empowerment and decision making. Special attention is given to detailing recommendations for economic empowerment (e.g. through enabling enterprise start ups) and several suggestions also relate to wider social issues without which economic empowerment cannot be sustained.

A Holistic View of Empowerment: The experiences of the four official and NGO implemented microfinance programmes showed that even minimalist microfinance programmes may have empowering effects, almost by default. For instance, women who begin to earn more money, also acquire the confidence to participate in greater decision making within and outside the household. However, several factors that disempower women are in the social realm and need collective action to ameliorate. One example is lack of access to property, even with a positive legal framework in place. Some microfinance programmes insist on women jointly owning the property, e.g. house, when it finances asset for the women, thereby ensuring that women not only take the credit liability but also have ownership over the asset created. When microfinance programmes do not address societal causes of gender inequality, the positive effects can be minimal, or even negative. For instance, in the above case, the woman may be indebted while the asset may be owned by the man, thus exacerbating gender inequality. Microfinance programmes can work towards greater equality not only in the 'condition' but also in the 'position' of women in society.

This calls for a holistic view of empowerment, which would require increasing confidence, women's awareness, literacy, vocational skills, management and entrepreneurial skills including negotiation for business or better official benefits providing opportunities for income generation and enterprise, extending microcredit and other financial services including social security. Women's property rights must receive special attention through the programmes, as well as access and control over their own savings.

Setting Up of Indicators of Women's Empowerment: The indicators monitored currently at the national level derive from internationally accepted Gender Development Index, which are quite comprehensive. However, microfinance programmes need to develop indicators which provide information on key variables affected by microfinance interventions. While microfinance impact studies of official and NGO programmes use a wide range of indicators, there is no agreed set of indicators at the national level for assessment of empowerment impact of microfinance programmes. The suggestions are for the government to initiate and undertake:

- Development of appropriate indicators of women's empowerment that can be used to evaluate impact of the policy at the national level, and against which each department and each programme of the government can report;
- The process of setting indicators must include a debate involving a wide range of stakeholders, especially organisations working with women's empowerment issues, both through action and research;
- Establishment of a system of monitoring and assessing impact in terms of empowerment. Such a set would not only help to elaborate a concept of empowerment of women through microfinance, but also establish a common base on which both government and non-government programmes can be assessed.

Regulation of SHGs: The women's SHG is the critical forum that has enabled the revolution in micro-lending to the poor. This forum is expected to work as a Joint Liability Group (JLG), whereby if one member cannot repay, others pool in and keep up the repayment schedule to the external agency, resulting in high repayment rates, and consequent reduction of risks of poverty lending.

While it has resulted in lower risks for the credit supplying agencies, the SHG pools in funds of poor women, and expects joint management of money in a manner that they have not done earlier. Typically, one or two women leaders control a group, and the competence and accountability of these determines the money management in groups. Where the members are able to hold their leaders accountable, and have transparency of money management, groups work well. By contrast, in many SHGs, leaders control funds, and if there are disputes, and if trust does not exist, groups disintegrate, and women are at the risk of losing their small savings.

Currently, the official system recognizes the positive aspects of SHG functioning, but does not pay heed to the risks and vulnerabilities created for the small saver. The RBI has taken a stand that groups are to be 'left to their own devices' and not regulated. This means that SHGs remain "informal" forums, with the savings and credit activities not being supervised under any law. They remain outside the ambit of legal supervision, e.g. the Co-operative Act, Moneylender Act, the Banking Regulation Act, or the Companies Act. This situation leaves the vulnerability unattended to.

In case operations of an SHG are not well managed, and collective finances have been misused by one or two members, currently the members do not have any recourse, and must resolve the issue among themselves. However, given the proliferation of SHGs, and the position they have come to occupy as a major link between formal organizations and women, it is time that the current discourse also included risks that women face to their savings because of joining SHGs, and find ways and means to address these.

There is a need to regulate SHGs, and ensure that at least one of the many intermediary agencies engaged in the MF chain: NGO, bank, MFI, RMK, SGSY or any other official agency like Women's Development Corporation, or even the village, taluk and district level Panchayati Raj Institutions are assigned the responsibility of supporting, monitoring and ensuring sustainability of SHGs.

Right to Ownership of Productive Resources: Women's access to economic resources is linked to their legal rights to property and other resources, and the Tenth Plan policy document, acknowledges that lack of ownership of property is a major factor constraining women's economic empowerment. Microfinance programmes are in a unique position to address this imbalance, as they provide credit mostly to women.

The recommendation, therefore, is that microfinance programmes must ensure that all women who are reached through microfinance are given such access by their parental and husband's homes. For instance, this can be done by insisting that the asset be created in the woman's name, e.g. cow, petty shop, and where housing loans are given, that these are registered in the joint names of women and men. Further, agricultural credit extended to women can have a condition that women share land ownership. Such links between microcredit provision and ownership of assets will go a long way in promoting gender equality and women's empowerment.

Access and Control Over Savings: One of the most impact creating aspects of MF programmes is the creation of the habit of savings, and the rotation of these as small credit among women. Increasingly, women have reported access and control over own savings as beneficial. It not only helps them to get small credit for consumption smoothening, health and education needs and income generating activities, it also helps to build the financial capital of the group, by pooling of savings and earning of interest at the group level.

The recommendation that arises from this is to ensure that women's savings stay with the SHGs as far as possible, and that NGOs/MFIs do not take these away from the groups. In case groups are to be federated and a second layer created, attention needs to be paid to the institutional form, as this determines women's access and control over their own savings. Cooperatives are more relevant as they allow women to manage their own money, whereas forms like MFIs tend to transfer control to external, 'professional' agencies and staff.

Streamlining and Convergence of Official Schemes: There is a realization that a large number of schemes result in increased costs of administration, leading to the need for rationalising the number of government schemes, and also transferring some responsibilities to the private sector (GoI, 1995).

Another important recommendation is to have links between schemes of different departments, which provide skill trainings, e.g. in agriculture, industry and services, and credit, to enable self-employment in the sectors in which the departments provide training. This link can be made through MWCD and banks by each of the line departments. In this regard, a critical question arises about whether microfinance extended to women should continue to flow through various departments as it currently does, or whether any benefit is to be derived from assigning MWCD not only a linking and monitoring role, but also coordination and implementation of all schemes involving women's microfinance. This issue is beyond the scope of this study and merits in-depth research and discussions among various stakeholders.

Duration of Programmes: Microcredit programmes like Swashakti and Swayamsidha have a five to six year duration, including the starting of the project, making partnerships, establishing the structures within the government and training them, making NGO partnerships and training them, and the project implementation on the ground. The latter, which involves establishment and training of groups and bank linkages, along with micro-enterprise promotion and marketing support, is spread over about two to three years at the maximum. This time is inadequate for establishing SHGs that would sustain beyond the project period. SGSY makes only a one time linkage with SHGs, to provide the grant, through the bank, and therefore does not envisage a continuing relationship of capacity building of SHGs, and assumes rather than ensures continuity of groups. Similarly, RMK assumes continued NGO support to SHGs, and engages primarily with the former for disbursement and repayment of loans.

Given that SHGs are forums managed by women, and new for them, women take time to learn the new methodology for coming together and accessing new resources. The processes and group dynamics offer learning opportunities and take time to settle down, with SHGs sometimes going through dissolution and reconstitution two or three times in as many years. As groups take time to settle down, and become accountable grassroots organizations, it is imperative that a MF programme allow for such social learning processes to take place. Thus the grassroots effort in any MF programme must be at least three years, with another two years of consolidation before the external agency withdraws from the work. The recommendation for longer duration, contact is contingent upon an empowering programme design and implementation processes.

SHG Capacity Building for Empowerment: With respect to credit related empowerment, the programmes are varied, and while some, like Swashakti and Swayamsidha claim empowerment as their objectives, others limit their stated objectives to provision of credit and grants. Swayamsidha provides Rs. 2,750 for group formation, and SGSY Rs. 10,000 as a one-time grant for group formation. The empowerment objective calls for emphasis on capacity building, which is resource intensive, and therefore is not an important part of government programmes.

There is a need to build capacities of SHGs, in book keeping, accountable and transparent management of own money, and training of leaders and well as members to ensure the managerial sustainability of the SHGs. SHGs and their members also need training in enterprise start-ups and marketing, and social empowerment aspects such as functional literacy, age of marriage, women's rights, workers' and citizens rights. The grants for capacity building need to be institutionalized, monitored, and funds disbursal needs to become more transparent and accountable. The government and banking sector should assess group sustainability and continued operations, not just one time linkage. If the microcredit movement is to be sustained on the basis of SHGs, this investment will need to be made.

In addition of capacity building for money and enterprise management, women also need special inputs for building their confidence to demand their rights, protect their access and enhance their ownership of productive assets including land and other property. They also need support to create joint representation and collective voice against other discrimination within households or in the community, e.g. domestic violence and lack of political representation. This would ensure that women not only enhance their economic livelihoods, but also their control over the livelihoods created.

Institutional Levels: SHG sustenance and long-term access to funds is related to the question of the levels at which SHGs are consolidated and the institutional form of such consolidation. Many large MF programmes envisage three levels: SHGs, cluster associations (5 to 20 SHGs), and federations (50 to 500 or more SHGs). Banks provide money to groups, whereas wholesale providers like RMK and FWWB provide credit through NGOs or federations. The consolidation of SHGs at a higher level makes access to large funding possible. However, each layer adds on an administrative cost, and therefore the need to be a profit centre. The tasks at each level need to be defined clearly, costed, and earnings ensured so that each level can become viable. Where SHGs can access bank funds directly to meet all their credit needs, they prefer not to have even a second layer, so that the difference between the interest payable to the bank, and that paid by the individual to the group, can be fully enjoyed by the SHG. Similarly, when NGOs or MFIs lend to SHGs, the groups have low or no margins on interest earnings. In these cases, SHGs do not perceive the need for a second layer. Second and third level organizations like cluster associations and federations have a rationale only when they can perform tasks like monitoring, auditing and capacity building of groups. Thus the decision about the levels of client-owned organizations varies according to the local situation, and in general, the lower the number of layers, the greater the benefit that SHGs can have.

Skill Training and Enterprise Promotion: Small credit is first used for household consumption, and to meet medical and education expense. Women meet their small needs for income generating activities in agriculture and other micro businesses from this money. However, potential for greater earning can be constrained by several factors. The first of these is low human capital, calling for skill training so women and youth can engage in activities that generate higher incomes than prevailing agricultural wage rates. The second is lack of business opportunities in the semi arid and poverty-ridden regions in which poor people live. Thus counselling and enterprise promotion inputs become relevant to help women to think through and plan individual and group level IGAs. These inputs need to be market oriented and demand based. Further, very poor women cannot give up wage labour and attend programmes; their skill training will need to be supported by paying stipends to enable them to attend the trainings offered.

Marketing Linkages: The government programme to hold exhibitions in which SHGs are provided to exhibit and sell their products are largely not utilized and not found useful by women beneficiaries. The SGSY impact study (CMD, 2003), showed that 42 per cent of the groups market the products on their own, only 5 per cent of the groups participated in the trade fairs/exhibitions organized by official and non-government agencies. The government invests resources in these exhibitions, which could be much better used by preparing the groups to do market research, identifying customers and teaching them how to market their own products, rather than by holding exhibitions. Thus the marketing support needs to be provided very differently from the way it is currently done. SHGs need to learn how to make their own marketing linkages, which is a more sustainable strategy in the long term. These are better served by involving women in market research using simple techniques, and through enterprise counselling services, rather than holding exhibitions or trade fairs, which are far more cost intensive but less effective in meeting women's needs.

Providing a Range of Financial Products/Services: The earlier discussion has brought out the need to have a range of financial products and services that meet the several needs of poor women.

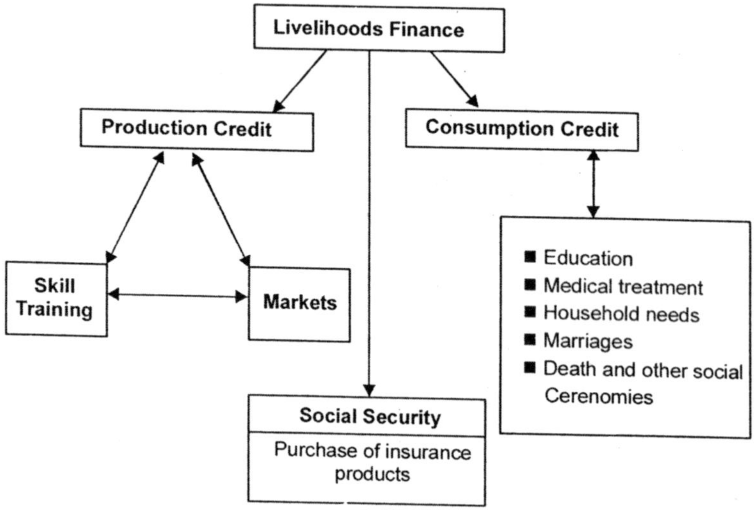

Fig. 10.2: Provision of range of financial products/services

The credit products need to cover consumption and livelihoods needs including food, education, medical care, and social expenses like birth, death and marriage ceremonies. Credit products need to be offered on terms acceptable to women, and need to be linked to skill training that women obtain, which needs to be in market-related vocations. Finally, women need insurance for life, medical care, accidents, and their assets and crops. There are now several schemes that ensure social security for members of SHGs. The linkage of SHG members with insurance can become much stronger as comprehensive insurance schemes become available for this segment of the population. A Microcredit programme of the government can incorporate social security as an essential element across the country.

Monitoring Outcomes and Impact: The programmes of the Indian government are monitored for performance but not for effect or impact. At the national level, for both RMK and Swayamsidha, no indicators have been set for assessing impact, either in terms of economic or other aspects of empowerment, and no monitoring system established. The national office of these two schemes does not even ask for reports of how many old SHGs have sustained their operations, whether skill training has been utilized, or income generating activities started.

However, there is an existing feedback mechanism for programme performance and review, within each department, and this permits some formal and informal feedback to bring about improvements at the programme level. For instance, the officers of SGSY and RMK have had discussion about how the SGSY grants are in fact providing guarantee support to the banking sector, and now there are talks of collaboration between RMK and SGSY so that reach of RMK can be increased, and government-to-government collaboration strengthened. Such examples, however, are *adhoc* and do not create evidence of a 'system'. There is need not only to monitor individual programmes but also systematically compare design, processes and impacts of various official programmes that include microfinance as a component.

In general, impact in terms of empowerment of women is not being measured by any of the Microcredit programmes reviewed in this study. Considerable work is still needed for setting of indicators and measurement of women's empowerment at the national level, for each programme. Once indicators are set, it would be possible to set up a system for periodic monitoring of these, and to be able to refine the monitoring system at the national level, which can be done through the Department of Women and Child Development Department.

Thus an approach to microfinance that seeks to empower women must leave the control of resources in their hands, and must invest the time and resources to develop women's capacities to manage their own resources and organizations. And any interventions, whether governmental or non-governmental, need to check regularly whether they are on the right track, whether the path chosen indeed leads to women's empowerment, and when corrective measures need to be taken to ensure that the movement is in the right direction.

NOTES

1. Premchander, Smita and V. Prameela, Empowering Women through Microfinance: A Policy and Programme Review. Delhi: CARE India.

This may be downloaded from: http://www.careindia.org/ManagePublications/VisitPublicationDetail.aspx?SectionID=114
2. Field experience during evaluation of PEBLISA project, 2005.
3. This case study is derived from a field visit to GRAM, for evaluating its programme.
4. A fictitious name assigned to the local broker NGO.

REFERENCES

AFC, (2005). Report on *Impact Evaluation of Swashakti*, MWCD, New Delhi: Agricultural Finance Corporation Ltd.

Batliwala, Srilatha (1995). "Education for Women's Empowerment", ASPBAE Position Paper for the Fourth World Conference on Women, Beijing, September 1995. New Delhi: Asia-South Pacific Bureau of Adult Education.

Bhatt, Ela R., Armaity Desai, R. Thamarajakshi, Mrinal Pande, Jaya Arunachalam and Veena Kohli (1988). Shramashakti: A Summary of the Report of the National Commission on Self-Employed Women and Women in the Informal Sector. Ahmedabad: *Self Employed Women's Association.*

Buch, Nirmala (2002). Poverty, Gender and Micro-Credit. *A Study of the Experience of Rashtriya Mahila Kosh*. New Delhi: Centre for Women's Development Studies.

Centre for Management Development, (2003). Concurrent Evaluation of *Swarnajayanti Gram Swarozgar Yojana*. Theruvanthapuram: Centre for Management Development.

Government of India, (1995). *Fourth World Conference on Women*. Beijing 1995. Country Report. New Delhi: Department of Women and Child Development. Ministry of Human Resource Development.

Government of India, (2001). National Policy for the Empowerment of Women New Delhi: Department of Women and Child Development, Ministry of Human Resource Development.

Government of India, (2002). *Five Year Plan 2002-2007*. Dimensions and Strategies. New Delhi: Planning Commission Government of India, Volume-I, II and III.

ILO, (2004). Strategies and Tools Against Social Exclusion and Poverty. India: Needs Assessment Survey: Identifying the Social Protection Priority Needs of Cooperative Societies' Members in Karnataka. New Delhi: *STEP Project*, ILO Sub Regional Office for South Asia.

Indian Institute for Human Research and Development (IIHRD), (2003). Impact Assessment Study of Rural Development Programmes in Ramanathapuram District, Tamil Nadu. Chengalpet: Ministry of Development, Government of India.

IUSSP, 1997. Seminar on Female Empowerment and Demographic Processes: Moving Beyond Cairo, 21-24 April 1997. Sweden: IUSSP Committee on Gender and Population, PROP and the Department of Sociology of the Lund university. http://www.iussp.org/Activities/scp-gen/gen-rep97.php, accessed on January 1, 2004.

Jain, Devaki (1997). In Karl Marilee 1997. Women and Rural Development. ISIS Women's International Information and Communication Service. Women in Development. A Resource Guide for Organisation and Action. Ahmedabad: Intermediate Technology Publications, India.

Jain, S.K., Srivastava, K. Mathur, M. Jaitly and N. Nair (1986). *Exploring possibilities*. A Review of the Women's Development Programme. Institute of Development Studies, Jaipur.

Kabeer, Naila (1995). *Reversed Realities: Gender Hierarchies in Development Thought*. London, Verso.

Kraus-Harper, U. (1998). *From Despondency to Ambitions: Women's Changing Perceptions of Self Employment: Cases from India and other developing countries*. Hants, England: Ashgate.

Mosedale, Sarah (2003). Towards a Framework For Assessing Empowerment, Paper prepared for the international conference, *New Directions in Impact Assessment for Development: Methods and Practice*, Manchester UK, 24 and 25 November 2003, EDIAIS, (Online). Available from: http://www.enterprise-impact.org.uk/pdf/Mosedale.pdf, (Accessed January 10, 2004).

NABARD, (2005). SHG-Bank Linkage Programme—Regional Spread of SHGs Financed. http://.www.nabard.org/roles/microfinance/files/others/statewise310305.hmt

Premchander, Smita (2003). NGOs: and Local MFIS: How to Increase Poverty Reduction through Women's Small and Micro-Enterprise. Futures 35 (2003: 361-378). Pergamon: *doi: 10.1016/S0016-3287 (02) 00086*.

Premchander, Smita (2005). Competing Perspectives of Women and Micro-finance Institutions: Rethinking Organisational Forms and Capacity Building: *Mainstream*, Vol. XLIII, No. 16, PP: 11-12.

Premchander Smita, Prasad Eswar K., Prameela V., Ben Laroquette, Jeyaseelan L. (2006). *Terminal Project Evaluation of Prevention and Elimination of Banded Labour in South Asia (PEBLISA) Project*. India Chapter, Phase 2, Bangalore.

Ranadive, Joy Deshmukh and Rajini K. Murthy (2005). Introduction: Linking the Triad. *In*: Neera Burra, Joy Deshmukh Ranadive, and Rajani K. Murthy, (eds). *Micro Credit, Poverty and Empowerment*, New Delhi: Sage Publications India Pvt. Ltd.

Sampark, (2006). Study on Microfinance and Self Help Groups (SHGs) of CARE-STEP Project in Andhra Pradesh, CARE India, Vishakapatnam, Andhra Pradesh.

Sankar, Kalpana (2005). Social Mobilization and Microfinance and Microfinance for Women's Empowerment—Lessons from the ASA Trust. In: Neera Burra, Joy Deshmukh-Ranadive, and Rajani K. Murthy, (eds). *Micro Credit, Poverty and Empowerment*, New Delhi: Sage Publications India Pvt. Ltd.

Index